DATE DUE

			PRINTED IN U.S.A.

The New Humanitarians

Recent Titles in
Social and Psychological Issues: Challenges and Solutions
Albert R. Roberts, Series Editor

Finding Meaning in Life, at Midlife and Beyond: Wisdom and Spirit from Logotherapy
David Guttmann

The New Humanitarians

Inspiration, Innovations, and Blueprints for Visionaries

Volume 1
Changing Global Health Inequities

Edited by Chris E. Stout, PsyD

Foreword by Mehmet Oz, MD

Social and Psychological Issues: Challenges and Solutions
Albert R. Roberts, Series Editor

Westport, Connecticut
London

Library of Congress Cataloging-in-Publication Data
The new humanitarians : inspiration, innovations, and blueprints for visionaries / edited
by Chris E. Stout ; foreword by Mehmet Oz.
    p. cm. — (Social and psychological issues: Challenges and solutions, ISSN
1941–7985)
  Includes bibliographical references and index.
  ISBN 978–0–275–99768–7 ((set) : alk. paper) — ISBN 978–0–275–99770–0 ((vol. 1) :
alk. paper) — ISBN 978–0–275–99772–4 ((vol. 2) : alk. paper) — ISBN
978–0–275–99774–8 ((vol. 3) : alk. paper)
  1. Philanthropists. 2. Humanitarianism. 3. Charities. 4. Social action. I. Stout, Chris E.
  HV27.N49 2009
  361.7'4—dc22   2008020797

British Library Cataloguing in Publication Data is available.

Library of Congress Catalog Card Number: 2008020797
ISBN: 978–0–275–99768–7 (set)
          978–0–275–99770–0 (vol. 1)
          978–0–275–99772–4 (vol. 2)
          978–0–275–99774–8 (vol. 3)
ISSN: 1941-7985

First published in 2009

Praeger Publishers, 88 Post Road West, Westport, CT 06881
An imprint of Greenwood Publishing Group, Inc.
www.praeger.com

Printed in the United States of America

The paper used in this book complies with the
Permanent Paper Standard issued by the National
Information Standards Organization (Z39.48–1984).

10   9   8   7   6   5   4   3   2   1

To all of those profiled herein and to all of those they help—you are all heroic.

Contents

Foreword: Honor Roll

From the time I first met Chris after our election as fellow Global Leaders of Tomorrow in Davos, Switzerland, for the World Economic Forum's Annual Meeting, I was impressed by his remarkable insight and diligence. Over the years, we have collaborated on various health-related projects, and we have shared profound sadness over many global tragedies.

Now Chris has embarked on a daunting challenge—that of compiling a Who's Who, or Honor Roll, of worldwide humanitarian organizations. Chris has taken his proverbial golden Rolodex of contacts and friends and compiled an impressive list that represents the "best of the best" in global human service organizations. Although Chris made his admittedly "biased" choices by going to the founders he already knew, he has nevertheless highlighted some of the best in the world–some well known, some almost unknown—but all that represent a sampling of the finest. Each is a testament to the power of the human spirit in the face of seemingly insurmountable challenges and deficits.

All the familiar bromides are absent from *The New Humanitarians*. Though it would be tempting to wring our collective hands at the enormity of the proverbial "world-going-to-hell-in-a-hand-basket," *The New Humanitarians* is a totem of real inspiration. Chris has highlighted organizations that favor results over standard protocol in accomplishing their work. Those herein are doing the difficult—not by following in other's footsteps, but by forging new paths and finding new solutions to mankind's humanitarian needs. The time has come for them to collectively tell their stories—a daunting task, but that is something Chris has experience with.

Someone once remarked that the core issue with Nazi Germany was *not* that there was a Hitler, but that there were *too few* Schindlers. *The New Humanitarians* gives us all hope that there is a new generation of Schindlers across the globe, and our imaginations can show us the differences they will make for the future.

Mehmet Oz, MD, MBA

Acknowledgments

First and foremost, I want to thank all of the people involved in the organizations profiled herein. Many people would not be alive or function at the levels they are without your vision and passion. Period. Full stop. It is your zeal that has so inspired me to publish these books. My thanks to each of you for taking the time to craft what has become this set. I am fortunate to call each of you my friend, and the world is blessed to have you. I also must apologize to those who lead organizations that are not included herein. It is a function of time and space—not having adequate amounts of either. Nevertheless, I hold a great and abiding respect for all of those working in the so-called humanitarian space. The world is in your debt.

Debbie Carvalko is my publisher extraordinaire at Praeger/Greenwood. Without her pitching my proposal, this project would not have been made into the reality that you are holding in your hand. She was a valued collaborator in the shepherding of the production of the manuscripts to final production. Debbie, you are amazing.

I was fortunate to gain valuable help in organizing, interviewing, and writing with a valued set of graduate student assistants: Annie Khan, Teresa Bartrum, Stephanie Benjamin, Mark Zissman, Valaria Levit, and Donald Bernovich. I would like especially to thank Patrick "Skully" Savaiano, who from the start displayed not only a keen sense of organization of the myriad of complexities that this project involved, but also demonstrated a wonderful balance of professionalism blended with a hip, e-mail-savvy communication style with some of the most prominent leaders in the humanitarian space. This is an incredible feat by an incredible person—tip-o-the-hat to you, Skully. And I would also like to particularly thank Myron Panchuk, who served as a fantastic resource and intellect to this project. I owe you my friend.

It was my mother who modeled rather than lectured about the importance of helping others. She provided me with an inspiring example that I can only hope to be able to mimic for my children. Thanks, Mom.

The support of my wife, Karen, is always invaluable, whether I am writing or not; and she was especially helpful in her ever-sharp review of many of the first drafts of what now appear herein, as well as tolerating my innumerable, long-winded, overly animated discourses about so many of the incredible stories and works of those profiled. Both of my children, Grayson and Annika, were valued partners in the early production steps of helping me stay organized with the chapters and whatnots of such a project. They were willing and able freelancers who could perforate pages as well as offer critique on some of my more complicated sentence-structuring problems. I thank and love you all.

Chris E. Stout
Kildeer, IL

Care to do more yourself? Please do! Here's how . . .

1. Visit CenterForGlobalInitiatives.org for more information on projects you can be a part of. If you don't see something you think you can help with, e-mail me at Chris@CenterForGlobalInitiatives.org and I may be able to connect you to another organization that can help, or we may be able to initiate work.
2. Consider suggesting *The New Humanitarians* to others and start a viral buzz! Think of all your contacts who may be interested in this book. If you go to www.Praeger.com and search for "The New Humanitarians" you can print a downloadable flyer for the book to give to interested others. You can also email the Praeger link to interested others as well as the CenterForGlobalInitiatives.org.
3. Inquire if your local or university library has *The New Humanitarians* in its collection, or on order. If you recommend it to them, they may add it and others can read it as well.
4. Request a presentation at your local college, university, public library, high school, church, mosque, synagogue, book seller, coffee shop, service organization (Rotary, Lyons, etc.), or book club by e-mailing a request to Chris@CenterForGlobalInitiatives.org or by calling 847.550.0092, ext. 2.
5. Request an interview by a broadcast, cable, or Internet television program, radio, newspaper, or magazine reporter. Media kits are also available by request to Chris@CenterForGlobalInitiatives.org or by calling 847.550.0092, ext. 2.

Introduction

Chris E. Stout

Welcome to a trip around the world. You will travel to six continents, led by men and women of various ages and backgrounds. Be warned: you may go to some fairly desperate places, but they all have a seed of hope. You will not be traveling as a tourist, but rather as an activist with more than three dozen organizations—each one incredible. Each chapter is a story, a story of need, of response, and of accomplishment. They are all at once different, but yet the same as being an inspirational account demonstrating the power of the individual triumphant over the challenges of poverty, illness, conflict, or a litany of injustices. My friend, Jonathan Granoff, President of the Global Security Institute, said of the project that it is a counter to the pervasive "pornography of the trivial" that infects much of what is in print these days. I suspect he is correct.

As a sad postscript but powerful testament to the seriousness of the work done by those profiled herein, a few days prior to this manuscript being sent in to the publisher, I was speaking with a representative with Médecins Sans Frontières who told me that three of their staff had been killed in a conflict zone in northwest Africa. My heart sunk on this news. Although I know such things happen—and with much more frequency than I usually let myself believe—I was more honored to get the stories of these heroic organizations out to a broader audience.

In these three volumes, readers will learn about individuals who have created organizations that:

- Break up human trafficking rings and teach citizens how to intervene in other injustices
- Go to conflict areas and put themselves at risk to end the conflict
- Help ensure elections are just
- Go to active war zones to administer emergency medical care
- Provide training and loans in order to empower people out of poverty

- Create a new language and then put it to use in developing education and job training programs
- Work to stop nuclear war and curb the development of weapons of mass destruction
- Create an ingenious for-profit organization that supports the not-for-profit work
- Solve a problem of medical supply shortages in the developing world while also alleviating medical waste problems in the developed world
- Export social services training into self-sustaining programs
- Create project-based trainings in order to increase capacity for global projects
- Treat immigrant and refugee survivors of torture in a culturally competent manner that is encompassing and holistic
- Help boys conscripted into being child soldiers adapt to a normal life
- Create the first not-for-profit pharmaceutical company to help in the battle of neglected diseases
- Advance education for girls where it is almost unheard of
- Integrate urban environmental design with democracy, civic participation, and social justice
- Bring the philosophy of "it takes a village to raise a child" to formative elementary school years, blend cultural heritage, and inspire students by mobilizing parents, teachers, and young adults
- Connect experts from a range of fields to work together on problems such as curing and preventing infectious and epidemic diseases, analyzing the risks of science and technology breakthroughs, and designing enforceable global health and environmental policies

CONTEXT FOR THE PROJECT

In developing my own nascent organization, the Center for Global Initiatives (profiled herein), I came to realize that there are many successful, groundbreaking models that already exist worldwide, but there really isn't a blueprint or a how-to on the subject. Although this is most likely due to the uniqueness of the organizations and their leadership examined herein, as well as their idiosyncratic approach to conducting their work, it is my hope that these volumes will provide readers a unique behind-the-scenes glimpse of the organizations and offer incredibly valuable insights, present insider experiences, and give advice that few would ever have access to from one organization, let alone from more than forty of the best-of-the-best.

I went about the selection process via the people I know. I met some in Davos at annual meetings of the World Economic Forum, or perhaps at a TED conference (back when Richard Saul Wurman still orchestrated them), or a Renaissance Weekend, or by being a co-nominee in the Fast Company Fast-50, or goodness knows where. I did not apply any scientific methods or algorithms to seek out the most cost-efficient organizations, those with the most stars on Charity Navigator, or those listed in a *Forbes* table. I was totally subjective and biased. I left my scientific method in the lab because I have been fortunate to have worked with some of the most innovative humanitarian organizations in the world, or to have collaborated with their incredibly talented founders/directors.

In fact, it is my experiences with these extraordinary people that led to my idea for this book project. There are many wonderful, long-standing organizations that do important work, but I found that many of the organizations I was working with were newer and, honestly, a bit more edgy. Many have more skin-in-the-game. These founders were on the ground and doing the work themselves, not remotely administrating from a comfortable office miles or a continent away. But don't let my capricious favoritism prevent you from researching the many, many other fantastic organizations that exist throughout the world. In fact, I hope this book may cause you to do exactly that. (I suppose I could have tried to get a book deal to compile the *Encyclopedia of New Humanitarians*, but I will leave that to someone with way more spunk than I.)

Though many of us are content in helping various causes by writing checks of support or perhaps even volunteering, the individuals profiled herein preferred to actually start their own organizations—to enact their passionate interests. So therein was the idea that crystallized the concept for this *New Humanitarians* project. I wanted to find out what makes these new humanitarians tick and how their brainchildren worked. Now, through this three-volume set, readers can, too.

From Braille Without Borders and Witness, to Geekcorps and ACCION, humanitarian groups are working worldwide largely in undeveloped countries to better people's lives. Whether they are empowering people with schools for the blind, intervening in human trafficking, giving the underserved access to technology, or helping individuals work out of poverty, the men and women of these innovative organizations offer their tremendous talent to their causes, along with great dedication and, sometimes, even personal risk to complete their missions. The work of these groups is remarkable. And so, too, are the stories of how they developed—including the defining moments when their founders felt they had to take action.

This project features a sampling of humanitarian groups across various areas: medicine, education, sustainable development, and social justice. These new humanitarians have been very successful with on-the-ground guerilla innovations without a lot of bureaucracy or baloney. They are rebels with a cause whose actions speak louder than words. They have all felt a moral duty to serve as vectors of change.

I did not want to be the author of *The Complete Idiot's Guide to Changing the World* or *Humanitarian Aid for Dummies,* but I did want to canvass the organizations whose founders I know personally and have had firsthand experiences with, as well as showcase others who are recognized pioneers, and have them describe in their own words where they gained their original idea, or what the tipping point was that so moved them to create their own organizations. I hope readers may gain not only inspiration, but also actionable approaches that are based on the real-world experiences of those profiled if they, too, care to take action.

Many of those appearing herein already hold world renown, so I hope this project will give readers the chance to learn the answers to questions rarely answered publicly, such as "How did you first get funding? Did you have false starts or failures? How creatively do you approach opportunities and obstacles—be they organizational or political? How do you create original solutions? What would you do differently today or what do you know now that you wish you knew then?"

COMMON DENOMINATORS

Even though the approaches of all these organizations are different, they do share a number of commonalities. At the time they formed their entities, each organization was novel in its approach to dealing with the problems it was addressing. The organizations were not restricted by past ways of thinking or acting. They created innovative approaches to produce something that was real and actionable from a concept and a vision. They developed practical approaches to solutions, some complex, some elegant, all robust and lasting. They were provocative. They were unhappy or unsatisfied with approaches others were using, and decided: if you can't join 'em, beat 'em. And they did just that—they cleared their own trails to sustainability for their organizations for the benefit of others.

They also either have a global reach or are at least not bound to the North or the West. These are "young" organizations with an average organizational age of fifteen years, with the majority being founded ten or fewer years ago. Thus, they are new enough to demonstrate generalizable methods to help readers in their own development of their work, while demonstrating sustainability and viability of their model and approach. Simply put, it is my goal to have this set of books demonstrate how these organizations make a difference. Each of them has taken an approach to their life and work by living like they mean it. While there is the essence of the power of one, it is one for all.

The organizations profiled in this three-volume book set differ in many other ways as well. Some have been recognized with many awards and accolades (MacArthur "Genius" Award recipients, fellows of institutes or think tanks, etc.), whereas others are newer or have such a low profile or are so remote as to not be picked up by any radar. I like that diversity. Some have incredible budgets and others almost none, but they all do amazing things with what they have. And with the increased exposure gained from being in this book set, they may be able to gain more people's awareness.

For example, Braille Without Borders is an organization created in 1998 by Sabriye Tenberken and Paul Kronenberg when they left Europe to establish the Rehabilitation and Training Centre for the Blind, a preparatory school for elementary-school children in the Tibet Autonomous Region (TAR). Before the center was opened, blind children there did not have access to education. These children were stigmatized outcasts who held little hope for integration or much of a future. Although there are many governmental and nongovernmental organizations that have set up eye clinics for surgery or eyeglasses, there is a large group of blind people that cannot be helped by these clinics. The center was created for them.

If this wasn't challenge enough, those in the TAR had no written form of communication. There was no Tibetan version of what many blind individuals use to read, known as Braille (invented in 1821 by Frenchman Louis Braille). So, of course, Sabriye *invented* a Tibetan script, or Braille if you will, for the blind. This script combines the principles of the Braille system with the special features of the Tibetan syllable-based script.

Impoverished countries worldwide account for nearly 6 million preschool and school-age children who are blind, and 90–95 percent of them have no access to education. Braille Without Borders wants to empower blind people in such countries so they can set up projects and schools for other blind people. In this way the concept can be spread across the globe so that more blind and visually impaired people have access to education and a better future.

It is people like Sabriye Tenberken and Paul Kronenberg and all of those herein who are taking the kind of action that William Easterly pines for in *The White Man's Burden*—they are interested in results and they deliver. They offer small-scale results that make a large-scale impact.

STRUCTURE

Readers will find that some of the chapters are authored by the founder or current leader of the organization profiled. Other chapters are the result of an interview. I wanted this book to be thematic and structured, but I also wanted to provide a wide berth for every organization to best tell its story. Thus, for some it is literally in their own voice, first-person. In other instances interviews were conducted and a story unfolds as told by the founder or current leader, the de facto coauthor.

I had established a set of standard questions that could be used as a guide, but not as a strict rule-set. I told every organization's leader that he or she could follow them or ignore them, or to choose whatever was appropriate. I was very pleased with the result. That is, most chapters cover similar thematic aspects—how they started, how they manage, and so forth. But I think I have been able to steer clear of the chapters looking like cookie-cutter templates with simply different content sprinkled in the right spots here and there. It was my hope to create a set of guidebooks, not cookbooks, and I hope you as a reader will enjoy a similarity between chapters in their construction, but great variability in their voice and creation.

I asked authors to sketch the background on their centers or organizations, when they started, canvass their history to current day, provide a description of their model, indicate how large they are, what type of corporate structure (non-for-profit, university based, etc.) they have, what metrics they use to track productivity or how they measure success, and biographical information about the founder.

I also had a set of curiosities myself: Where did the idea came from? What was the inspiration/motivation for the starting the organization? Was there "that one incident" (or the first, or the many events) that so moved the founder to no longer "do nothing" and take action. I felt that reading about specific cases or vignettes of groups or individuals who were helped would give a finer grain as to outcomes and impacts of such organizations. But I also wanted to learn how these organizations defined success. I think readers will be not only pleased, but inspired. I hope that readers will have their own passions sparked and have their desire to know (and perhaps, to do) more increased.

Organizing the chapters was a bit of a challenge. As you will see, there is much overlap between their activities, and many somewhat defy an easy categorization (which I like, actually), so I did the best I could to make what I hope readers will consider to be reasonable groupings. Or, perhaps this will at least cause readers to look at all three volumes!

And now, it is with great pleasure (and awe) that I introduce the *new humanitarians*.

VOLUME 1: CHANGING GLOBAL HEALTH INEQUITIES
Médecins Sans Frontières/Founded in 1971

I was in Geneva when I first met Doris Schopper, a physician who was involved in the founding of Médecins Sans Frontières (MSF), and she was an incredible person filled with energy and stories. As readers will find, this chapter provides a frank and transparent description of the chaos involved in the nascent years of MSF—quite the shift to the Nobel Prize–winning organization and operation of today. Médecins Sans Frontières is an independent humanitarian medical aid agency committed to two objectives: providing medical aid wherever needed, regardless of race, religion, politics, or sex, and raising awareness of the plight of people it helps.

Unite For Sight/Founded in 2000

If you ever want to feel inadequate, just look up Jennifer Staple. While most of us were struggling to get through undergraduate school, Jennifer, while at Yale, formed what has become an award-winning global enterprise doing incredible work. The organization's model serves as an inspiration regarding the power of making and acting upon connections. Unite For Sight implements vision screening and educa-tion programs in North America and in developing countries. In North America, patients are connected with free health coverage programs so that they can receive an eye exam by a doctor. In Africa and Asia, Unite For Sight volunteers work with partner eye clinics to implement screening and free surgery programs.

Scojo Foundation/Founded in 2001

In the small world of global efforts, I read a piece by Jordan Kassalow, OD, MPH, and I called him while he was at the Global Health Policy Program at the Council on Foreign Relations in New York, serving as an adjunct senior fellow. We had a wonderful conversation, and I have referenced his keen points on the deadly reciprocity of illness and warfare in subsequent talks I have given. He and Scott Berrie went on to found the Scojo Foundation. Their mission is to reduce poverty and generate opportunity through the sale of affordable eyeglasses and complementary products. Scojo Vision Entrepreneurs are low-income men and women living in rural villages who are trained to conduct vision screenings within their communities, sell affordable reading glasses, and refer those who require advanced eye care to reputable clinics.

Sustainable Sciences Institute/Founded in 1998

I tell people that Eva Harris, PhD, could make a lab out of a Jeep and that she is the spiritual cousin of MacGyver. I have read her seminal book, *A Low-Cost Approach to PCR*, and though not a biologist, I was astounded. We first spoke on the phone some years ago about the possibility of collaborating on a project together, and my astonishment continued. She developed the Sustainable Sciences Institute (SSI) and holds a mission to develop scientific research capacity in areas with pressing public health problems. To that end, SSI helps local biomedical scientists gain access to training, funding, information, equipment, and supplies, so that they can better meet the public health needs of their communities.

Institute for OneWorld Health/Founded in 2000

I first spoke to Victoria Hale, PhD, after she and her attorneys had been meeting with Internal Revenue Service attorneys to convince them that the Institute for OneWorld Health was indeed a NOT-for-profit pharmaceutical company. We were looking to collaborate on a pharmacogenomic project in which my Center would do the "R" of R&D and she would work on the "D," or development. We first met face-to-face in Geneva at the World Economic Forum headquarters. Today, the Institute for OneWorld Health develops safe, effective, and affordable new medicines for people with infectious diseases in the developing world.

Jamkhed (aka Comprehensive Rural Health Project — CRHP)/Founded in 1970

Shobha Arole, MD, came looking for me in Davos at a World Economic Forum Annual Meeting. I will never forget that, in our conversation, I presumed she needed help with getting some doctors to Jamkhed, but she quickly, and ever so kindly, told me that she was in the market for *students* so she could help train them before they developed their bad habits. And she and her father, Raj Arole, MD, are doing so, and quite successfully. Their Comprehensive Rural Health Project (CRHP) was started to provide healthcare to rural communities, keeping in mind the realities described above. It developed a comprehensive, community-based primary healthcare (CBPHC) approach. CRHP is located at Jamkhed, which is far away from a major city and is typically rural, drought-prone, and poverty stricken. One of the main aims of the project is to reach the poorest and most marginalized and to improve their health. In reality, perhaps not everyone in the world will be able to have equal healthcare. However, it *is* possible to make sure that all people have access to necessary and relevant healthcare. This concept is known as equity, and it is an important principle of CRHP. Health is not only absence of disease; it also includes social, economic, spiritual, physical, and mental well-being. With this comprehensive understanding of health, the project focuses on improving the socioeconomic well-being of the people as well as other aspects of health. Health does not exist in isolation: it is greatly related to education, environment, sanitation, socioeconomic status, and agriculture. Therefore, improvement in these areas by the communities in turn improves the health of the people. Healthcare includes promotive, preventive, curative, and rehabilitative aspects. These areas of integration bring about effective healthcare.

International Center for Equal Healthcare Access/Founded in 2001

I met Marie Charles, MD, MIA, in Quebec City at a Renaissance Weekend. I listened to her presentation on her Center's work, and I knew I had found a kindred spirit. In fact, at the time of this writing, it is looking promising that we will be working collaboratively together in Cambodia. Marie founded the International Center for Equal Healthcare Access (ICEHA), which is a truly remarkable nonprofit organization of 650+ volunteer physicians and nurses who transfer their medical expertise in HIV and infectious diseases (>7,000 aggregate man-years of human capital) to colleagues in more than twelve countries in the developing world. Rather than perpetuating a continued dependence on Western charity, this creates a sustainable system that allows these countries to provide healthcare to their own patients at the highest possible standards and yet within the existing resource limitations. As an interesting but crucially important side-note, the recipient developing countries themselves shoulder the major share of the program implementation costs, giving them a true sense of proprietary pride, value, and ownership as opposed to "receiving charity." ICEHA turns the paradigm of international development on its head.

Flying Doctors of America/Founded in 1990

Allan Gathercoal, DDiv, and I have been through a lot together—stuck in Nairobi, stuck in Burundi, bribing airport officials with lighters in Hanoi to bring medicines in, working in Bolivian prisons together; and, most recently, we met in

Cambodia. Allan is the founder of Flying Doctors of America, and his organization runs short-term medical/dental missions to the rural regions of Third World countries.

Marjorie Kovler Center of Heartland Alliance/Founded 1987

I'd speculate that Mary Fabri, PsyD, spends more time some years in Rwanda than in Chicago. She goes to where the needs are, and when in Chicago, the needs are at the Marjorie Kovler Center, where she is director and one of the clinical co-founders. The Kovler Center provides comprehensive, community-based services in which survivors work together with staff and volunteers to identify needs and overcome obstacles to healing. Services include Mental Health (individual or group psychotherapy, counseling, psychiatric services, and a range of culturally appropriate services on-site in the community), Health Care (primary healthcare and specialized medical treatment by medical professionals specifically trained to work with torture survivors), Case Management (access to community resources, including tutoring, ESL, food, transportation, special events), Interpretation and Translation (bridging cultural and linguistic barriers in medical, mental health, and community settings), and Legal Referral (referral and collaboration with immigration attorneys and organizations).

International Center on Responses to Catastrophes/Founded in 2002

Stevan Weine, MD, is a renaissance kind of guy. He can gain impressive NIH grants and awards while also writing about Alan Ginsberg and Bruce Springsteen (and take time to coauthor and present with me as well). I have had the pleasure of traveling to all sorts of places with Steve and meeting a fascinating group of activists, scientists, and intellectuals, all the while listening to some great music. He is a mentor, a role model, and a good friend. He also is the founder of the Center at the University of Illinois–Chicago, whose primary mission is to promote multi-disciplinary research and scholarship that contributes to improved helping efforts for those affected by catastrophes.

International Trauma Studies Program/Founded in 1997

It was Stevan Weine who introduced me to Jack Saul, PhD, and took me to visit Jack's International Trauma Studies Program (ITSP), now at Columbia University. Jack's perspective is that recent natural and human-made catastrophes have highlighted the need for a multidisciplinary approach to the study, treatment, and prevention of trauma-related suffering. So, at New York University in 1997, he founded the original program. It is now a training and research program at Columbia University's Mailman School of Public Health. The program has been enriched by the participation of a diverse student body, ranging from mental health professionals, healthcare providers, attorneys, and human rights advocates, to journalists and media professionals, academicians, oral historians, and artists. Students and professionals are given the opportunity to develop and share innovative approaches to address the psychosocial needs of trauma survivors, their families, and communities. ITSP offers a dynamic combination of academic studies, research, and practical experience working with trauma survivors in New York City, the United States, and abroad.

Center for Health, Intervention, and Prevention @UConn/Founded in 2002

Jeff Fisher, PhD, invited me to his Center at UConn, and I had the flu. I would not have missed such an opportunity for the world. You see, the University of Connecticut Psychology Department's Center for Health, Intervention, and Prevention (CHIP) creates new scientific knowledge in the areas of health behavior, health behavior change, and health risk prevention and intervention. CHIP provides theory-based health behavior and health behavior change expertise and services at the international, national, state, university, and community levels.

REMEDY/Founded in 1991

REMEDY, Recovered Medical Equipment for the Developing World, is a nonprofit organization committed to teaching and promoting the recovery of surplus operating-room supplies. Proven recovery protocols were designed to be quickly adapted to the everyday operating room or critical care routine. As of June 2006, the REMEDY at Yale program alone had donated more than 50 tons of medical supplies! It is estimated that at least $200 million worth of supplies could be recovered from U.S. hospitals each year, resulting in an increase of 50 percent of the medical aid sent from the United States to the developing world.

Center for Global Initiatives/Founded in 2004

The Center for Global Initiatives (CGI) is my baby. It is the first Center devoted to training multidisciplinary healthcare professionals and students to bring services that are integrated, sustainable, resiliency based, and that have publicly accountable outcomes to areas of need, worldwide, via multiple, small, context-specific collaboratives that integrate primary care, behavioral healthcare, systems development, public health, and social justice. The word "global" is not used herein as a synonym for overseas or international, but rather local as well as transnational disparities and inequities of health risk and illness outcomes. The Center seeks to eschew the many disconnects between separation of body/mind, physical/mental, individual/community, and to offer a synthetic model of integration. CGI's philosophy and approach is always that of a collaborator and colleague. No West-Knows-Best hubris. Perhaps the most important aspects of the Center for Global Initiatives are the simplest: it serves as an incubator and hothouse for new projects; it helps to nurture, grow, and launch those projects as self-sustaining, ongoing interests; and after a project has taken hold, it serves as pro bono consultant to help those now managing the work with whatever they may need—materials, medicines, case consultation. About 90 percent of all CGI's projects have come about as a result of being invited to do the work. As best can be done, depending on the project, CGI seeks to blend primary care, behavioral health, and public health into an ultimately self-sustaining, outcomes-accountable, culturally consonant result.

VOLUME 2: CHANGING EDUCATION AND RELIEF
Braille Without Borders/Founded in 1997

Sabriye, Paul, and I used to joke about how we were likely the poorest attendees in Davos at the World Economic Forum. And in spite of our modest bank balances, I can tell you that they were two of the most powerful of the movers and shakers there. Braille Without Borders wants to empower blind people in these countries so they themselves can set up projects and schools for other blind people. In this way the concept can be spread across the globe so other blind and visually impaired people have access to education and a better future.

Room to Read/Founded in 2000

I heard John Wood talk about his post-Microsoft adventure of founding Room to Read. His brainchild partners with local communities throughout the developing world to establish schools, libraries, and other educational infrastructure. They seek to intervene early in the lives of children in the belief that education is a lifelong gift that empowers people to ultimately improve socioeconomic conditions for their families, communities, countries, and future generations. Through the opportunities that only an education can provide, they strive to break the cycle of poverty, one child at a time. Since its inception, Room to Read has impacted the lives of over 1.3 million children by constructing 287 schools, establishing over 3,870 libraries, publishing 146 new local language children's titles representing more than 1.3 million books, donating more than 1.4 million English language children's books, funding 3,448 long-term girls' scholarships, and establishing 136 computer and language labs.

Global Village Engineers/Founded in 1992

Chris Shimkus is a good guy and a good friend with whom I first connected in Geneva at the WEF Headquarters. He took one of those proverbial leaps of faith and left his "day job" to devote himself to the work of Global Village Engineers (GVE). GVE is a volunteer corps of professional engineers supporting the local capacity of rural communities in developing countries to influence public infrastructure and environmental protection. Its engineers choose to volunteer their skills to ensure the livelihood of these communities by building long-term local capacity, especially in situations of disaster prevention and rehabilitation and the need for environmental protection. They believe that infrastructure will best serve communities when they have the capacity to become involved from project inception through construction. Governments and project sponsors often do not invest in communicating basic facts to the community about design, construction, and maintenance. The mission of Global Village Engineers is to find these facts and develop the local capacity to understand such facts.

Common Bond Institute/Founded in 1995

I first met Steve Olweean, PhD, in an airport in Oslo—or was it Helsinki? We were on our way to St. Petersburg to the conference he founded. That conference was a lightning rod of connections with people I continue to work with around the world, from Sri Lanka to Tel Aviv, and that's just the tip of the iceberg of what Steve does. He founded the Common Bond Institute (CBI), which is a U.S.-based NGO that grew out of the Association for Humanistic Psychology's *International (Soviet-American) Professional Exchange.* The Professional Exchange was initiated in 1982 as one of the first Soviet-American nongovernmental human service exchanges. CBI organizes and sponsors conferences, professional training programs, relief efforts, and professional exchanges internationally, and it actively provides networking and coordination support to assist newly emerging human service and civil society organizations in developing countries. Its mission is cultivating the fundamental elements of a consciousness of peace and local capacity building, which are seen as natural, effective antidotes to small-group radical extremism and large-group despair, as well as to hardship and suffering in the human condition. To this end, enabling each society to effectively resolve and transform conflicts, satisfy core human needs within their communities, and construct effective, holistic mechanisms for self-determination, self-esteem, and fundamental human dignity and worth is the purpose of their work.

SWEEP/Founded in 2004

The Jane Addams College of Social Work, University of Illinois at Chicago (UIC), Addis Ababa University (AAU), The Council of International Programs USA (CIPUSA), and a network of nonprofit agencies are engaged in an exciting effort to develop the first-ever master's degree in social work in Ethiopia, through a project known as the Social Work Education in Ethiopia Partnership, or SWEEP. The undergraduate social work program at AAU was closed in 1976, when a military regime ruled the country. Now, with a democratic government in place since the early 1990s, the SWEEP project is working in collaboration with AAU's new School of Social Work and nongovernmental agencies in Ethiopia to develop social work education and practice.

CUP/Founded in 1997

The Center for Urban Pedagogy (CUP) makes educational projects about places and how they change. Its projects bring together art and design professionals—artists, graphic designers, architects, urban planners—with community-based advocates and researchers—organizers, government officials, academics, service providers and policymakers. These partners work with CUP staff to create projects ranging from high-school curricula to educational exhibitions. Their work grows from a belief that the power of imagination is central to the practice of democracy, and that the work of governing must engage the dreams and visions of citizens. CUP believes in the legibility of the world around us. It is the CUP philosophy that, by learning how to investigate, we train ourselves to change what we see.

Endeavor/Founded in 1997

Linda Rottenberg, who co-founded Endeavor, is a Roman candle of energy, enthusiasm, and brainpower. I met her through the World Economic Forum as a Global Leader of Tomorrow. She is amazing at delivering on what's needed in creatively intelligent ways. Endeavor targets emerging-market countries transitioning from international aid to international investment. Endeavor then seeks out local partners to build country boards and benefactors to launch local Endeavor affiliates.

ACCION/Founded in 1961

ACCION International is a private, nonprofit organization with the mission of giving people the financial tools they need—micro enterprise loans, business training, and other financial services—to work their way out of poverty. A world pioneer in microfinance, ACCION was founded in 1961 and issued its first micro-loan in 1973 in Brazil. ACCION International's partner microfinance institutions today are providing loans as low as $100 to poor men and women entrepreneurs in twenty-five countries in Latin America, the Caribbean, Asia, and sub-Saharan Africa, as well as in the United States.

Invisible Conflicts/Dwon Madiki Partnership/Founded in 2006

I just met Evan Ledyard at a talk I gave at Loyola University in Chicago, and he introduced me to the work he has done with an incredible group of students. Invisible Conflicts is a student organization that sponsors the education, mentorship, and empowerment of twenty Ugandan orphans and vulnerable children. A twenty-one-year civil war in northern Uganda, between the government and a rebel faction called the Lord's Resistance Army (LRA), has led to the forced displacement of over 1.7 million people into internal refugee camps. To support their rebellion, the LRA abducted more than 30,000 Ugandan children, forcing them to be sex slaves and to fight as child soldiers. Because of these atrocities, all of the DMP-sponsored children live in squalid conditions in and around the many displacement camps. Because life around these camps is marked by poverty, hunger, and little or no access to education, an entire generation of children find themselves denied a childhood and a chance to succeed in life.

BELL/Founded in 1992

Building Educated Leaders for Life, or BELL, recognizes that the pathway to opportunity for children lies in education. BELL transforms children into scholars and leaders through the delivery of nationally recognized, high-impact after-school and summer educational programs. By helping children achieve academic and social proficiency during their formative elementary-school years and embrace their rich cultural heritage, BELL is inspiring the next generation of great teachers, doctors, lawyers, artists, and community leaders. By mobilizing parents, teachers, and young adults, BELL is living the idea that "it takes a village to raise a child."

Hybrid Vigor Institute/Founded in 2000

I first met Denise Caruso at a TED Conference. She was just stepping down from her position as technology columnist at the *New York Times*, just before the tech bubble burst. Smart gal. I was immediately smitten by her intellect, and in subsequent emails and conversations, she agreed to help me in the pondering of my nascent ideas for my Center as she was building her Institute in the form of Hybrid Vigor. The Hybrid Vigor Institute is focused on three ambitious goals: (1) to make a significant contribution toward solving some of today's most intractable problems in the areas of health, the environment, and human potential, both by producing innovative knowledge and by developing processes for sharing expertise; (2) to develop new methods and tools for research and analysis that respect and use appropriately both the quantitative methods of the natural sciences and the subjective inquiries of the social and political sciences, arts, and humanities, and to establish metrics and best practices for these new methods of collaboration and knowledge sharing; (3) to deploy cutting-edge collaboration, information extraction, and knowledge management technologies, so that working researchers from any discipline may easily acquire and share relevant work and information about their areas of interest.

Our Voices Together/Founded in 2005

Marianne Scott and I had a wonderful conversation one Sunday night that I will never forget. Without repeating it, I do want to say I was touched by her humanity in a very powerful and lasting way, and I knew then that she needed to be represented in this project. Our Voices Together holds a vision of a world in which the appeal of lives lived in dignity, opportunity, and safety triumphs over the allure of extremism and its terrorist tactics. The people of this organization see a future where terrorist tactics are not condoned by any community worldwide. They understand that to achieve this, trust must be built on mutual trust and respect around the globe. They recognize the vast potential in engaging the United States in diplomacy by connecting communities. To this end, they promote the vital role of people-to-people efforts to help build better, safer lives and futures around the world.

Geekcorps/Founded in 1999

Ethan Zuckerman has a wicked sense of humor, and he is not afraid to use it. I last saw Ethan in Madrid at an anti-terrorism conference, and we spoke of wikis as a solution to a puzzle I was working on about Amazonian medical services. How obvious. Ethan is the founder of Geekcorps, which has evolved into the IESC Geekcorps, which is an international 501(c)(3) nonprofit organization that promotes stability and prosperity in the developing world through information and communication technology (ICT). Geekcorps' international technology experts teach communities how to be digitally independent: able to create and expand private enterprise with innovative, appropriate, and affordable information and communication technologies. To increase the capacity of small and medium-sized business, local government, and supporting organizations to be more profitable and efficient using technology, Geekcorps draws on a database of more than 3,500 technical experts willing to share their talents and experience in developing nations.

VOLUME 3: CHANGING SUSTAINABLE DEVELOPMENT AND SOCIAL JUSTICE
Witness/Founded in 1992

I first saw some of the work of Witness at the Contemporary Museum of Art in Chicago, and I was quite disturbed and moved by the images I saw— which was the point. I then contacted Gillian Caldwell of Witness about this book project, and I got the distinct impression that she wondered "who is this guy, and is he on the level?" So, with some emails back and forth, and the good timing of the WEF Annual Meeting, where she happened to be going, I gained some street cred with her as I'd been an invited faculty, gone to Davos a number of years, and knew Klaus Schwab, who had also written the foreword for one of my other books. Then she let me into the tent, and I am very glad she did. Witness does incredible work by using video and online technologies to open the eyes of the world to human rights violations. It empowers people to transform personal stories of abuse into powerful tools for justice, promoting public engagement and policy change. It envisions a just and equitable world where all individuals and communities are able to defend and uphold human rights.

The Community Relations Council/Founded in 1986

I worked on a three-volume book set (*The Psychology of Resolving Global Conflicts: From War to Peace*, Praeger, 2005) with Mari Fitzduff, PhD, and I had no idea of the violence she was exposed to in Belfast as a child growing up there. Now it makes perfect sense as to her development of the Community Relations Council. Its aim is to assist the people of Northern Ireland to recognize and counter the effects of communal division. The Community Relations Council originated as a proposal of a research report commissioned by the NI Standing Advisory Committee on Human Rights. The Community Relations Council was set up to promote better community relations between Protestants and Catholics in Northern Ireland and, equally, to promote recognition of cultural diversity. Its strategic aim is to promote a peaceful and fair society based on reconciliation and mutual trust. It does so by providing support (finance, training, advice, information) for local groups and organizations; developing opportunities for cross-community understanding; increasing public awareness of community relations work; and encouraging constructive debate throughout Northern Ireland.

Amnesty International/Founded in 1961

Amnesty International's (AI's) vision is of a world in which every person enjoys all of the human rights enshrined in the Universal Declaration of Human Rights and other international human rights standards. In pursuit of this vision, AI's mission is to undertake research and action focused on preventing and ending grave abuses of the rights to physical and mental integrity, freedom of conscience and expression, and freedom from discrimination, within the context of its work to promote all human rights. AI has a varied network of members and supporters around the world. At the latest count, there were more than 1.8 million members, supporters, and subscribers in over 150 countries and territories in every region of the world. Although they come from many different backgrounds and have widely different political and religious beliefs, they are united by a determination to work for a world where everyone enjoys human rights.

PeaceWorks Foundation and OneVoice/Founded in 2002

Daniel Lubetzky is one of those incredible people who turn on a room when they enter it. He does so not with bravado and brashness, but rather with a quiet power that captures those around him. He is a compelling person with a compelling mission. He founded OneVoice with the aim to amplify the voice of the overwhelming but heretofore silent majority of Israelis and Palestinians who wish to end the conflict. Since its inception, OneVoice has empowered ordinary citizens to demand accountability from elected representatives and ensure that the political agenda is not hijacked by extremists. OneVoice works to reframe the conflict by transcending the "left vs. right" and "Israeli vs. Palestinian" paradigms and by demonstrating that the moderate majority can prevail over the extremist minority. Although the needs and concerns of the Israeli and Palestinian peoples are different—Israelis wish to end terror and the existential threat to Israel; Palestinians wish to end the occupation and achieve an independent Palestinian state—the vast majority on each side agree that these goals are achievable only by reaching a two-state solution. OneVoice is unique in that it has independent Israeli and Palestinian offices appealing to the national interests of their own sides with credentials enabling them to unite people across the religious and political spectrum. It recognizes the essential work many other groups do in the field of dialogue and understanding, but OneVoice is action oriented and advocacy driven. It is about the process and demanding accountability from its members and from political leaders. A peace agreement, no matter how comprehensive, will be ineffective without populations ready to support it. The focus is on giving citizens a voice and a direct role in conflict resolution.

Nonviolent Peaceforce/Founded in 1998

Nonviolent Peaceforce is a federation of more than ninety member organizations from around the world. In partnership with local groups, unarmed Nonviolent Peaceforce Field Team members apply proven strategies to protect human rights, deter violence, and help create space for local peacemakers to carry out their work. The mission of the Nonviolent Peaceforce is to build a trained, international civilian peaceforce committed to third-party nonviolent intervention.

Peace Brigades/Founded in 1981

Peace Brigades International (PBI) is an NGO that protects human rights and promotes nonviolent transformation of conflicts. When invited, it sends teams of volunteers into areas of repression and conflict. The volunteers accompany human rights defenders, their organizations, and others threatened by political violence. Perpetrators of human rights abuses usually do not want the world to witness their actions. The presence of volunteers backed by a support network helps to deter violence. They create space for local activists to work for social justice and human rights.

Witness for Peace/Founded in 1983

Witness for Peace (WFP) is a politically independent, nationwide grassroots organization of people committed to nonviolence and led by faith and conscience. WFP's mission is to support peace, justice, and sustainable economies in the Americas by changing U.S. policies and corporate practices that contribute to poverty and oppression in Latin America and the Caribbean.

Southern Poverty Law Center/Founded in 1971

Throughout its history, the Center has worked to make the nation's Constitutional ideals a reality. The Center's legal department fights all forms of discrimination and works to protect society's most vulnerable members, handling innovative cases that few lawyers are willing to take. Over three decades, it has achieved significant legal victories, including landmark Supreme Court decisions and crushing jury verdicts against hate groups.

Human Rights Campaign/Founded in 1980

After having served as a federal advocacy coordinator on the Hill for the American Psychological Association for twelve years, and at the state level even longer, I have come to know and very much appreciate the twists and turns of law making and the body politic. I have also come to know and respect the impressive work of those in the Human Rights Campaign (HRC). They have evolved from battling stigma to being a political force to contend with—no easy task in the Beltway or on Main Street USA. The Human Rights Campaign is America's largest civil rights organization working to achieve gay, lesbian, bisexual, and transgender (GLBT) equality. By inspiring and engaging all Americans, HRC strives to end discrimination against GLBT citizens and realize a nation that achieves fundamental fairness and equality for all. HRC seeks to improve the lives of GLBT Americans by advocating for equal rights and benefits in the workplace, ensuring that families are treated equally under the law, and increasing public support among all Americans through innovative advocacy, education, and outreach programs. HRC works to secure equal rights for GLBT individuals and families at the federal and state levels by lobbying elected officials, mobilizing grassroots supporters, educating Americans, investing strategically to elect fairminded officials, and partnering with other GLBT organizations.

Global Security Institute/Founded in 1999

Back in the late 1990s, as a member of Psychologists for Social Responsibility and living in Chicago, I was asked to represent that organization at a meeting called Abolition 2000. The goal of that group was to have abolished nuclear weapons by 2000. I had the chance to meet its founder, the late Senator Alan Cranston, and I was smitten. That movement evolved into the organization Jonathan Granoff now leads, known as the Global Security Institute (GSI). It is dedicated to strengthening international cooperation and security based on the rule of law with a particular focus on nuclear arms control, nonproliferation, and disarmament. GSI was founded by Senator Alan Cranston, whose insight that nuclear weapons are impractical, unacceptably risky, and unworthy of civilization continues to inspire GSI's efforts to contribute to a safer world. GSI has developed an exceptional team that includes former heads of state and government, distinguished diplomats, effective politicians, committed celebrities, religious leaders, Nobel Peace laureates, disarmament and legal experts, and concerned citizens.

Search for Common Ground/Founded in 1982

I first had the pleasure of meeting Susan Marks in Davos at a breakfast meeting in which we were to co-facilitate a discussion. I could not keep up with her! She had us all enthralled with her perspectives and experiences, and I was astonished. She and her husband John started the Search for Common Ground as a vehicle to transform the way the world deals with conflict: away from adversarial approaches, toward cooperative solutions. Although the world is overly polarized and violence is much too prevalent, they remain essentially optimistic. Their view is that, on the whole, history is moving in positive directions. Although some of the conflicts currently being dealt with may seem intractable, there are successful examples of cooperative conflict resolution that can be looked to for inspiration—such as in South Africa, where an unjust system was transformed through negotiations and an inclusive peace process.

Project on Justice in Times of Transition/Founded in 1992

Mari Fitzduff introduced me to Timothy Phillips in the context of working on this project, and needless to say, I was taken aback by their work. The Project on Justice in Times of Transition brings together individuals from a broad spectrum of countries to share experiences in ending conflict, building civil society, and fostering peaceful coexistence. It currently operates in affiliation with the Foundation for a Civil Society in New York and the Institute for Global Leadership at Tufts University. Since its creation in 1992 by co-chairs Wendy Luers and Timothy Phillips, the Project has conducted more than fifty programs for a variety of leaders throughout the world and has utilized its methodology to assist them in addressing such difficult issues as the demobilization of combatants, the status of security files, police reform, developing effective negotiating skills, political demonstrations, and preserving or constructing the tenets of democracy in a heterogeneous society. Through its innovative programming, the Project has exposed a broad cross-section of communities in transition to comparable situations elsewhere, and it has contributed to the broadening of international public discourse on transitional processes.

In recent years the Project has conducted programs that have helped practitioners and political leaders strategize solutions in a variety of countries and regions, including Afghanistan, Colombia, East Timor, Guatemala, Kosovo, Northern Ireland, Palestine, and Peru.

Exodus World Service/Founded in 1988

Heidi Moll was cheering my son and me on last fall in a five-kilometer run that was a fundraiser for Exodus World Service and other agencies. I first came to know of their refugee work via a church we used to attend, and it was remarkable. Exodus World Service transforms the lives of refugees and of volunteers. It educates local churches about refugee ministry, connects volunteers in relationship with refugee families through practical service projects, and equips leaders to speak up on behalf of refugees. The end result is that wounded hearts are healed, loneliness is replaced with companionship, and fear is transformed into hope. Exodus recruits local volunteers, equips them with information and training, and then links them directly with refugee families newly arrived in the Chicago metropolitan area. It also provides training and tools for front-line staff of other refugee service agencies. In addition, Exodus has developed several innovative programs for use by volunteers in their work with refugees.

International Institute for Sustainable Development/Founded in 1990

The International Institute for Sustainable Development (IISD) contributes to sustainable development by advancing policy recommendations on international trade and investment, economic policy, climate change, measurement and assessment, and natural resources management. By using Internet communications, it is able to report on international negotiations and broker knowledge gained through collaborative projects with global partners, resulting in more rigorous research, capacity building in developing countries, and better dialogue between North and South. IISD is in the business of promoting change toward sustainable development. Through research and through effective communication of their findings, it engages decision makers in government, business, NGOs, and other sectors to develop and implement policies that are simultaneously beneficial to the global economy, to the global environment, and to social well-being. IISD also believes fervently in the importance of building its own institutional capacity while helping its partner organizations in the developing world to excel.

LET'S GET GOING

I hope you enjoy learning more about these amazing individuals and their work. I certainly have enjoyed working with them and in completing this remarkable writing project. They all have the common denominator of changing people's lives, and isn't that truly the way to change the world?

From an Idea to Action: The Evolution of Médecins Sans Frontières

Kevin P. Q. Phelan

Today, Médecins Sans Frontières/Doctors Without Borders (MSF) is one of the world's leading independent humanitarian medical aid organizations, responding to the emergency medical needs of people affected by armed conflict, natural disasters, and such medical catastrophes as malnutrition, malaria, AIDS, tuberculosis (TB), kala-azar, other neglected diseases, and epidemic outbreaks of meningitis and cholera. MSF is an association with individual sections in nineteen countries and thousands of members. Each year, MSF doctors, nurses, logisticians, water and sanitation experts, administrators, and other medical and non-medical professionals depart on more than 4,700 aid assignments in more than seventy countries. They work alongside more than 25,800 locally hired staff to provide medical care.

Before December 20, 1971, though, MSF was just an idea. On that day, a group of French doctors (Xavier Emmanuelli, Marcel Delcourt, Max Recamier, Gérard Pigeon, Jean Cabrol, Jean-Michel Wild, Bernard Kouchner, Pascal Greletty-Bosviel, and Jacques Beres) joined several medical journalists (Raymond Borel, Vladan Radoman, Gérard Illiouz, and Philippe Bernier) at the Paris offices of the medical journal *Tonus* to form the organization.

Some of the doctors had worked from 1968 to 1970 in Biafra, a region of Nigeria torn apart by a brutal civil war, on behalf of the French Red Cross. Others had volunteered in 1970 to treat the victims of a tidal wave in eastern Pakistan (now Bangladesh). Independently, these groups discovered—the first during a war, the second during the aftermath of a natural disaster—the shortcomings of international aid as it was then configured. By forming MSF, this core group intended to change the way humanitarian aid was delivered by providing more medical assistance more rapidly and by being less deterred by national borders during times of crisis.[1]

Throughout the next several decades, MSF hewed close to its basic, founding ideas, but it would learn by doing and adapt to the changing international environment, struggling to refine its response to crises and exploring the place and role of humanitarian action.

MSF IN THE 1970s: ROOTS, FIRST ACTIONS, AND COMPETING VISIONS
Activist Underpinnings

In addition to their medical training, many of MSF's founders were active in left-wing, anticolonial, and activist causes during France's turbulent 1960s. Bernard Kouchner was an ex-militant from the Communist Students Union, while Xavier Emmanuelli, an anaesthetist, was a member of the French Communist Party. Later influential members also shared these political leanings, including Claude Malhuret, a fiercely left-wing student from Cochin University Hospital, known in May 1968 as the "Red college," and Rony Brauman, a former Maoist militant from Cochin and a graduate in tropical medicine.

Soon after the heavily televised revolt of May 1968, far more disturbing images were brought to the French public. For the first time, television broadcasted scenes of children dying of hunger. The southern Nigeria province of Biafra had seceded. The territory was surrounded by the Nigerian army, and the Biafrans, victims of one of the very first oil conflicts, were decimated by famine.[2]

Red Cross Roots[3]

MSF's creation was also partly the culmination of a trend initiated ten years earlier by the International Committee of the Red Cross (ICRC), a trend that was itself a response to the work of Red Cross societies. During the early part of the twentieth century, humanitarian emergency aid was provided primarily by the Red Cross movement. But the effectiveness of its actions was compromised by slow transport facilities and cumbersome administrative and diplomatic formalities.

In times of war, the ICRC intervened. Its main role was to make sure that the belligerent nations complied with the Geneva Conventions providing for the protection of and assistance to prisoners and civilians in time of war. Until the beginning of the 1960s, the Geneva-based ICRC carried out its duties without sending medical units to battle sites.

It took the multiplication of civil wars in the developing world after the era of decolonization (Katanga in 1960, Yemen in 1962, Biafra in 1967) to prompt the ICRC to add medical assistance to its roster of help. These new conflicts were much harder on the civilian population than earlier wars because of food blockades, and because guerrilla and counter-guerrilla strategies caused massive flows of refugees and put large numbers of internally displaced persons in very precarious circumstances.

The ICRC began its emergency medical efforts by sending out a few doctors, whom it hired temporarily for renewable, three-month terms. These doctors were recruited by the national Red Cross societies. During the summer of 1968, the ICRC offered the French Red Cross (FRC) the opportunity to run its own independent medical mission in Biafra. The FRC accepted readily, particularly since its acceptance enabled the French government to support the Biafra secession without too much compromise.

From September 1968 until January 1970, under extremely dangerous circumstances, the FRC managed to send some fifty doctors to Biafra. For many, the conflict over Biafra meant the discovery of the "Third World," of a little-known conflict, and of the inability of humanitarian action to solve crises of enormous proportions. The Biafran war, which ended in 1970 with the Nigerian government's victory and the deaths of 1 million people, clearly revealed the shortcomings of the Red Cross in responding to emergencies.

Speaking Out as a Defining Characteristic of MSF: The Myth and Reality of Biafra[4]

During the war in Biafra, some of the future founders of MSF opposed ICRC strictures in providing assistance. In return for access, particularly to the POWs who are at the heart of its mandate, the ICRC typically promises that its findings will remain confidential. Thus, ICRC personnel take a reserved public attitude toward the events they witness during an assignment.

In addition, the ICRC interpreted neutrality in such a way that its intervention on any part of a country's territory required the approval of the central authorities. This essentially placed ICRC's aid to a break-away region such as Biafra at the mercy of the Nigerian government.

Several doctors defied this prohibition by organizing a "committee against the Biafran genocide" as soon as they were back in France—less to make the public aware of the plight of the Biafran population than to denounce the political sources of this conflict, which were too often hidden by the journalistic accounts of the war.

By dropping their apolitical stance, though, the French doctors gave legitimacy to the rebels' secessionist cause. In the media, the doctors offered sensationalist accounts, speculated wildly about death tolls, and invoked the Holocaust and genocide to describe the situation. The doctors' one-sided denunciations of the Nigerian government also led them to overlook serious rebel abuses, such as their refusal to accept aid that transited through Nigerian federal territory, which amounted to starving their own people to publicize their cause as victims. These actions unwittingly played into the hands of the rebels and their supporters, chief among them the French government, which hired a PR firm to generate publicity for the rebellion.

But this new wave of doctors was haunted by the passivity of the ICRC during World War II when confronted by the Holocaust, and wanted to avoid at all costs the sense that aid organizations were abetting the ultimate crime.

This activity attracted a group of approximately fifty people who were persuaded that conflicts such as Biafra would happen again and needed to be anticipated. Thus, the Biafra veterans began meeting once a month to share and refresh their memories. In 1970 they organized the Groupe d'Intervention Medical et Chirurgical d'Urgence (Emergency Medical and Surgical Intervention Group, or GIMCU), in the hope of setting up an independent association specializing in providing medical emergency assistance free from the administrative and legal constraints facing the ICRC.

At the same time as the conflict in Biafra, another group of doctors in France formed at the initiative of the medical journal *Tonus*. In 1970 *Tonus'* editor, Raymond Borel, had spoken on television about the distress of tidal wave victims in eastern Pakistan (now Bangladesh) and the lack of French doctors at the site of the disaster. On November 23, 1970, he published an appeal in the columns of his journal to establish an association: Secours Medical Français (French Medical Relief, or SMF).

Doctors responded to Borel's call to action for many reasons: a bad conscience in the wake of the disturbing television images; the feeling that France, because of its history, had a duty to cooperate with decolonized countries; or simply the desire to get away from routine medicine and benign pathologies in order to practice presumably more useful medicine under more stimulating conditions. In 1971 MSF arose from a merger of GIMCU and SMF.

The notion of *témoignage,* or speaking out, coupled with appeals to the mass media became an integral part of MSF's concept of modern humanitarian action. Ironically, though, until 1977 MSF actually forbade its members to talk about what they had witnessed during their missions, despite an early record of opposition to the ICRC's reserved policy. This silence was intended as a strong symbol of political neutrality as well as a strategic posture to ensure its ability to perform "border-free" operations, since it was thought that no state would accept the presence of overly garrulous doctors on its territory. Bernard Kouchner explained this as concession to the *Tonus* doctors.

MSF's First Interventions[5]

MSF was formed as a nonprofit organization according to the 1901 French law "Associations de loi." MSF would legally be a group of people "who have come together to act" (*associés pour agir*) and who would participate in the ownership of the organization. Members would essentially be former field staff, and the majority of the board, including the president, would be elected from and by the association members.

MSF's creation coincided with an era of increasing air transport, electronics, and satellites, and with the growing perception of the world as a global village. These factors made it possible to intervene increasingly rapidly at disaster sites. The instantaneous visibility of disasters and conflicts on television made it less

Médecins Sans Frontières (MSF) is a private international association. The association is made up mainly of doctors and health sector workers and is also open to all other professions which might help in achieving its aims. All of its members agree to honor the following principles:

Médecins Sans Frontières provides assistance to populations in distress, to victims of natural or man-made disasters, and to victims of armed conflict. They do so irrespective of race, religion, creed, or political convictions.

Médecins Sans Frontières observes neutrality and impartiality in the name of universal medical ethics and the right to humanitarian assistance, and claims full and unhindered freedom in the exercise of its functions.

Members undertake to respect their professional code of ethics and to maintain complete independence from all political, economic, or religious powers.

As volunteers, members understand the risks and dangers of the missions they carry out, and make no claim for themselves or their assigns for any form of compensation other than that which the association might be able to afford them.

Figure 1.1   MSF Charter

and less acceptable either to do nothing or to offer only a confused effort at emergency assistance.

From its beginning, MSF hoped to benefit from the experience of its "Biafran" firebrands and the infrastructures (offices and secretariat) of its *Tonus* group. But the first steps were difficult. Between 1971 and 1976, MSF was more like a pool of doctors at the disposal of large development aid organizations than a truly independent medical emergency organization. Its budget was limited to a few hundred thousand francs, and its assignments, with a few exceptions, were not independent: in Nicaragua after the 1972 earthquake, for example, and Honduras after the 1974 hurricane, the doctors actually traveled with the French military. For lack of resources and experience, these early and limited interventions were highly ineffective.

MSF remained a very small organization in the 1970s for several reasons. First, it consisted exclusively of volunteers, each of whom was employed outside MSF. In the circles of established international organizations, the MSF volunteers were considered amateurs and medical tourists. Second, MSF's members refused to ask for charity from the public or to "sell" humanitarian services as a commercial product, a policy that was not conducive to growth.

MSF flourished for the first time from 1976 to 1979. A 1976 war intervention in Lebanon in a Shi'ite neighborhood encircled by Christian militia, and a free advertising campaign offered by an advertising agency in 1977, gave MSF an identity as an organization that dealt with dangerous emergencies and its first public recognition. MSF was of interest not only in France but also in the United States, largely because the American press reported on the actions of the French doctors in Lebanon.

Despite its interventions during a widely reported war and the fruits of an advertising campaign (including one ad proclaiming with hyperbole that there were "two billion people in our waiting room"), in 1978 there remained a large gap between the association's reputation in France and its actual impact. And despite its strong showing in the media, the organization's existence was more symbolic than operational: it sent out only a few dozen doctors per year.

Competing Visions Lead to a Split

Throughout the 1970s, many of the physicians sent out by MSF returned from their aid assignments content with the experience, but frustrated by lack of adequate means with which to treat their patients.[6] Many drew broad conclusions that medical effectiveness was not at the heart of MSF's concerns. There was constant improvisation in the way humanitarian missions were selected and carried out: for Kouchner and his allies, MSF's strength resided in its informality, in its capacity to generate indignation and attention by carrying out symbolic missions in places that journalists and politicians could not reach. Kouchner argued that when people were dying by the hundreds, a team of doctors, however competent they may be, cannot really make a difference, and that building MSF into a structured organization would only further the illusion that they could.

In 1977 Dr. Claude Malhuret, sent by MSF to work for a year with the International Rescue Committee (IRC) in a Cambodian refugee camp in Thailand, returned to Paris with an experience shared by many others. Deeply critical of Kouchner, he argued that MSF needed to develop an independent structure to deploy multidisciplinary teams and to give them appropriate medical and logistical means in order to be effective in the field. "We are doctors," he said, "and if we organize ourselves and become a medical organization, we will really be useful."[7]

The opposition between these sharply contrasting visions about the very identity of the organization came to a head, and the outcome continues to shape MSF's evolution today. In 1978 Malhuret was elected president of MSF during the annual general assembly, and in 1979, a bitter dispute over MSF's participation in an initiative by leading French intellectuals to send a boat to rescue Vietnamese refugees in the South China Sea culminated in a split. Kouchner, who was part of the committee that launched "a boat for Vietnam," saw this as a spectacular way to unite the most influential French thinkers— Jean-Paul Sartre and Raymond Aron, who had often been at odds—in a common cause to shine a spotlight on the problem.

Although they did not underestimate the media and symbolic impact of this initiative, for the refugees and MSF, Malhuret and Emmanuelli disputed its technical legitimacy: they considered a single ship—whose very presence encouraged people to flee—insufficient to receive the refugees. In an article titled "A Boat for Saint-Germain-des-Prés," Emmanuelli went further in denouncing the ship as a self-serving stunt to give Parisian intellectuals a good conscience, when the plight of refugees around the world called for sustained commitment and practical action. In the 1979 MSF General Assembly, Malhuret's call to transform MSF into an effective medical organization, including by compensating volunteers who took on six-month assignments, defeated Kouchner's warning of MSF's impending death at the hands of "bureaucrats of charity."[8] Kouchner and his friends left MSF and went on to found Médecins du Monde/Doctors of the World, with key objectives intended as a rebuttal of MSF's new direction: "to denounce the intolerable and work without any compensation."

Efficiency, pragmatism, and professionalism, though, would be the watchwords of the team formed by Malhuret, Francis Charhon, and Dr. Rony Brauman, who transformed MSF in the 1980s and set the groundwork for its current actions and focus.

MSF IN THE 1980s: EFFICIENCY, PRAGMATISM, PROFESSIONALISM, AND THE LIMITS OF HUMANITARIAN ACTION IN THE CONTEXT OF THE COLD WAR
The Refugee Camp Factor

The multiplication of refugee camps at the end of the 1970s accelerated the growth of MSF after 1978 and defined MSF's main fields of intervention. Although the global refugee population remained stable between 1970 and 1976, it doubled between 1976 and 1979, from 2.7 million to 5.7 million. It doubled again between 1979 and 1982, settling at 11 million people until 1985. This increase was caused by a spike in the number of conflicts in the Southern Hemisphere after 1975, fueled largely by the reemergence, after the era of decolonization, of old national antagonisms and ethnic rivalries, as well as the fact that the East-West confrontation had moved out of Europe.

At the same time, the Soviet Union began to increase its influence in several developing countries, profiting from 1975 onward from the U.S. withdrawal from Vietnam and the instability brought about in southern and eastern Africa because of the Portuguese decolonization and the fall of the Ethiopian Negus. The Soviet expansion fueled a number of conflicts in Angola and Mozambique between pro-Soviet regimes and counterrevolutionary guerrillas, as well as in the Horn of Africa. There, Somalia and Ethiopia began to fight in 1977 over control of the Ogaden region, an Ethiopian territory inhabited mostly by Somalis. In addition, the 1975 communist takeover of Indochina led to the exodus of hundreds of thousands of boat people and other refugees to Thailand, Malaysia, and Indonesia. Meanwhile, ethnic and religious minorities in Eritrea and Lebanon began or continued civil wars to obtain their independence or more power. Millions of people were packed in camps along the borders of these warring countries, often under very poor sanitary conditions. Although the Office of the United Nations High Commissioner for Refugees (UNHCR) assumed responsibility for the refugees, and built and supplied camps, it had tremendous difficulty finding medical personnel willing to work in these areas.

MSF saw the increasing number of refugee settlements in the world as a fertile field of action. In contrast to the UNHCR, MSF did not lack doctors. In the second half of the 1960s, the French job market had been flooded by doctors from the baby-boom generation who did not have to repay their student loans (as they did in the United States) and who often had had their first taste of the "Third World" during their military service. Many general practitioners of this generation were experiencing an identity crisis. Faced in their daily practice with benign pathologies that did not interest them and unsolvable problems that they could only refer to specialists, many of them were tempted to practice what they saw as a "more authentic" form of medicine in the developing world.

From 1976 to 1979, MSF aided Angolan refugees in the former Zaire; Somali refugees in Djibouti; Saharan refugees in Algeria and Eritrea; and, above all, Vietnamese, Cambodian, and Laotian refugees in Thailand. Initially, MSF offered modest help to the American humanitarian organizations that had already been on the scene for over a year (particularly the International Rescue Committee and World Vision). Yet the French doctors sometimes questioned the motivations of the organizations for which they were working, suspecting them of acting as much for political objectives (anticommunism) and religious reasons (proselytizing) as for humanitarian goals.

During this period, MSF gradually expanded its operations in Thailand, slowly replacing the American organizations, which began to withdraw from the refugee camps as the memory of the Vietnam War began to fade. In December 1979, MSF also sent 100 doctors and nurses to the Cambodian border.

Logistics Revolution and Creating Medical Guidelines and Protocols

The transformation of MSF in the 1980s was prompted by a realization of how ineffective and poorly adapted the organization was in responding to the large-scale refugee movements and camps.

The nature of the humanitarian and medical challenges posed by large refugee camps led MSF leaders to turn to public health. In addition to delivering primary health care and carrying out medical consultations, the importance of implementing vaccination campaigns and providing water and sanitation became apparent. This diversification of activities that had to be carried out on a large scale prompted organizational transformation in several ways.

To begin with, improving the health of refugees required skills beyond those of the medical doctor, and this led to the constitution of multidisciplinary teams with other medical professionals including nurses, midwives, and lab technicians. But perhaps the key innovation that would revolutionize MSF's work was the "invention of the logistician." The first full-time logistics manager, the pharmacist Jacques Pinel, began to see the importance of logistics during an aid assignment assisting refugees on the Thai-Cambodian border in 1980. Following his experience, Pinel returned to Paris to work with other logistics and medical experts to develop a sophisticated inventory of medical and field supplies.

Given the nature of MSF's activities, the first logistical priority was the pharmacy: improving the way drugs were ordered, supplied, stored, and managed. This led to the development of standardized "kits" that included selected drugs and medical materials adapted to a particular situation, such as the now widely used 10,000 patients for 3 months' kit.

Logistics were also essential in other aspects: from the most basic such as organizing the accommodations and food for the medical teams, to more program-related activities such as the delivery of water in the medical structures or the building of latrines. The realization that strong logistics was the backbone of any effective aid operation further led to the constitution of specialized "logistical centers" in Europe that tested, purchased, and warehoused all items necessary for a medical humanitarian mission, a list that expanded over the years to include radio-telecommunication material, computers, and vehicles.

Epidemiological measures of effectiveness adapted to refugee camp settings, such as a target mortality rate of less than 1 person/10,000 people/day, emerged as program objectives. To reach these objectives, MSF developed protocols and guidelines in order to guide volunteers in carrying out medical work in contexts far different from the ones they were used to. In the 1980s, MSF produced a great number of medical guidelines, ranging from the now ubiquitous Essential Drugs and Clinical Guidelines to those dealing with sanitation, the priorities in refugee health, and responding to cholera outbreaks. These books helped standardize the medical response and served as training tools for volunteers.

Survival and Growth

The increasing number of programs throughout the 1980s required guidance and support from headquarters. The early days when practicing doctors would volunteer to spend one afternoon a week in the office to undertake a range of support activities were over. Permanent staff was hired to organize and supervise field operations. Over time, specialized functions beyond program support were developed—human resources management, communications and fundraising, financial oversight and accounting—as headquarters grew.

For MSF, a critical development was international expansion beyond the original French organization. In 1980, Belgian doctors who had been in the field with MSF created their own organization. This occurred with the support of Paris, which saw the creation of MSF-Belgium as a positive extension into a country with strong human resource and fundraising potential. For legal reasons however, MSF-Belgium was set up as an independent organization. The Belgian group soon developed its own dynamic: it ran its own programs, and its interpretation of

MSF's mission sharply contrasted with that espoused in Paris. Policy differences culminated in an open split and a failed attempt by MSF-France to strip MSF-Belgium of its name in 1985.

Other MSF national sections were then created—MSF-Holland, Switzerland, and Spain—in the mid to late 1980s, all of which ran their own programs. In practical terms, this meant that it was possible for five MSFs to be in one country sharing the same name but running distinct programs. While the diversity of approaches allowed more ground to be covered, it also created issues of internal coordination.

The late 1980s and early 1990s saw a next phase of organizational development. In some countries, such as Sweden, sections were created at the urging of doctors from that country. In other countries, offices were set up under the aegis of existing MSF sections. All of the MSF sections were formed as private, nonprofit organizations with different legal structures depending on the country in which they were formed. Several of these new entities, though, were associations in line with the spirit of MSF's original founding.

The intent of opening an office in the United States, as well as in other countries such as Japan, Australia, Canada, Sweden, or Hong Kong, was primarily to tap into the resources required to support growing field programs. Private funding in particular was a key consideration in this organizational expansion. These "partner sections," which today number fourteen, were designed as support offices that would not run field programs.[9]

Over the years, MSF has also helped to create several affiliated organizations that are devoted to pursuing specific areas of research in the field of emergency medicine and relief. In 1986 in Paris, MSF created Epicentre, a group of epidemiologists charged with epidemiological research and evaluation of the work of MSF and other aid organizations. Today, MSF and Epicentre are often called on to monitor, diagnose, and control outbreaks of diseases, such as cholera, meningitis, and measles.

In short, "professionalization" at MSF originated from the goal of developing field programs that would be more effective and better adapted to the needs of the populations the organization intended to serve, particularly refugees. Multidisciplinary field teams and the creation of specialized and permanent functions at headquarters were means that were considered necessary to make progress toward that end. MSF's further organizational development, particularly the setting up of offices worldwide to expand human and financial support, was an additional step in the same direction. The process and ensuing result has led to unforeseen consequences in organizational terms, particularly the large degree of interdependence between nominally independent entities.

Humanitarian Aid in the Cold War: On the Side of Freedom?

Although MSF's experience in refugee camps was critically important in defining its role and responsibility, it also led to reflection about humanitarian aid in Cold War. Many of the leftists who founded MSF began to realize that most of the refugees in the world were fleeing "socialist" or "communist" regimes. For Rony Brauman, it became apparent that "defending human rights and humanitarian principles required criticizing totalitarianism and defending democracy."[10]

The French section of MSF even created a short-lived think tank called "Libertés Sans Frontières," devoted to publicizing what was felt to be the root causes of the massive humanitarian crises of the 1980s: namely, totalitarianism and the lack of freedom. During this period, the group also organized a conference to critique "third-worldism," a doctrine that placed blame on Western neocolonialism as the fuel for many wars.

But taking a firmly anticommunist stand was no guarantee of avoiding misjudgments similar to those the original founders had made in Biafra. In their 1979 March for Cambodia, which staged a public protest on the Thai border demanding access to Cambodia, Malhuret and Brauman denounced "famine" in Cambodia based on the terrible shape of tens of thousands of refugees arriving in Thailand after the Khmer Rouge genocide. In reality, the refugees MSF treated were not representative of the situation for the Cambodian population, but were rather Khmer Rouge fighters and civilians who had been used as slaves. In Phnom Penh, Viet Nam had replaced a regime of terror with a dictatorship that stoked rumors of possible famine in order to receive international aid funds. The few international groups allowed to work in Cambodia were severely restricted, and the new regime manipulated incoming aid to gain international recognition. The famine never occurred.

In 1980 in Afghanistan, MSF ran clandestine cross-border programs to provide medical and surgical care for civilians affected by the Soviet invasion. Bringing their medical supplies on risky donkey caravans from Pakistan with the "mujahideen" resistance, MSF teams spent a year working in medical outposts in rural, isolated parts of Afghanistan before making the trip back. Keen to hear eye-witness accounts, the U.S. Congress invited MSF to testify for the first time, but it became clear that the primary objective was less to understand the medical and humanitarian conditions faced by the Afghan people than to denounce the Soviet occupation.

More Harm than Good? Confronting the Diversion and Manipulation of Aid

The drive toward professionalism and efficiency allowed MSF to respond more quickly and effectively to crises around the world. As the organization grew in size and capacity, though, it faced more complex political situations and confronted the limits of humanitarian action. In particular, the group was forced to ask this question: when do humanitarian organizations do more harm than good? Nowhere was this question more acute than in Ethiopia.

As a famine raged in 1984, the Ethiopian government began a policy of forcibly relocating hundreds of thousands of people in the country from areas most affected by the drought to more fertile regions. When MSF assisted with the first transfer, it saw no reason for criticism. But it became clear over time that the transfers had two nefarious aims: (1) to weaken the guerrilla movements in the north (in Eritrea and Tigre) by removing their grassroots supporters, and (2) to place these populations in villages in order to bring them ideologically in line with government policy. Under this scheme, humanitarian aid actually became a trap, used to attract vulnerable villagers and blackmail them into going along with the program.

By early 1985, the transfers became more authoritarian and violent. MSF members witnessed roundups of the hospitalized, and noticed that no efforts were made to keep families together. Many persons died during the transfers. The areas where people were forcibly relocated to frequently had inadequate facilities or assistance, while the Ethiopian authorities established food quotas in Addis Ababa. Furthermore, the transfers diverted many resources from the MSF rescue operations.

After lodging many fruitless protests with the Ethiopian authorities, MSF decided in November 1985 that, regardless of the consequences to its ability to remain in the country, the organization could no longer remain silent. If it did so, MSF could appear to be condoning the brutality of these transfers, already responsible for more deaths than the famine.

The presence of a host of aid organizations in Ethiopia made it less difficult for MSF to denounce the transfer practices in public and enabled MSF to take the risk of expulsion. In explaining this position, MSF operations advisor, François Jean, wrote that nongovernmental organizations (NGOs) must not help "fund a lunatic project of social transformation."[11] A few days after officially calling for a halt to the transfers, MSF was expelled from Ethiopia. MSF immediately briefed the media on the diversion of aid, used to oppress instead of help. A few days after MSF's expulsion, the European Economic Community and the United States decided to make further aid conditional on the discontinuance of these forced population transfers. Thus pressured, the Ethiopian government announced in early 1986 that it would cease its resettlement programs.

The experience in Ethiopia continues to echo within the organization. No longer could the humanitarian act be considered good in and of itself. Nor could humanitarian actors simply be content with developing technocratic proficiency without a deeper understanding of political developments. Rather, MSF needed to practice a humanitarian action that valued self-criticism and admitted the limits of what it could accomplish in the face of forces using means—blunt or subtle, crude or sophisticated—to manipulate and divert assistance. Such a critical and reflective stance would be needed for the crises in the decades ahead.

This experience was seminal for MSF. No longer was *témoignage* only about denouncing perpetrated crimes. Rather it was anchored in analysis about the responsibilities of aid agencies themselves—the impact, both positive and negative, of their presence and their work, which can reach the extreme of aiding and abetting crime.

Since Ethiopia, MSF has been confronted with a handful of extreme situations, where abstaining from providing aid has been seen as preferable to intervening, either because the minimum conditions for ensuring that victims would benefit from the assistance did not exist (Iraq under Saddam Hussein, North Korea) or because the negatives outweighed the positives, as when aid was used against the interests of its intended beneficiaries (Rwandan refugee camps in Zaire and Tanzania, see below; Rwandan refugees in Zaire 1996).

In North Korea in 1998, MSF felt leaving the country was preferable to continued action despite urgent medical and nutritional needs. After years of trying to negotiate to have free access, to independently assess the needs, to bring humanitarian assistance to those most in need, and to monitor its aid, there was a clear government policy to restrict and limit effective assistance, making it impossible to deliver aid in a principled and accountable manner. The government refused to acknowledge an emergency and would only allow structural support to rebuild the national pharmaceutical industry. At the time, MSF also called on all donor governments to review their aid policies toward North Korea to ensure more accountability and impartiality in delivering aid.

MSF IN THE 1990s: RESPONDING TO GENOCIDE AND MILITARY-HUMANITARIANISM LEADS TO AN INTERNAL CRISIS
Kurdistan, Somalia, and Bosnia—The Promise and Pitfalls of "Humanitarian Intervention"

The collapse of the Cold War's ideological divide brought hope of a quick end to what were seen as "proxy wars" throughout the Third World. Instead, a newly unified "international community" under the aegis of the UN was faced with the transformation of persistent wars in places such as Afghanistan and Angola and the eruption of new conflicts from Bosnia to Somalia. As MSF increasingly deployed in the midst of these wars, it found itself confronted with the novel doctrine of "humanitarian intervention," in which Western governments used military force ostensibly for humanitarian purposes. The selective application of the doctrine would range from abstention in the face of genocide (Rwanda) to "humanitarian war" (Kosovo). After overcoming profound internal divisions over its response to the Rwandan refugee crisis, MSF emerged from the decade with few illusions but a reinforced conviction about the value of independent humanitarian action.

In 1991, what President George H. W. Bush termed the "new world order" was inaugurated when a thirty-seven-nation-strong military coalition, duly endorsed by the UN Security Council, expelled Iraqi forces that had invaded Kuwait the year before. As the war was ending, hundreds of thousands of Kurds—with memories of massacres at the hands of Saddam Hussein's army still fresh in their minds—fled toward the border with Iran and Turkey.

Returning from an assessment mission in late March 1991, MSF's Dr. Marcel Roux spoke in vivid terms of the catastrophic situation of the Kurds, traumatized and fearful of further Iraqi atrocities, isolated in the mountains, and in dire need of shelter, food, and medical care. The UN Security Council adopted Resolution 688, which opened the way for a U.S.-led military operation that would both drop food to refugees on the border and establish a "safe zone" in Northern Iraq to facilitate their return.

Operation Provide Comfort was the first manifestation of the phrase coined by Bernard Kouchner, now France's "Minister for Humanitarian Affairs," as "right to intervene" (*droit d'ingerence*). This was a call for military intervention to protect and assist civilians at risk preferably with, but if need be without, the consent of the state on whose territory it would take place. While MSF mounted its largest ever relief operation on the ground—combining its French, Dutch, and Belgian sections, sending seventy-five cargo planes in ten days, and bringing supplies to the mountains by truck—the U.S. air force preferred to conduct airdrops. Xavier Emmanuelli, one of MSF's founders leading the field operations, was shocked at what he felt was a "show" mainly done for the cameras: planes were used even though trucks could reach the affected areas.

Eventually, the massive relief operation and especially the establishment of a "safe zone" secured by a credible military threat defused the crisis and allowed the Kurds to return to their homes. For many in MSF, though, there was a bitter aftertaste in what they saw as the hypocrisy of major powers that allowed the crisis to unfold before taking action in the name of humanitarian morality. It would also give a flavor of things to come.

At the same time, far from the media spotlight, a devastating crisis was unfolding in Somalia. After the ouster of the dictator Siad Barre in January 1991, internecine rivalry erupted between the rebel groups that had toppled him. Fierce fighting in the capital, Mogadishu, divided the city, caused thousands of casualties, and displaced countless more. MSF was one of the few organizations, along with the ICRC and Save the Children-UK, which managed to maintain a presence in the war-torn city, providing surgical services in highly insecure conditions. People in distress congregated in towns searching for food due to the combined effects of war and drought, and famine spread throughout southern and central Somalia.

Providing assistance during this massive crisis was extremely difficult. Anarchical violence and the absence of any system of social order extending to foreigners in Somalia compelled MSF (and other organizations) to use armed guards, a "necessary evil" whose costs would become increasingly apparent. In time, MSF teams would have a small militia on hire to protect their travel and work, fuelling the "war economy." But the benefits of MSF's surgical and nutritional programs in this massive crisis overrode these concerns.

MSF and other organizations, including the ICRC, attempted to publicize the Somali emergency. Ironically, as the famine was already receding from its peak of early to mid-1992, the United States launched Operation Restore Hope in the waning days of the Bush administration. The UN Security Council authorized the U.S.-led coalition to use all necessary means "to establish a secure environment for humanitarian relief operations in Somalia as soon as possible."[12] In December, U.S. marines staged a dramatic landing on a Mogadishu beach—already secured by UN forces—for the waiting TV crews and journalists.

Whether the U.S.-led coalition, operating under a "shoot to feed" policy, helped turn the corner by increasing relief supplies or whether only few people remained to be rescued is still debated. In any event, by early 1993, the worst of the famine was over, but Somalia's conflict over power and resources was not. The United States and its allies became embroiled in the war in the name of promoting political reconciliation. Soon, insecurity increased, U.S. forces fired at hospitals, and Somali forces captured and killed eighteen U.S. soldiers in October 1993.

MSF activities in the former Yugoslavia began in 1991 with an evacuation of the wounded from Vukovar, then under siege. For the next several years, MSF ran surgery programs, distributed medical supplies and drugs to hospitals and clinics, operated mobile clinics, and worked in refugee camps throughout the region. MSF also implemented a comprehensive mental health program in several areas because of the intense traumas experienced by the population.

MSF and other aid organizations were confronted with serious dilemmas of ethnic cleansing, and the events in Bosnia represented the culmination of the "humanitarian alibi," or the use of humanitarian aid to avoid making political decisions. First, the UN force was mandated to strictly protect humanitarian convoys, not populations. Then, the UN set up enclaves that were supposed to be UN "safe havens" for populations under assault. But MSF directly witnessed a massacre during the Bosnian Serbs' attack on Srebrenica on July 11, 1995, which led to the deportation of approximately 40,000 people and the execution of an estimated 7,000. Twenty-two local members of MSF's personnel and approximately 10 of the sick and wounded were also executed. The fall of the "safe haven" occurred in the face of NATO and UN paralysis, and would lead MSF to be actively involved, years later, in efforts to establish who had been responsible in France and Holland.

For MSF, as for other aid organizations, these three interventions ended the illusion that the "international community" would effectively take the side of victims and protect them from imminent danger. Instead, MSF recognized how humanitarian aid was used as a fig leaf to hide political inaction, or break the promise to protect civilians.

Rwanda — Genocide, Then the Hijacking of Aid

International powers abandoned Rwanda during the genocide in 1994, and humanitarian organizations were powerless. MSF managed to maintain a presence in Kigali at the height of the killings with a group of medical staff working with the ICRC to transform the ICRC compound into a hospital. Another MSF team worked at the King Faycal Hospital under UN military protection. These interventions helped save several hundred people, but were futile overall. Patients were slaughtered soon after they were discharged, or in ambulances as they were being transferred to the hospital. In Butare, MSF international personnel were powerless as their Rwandan colleagues were executed in the hospital. In fact, most of MSF's Rwandan colleagues, except for a handful of heroic exceptions, could not be evacuated and were killed. Humanitarian aid in this situation had been rendered meaningless. The situation led to MSF's belated, yet unprecedented, call in June 1994 for military intervention to stop the killings, coining the phrase "doctors and nurses cannot stop genocide." No effective military intervention occurred except for the Operation Turquoise by the French army in southwestern Rwanda, serving as much to protect the flight of the *genocidaires* as to protect remaining groups of Tutsi from genocidal onslaught.

Following the Rwandan army's defeats at the hands of the Rwandan Patriotic Front, the authorities responsible for the massacres orchestrated a mass exodus, first in late April into Tanzania and then of more than one million people into the Democratic Republic of Congo (former Zaire) in early July. The crisis continued to escalate when a cholera epidemic broke out in the refugee camps of eastern Congo, prompting the largest intervention in MSF's history. It soon became clear, though, that those responsible for the genocide were creating a climate of fear in these massive camps, with the *genocidaires* being bolstered by international relief operations that in turn strengthened the iron grip they maintained over the refugee population through the distribution of humanitarian relief. There was also growing evidence that the refugee camps located right on the Rwandan border were becoming training bases for members of the "interahamwe" militia and the former Rwandan armed forces (FAR), which had not been separated from the refugee population. Aid workers became increasingly outraged that they were turning into unwilling accomplices to the perpetrators of genocide.

A few months after the camps were established, MSF was divided on what do to—some felt MSF should leave and denounce the situation, while others felt that MSF's role was to provide medical services to vulnerable refugees, particularly women and children, while carrying out communication and advocacy to try to improve the situation. The sharp debate was thus not about the analysis of the camps' nature, but rather about MSF's responsibility, and three main positions crystallized. The French section took the drastic step of halting its aid operations at the end of 1994 in Zaire and Tanzania rather than participate in what it considered a perversion of humanitarian action, as assistance was propping up leaders intent on "finishing the genocide." The Belgian section decided to carry out "humanitarian resistance," aiming to undermine the clout of the leaders through its program implementation, for instance by providing information to refugees about returning to Rwanda in a way that undercut propaganda from the leaders. These efforts "managed to reduce the quantity of aid resources that were diverted to the military."[13] The Dutch section focused on its maintaining medical services, which it complemented with reports and "silent diplomacy." In late 1995, all had come to the conclusion that the situation was entrenched and untenable, and finally decided to leave.

Chantilly: Internal Crisis and Back from the Brink

The division among MSF sections about how to respond to the dilemma posed by the Rwandan refugee camps in Zaire and Tanzania was serious and profound. It resulted in an international process of reflection to attempt to resolve these differences and come to a common understanding. After a series of meetings, leaders of various MSF sections eventually agreed on a definition of what MSF stands for, aims to achieve, and the key principles it follows. While placing "medical action" in "crisis periods, where the very survival of the population is threatened" first and foremost, the Chantilly Principles also made *témoignage*—from raising public awareness to the possibility of openly criticizing and denouncing—an "indispensable complement" of MSF's medical action, putting an end to the debates about "silent diplomacy."[14] Organizational rules were created as well as the goal of being 50 percent privately funded in order to maintain an independence of action.

At this time, MSF also created an International Council (IC), regrouping all nineteen board presidents as the highest international policy-making forum. The IC instituted a moratorium on the opening of new sections, and decided on the transformation of all sections into "associations" according to France's "Association de loi" of 1901. This was done for reasons of principle as well governance. The associative spirit gave former field staff a democratic voice within the movement and ownership over MSF's direction and decisions. The governance structure put a premium on programmatic legitimacy, with leadership that was constituted of people who have carried out the core responsibility of designing and implementing medical humanitarian programs.

The Chantilly document states: "The commitment of each volunteer to the MSF movement goes beyond completing a mission; it also assumes an active participation in the associative life of the organization and an adherence to the Charter and Principles of MSF . . . the associative character of MSF permits an openness towards our societies and a capacity for questioning ourselves."[15]

The agreement at Chantilly also established an international office based in Brussels (today it is in Geneva.) It has a small staff led by the international secretary, and it orchestrates collaboration in areas such as pharmaceutical validation, quality control, medical guidelines, financial reporting, and representation and advocacy toward the UN or other international and national bodies.

Chantilly having brought MSF back from the brink, attempts were made to solidify the reaffirmation of the organization's international character through concrete collaboration. One was to organize a concerted emergency response system with a single operational leader for the whole of MSF. Although a few major programs, such as a mass meningitis vaccination campaign in Nigeria in 1996, were implemented, in the end, all of the sections agreed that MSF's reactivity was best served by the diversity of approaches among sections.

Nobel Peace Prize—An Ambiguous Recognition

As the twentieth century came to a close, MSF's work gained recognition from the Nobel Peace Prize Committee. Some felt that it offered hope for the recognition of independent humanitarian action. In his acceptance speech on behalf of the organization, Dr. James Orbinski, president of MSF's International Council said, "Humanitarian action is more than simple generosity, simple charity. It aims to build spaces of normalcy in the midst of what is profoundly abnormal. More than offering material assistance, we aim to enable individuals to regain their rights and dignity as human beings."[16]

But the recognition was ambiguous at best. MSF was keen to distance itself from having the Nobel Prize misconstrued as a triumph of the idea of military "humanitarian interventions" waged in the name of humanitarian ideals or motives. In Kosovo, NATO had used MSF data as one of the justifications for its military campaign, while other aid organizations were becoming "subcontractors" to the Western nations waging the war. Increasingly uneasy about humanitarian action being co-opted in a war effort, MSF took further measures to assert its independence.

HUMANITARIAN ACTION IN THE TWENTY-FIRST CENTURY
Medical Catastrophes: Struggling to Respond to HIV/AIDS

As the global HIV/AIDS pandemic raged throughout the 1990s, MSF was forced to reexamine the limits of its humanitarian action and what constituted an emergency. By 1999, HIV/AIDS had laid waste to millions of lives in villages, towns, and cities throughout Africa, Asia, and Latin America. The sick were arriving at MSF clinics and hospitals in increasing numbers, only to be told they had a deadly disease and that nothing could be done.

Debate had been going on within MSF for years about how to address the needs of people living with HIV/AIDS it was seeing in its field hospitals. Treatment on the scale needed seemed impossible. The magnitude of the problem dwarfed what one aid organization could handle, while the sophisticated, lifelong, daily regimen—based on the technologically heavy model of diagnosis and care implemented in European or North American hospitals—was ill suited for the remote, sometimes war-ravaged, infrastructure-less settings where MSF worked. The cost of the drugs ($10–$15,000 dollars per patient per year in 2000) could never be afforded by ministries of health, let alone by most people living with HIV/AIDS, and the long-term commitment needed to sustain treatment programs went far beyond the usual scope of a medical organization geared toward responding to acute crises that required immediate, but short-term, action. Doctors and nurses continued to return from their aid assignments frustrated and angry that they could do little for their patients who were dying in catastrophic numbers.

As obstacles to treatment seemed intractable, many MSF aid workers tried to integrate a variety of prevention programs or treatment of opportunistic infections into their projects in the mid- and late 1990s. But the pandemic spread with no end in sight. As the 1990s drew to a close, frustrations over the impotent medical response in the face of rising death tolls boiled over, and many within MSF began to push for solutions.

MSF's HIV project in Thailand began in 1995. As elsewhere, this largely consisted of providing palliative care and treatment for opportunistic infections. In Thailand a large network of people living with HIV/AIDS (PLWHAs), health professionals, and other NGOs had been fighting for better care for PLWHA, including having TB care provided in district hospitals so patients could be treated closer to home.

In Europe a group of MSF doctors and nurses were in the early stages of forming a campaign to help overcome obstacles such as high prices and patent restrictions preventing field doctors from providing life-saving medicines to their patients. They contacted Dr. Wilson, the medical coordinator of MSF's Thai program, and in turn linked the team up with a number of experts and activists. With coalitions building within Thailand and worldwide, HIV/AIDS treatment was soon possible.

Since the Thai health care system functioned well, the team decided to work within Ministry of Health structures, and began a treatment program in a district hospital on the outskirts of Bangkok. In 2000 Dr. Wilson became one of the first MSF physicians to provide ARV treatment. The subsequent project relied heavily on the involvement of PLWHAs, which would become a hallmark of successful HIV/AIDS treatment programs throughout the world.

Halfway across the world in 1999, Dr. Eric Goemaere and his colleagues were trying to open a treatment program in South Africa. The country had the world's highest prevalence of HIV/AIDS, and people living with HIV/AIDS took an active, and growing, part in community efforts to address the epidemic.

After a project site outside of Johannesburg was blocked by government health officials at the end of 1999, a clinic in Khayletshia, a sprawling slum near Cape Town, gave Dr. Goemaere some dilapidated space to set up.

The team felt strongly that the only viable solution was to rely on generic versions of the medicines, most likely from manufacturers in India and Brazil. Overcoming patent barriers to using generic medicines would be another hallmark of successful treatment programs. In the seven years since generic competition emerged, the price for ARVs has dropped to a much more affordable level—less than US$150—and has allowed for more massive scale-up of programs throughout the world.

The first patient was put on treatment in Khayletshia in May 2001. Over the next six years, MSF drastically scaled up its treatment programs, and by the end of 2007, MSF was treating more than 100,000 people living with HIV/AIDS—including more than 7,000 children—in more than thirty-two countries. While still barely a drop in the ocean of needs, international efforts have been growing as well. New obstacles have arisen, though, including a dangerous shortage of healthcare workers contributing to the inability of many countries to scale up HIV/AIDS programs.

The experience in trying to respond to HIV/AIDS led MSF to incorporate responding to medical catastrophes into its self-defined mandate.

Access to Essential Medicines Campaign

For years, there was growing recognition in MSF that medical staff faced major problems trying to treat their patients. This was not just a technical issue, but also a political one. Medicines were inaccessible to poor people living in resource-poor countries because they did not represent a market for the pharmaceutical industry nor a political constituency. Lack of access to ARVs was the most egregious example, but others multiplied. The production of a useful drug for treating meningitis, oily chloramphenicol, had been abandoned because no other uses had been found. The same held true for eflornithine, which proved effective in treating human African trypanosomiasis, also known as sleeping sickness. Every day in the field, doctors and nurses were forced to make choices that conflicted with medical ethics, such as rationing treatments or not providing ARVs.

In 2000 MSF, led by Dr. Bernard Pécoul, launched the Access to Essential Medicines Campaign to understand and overcome select obstacles, hoping to obtain the medicines needed to transform medical practice in the field. The campaign would focus on patients in MSF programs, but advocate for solutions that would also benefit others. The campaign was critical of donation programs from the pharmaceutical industry, and pushed for generic production to lower prices through competition. It also called for greater public involvement in R&D as private incentives would not stimulate research where no market existed. Analysis of price issues pushed MSF to learn about areas far from its core expertise: for example, how patent protections (TRIPS) were included in international trade agreements as an obligation for countries wanting to join the World Trade Organization, or how generic production was threatened in countries such as India that had not issued patents on pharmaceuticals. MSF and others pushed for the public health safeguards included in TRIPS to be effectively used to increase access to medicines. MSF confronted international policies detrimental to public health and access, often linking with and supporting national activists, as in the 2001 South Africa court case.

MSF used the proceeds from the Nobel Peace Prize to support this new Access to Essential Medicines Campaign as well as to fund a working group to investigate how best to spark research and development into diseases neglected by most of the pharmaceutical industry. This working group led to the creation of the Drugs for Neglected Diseases initiative (DNDi), which today is an independent organization led by Dr. Pécoul, of which MSF is a co-founder, along with several public-sector research institutions mainly in endemic countries (Brazil, India, and Kenya, in addition to the Pasteur Institute). DNDi fosters collaboration both among developing countries and between developing and developed countries, focusing on needs-based, field-adapted research to develop new treatments for neglected diseases such as human African trypanosomiasis, or sleeping sickness, visceral leishmaniasis, and Chagas disease.

No to "Coherence"—Independence of Action

In Angola in 2002, following a negotiated surrender of UNITA after the death of Jonas Savimbi, MSF responded to the discovery of starving populations emerging from war zones throughout the country. MSF struggled to expand nutritional and medical programs to deal with the emergency at a time when the UN was focused on negotiating with the Angolan government for a comprehensive approach, not just assistance but also disarmament and the creation of a political process. The UN did not push the humanitarian imperative independently, and put pressure on MSF not to break ranks, resulting in a serious delay in providing assistance.

The humanitarian failure in Angola was part of a trend that had begun a decade earlier in which international interventions increasingly combined political, military, and assistance programs under one umbrella. In several instances, the UN led robust peacekeeping operations that subordinated relief efforts to broader political aims. MSF was skeptical of the trend, as the very essence of humanitarian action is to provide aid without conditions, and many within MSF felt that impartial assistance would take a back seat to other concerns. MSF's field experience confirmed these fears.

In Liberia in the late 1990s, the UN peacekeeping force bombed MSF convoys. In Sierra Leone, as well, the UN and international organizations withdrew from the country to protest the RUF/AFRC takeover, in effect creating a situation of collective punishment. The Henry Dunant Center called this "one of the most shameful episodes regarding international humanitarian action in modern times."[17] Only MSF, ICRC, and Action Against Hunger stayed.

This trend of associating humanitarian aid with broader strategic goals was intensified in the "global war on terror" launched in response to the terrorist attacks on New York City in 2001. Recent wars waged by Western powers put forward a variety of objectives for taking military action, such as restoring peace, democratic political order, and economic development. Relief operations in these contexts have aspects of propaganda and public relations, both in the war zone and at home, in helping to depict the overall mission as altruistic or humanitarian. United States–backed coalition forces have consistently sought to further U.S. military and political ambitions by using aid to "win hearts and minds" and gather intelligence.

It has always been difficult to work in war zones. Humanitarian principles such as impartiality—providing aid based on need alone, without any kind of discrimination—and neutrality—the refusal to take political sides—help aid workers navigate between warring groups, gain acceptance from all groups, and help reduce security risks while delivering much-needed assistance in volatile and sensitive environments. By definition, humanitarian assistance is a suspect activity in many contexts. In MSF's experience, the most effective way to gain acceptance and a measure of trust in conflict settings is to have a very clear and transparent humanitarian identity to defuse suspicion and to provide quality medical care to build support. It is, however, never a guarantee.

Given the overt attempts of Western-based military interventions to enlist humanitarian aid, MSF has taken steps to remain independent and distinct. MSF denounced several of the coalition's attempts to co-opt humanitarian aid, particularly dropping "humanitarian" food packets during the initial aerial strikes in Afghanistan, calling aid workers "force multipliers," and distributing leaflets that conditioned aid based on civilians providing intelligence about the Taliban and al Qaeda. Because of such actions, MSF's fear was that the provision of aid would no longer be seen as an impartial and neutral act, thus endangering the lives of humanitarian volunteers and jeopardizing the aid to people in need.

Despite these efforts, some radical groups may never see MSF or other groups as strictly humanitarian and may continue to target aid workers and civilian groups, especially in situations involving Western military intervention.

"MSF does not object to militaries building village clinics or offering medical help. But these are legal obligations under the Geneva Conventions, not humanitarian assistance," wrote Dr. Rowan Gillies, the president of MSF's International Council in 2004. "People in crisis deserve to have access to impartial, independent humanitarian aid based on needs alone, without regard to military political objectives. In the 'war against terror' all factions want us to choose sides. We refuse to choose sides, just as we refuse to accept a vision of a future where civilians trapped in the hell of war can only receive life-saving aid from the armies that wage it."[18]

Aid Workers Face Increasing Risks

As aid has moved from the periphery to the center of war zones and the multiplication of actors, aid workers face increased exposure. In 1989 a missile destroyed an Avions Sans Frontières airplane in Sudan, killing two MSF members on board. In 1990 an MSF logistics expert was assassinated in Afghanistan, and in 1997, an MSF doctor was murdered in Somalia. The organization faced kidnappings in Colombia, Ingushetia, and Sierra Leone as well as grave security concerns in the former Yugoslavia, Liberia, Chechnya, Rwanda, and Congo (former Zaire).

In July 2004 in Afghanistan, MSF closed all medical programs in the aftermath of the killing of five MSF aid workers in a deliberate attack on June 2, 2004, when a clearly marked MSF vehicle was ambushed in the northwestern province of Badghis. Five MSF colleagues were mercilessly shot in the attack. This targeted killing, the government's failure to at first arrest the primary suspects and then credibly prosecute them, as well as declarations by the Taliban claiming responsibility and threatening further attacks made it impossible for MSF to continue providing assistance to the Afghan people.

MSF is not alone. More than thirty aid workers had been killed in Afghanistan since the beginning of 2003. The association of aid with broader political and military goals has heightened the likelihood that aid workers will become targets and will be attacked.

"MSF, as a medical humanitarian organization, provides unconditional assistance to people in Afghanistan and elsewhere around the world based on needs alone, regardless of political beliefs or relations with any military or political groups," said Nicolas de Torrente, executive director of MSF-USA in 2004. "When warring parties do not respect the integrity of impartial needs-based humanitarian action, aid workers are put at serious risk. In the end, the result is that people do not get the aid they badly need."[19]

The kidnapping of Arjan Erkel in the northern Caucasus and its aftermath highlighted the increasing dangers aid workers faced in several conflict zones and the willingness of many armed groups and governments to undermine legal protections shielding civilians and aid workers alike from violence during war, as set down in International Humanitarian Law (IHL). "Since 1994, 15 humanitarian aid workers have been abducted in the Caucasus including four MSF aid workers," said MSF program officer Patrice Pagé in 2003. "The violence towards civilians is clearly extending to humanitarian aid workers."[20]

Arjan Erkel was held for twenty months. Afterward, the Dutch government sued MSF in a Swiss court—they wanted to recoup funds they had paid as ransom after having negotiated with Russian security services. In March 2007, a Swiss judge ruled in MSF's favor, a judgment that was upheld by a higher court in March 2008 after the Dutch government appealed the initial verdict. Especially troubling in this episode, though, was the Dutch government's argument that it does not have any specific obligations related to Arjan Erkel's status as an aid worker—in their view, he was no different than an employee of a private company.

Private Funding Helps Maintain Independence of Action

Responding on the basis of need and reducing security risks for teams are two of the reasons why MSF has insisted on building and defending the independence of its medical humanitarian action. It is impossible to act independently, though, without the resources to do so.

MSF took a strategic decision in the mid-1990s to move away from institutional and government funding. Today, it relies on the general public for well over 80 percent of its operating funds. The remaining funds come from international agencies and governments. The organization counted more than 3.3 million individuals, foundations, corporations, and nonprofit organizations among its donors worldwide in 2006 for $714 million of income. The organization continues to exert significant effort at building unrestricted, stable, and diverse revenue sources.

This independence of funding is critical to a rapid response, flexibly, and innovation. Political and other interests can sometimes drive government funding decisions, and MSF does not want to be considered as implementing agents, or "subcontractors," for government interventions. If MSF relied primarily on government funding, for example, it would not have been able to start ARV treatments for people living with HIV/AIDS.

Relying on media-driven private funding has its drawbacks as well: neglected crises without media coverage do not generate donations, while highly exposed crises can sometimes lead to an overreaction in response. Following the tsunami that devastated many parts of South Asia in 2004, MSF was able to set up medical clinics in Aceh, Indonesia, within seventy-two hours. MSF quickly realized, however, that emergency needs in the region would be limited, and that the local response, particularly in Sri Lanka, was significant. Faced with a massive, unprecedented, spontaneous outpouring of support, MSF decided to stop accepting earmarked funds within days of the catastrophe. MSF asked donors to "de-restrict" their gifts. Nearly all of them agreed to do so, while the others were reimbursed. This allowed MSF to have sufficient resources to respond to other crises, most notably a nutritional crisis in Niger, where MSF teams effectively treated nearly 70,000 severely malnourished children.

"In 2006, MSF undertook over 9 million medical consultations, and hospitalized almost half a million patients," said Dr. Christophe Fournier, president of MSF's International Council. "For this work and commitment to remain constant, the massive support we receive from individual donors worldwide remains crucial. It allows us to preserve our humanitarian identity and to maintain our independence to make decisions about where and how we will work, guided by the needs of our patients and independent from any power other than the medical-humanitarian imperative."[21]

Treating Victims of Today's Armed Conflicts

Beginning with its intervention during Lebanon's civil war in the 1970s, the commitment to treating victims of armed conflict has been central to MSF's work throughout its history.

MSF has moved from the periphery of conflicts in refugee camps to try to be closer to the violence directly and indirectly affecting civilians. The number of internally displaced persons has been increasing as borders become closed to those trying to flee war, as in the DR Congo. Many conflicts today are also in urban areas, as in Port-au-Prince, Haiti; Mogadishu, Somalia; and Port Harcourt, Nigeria; in these locations, MSF has tried to offer more comprehensive services, including surgery for victims of direct violence, physical rehabilitation, and mental health services for trauma victims.

One of MSF's largest operations has been in the Darfur region of Sudan. A brutal, scorched-earth counterinsurgency campaign in 2003 and 2004 left tens of thousands dead and hundreds of thousands of people displaced. For the next several years, hundreds of international MSF staff and thousands of Sudanese personnel brought aid to people in North, South, and West Darfur as well as to hundreds of thousands of refugees in Chad. Security conditions have deteriorated over the last several years, with armed groups fragmenting and banditry becoming rife, putting at risk humanitarian aid to hundreds of thousands of people.

In Iraq, there are specific operational dilemmas. In order to provide critical medical and surgical care to victims of the violence there, it is necessary to reach them quickly, which means providing appropriate services as close as possible to where the violence is occurring. However, it is precisely those violence-affected areas that are the most unsafe for patients and for medical personnel, particularly for international staff.

MSF has taken two different approaches to deal with this dilemma in order to support medical personnel inside Iraq who are dealing with the bulk of casualties.

One is trying to provide medical supplies and training from Jordan to Iraqi medical staff still on the front lines.

The other is to provide care to patients in more stable and safe environments. The MSF project in Amman, Jordan, attempts to help rehabilitate stabilized Iraqi patients who require complex orthopedic, maxillo-facial, or plastic surgery services. While the project does provide hands-on care to Iraqi patients, it faces a number of limits and challenges such as administrative or political barriers to entering Jordan and lengthy treatment. MSF is also trying to help Iraqi doctors who are still working in the country despite the threats they are facing.

Both approaches, while important, have serious drawbacks. "In the worst war zone of the new century, international assistance is absent on the ground," said Christopher Stokes, secretary general of MSF International. "In contrast, the deployment—albeit fragile and often threatened—of over one hundred MSF international aid workers in Darfur is a painful reminder of the impotence of humanitarian aid agencies. The struggle to assist victims of conflict is not one MSF can abandon, but it will be a long, hard struggle to achieve a real operational space in Iraq."[22]

Critical Reflection Leads MSF to Treat Victims of Sexual Violence

What is an effective humanitarian aid operation? How can we improve the aid we provide to victims of armed conflict? Questions such as these often confront aid workers in the course of their work, and struggling to answer them helps MSF strive to improve its emergency medical care. A culture of reflection led MSF to critique its operations during the civil war in Congo-Brazzaville 1998–2000, which illustrates the risk that policy "lenses" can lead to pressing medical needs being neglected.[23]

During an intervention that assisted displaced Congolese returning to Brazzaville in dire nutritional and medical condition, a large number of women who had been assaulted and raped did not receive appropriate care. Although the field team was aware of the severity and extent of the problem, it focused its limited means in a tense security environment on nutritional assistance. The people in head-quarters also did not devote sufficient attention to the issue, and did not move to ensure adequate care was provided, in particular, post-exposure prophylaxis against HIV/AIDS. The reason was largely that sexual violence was then not considered a policy priority in conflicts. In fact, it is largely the experience garnered in Congo-Brazzaville that has resulted in sexual violence becoming a key concern of MSF's in all conflict settings, along with the development of specialized medical and psychological approaches and tools.

By 2007 the treatment of sexual violence victims had been integrated into most of MSF's interventions. At the Bon Marché hospital in Bunia, capital of the Ituri region in eastern Democratic Republic of Congo (DRC), for example, MSF teams treated 7,400 rape victims over a four year period, thus revealing the brutal targeting of women in that war.

The Need for Innovative Medical Tools

There is an urgent need for innovative medical tools adapted to the conditions faced by people in resource-poor settings. Tuberculosis (TB), malaria, HIV/AIDS, sleeping sickness, Chagas disease, kala-azar, and many other diseases have been all but abandoned by the current for-profit research and development system. The drugs to treat TB, for example, all date from the 1960s even though the most widely used TB diagnostic test was invented in the 1880s.

When an innovative medical tool is adapted to people's needs in resource-poor settings, the result can be stark. The innovative three-in-one fixed-dose combination ARV created by an Indian generic manufacturer, for example, has allowed the scale-up of treatment for people living with HIV/AIDS.

MSF also began an innovative nutritional program in the vast, landlocked West African nation of Niger adapted to the needs of severely malnourished children, who are mostly poor and from rural areas. Based in large part on the provision of new therapeutic ready-to-use foods (RUF) such as BP 100 or Plumpy'nut, the vast majority of malnourished children can now take treatment at home, under the supervision of their mothers or other caregivers, instead of in a hospital.[24]

The value of this approach became most evident in 2005, when a nutritional emergency ravaged impoverished families throughout rural parts of the country. MSF teams successfully treated nearly 60,000 severely malnourished children during the crisis.

In previous nutritional crises, MSF and others could reach only a fraction of those in need because of the limitations inherent in the tools available at the time. The famine in southern Sudan in 1998 produced mortality rates that in some areas equaled or exceeded those reported in Ethiopia during the crisis of 1985. MSF encountered catastrophic levels of malnutrition and mortality in Bahr el Ghazal, with more than 100 people dying every day in some areas. Although MSF was late in responding to the initial signs of the crisis, teams quickly set up throughout the region and were able to treat thousands of children.

"Before, we wouldn't have been able to treat nearly as many children," said Dr. Milton Tectonidis. "Angola in 2002 was MSF's last big nutritional response that did not include outpatient care, and we treated 8,600 children. So it's a huge difference. Therapeutic foods should be considered an essential medicine and not just during emergencies. I don't think we can go back again."[25]

Since outpatient treatment based on RUF proved so effective the previous two years, MSF decided in 2007 to provide a modified version as a supplement to the staple of the daily diet for young Nigerian children in the hopes of preventing severe malnutrition in high-prevalence areas. Initial results have shown great promise.

The "La Mancha" Process and Challenges Ahead

Nearly forty years after its creation, both MSF and the international environment in which it works have changed significantly. In 2006 the group undertook a consultative process to reflect on its roles and responsibilities, to define a common ambition among its various sections, and to clarify issues of internal governance. The "La Mancha" process, as it was known internally, is emblematic of MSF's emphasis on critical review and an effort to learn from successes as well as failures. The resulting text serves as a companion to the original MSF Charter and the more recent Chantilly Principles, and was written to help guide MSF in the years ahead.

Concerning MSF's social mission, La Mancha reaffirmed that the core of the group's work would continue to be responding to emergency medical needs arising from conflict or medical catastrophes. Top priority should also be given to improving the effectiveness, relevance, and quality of operations. Speaking out to highlight and confront political responsibilities would remain central to MSF's identity, but the group would refrain from proposing global solutions. MSF would, however, be committed to transparently documenting its results and exposing obstacles that could contribute to a response that can benefit others. There will be an effort at consensus in public positions, but not at the total exclusion of minority points of view. And because of the disillusionment with international efforts to "coherently" respond to crises, MSF would stress the independent and humanitarian nature of its work.

Organizationally, La Mancha strengthened MSF's international governance and reaffirmed its international, associative character. Few colleagues from the countries where MSF works were present at the La Mancha conference, but they made their voice heard. There was a strong consensus that MSF had failed to integrate national staff appropriately, and that urgent action was needed to address this shortcoming in the years ahead.

The transformation of MSF from an idea to a single section in France to today's international network in nineteen countries has been profound. This interdependence has enabled the continued expansion of field operations by providing much-needed human and financial resources. Mutual accountability and active transparency will be key elements as MSF moves forward.

For the people who make up the organization, maintaining creativity and innovation as the group continues to grow with strong public support will require a major commitment. As future transformations are inevitable, the culture of debate and participation that helped MSF adapt in previous years will help guide its members as they provide emergency medical assistance to people struggling to survive crises around the world.

ORGANIZATIONAL SNAPSHOT

Organization: Médecins Sans Frontières/Doctors Without Borders (MSF)

Founders: Xavier Emmanuelli, Marcel Delcourt, Max Recamier, Gérard Pigeon, Jean Cabrol, Jean-Michel Wild, Bernard Kouchner, Pascal Greletty-Bosviel,

Jacques Beres, Raymond Borel, Vladan Radoman, Gérard Illiouz, and Philippe Bernier

President of U.S. Board of Directors, & President of Officers of the Organization: Darin Portnoy, MD, MPH

Mission/Description: Doctors Without Borders/Médecins Sans Frontières (MSF) is an independent international medical humanitarian organization that delivers emergency aid to people affected by armed conflict, epidemics, natural and man-made disasters, or exclusion from health care in more than 70 countries.

Each year, MSF doctors, nurses, logisticians, water-and-sanitation experts, administrators, and other medical and non-medical professionals depart on more than 4,700 aid assignments. They work alongside more than 25,800 locally hired staff to provide medical care.

In emergencies and their aftermath, MSF provides essential health care, rehabilitates and runs hospitals and clinics, performs surgery, battles epidemics, carries out vaccination campaigns, operates feeding centers for malnourished children, and offers mental health care. When needed, MSF also constructs wells and dispenses clean drinking water, and provides shelter materials like blankets and plastic sheeting.

Through longer-term programs, MSF treats patients with infectious diseases such as tuberculosis, sleeping sickness, and HIV/AIDS, and provides medical and psychological care to marginalized groups such as street children.

MSF was founded in 1971 as the first nongovernmental organization to both provide emergency medical assistance and bear witness publicly to the plight of the people it assists. A private nonprofit association, MSF is an international network with sections in 19 countries.

Website: www.doctorswithoutborders.org

Address: 333 7th Avenue, 2nd Floor

New York, NY 10001-5004

Phone: (212) 679-6800

Fax: (212) 679-7016

E-mail: Kevin.phelan@newyork.msf.org

NOTES

1. Section adapted from Rony Brauman and Joelle Tanguy, "The Médecins Sans Frontières Experience" (http://www.doctorswithoutborders.org/volunteer/field/themsf experience.cfm).

2. *The MSF Adventure*, a documentary by Anne Vallaeys and Patrick Benquet (2006).

3. Section adapted from Rony Brauman and Joelle Tanguy, "The Médecins Sans Frontières Experience" (http://www.doctorswithoutborders.org/volunteer/field/themsf experience.cfm).

4. Section adapted from Rony Brauman and Joelle Tanguy, "The Médecins Sans Frontières Experience" (http://www.doctorswithoutborders.org/volunteer/field/themsf experience.cfm).

5. Section adapted from Rony Brauman and Joelle Tanguy, "The Médecins Sans Frontières Experience" (http://www.doctorswithoutborders.org/volunteer/field/themsf experience.cfm).

6. Anne Vallaeys, *Médecins sans Frontières: la biographie* (Paris: Fayard, 2004), pp. 150–55.

7. Vallaeys, p. 248.

8. See Rony Brauman and Joelle Tanguy, "The Médecins Sans Frontières Experience."

9. The exception is MSF-Greece, which was created with the intention of running field programs. It did so for a number of years before being expelled from the MSF movement in 1999 over its stance during the Kosovo crisis. MSF-Greece has been reintegrated within MSF in early 2005, but its operations have been folded under the authority of MSF-Spain.

10. See Rony Brauman and Joelle Tanguy, "The Médecins Sans Frontières Experience."

11. Francois Jean, *From Ethiopia to Chechnya: Reflections on Humanitarian Action, 1988–1999* (New York: MSF, 2008), p. 23.

12. U.N. Security Resolution 794, December 1992 (http://daccessdds.un.org/doc/ UNDOC/GEN/N92/772/11/PDF/N9277211.pdf?OpenElement).

13. Fiona Terry, *Condemned to Repeat* (Ithaca, NY: Cornell University Press, 2002), p. 201.

14. *Who Are Médecins Sans Frontières?*, MSF Internal document (1997).

15. *Who Are Médecins Sans Frontières?*

16. Nobel Lecture by James Orbinski, Médecins Sans Frontières, Oslo, December 10, 1999 (http://nobelprize.org/nobel_prizes/peace/laureates/1999/msf-lecture.html).

17. Henry Dunant Centre for Humanitarian Dialogue, "Politics and Humanitarianism Coherence in Crisis?" (February 2003), p. 11 (http://www.reliefweb.int/ rw/lib.nsf/db900sid/RURI-6N4RYU/$file/politics%20and%20humanitarianism.pdf? openelement).

18. Dr. Rowan Gillies, *Wall Street Journal*, August 19, 2004, p. A13.

19. Nicolas de Torrente, "Our Distress and Grief are Compounded by Outrage": On the Killing of Five MSF Aid Workers in Afghanistan (June 2004) (http://www.doctors withoutborders.org/publications/ideas/opinion_nicolasdetorrente_06-04.cfm).

20. Patrice Pagé, presentation at the U.S. Holocaust Memorial Museum (September 2003) (http://www.ushmm.org/conscience/analysis/details.php?content=2003-09-15).

21. Dr. Christophe Fournier, MSF International Activity Report (2007) (http://www. doctorswithoutborders.org/publications/ar/report.cfm?id=2382).

22. Christopher Stokes, MSF International Activity Report (2007) (http://www.doctors withoutborders.org/publications/ar/report.cfm?id=2383).

23. Marc le Pape and Pierre Salignon, eds., *Civilians under Fire—Humanitarian Practices in the Congo Republic 1998–2000* (n.p.: MSF/L'Harmattan, 2002).

24. *Community-Based Management of Severe Acute Malnutrition: A Joint Statement by the World Health Organization, the World Food Programme, the United Nations Standing Committee on Nutrition and the United Nations Children's Fund* (May 2007). (http://www.who.int/child-adolescent-health/New_Publications/CHILD_HEALTH/ Severe_Acute_Malnutrition_en.pdf).

25. Milton Tectonidis, MSF Voices from the Field (August 2005) (http://www.doctorswith outborders.org/news/voices/2005/08-2005_niger.cfm).

2

Unite For Sight

Jennifer Staple*

Unite For Sight is the only organization that has been able to give free treatment in this settlement since I have been on this refugee camp, and right now there are people coming all the way from Liberia here for help from Unite For Sight. Many of our patients have returned to Liberia with the good news about Unite For Sight in the refugee camp in Ghana.

—Karrus Hayes, President of Unite For Sight
Chapter at Buduburam Refugee Camp

The question I have always asked myself is "what would have happened to all these people who have benefited from Unite For Sight programs had the organization not come to their aid?" It is likely that many would have perished in their agony.

—Dr. James Clarke, Crystal Eye Clinic, Unite For Sight
Partner Ophthalmologist in Ghana

There are an estimated 45 million blind people and 135 million visually impaired individuals worldwide.[1] The World Health Organization (WHO) indicates that 90 percent of people who are blind live in developing countries, and 80 percent of blindness is curable or preventable.[2] The major barriers to eye care in developing countries include education and awareness, expense, distance and transportation, and poor quality of services by untrained or under-trained doctors. With 45 ophthalmologists, Ghana has one of the highest number of ophthalmologists in Africa: there is approximately one ophthalmologist for every 59,146 people. Liberia, in contrast, has only a handful of ophthalmologists for the entire

---

*The author is grateful to Buduburam Refugee Camp resident Karrus Hayes's work as her research assistant for this chapter.

population of 3.5 million. In the United States, there is one optometrist or ophthalmologist for every 5,000 people,[3] with an estimated 59,146 eye doctors for the population. Yet, despite the prevalence of doctors in the United States, we know that more than 40 million people remain uninsured and medically underserved in general health care. Countries such as Ghana and Liberia, with many fewer ophthalmologists, cannot meet the eye care needs of the majority of the population.

Further complicating the lack of eye care professionals is the fact that poor patients in rural areas are usually unaware that their blindness may be curable or preventable. Even those aware of eye care services will often not pursue treatment because of fear or expense. Quality eye care and innovative outreach programs are vital in order to achieve the Vision 2020 goals of the WHO and the International Agency for Preventable Blindness. With a mission statement of "The Right to Sight," Vision 2020 seeks to eliminate avoidable blindness worldwide by the year 2020.[4]

Eight years ago, I founded Unite For Sight, a 501(c)(3) nonprofit organization that improves eye health and eliminates preventable blindness. I founded the organization when I was a sophomore at Yale University. During the previous summer, I had worked as a clinical ophthalmology research associate in Connecticut. While interacting with low-income patients, I learned about eye diseases that could have been prevented by early medical intervention. Their poignant stories made me recognize the need for community programs to promote eye health, motivating me to found Unite For Sight. What started with a single volunteer has now grown to a force of 4,000 volunteers worldwide, who are dedicated to targeting the more than 36 million people with undiagnosed and untreated cases of preventable blindness, including those suffering eye damage as a result of atrocities committed against them. In April of each year, Unite For Sight volunteers from throughout the world, as well as others among the general public who are interested in global health, convene for Unite For Sight's annual Global Health Conference. The goal of the conference is to exchange ideas across disciplines—from international service and public health to microfinance and international development—about best practices to achieve global goals in health and development. The Unite For Sight conference has become a key to continuous enhancement of the organization's eye care programming within the context of international development, social entrepreneurship, and global health.

Unite For Sight works with eye clinics worldwide that previously have attempted to provide free cataract surgeries and other eye care services in their community, but have been precluded from doing so by lack of staffing and funding. Unite For Sight's model is unique among global health and volunteer organizations in that it involves local and visiting volunteers who serve as support staff to eye doctors in the field. Additionally, Unite For Sight provides grants to its partner eye clinics to hire local ophthalmic nurses, optometrists, translators, and coordinators to assist in remote, rural village outreach programs. The clinics' eye doctors diagnose and treat eye disease in the field, and surgical patients are brought to the eye clinics for surgery. The Unite For Sight-sponsored patients receive surgical care in the same facilities as the private patients, who are able to pay for their own surgeries. To ensure that all patients receive high quality care, Unite For Sight monitors the postoperative outcomes of patients receiving eye care through its programs with partner eye clinics. The goal of Unite For Sight is to create eye disease-free communities and to achieve the Vision 2020 goals of the World Health Organization and the International Agency for Prevention of Blindness. Since Unite For Sight's international launching in 2004, its programs have provided services to more than 600,000 people worldwide, and a total of 19,000 sight-restoring surgeries are anticipated by the end of 2008.

The Unite For Sight model coincides with the World Health Organization's Vision 2020 strategy that aims to eliminate preventable blindness by the year 2020, which is as follows:

1. Creating professional, public and political awareness of:
   a. the magnitude of blindness and visual impairment;
   b. the fact that at least 75% can be prevented or cured using existing knowledge and technology;
   c. that existing interventions for cataract, refractive errors, vitamin A deficiency, onchocerciasis, and trachoma, are some of the most cost-effective in health-care.
2. More efficient use of existing resources and mobilising [*sic*] new resources for the development of eye care services. These resources come from a variety of sources including Ministries of Health, NGOs, private, and corporate sectors of society.
3. Implementing comprehensive eye care services at the "district" level (population varies from 100,000 to 1 million) involving human resource development (eye care teams with different cadres of staff), and infrastructure development (facilities, equipment, and consumables). These services should be sustainable and equitable.
4. Prioritising [*sic*] available resources on control of the avoidable causes of blindness and visual impairment in that community. This will vary from country to country and even from district to district in some countries.[5]

Sasikumar et al. conducted an analysis during 1998 of eye screening camps for 90,000 people in an area of 190 square kilometers in Kolenchery, Kerala, India. The researchers reported that while 20 percent of those who attended the camps had operable cataracts, fewer than 10 percent reported for surgery at the base hospital. Reported barriers included "lack of escort, fear of surgery, socio-economic reasons, adverse media reports of isolated failures in eye surgeries."[6] Unite For Sight's model aims to reduce these identified barriers by providing patients with transportation, education, and financing for their surgeries. A previous cataract patient at Buduburam Refugee Camp in Ghana said, "Unite For Sight is popular here because of the dedicated services it gives to the community. This is something that many of us cannot comprehend since we have been here as refugees. No one has ever come over here to pay for patient treatments and transport them at the same time to the eye clinic for their treatment. This is wonderful thing that we have seen and led from Unite For Sight."[7]

Since Unite For Sight's international launching, its programs have evolved into a standardized model at thirteen eye clinics worldwide, which have provided eye care to more than 600,000 people thus far, including thousands of sight-restoring cataract surgeries and other types of eye care to thousands more. The global programs are based in rural villages and urban locations, as well as in refugee camps.

Unite For Sight's volunteers make a significant, meaningful, tangible impact in the lives of children and adults. The volunteers immediately see the joy on people's faces when their sight is restored after years of blindness. In addition to helping the community, volunteers are also in a position to witness and draw conclusions about the failures and inequities of global health systems, as well as the impacts of atrocities. The experience broadens their view of what works, and what role they can have to ensure a health system that works for everyone and that leaves no person blind in the future. Unite For Sight believes that anyone can become part of a global solution. Walid Mangal, a medical student and Unite For Sight volunteer in Chennai, India, wrote:

> The satisfaction of giving the gift of sight back to someone who was practically blind is immeasurable. For the first time in over 10 years, a frail and elderly female villager was able to see her reflection in the mirror. She stood up and walked out of the hospital without the help of the nurses, holding a small plastic bag filled with her life belongings, close against her green sari. This memory I will never forget. It was at that point that I realized the significance of why we were there and what we had done. We made a difference.[8]

In addition to their generous donation of time and energy to Unite For Sight's programs in developing countries, the volunteers also fundraise for the eye care programs. The fundraising efforts of Unite For Sight's volunteers provide poor patients worldwide with free eye care and sight-restoring surgeries. Each cataract surgery costs $50 on average, so every dollar raised makes a tremendous impact on the lives of children and adults. Jaci Theis, a recent Unite For Sight volunteer in Ghana, wrote about her fundraising and volunteer experience:

> In the surgery room, people were prepped and operated on at amazing efficiency, as the surgery itself took but seven minutes. Seven miraculous minutes was all it took for people to get their sight back. A miracle not only for them, but an eye opener for me, for I had fundraised enough money for 57 of these people to have this chance to regain their sight, a chance they would not have had without the financial support of Unite For Sight. My experience in Ghana was nothing short of amazing. Not only did I get a hands-on experience in the medical field as an undergraduate, but I realized how preventable blindness can be in many developing countries—so preventable that I, a mere college student, could change 57 lives.

Additionally, these fundraising efforts help create public awareness about global eye care needs. In addition to a network of volunteer fundraisers, Unite For Sight also receives donations from individuals, organizations, and corporations.

ESTABLISHING EYE CARE PROGRAMS WHERE THERE WERE NONE

There are hundreds of communities worldwide that are in need of eye care. In Tamale, Ghana, Dr. Seth Wanye is the only ophthalmologist for 2 million people in the entire region. Prior to a partnership with Unite For Sight, Dr. Wanye often went months without providing a single cataract surgery because the community members could not access or afford eye care. Unite For Sight volunteers now work with his ophthalmic staff to assist with screening outreach programs, ophthalmologist volunteers participate with Dr. Wanye to provide training and surgery, and Unite For Sight provides necessary equipment and also funds all of the eye care expenses for the patients. Since Unite For Sight's partnership began with Dr. Wanye and the Eye Clinic of Tamale Teaching Hospital, more than 40,000 patients have been screened in rural villages, and thousands have received sight-restoring surgery sponsored by Unite For Sight.

Ten hours away from Tamale is Buduburam Refugee Camp. In January 2005, Unite For Sight established an eye care program at this camp in Gomoa, Ghana. This 120-acre camp, located one hour from Ghana's capital city of Accra, was established in early 1990 by the government of Ghana to host a population of Liberian refugees fleeing the civil war in Liberia. Today, the camp has a total population of 77,398, which includes 42,398 resident refugees from Liberia, Sierra Leone, and Ivory Coast, as well as a Ghanaian villager population of 35,000. Buduburam has a total of 19,000 children, including 15,000 students and 4,000 children who are unable to attend school because of financial or other barriers. Although there are forty-eight primary and junior secondary schools with 13,700 students, the camp includes just three high schools with a total of 1,300 students.

Prior to January 2005, eye care had never been provided at the refugee camp. Even today, health care at the camp continues to be scarce. Initially, the Office of the United Nations High Commissioner for Refugees (UNHCR) provided assistance to the massive influx of Liberian refugees by implementing assistance programs, accommodations, health services, education, food distribution, and sanitation. In June 2000, though, UNHCR withdrew all services from Buduburam and instead encouraged repatriation after the elections in Liberia during 1997. In June 2002, however, when the political situation in Liberia worsened, UNHCR returned humanitarian aid to Buduburam.[9] Currently, there is one health center at Buduburam with a single primary care physician for the entire population. Patients requiring primary care pay a nominal fee for the doctor's services. Specialty care such as ophthalmology, however, is not provided at the small clinic.

Like all Unite For Sight programs, this program at Buduburam originated from an urgent community need. Karrus Hayes, a schoolteacher at the refugee camp, learned about Unite For Sight while searching for health care resources on the Internet. He contacted Unite For Sight, which then worked with Karrus and other members of the community to establish an eye care presence at the refugee camp. Dr. James Clarke, ophthalmologist and medical director of the Crystal Eye Clinic, who is also a member of Unite For Sight's medical advisory board, leads the program locally. Crystal Eye Clinic is a private clinic in Accra, Ghana, which has been devoted to service outreach programs for years despite very limited resources and staffing. A partnership with Unite For Sight to assist with regular community eye care programs and funding for surgeries was immediately a mutually beneficial affiliation.

By the first day Unite For Sight's volunteers had arrived at Buduburam, hundreds of people had already signed up to receive eye care screenings. Patients presented with cataracts, glaucoma, corneal opacities and scarring, macular scarring, and a range of other ailments. As patients continued flooding into the eye clinic, Unite For Sight's volunteer team trained the local refugees to assist with the vision screenings so that they could help identify patients requiring diagnosis, treatment, and surgery at Crystal Eye Clinic. Karrus, the teacher who originally had contacted Unite For Sight, was appointed the leader of the local Buduburam Refugee Camp chapter of Unite For Sight. He mobilized a large contingent of dedicated, motivated, and dependable volunteers to assist with the daily Unite For Sight activities. Over the course of six months, Unite For Sight's volunteers from the United States, Canada, and Europe trained staff of the local chapter to provide the screenings without the need for outside aid from international Unite For Sight volunteers. By September 2005, the local chapter had taken the lead in the eye care program and has continued daily screenings at the refugee camp. Margaret Duah-Mensah, an eye nurse at Crystal Eye Clinic, visits Buduburam Refugee Camp regularly to diagnose and treat patients, and also to identify those requiring advanced treatment and surgery by Dr. Clarke at his eye clinic, which is located two hours away.

In addition to training the local chapter's volunteers to provide daily vision screenings, Unite For Sight's international volunteers also implemented a train-the-trainer program for teachers in the refugee camp's schools. Teachers learned basic visual acuity testing and participated in seminars about eye health and infectious disease so that they could recognize potential eye disease or vision problems among their students as well as to be introduced to Unite For Sight's classroom curriculum. Additionally, the teachers learned about the important distinction between visual deficiencies and learning disabilities. After completing each level of training, the teachers participated in graduation ceremonies and received certificates.

Today, the local refugees continue regular educational workshops for children and teachers at the settlement. A recent one-day workshop brought together teachers from five elementary schools and three junior high schools, as well as health workers, at Buduburam to learn about the causes and prevention of blindness.

THE TRAGEDY OF BLINDNESS AT BUDUBURAM

When Unite For Sight first began its work at Buduburam Refugee Camp, the urgent need was immediately apparent. Many patients presented with blinding cataracts that could be removed with sight restored after a short, fifteen-minute operation by Dr. Clarke. Mr. and Mrs. S., for example, were both blind from cataracts before Unite For Sight began its programs. Mr. S. had surgery on one eye in February 2006, and the other eye was operated on during April 2006. His wife had been blind for years and had tried herbs in her eyes, hoping that she would recover her sight. However, her condition only worsened. As she reported in 2006, "When I was completely blind, I was myself being useless because I never got the respect of my family. I felt like just dying and leaving this earth, the fact is that there was pain always in my heart. Blindness is hell. I am happy today because I am back to life." Mrs. S. had her first eye operated on during February 2006, and the patch was removed the next day. After she came out of the surgery room and was able to see for the first time in eighteen years, she said, "I can see the television light and God's creations, oh my God! You are great!" When she returned to Buduburam Refugee Camp from Crystal Eye Clinic, she said, "Is this the camp? I can see many people passing by now, and can see what the refugee camp is like." When she returned home, she shouted, "I can see my family again, my husband, children, and my grandchildren. I have never seen them before! Oh God, I was in darkness and now you have used these people to recover my sight, praise be to the Lord God. I was dead, but I am now alive" (S., 2006).

Beyond the predicted types of eye disease at Buduburam, there were also a multitude of other complicated eye diseases, many of which were uncommon in other locations where Unite For Sight works. The operable cataract rate at Buduburam was much lower than expected because of compounding trauma-related eye disease, including macular scarring, corneal scarring, and uveitis. Unfortunately, when patients have these conditions, removing cataracts will not improve their vision. These conditions, which were mostly caused by physical abuse in Liberia prior to arrival at Buduburam, are infrequent in other non-refugee settings where Unite For Sight works. Macular scarring was found to be caused by an unusual form of abuse that has received little, if any, documentation. The rebels in Liberia forced scores of people to stare at the sun for long periods of time. If they looked away from the sun, they were immediately shot.[10] This form of abuse resulted in blindness because staring at the sun causes severe, irreversible retinal damage and macular scarring. Complicated eye conditions resulted in a low operable cataract rate of 2.6 percent at Buduburam Refugee Camp. Thirty-five percent of those with inoperable cataracts had corneal scarring, 14 percent had macular scarring, and 14 percent had uveitis.

ATROCITIES AND BLINDNESS

Thousands suffered human rights abuses by the rebels when civil war began in Liberia during 1989. The victims experienced brutal killings, mass rape, torture, and limb amputation. Survivors fled to neighboring countries, with the majority escaping to Ghana, where Buduburam Refugee Camp was established. Thousands of additional refugees were forced to flee when civil war again broke out a decade later in 1999, when warlord Charles Taylor led the atrocities. In total, since 1989, 250,000 have been killed[11], and 200,000 have been displaced from Liberia, 80 percent of whom are children and women who had witnessed and endured atrocities.[12]

The refugees at Buduburam in Ghana suffered crimes against humanity, resulting in physical and emotional scars. In 1992, rebels forced a fifty-seven-year-old Buduburam resident to look at the sun for over two hours. "I could not see anything very clear, everything was looking dark to me, and when the breeze hit my eye, I could feel so much pain," she said. "I therefore got the knowledge that I lost my sight due to my eye being exposed to the sun." She continued:

> It all started in 1992 when rebels entered our village. They forced us to beat a truck of seed rice with our hands. We were all given mortar and pestle to beat the rice. We started from the morning hour, and one was not allowed rest as we continued. Many of our hands got cut, blood running down from our hands, and could no longer hold the pestle to continue the beating of the rice. We were no longer efficient on the job. One of the rebels came close to me and said, "Why are you standing?" And we answered there was sore all over our hands, we could no longer beat the rice, but they said for us complaining was the act of wickedness. Therefore, they were left with no option but to start beating us all. And they later put us all in a dark room till night and we slept there. The next morning, we were brought outside, placed under the sun and asked to open our eyes directly to the sun. Afterward we should tell them how the sun operates in the sky. We should be the first scientists from Africa that have studied the sun. We spent the whole day looking at the sun. If anyone tries to remove or close their eyes, they will be killed. There was a 32-year-old young lady that was killed since she refused to look at the sun. When evening came, one of their commanders came into the village, and when he saw us, he asked his men what was going on. And they told him that we have refused to beat the rice. He was also angry, but when he got close to us and asked, we all showed our hands. When he saw it, he commanded his men to allow us to go and take our bath that the next day we would continue the beating of the rice. We all moved toward the riverside to bathe, but when we got there, one of the ladies said we have to leave this place, if not we will be killed one day. We all therefore took the risk to escape, and we did. And later came to Ghana. Since that time, my eyes started suffering.

An 80-year-old woman at Buduburam was physically beaten by rebels in Liberia in 1991 because of her tribal background. Now permanently blind, she experienced physical trauma to her eyes when she was forced to stare at the sun. Likewise, another patient at Buduburam was beaten in 1990 and experienced problems with his eyes immediately thereafter, as he describes:

> When the rebel[s] entered our town, that was some minute[s] after 9 AM and we were all in the door. They were firing the gun in every direction, and after a few hours, the firing ceased and we were asked to come out of the houses, and we did. We came out with our hands on our head, and we were asked to sit down. They were moving from person to person, and when they reached me, they asked where is the money you got? I answered there is no money. But they said that if I don't bring the money, they were going to kill me. I started crying, begging because they have already killed two people. I was very much afraid and asked them to please

allow me to live. One of them said let's kill me, but another said that I had to suffer first. I remember one of them hit me with the gun, and everyone started beating me with the gun. One of them asked for a cup, and it was given to me. They asked me to urinate into the cup with the gun in my ear, and I did. They therefore gave it to me to drink, and I drank it. In that process, one of my brothers got up and said we have done no wrong, why are you treating us like this? The word did not end from him, and he was shot. I was then ordered to be tied, and they did and placed me in the middle of the town with facing the sun. They also placed a rock in my mouth, and they started urinating on me in my face and my mouth. I was placed in the sun for over five hours. While undergoing that pain, there came a firing from the government troops, and they left us running to the direction they came from. When the government troops reentered the town, they untied me and others, and they asked us to go behind them, and we did. When I got untied, the only person from my family was my daughter, who was found in the house by the army. We were taken to the government control area, and we later moved across into Ivory Coast where we lived over four years before coming to Ghana.

For these and countless other patients who suffered torture and abuse, Unite For Sight is not able to provide any treatment that will improve or restore their vision. Some patients, however, are able to receive sight-restoring surgery for eye complications caused by torture during the war. Many people with physical abuse to the eye develop trauma-induced cataracts. If patients do not have any other type of complicating eye problems related to the trauma, then cataracts can be removed to restore their sight.

A nineteen-year-old man became blind when he was living as a refugee in Ivory Coast. He had been hit in the right eye during the Liberian civil war and had no access to treatment. As time went by, he started experiencing periodic blindness and finally lost his sight in 1999. While he was in Ivory Coast, he met another refugee who had received sight-restoring surgery from Unite For Sight; this refugee advised him to go quickly to Buduburam Refugee Camp for an evaluation by Unite For Sight. He arrived at Buduburam and had his sight restored in June 2006 by Dr. Clarke. Karrus explained that the patient considers his recovery of sight a miracle. "He said that he has been considered as a disabled person, and no one had regard for him as a human being. There were a lot of struggles he underwent. He felt rejected by others, all of his friends he knew never had interest in him when he got blind." After his surgery, he asked Habib (another refugee at Buduburam who volunteers daily for Unite For Sight) to write something for him to read, and he read it without making any mistakes. The patient then said, "Today my life is changed. I am no more disabled. I can see clearly and do everything others do. I am sure I will be respected by my fellow men again. May God bless Unite For Sight and all their team volunteers and donate; they have made me proud and have brought me back to the world of life" (Habib, 2006).

A sixty-year-old woman at Buduburam Refugee Camp has a similar story. She had been beaten by rebels in Liberia in 1990 because she refused to relinquish land that she owned. Later, during the war, she was attacked by those wanting to claim the land. It was not until years later that she was able to have her vision restored. She tells her story:

> One morning, I went to buy goods in a waterside market, and the rebel took control of the area in my absence. On my way back home, there were so many people in the street running toward the city center, but since I left my children behind, I decided to rush back to get my children to move to a safer zone. Before reaching to my house, I saw groups of neighbors, but I could not see my children. I was asking at the same time I saw a lady who told me that rebels had entered our house and there was a gun fire there. But I tried to go there by all means to get my children when I got at the back of the house watching carefully before moving closer. I just heard from my back, "Put your hands on your head and move forward. If you want to run away, it's up to you." He used the word God [and said that] today you will either lose your land or your life. Right away, I was hit with the gun from my back and felt my face on the ground, and he stepped on my back and started calling his friends. And one of them gripped my hand and started dragging me toward the front of the house. My nephew's dead body was lying there, and all my children were on the ground without clothing, with their faces down. They said now your nephew is dead, we want you to celebrate over his death by dancing, singing, and asking for mercy. One of them slapped me in the face and others started kicking my face side. My daughter was ordered to get up and bring pepper from the house, and she was then told to mix the pepper, and she did. They took it and urinated inside and gave it to me to drink. When I was drinking it, they took it from me again and told me to lay down on the floor with my face up. Before I could try to do so, three men threw me down. One sat in my chest, one held my head and the other one put pepper mixed with urine in my eyes. They held me forever so long at the same time, peppering me till it got finished. I fought and cried till I got very weak and helpless. One of them said they wanted to remove my eye. He took the belt and started beating my eye. Within that process, darkness covered my whole eye, and it was very painful. I could no longer realize anyone nor expose my eye to light. He asked should I lose my life or the land? I said my land. They brought a written statement that I no longer in need of the land, that I have finally turned it over to the brother. I told them to allow my daughter to bring it for them and let her write for me since I could not see anything now. My daughter brought the deed and gave it to them, and she made the document that as of that date, all property was now for the brother, but not for me. I put my thumbprint on the document and turned it over to them. And we were released and asked never to come back to our house. We were able to find our way to the neighboring country Guinea. The only thing I was using in my eye was sugar water, there was no medication. Until I came to the Unite For Sight eye clinic where I had surgery and now can see.

ENTREPRENEURIAL SKILL BUILDING AND MICROFINANCE AT BUDUBURAM REFUGEE CAMP

Unite For Sight not only eradicates blindness and eye disease, but we also boost incomes through entrepreneurial skill building. We developed an educational scholarship fund that enables the children of blind patients to attend school. We also work with blind patients and women to develop small businesses so that they can support their families.

The residents of Buduburam Refugee Camp have very little money, and many barely earn enough money to feed their families. A blind man named A. is one such individual, and Unite For Sight worked with him to start a water-selling business at Buduburam. A. is a very shy, quiet man, who always looks at his feet when he speaks. He shuffles his feet in the dust when he walks because he has very low visual acuity as a result of a permanently blinding condition called retinitis pigmentosa. This eye disease is incurable even for the most well-equipped eye clinics in the developed world. Born in 1965 in Monrovia, Liberia, A. is married with four children of his own, in addition to caring for his brothers' three children. A. was well educated and taught math until January 1990, when fighting in Liberia forced him, his wife, and their baby daughter to flee to the Ivory Coast. He was safe in that country and began to teach math again, unaware that several of his remaining family members had stayed in Liberia and had faced torture and death. He served as director of an education project until war erupted in the Ivory Coast on September 20, 2002. Rebels targeted the Liberian refugees in the Ivory Coast, forcing A. and his family to flee to Buduburam Refugee Camp in Ghana. There, reunited with two brothers and one sister, he learned that his father and siblings had been killed in the war years earlier. His father, a popular local businessman, had been removed from his house early one morning in June 1990. He was arrested and jailed for selling rice to rebels, although it is believed that the true reason for his arrest was his tribal affiliation and ethnicity. When local supporters appealed for A.'s father's release, he was taken out of the jail, and shot and killed in front of the supporters.

A. was one of the first patients to arrive at the Unite For Sight clinic at Buduburam Refugee Camp. His retina appeared speckled with yellow, black, and red spots, indicating the genetic condition retinitis pigmentosa. A. was devastated when he was informed by the ophthalmologist that his condition was untreatable. He asked to speak privately with Julie, Unite For Sight's Ghana program coordinator. Looking down, he quietly asked Julie how he would study if he could not see. He also explained his family situation. He could not afford to support his family of thirteen people. They all lived in a small, eight feet by ten feet room and could not afford food. Julie said she had never felt so helpless; she wanted to cry for him. Julie immediately developed a plan to help A. generate an income for his family: he would sell purified water at the refugee camp. For A., Unite For Sight purchased a freezer, voltage regulator, cooler, extension cord, water sachets, and electrical current registration. With his water-selling business established, A. has been able to better support his family. Unfortunately, his sight will never be restored without a medical breakthrough.

In addition to working with individuals such as A. to create small local businesses, Unite For Sight also promotes the financial success of communities by linking them to world markets. One hundred percent of the proceeds to Unite For Sight directly fund eye care expenses at Buduburam Refugee Camp, thus helping the program to become locally sustainable. As female heads of household with limited or no income, several women were invited by Unite For Sight to participate in a unique microenterprise program. The women create beautiful, vibrant jewelry and eyeglass cases at Buduburam Refugee Camp, and they earn an income when Unite For Sight purchases jewelry and eyeglass cases. Unite For Sight then introduces the jewelry and eyeglass cases to world markets through sales on the Internet and at universities.

CONCLUSION

The provision of eye care is often overlooked in communities worldwide, from suburban North America to refugee camps in Africa and Asia. Although many are aware of a myriad of atrocities endured by refugees throughout the world, few are aware of the abuses to the eye, or the consequences of blindness. As a result of its remarkable volunteer force of refugees at Buduburam Refugee Camp, as well as the work of Dr. James Clarke and Margaret Duah-Mensah of Crystal Eye Clinic, and more than forty international volunteers who provided training for the local refugees during the first six months of programming in 2005, Unite For Sight is making a profound difference in the lives of thousands of patients at Buduburam Refugee Camp. With the election of a new president of Liberia in 2006, refugees at Buduburam are beginning to move back to their home country. Unite For Sight hopes to provide eye care to thousands more at Buduburam before they return to Liberia.

Unite For Sight encourages students, youth, eye care professionals, and physicians to become social entrepreneurs and join forces to prevent blindness in their local communities, as well as in communities abroad. Unite For Sight's rapid expansion and program enhancement has occurred because of several important steps that were taken to build the organization. First, I took advantage of established networks to grow the organization. Unite For Sight expanded its chapters and international programs by linking with existing networks, including eye clinics, university organizations, medical school dean's offices, international health networks, and nonprofit organizations. The next important step in the organization's development was to create a welcoming website and informative e-newsletter to increase effectiveness in recruitment, fundraising, training of volunteers, and working with communities. I continue to spend much of my time communicating with our partners and volunteers, as well as contacting and recruiting new volunteers. The website is a useful way for people to learn how they can become part of a global solution to improve eye health.

The website also has significantly expanded to provide extensive training for the more than 4,000 volunteers who have joined Unite For Sight to provide eye care services in their local community and abroad. We devote much of our effort to educating and training our volunteers, who are the heart and soul of Unite For Sight. All volunteers traveling abroad view Unite For Sight cultural competency and eye health training videos, study the Unite For Sight online Eye Health

Course, and complete a final exam; complete required reading and videos about professionalism, international volunteerism, and community eye health; pursue training with eye doctors in their home communities; and receive additional training by the partner eye clinic abroad. This prepares the volunteers to best assist the eye clinic's staff in the field. In addition to serving as support staff at eye clinics worldwide, the volunteers are also vital to the organization's fundraising capacity. The volunteers encourage friends and family to donate for eye care programs abroad. This network of volunteer fundraisers also helps promote public awareness about global eye care needs and ways that the general public can become involved with implementing a solution.

Possibly the most important advice for anyone interested in developing a nonprofit organization is to be dedicated to the continuous enhancement of programs. One should focus attention on listening carefully to the needs and advice of local communities and partners because their advice is crucial to the sustainability and effectiveness of an organization.

Acknowledgments

Unite For Sight is especially indebted to Dr. James Clarke and Margaret Duah-Mensah of Crystal Eye Clinic, as well as the leaders of Unite For Sight's chapter at Buduburam Refugee Camp: Karrus Hayes, Habib Kamara, and Joseph Muhlenberg. Each selflessly devotes every day to preventing blindness and restoring sight. Additionally, two of Unite For Sight's previous international volunteers from the United States, Julie R. Harris, MPH, PhD, and Valda Boyd Ford, MPH, RN, MS, are directly responsible for establishing a sustainable, long-term eye program at Buduburam Refugee Camp. Their dedication and leadership were invaluable to the community and to Unite For Sight.

ORGANIZATIONAL SNAPSHOT

Organization: Unite For Sight

Founder and/or Executive Director: Jennifer Staple

Mission/Description: Unite For Sight is a nonprofit organization that empowers communities worldwide to improve eye health and eliminate preventable blindness. Local and visiting volunteers work with partner eye clinics to provide eye care in communities without previous access, with the goal of creating eye disease–free communities. In North America, patients are connected with free health coverage programs so that they can receive eye exams by doctors. In Africa and Asia, Unite For Sight volunteers work with partner eye clinics to implement screening and free surgery programs.

Website: www.uniteforsight.org

Address: 31 Brookwood Dr.

Newtown, CT 06470

E-mail: jstaple@uniteforsight.org

Phone: 203-404-4900

Fax: 203-404-4975

NOTES

1. World Health Organization (1997), *Global Initiative for the Prevention of Avoidable Blindness,*_WHO/PBL/97.61 (Geneva: WHO, 1997).

2. Ibid.

3. Low Cost Eyeglasses: The Problem (http://www.lowcosteyeglasses.net/stuck.htm).

4. Vision 2020: The Right to Sight (http://www.v2020.org).

5. A. Foster and S. Resnikoff, "The Impact of Vision 2020 on Global Blindness," *Eye* 19 (2005): 1133–1135.

6. S. Sasikumar, N. Mohamed, and S. J. Saikumar, "Cataract Surgical Coverage in Kolenchery, Kerala, India," *Community Eye Health Journal* 11 (1998): 7.

7. Interview at Buduburam Refugee Camp, June 23, 2006.

8. http://uniteforsight.org/image/walidmangal.jpg.

9. Saah Charles N'Tow, "How Liberians Live on the Camp at Buduburam in Ghana," The Perspective (http://www.theperspective.org/2004/june/buduburamcamp.html).

10. Human Rights Watch, *Easy Prey: Child Soldiers in Liberia* (http://www.hrw.org/reports/1994/liberia2/).

11. BBC News, *Country Profile: Liberia* (http://news.bbc.co.uk/1/hi/world/africa/country_profiles/1043500.stm).

12. Abdullah Dukully, "Rights-Liberia: War Threatens Survival Of Children," *Inter Press Service,* (http://www.aegis.org/news/ips/2003/IP030415.html).

3

Achieving Social Goals through Business Discipline: Scojo Foundation

Jordan Kassalow, Graham Macmillan, Miriam Stone, Katherine Katcher, Patrick Savaiano, and Annie Khan

When we first started thinking about how to address the challenge of providing reading glasses to the millions of people across the globe who need them, we knew we had a steep hill to climb. Countless organizations start out with similarly ambitious ideas but often fail to implement them properly to form a sustainable, effective business model. Although we continue the climb that began when we started six years ago, we know we have developed a truly innovative social enterprise with great promise for success. Our customers around the world—in India, El Salvador, Guatemala, Bangladesh, and Ghana—have seen huge transformations in their lives because of a simple pair of Scojo Foundation reading glasses.

Who could have imagined that a simple pair of reading glasses could have such an effect? Well, we did. We saw that this basic and critical tool was unavailable to most in the developing world, and we sought a market-based solution to this problem—a solution that would not create a dynamic of dependency, but would empower individuals to transform their lives. Before starting our first program, we researched, studied, and tested our programs inside and out. We believe that it is Scojo Foundation's responsibility to provide a product and service that is of the highest quality for our customers.

For too long, the global economy has failed to recognize the power and influence that people living on only a few dollars a day can have. Scojo Foundation is working to change this perception by providing simple pairs of reading glasses to our customers and training new, determined Vision Entrepreneurs to sell our products. We know it is possible to empower the poor in developing countries because we have witnessed this transformation in the people we serve: the Scojo Vision Entrepreneurs and their customers.

BACKGROUND, MODEL, AND SIZE OF SCOJO FOUNDATION

Scojo Foundation derived its name as a composite of the first letters of the names of co-founders Dr. Jordan Kassalow and Scott Berrie. The organization began in 2001 with a six-month pilot program in India and was officially incorporated one year later in New York. Our goal is to reduce poverty and generate opportunities for our customers and our Vision Entrepreneurs through the sale of affordable reading glasses in the developing world. As we age, almost all of us will lose our ability to see up close. But for the more than 700 million people living in poverty who don't have access to reading glasses, the loss of near vision can mean the loss of livelihood. For tailors, electricians, goldsmiths, and others whose precarious working lives depend on their ability to see up close, the lack of access to reading glasses can have disastrous economic consequences. A pair of low-cost reading glasses, long available in every drugstore in the United States, can restore their vision and double their productivity, yet this simple, life-changing product has not yet made its way into the hands of those who live on less than $4 a day.

Committed to employing market-based solutions to solve this global issue, Scojo Foundation developed a replicable, scalable, microfranchise model. Crucial to our model are our Vision Entrepreneurs. These low-income men and women are trained to conduct vision screenings within their communities, sell affordable reading glasses, and refer those who require advanced eye care to reputable clinics. Each Scojo Vision Entrepreneur receives his or her own "Business in a Bag," a backpack that is branded with the Scojo logo and contains twenty to thirty pairs of reading glasses in four different styles and five different powers of magnification. Also included are three different styles of sunglasses and other accessories such as cleaning cloths, cords, and cases. These backpacks are sales kits containing all the products and materials needed for vision screening, sales, data collection, and marketing. This backpack is the cornerstone of the microfranchise owned by each of our entrepreneurs. With blueprints for success, Scojo Vision Entrepreneurs run profitable businesses, earning more than twice their previous daily income on each pair of glasses sold. Through the sales of these glasses, our entrepreneurs help us to create a sustainable business model. By employing a market-based model rather than by giving away glasses for free, we are able to become increasingly self-sustaining while creating sustainable jobs for local entrepreneurs.

Recognizing the massive numbers of people in need of reading glasses, Scojo Foundation also teaches Franchise Partners, or partner organizations with existing distribution networks, to reach the rural poor and add our Vision Entrepreneur model to their own operations. Partnering with these established programs makes it possible for Scojo Foundation to impact more people in a shorter period of time and bring us closer to our goal of providing glasses to all 700 million people in need. We support our Franchise Partners by providing the tools, knowledge, and products they need to successfully implement Scojo microfranchises, adding both profit and social value to established programs. Scojo Foundation currently works with nearly thirty Franchise Partners, from small nongovernmental organizations

(NGOs) to large multinational corporations, in India, Bangladesh, Ghana, El Salvador, Guatemala, and Paraguay. Thanks to our Franchise Partner model, we are able to greatly expand our reach and impact without building up our own costly infrastructure.

Our reading glasses are sourced from China, where the price-to-quality ratio is the most attractive, enabling us to deliver our products anywhere in the world for approximately $1.50, including the cost of transportation and customs duties. Through this process, Scojo Foundation is able to make reading glasses affordable, fashionable, and available to people in need. Today, we support over 1,000 Vision Entrepreneurs, we have sold more than 85,000 pairs of reading glasses, and we have referred over 80,000 people for advanced eye care.

TRAINING FOR SCOJO VISION ENTREPRENEURS

In order for our social business model to succeed, Scojo Foundation must ensure that our entrepreneurs are effectively trained. Our training process focuses on several areas, including business management, marketing, inventory sales figures, and vision screening. We teach business skills in accounting, marketing, and sales. Training lasts three days, with two days devoted to learning in a classroom setting and one day spent in the field shadowing an already-established entrepreneur. Our training process empowers our entrepreneurs with the knowledge, skills, and confidence they will need in the field.

Scojo Foundation maintains an organized system of training and support for our entrepreneurs in order to increase their chances of success. Teams of two or three full-time Vision Entrepreneur training and identification managers work at the district level to identify prospective Vision Entrepreneurs and provide them with initial training before handing them off to their district coordinator. Based in each region, district coordinators meet with each individual entrepreneur twice a month—once to restock inventory and collect payment for glasses sold, and once for additional training and support. Every quarter, regional groups of Scojo Vision Entrepreneurs come together to discuss their past experiences and share new ideas they may have to improve their systems.

FEMALE EMPOWERMENT

One of the most important aspects of Scojo Foundation's mission is our focus on empowering women. Research shows that women are much more likely than their male counterparts to invest in their children's education and health, thereby promoting further positive development. However, we have faced several obstacles that have made our focus on women challenging. For example, in rural India, women are not supposed to travel on their own, which is a key component of our sales model. Thus, Scojo Foundation decided to train male entrepreneurs as well as females, and we often train teams of husbands and wives and mothers and sons so that they can travel together as pairs. Our network in India is thus a mix of men and women working together, while in most of the other countries in which we work, our Vision Entrepreneurs are mainly women.

CONCEPTION OF SCOJO FOUNDATION

Before co-founding Scojo Foundation, Dr. Jordan Kassalow spent time as an ophthalmology student participating in missions for Volunteer Ophthalmic Services to Humanity (VOSH). In these missions, doctors would provide eye exams, glasses, surgeries, and other ophthalmic needs to low-income people in countries that did not have such services. Dr. Kassalow noticed, however, that these missions were geared toward more complicated conditions and did not cater to the most common and ubiquitous eye care problems. Of the people who need eye care service, 36 percent need treatment for presbyopia, a natural condition caused by the aging of the eye, in which the eye has difficulty focusing on nearby objects. The lack of basic services to treat presbyopia, which simply requires nonprescription reading glasses, inspired Dr. Kassalow to make a difference.

Through his early experiences providing reading glasses to those in need, Dr. Kassalow realized the tremendous effect this service could have. On one particular trip to Mexico, Dr. Kassalow's passion for providing low-cost eye care on a massive scale was transformed from a dream to reality. Dr. Kassalow provided a woman who hadn't been able to read her Bible for years with a pair of simple drugstore reading glasses. Overcome with gratitude, she returned the next day to give Dr. Kassalow twenty chickens to thank him for reviving her sight and changing her life. He knew right then that if he could help millions of people just like her to see, he could change the world. It was at that moment that Scojo Foundation was born.

Scott Berrie, Dr. Kassalow's business partner, also recognized that an opportunity was in place to create a socially responsible company that could work to support Scojo Foundations efforts. Together, they created a for-profit company called Scojo Vision LLC. The company sells fashionable reading glasses to high-end department stores, and 5 percent of the revenue generated by Scojo Vision LLC is donated to Scojo Foundation. Scojo Vision LLC has been sold, but the purchasing company continues to give 5 percent of its Scojo New York line to Scojo Foundation.

SCOJO FOUNDATION MEASURES OF SUCCESS

Scojo Foundation measures its success by monitoring three main areas. First, we keep close track on the number of glasses that are sold worldwide by our entrepreneurs, as well as the number of customers Scojo Vision Entrepreneurs screen before making a sale. Initially, an entrepreneur had to screen eight people to sell one pair of glasses, but that ratio has since improved to three to one thanks to our improved sales and marketing techniques. Secondly, we track the number of entrepreneurs who remain active salespeople, as compared to the number of entrepreneurs who have been trained since inception. Finally, Scojo Foundation tracks the number of clients we refer to hospitals and clinics for more advanced eye care. This is a critical component of our system since it allows us to provide a service to those with more serious eye conditions by connecting them to partner eye care hospitals offering free or low-cost care. It also reduces the burden on the eye care system by funneling only those who require a doctor's attention to more advanced care facilities.

BENEFIT TO OTHERS

At the core of our mission is the desire to benefit the greatest number of people possible. Scojo Foundation knows that the customers who wear our reading glasses have benefited tremendously. Their productivity has increased, their earnings have increased, and they are better able to invest in their families. In our line of work, we also challenge the flawed assumptions that the poor do not want a product or service that is of value, that they do not have the right to choose as a regular consumer, or that they do not care how they look or how they feel. All people want to be offered choices, and it is exactly this dignity of choice that we offer to our customers. For example, of the four styles of glasses we offer, 85 percent of our customers choose to buy our second most expensive product. This is quantifiable proof that the poor care about the quality and style of the products they are purchasing. It is an empowering experience for anyone to have the ability to choose.

SUCCESS STORIES
Noel Flores Alvardo (age sixty-four), Atiquizaya, Ahuachapan, El Salvador

Noel came to a mini-campaign organized by local Vision Entrepreneurs in El Salvador with the assistance of his daughter and a broomstick he used as a cane. He was completely blind in his right eye, and the sight in his left eye was rapidly deteriorating. During his vision screening, the Vision Entrepreneurs immediately realized that Noel needed treatment far beyond reading glasses. The Vision Entrepreneur was able to refer him to the local clinic and organize transportation for him to get there. At the eye clinic, Noel was seen by a board-certified ophthalmologist and was diagnosed with glaucoma. Both the consultation and the medicine Noel was prescribed were given to him free of charge. Ultimately, this intervention prevented him from going completely blind.

Vijaya Laxmi (age fifty-three), Andhra Pradesh, India

Vijaya Laxmi is a seamstress in the rural Tandur district of Andhra Pradesh, India. Six years ago, her shirt-making business was her primary source of income. She would sew an average of ten shirts per week, bringing in an income of $8. As presbyopia set in, it became all but impossible for Vijaya to thread a needle or do the necessary detailed work that her profession demanded. She began to rely on her granddaughter for help, but was alone during the daylight hours when her granddaughter was at school. As her output diminished, the stores where Vijaya sold her shirts began to source them elsewhere. She did not know of any place to purchase glasses locally, and she could not afford to take the day-long trip to Hyderabad to seek help. Vijaya then learned of a woman in her village selling eyeglasses through Scojo Foundation's rural distribution initiative. Vijaya went to her to have her eyes checked and bought a pair of gold-rimmed reading glasses. Since then, Vijaya Laxmi has begun sewing again and is once again earning a living. She finds the glasses comfortable to wear and also uses them to perform everyday household tasks without requiring the help of her family. Scojo Foundation was able to help Vijaya reclaim her livelihood.

Don Felipe (age forty), Nebaj, Guatemala*

A little over a year ago I was making a visit up to Nebaj to see how things were going. Night after night I noticed that a small Ixil man with huge glasses would come into El Descanso, the restaurant in Nebaj we support, and sit and pretend to read the old English language magazines that we have for clients. It struck me as odd for two reasons: one, he looked like a bug with his giant glasses, and two, it is rare that a farmer from Nebaj can read, especially *Newsweek* magazine.

So I asked the manager who this man was; he told me that he was Don Felipe, the newest guide of Guias Ixiles, a small trekking business that we support. Don Felipe, who is a wonderful man, did very well with the tourists and was able to make a decent living as a guide. However, we did start to receive some complaints from clients: they loved his tours but noticed that he could barely see. At this time we, Soluciones Comunitarias, were not yet involved with Scojo Foundation and did not know what could be done, but things did not look good for Don Felipe. One day, we sent Don Felipe out with two tourists on an easy day's hike. The tourists arrived back in Nebaj about an hour before Felipe, who had gotten himself lost. We felt that something had to be done about his vision if he were to continue working.

Luckily, right around this time, we began working with Scojo Foundation and an eye care clinic called Visualiza, in Guatemala, to work out a referral system for our Vision Entrepreneurs. We sent Don Felipe for an exam. They discovered that Don Felipe had been born with cataracts and had never been able to see correctly; because he had been born into extreme poverty, he had never had an eye exam as a child. The doctor told him that he would probably be completely blind within the next couple of years if he did not do something about it. They recommended two minor surgeries, one on each eye, to remove the cataracts (at a cost of Q500 per eye, about $65 each).

---

*Text by George Glickley of Soluciones Comunitarias, Scojo Foundation's Franchise Partner in Guatemala.

Don Felipe decided to go forward with the surgeries. Imagine a man who has spent the greater part of his forty some odd years (Guatemalans often have only a vague idea of how old they are) seeing through a cloud. Now, for the first time, he could see the faces of his loved ones, the crops that he grows for food to maintain his family, and the mountains and forests where he lives and works.

On his last night, he came to me, extended me his right hand, and in his best Spanish (Felipe's first language is Ixil, a Maya dialect) told me this: "When you and Greg showed me the new glasses from Scojo and told me that one day I would be able to see the beautiful mountains that all of the tourists come to see, I would have never imagined that it would be possible. Thank you for giving me this opportunity. My life will be much better now, I can already tell. I cannot wait to get back to Nebaj." Then, for the first time since we met, he actually looked me in the eye and shook my hand. And with that, he shuffled off to bed.

OVERCOMING FALSE STARTS AND OUR APPROACH TO OBSTACLES

It is inevitable in starting an organization that one will confront obstacles. In order to continue growing in the face of these obstacles, we have had to create new and innovative solutions. We learned many lessons from our initial projects in El Salvador. Consistent with our mission, this project involved training low-income women to start their own businesses selling glasses. Initially, the women were provided with the backpack of supplies that they rented for a monthly fee over a seven- to eight-month period. We made the faulty assumption that, by selling their glasses, the women would be able to pay off the loan and make a profit. Instead, we found that the women would not show up to the monthly meetings because they could not afford to pay the fee. As a result, a large portion of our inventory was not accounted for. To make matters worse, we were not selling many pairs of glasses, and we were not expanding as we had hoped. Essentially, Scojo Foundation had become a group of loan administrators, which diluted our efforts to distribute reading glasses. With help from our local partner, New Development Solutions, we changed our strategy to a consignment model, whereby we provided the supplies to our entrepreneurs at no cost, and they repaid us for the glasses that they sold. If the entrepreneurs were not successful in their business, or if it simply was not the right fit for them, they did not owe us any money. They would simply return the kit, and Scojo Foundation would not lose out on inventory.

Another major problem we encountered was that we were too wedded to our business plans. Because we were starting something completely new and different, our business plans were nothing more than numbers and words on paper. Moving from our plans to reality was a very different story. Fortunately, we had hired smart, hardworking, motivated, and passionate people, who were able to transform these plans into systems that worked on the ground. We stayed flexible, and have remained an efficient and highly productive organization, impacting a great number of people with a limited number of employees.

Scojo Foundation remains a "learning" organization to this day. We are relatively small and do not operate bureaucratically. Our decision-making process is decentralized, so each employee takes part in our businesses decisions. We also learned very early on to listen and learn from our entrepreneurs. As our agents in the field, the entrepreneurs have the best sense of our needs as an organization. For example, when Dr. Kassalow was in El Salvador visiting a project site, he noticed a Scojo Vision Entrepreneur selling sunglasses, even though Scojo Foundation was not providing its entrepreneurs with sunglasses at the time. The entrepreneur told Dr. Kassalow that she had received multiple requests from customers for sunglasses. Since she was unable to obtain sunglasses from us, she had purchased them on her own in order to make her customers happy. We learned from her and other Vision Entrepreneurs that sunglasses were an important product for many of their clients, and we began to manufacture them and offer them in our product line. Stories like these have taught us that it is essential to remain open and receptive to the ideas and desires of our employees, our staff, our Vision Entrepreneurs, and our customers.

We faced another major obstacle in reaching our goal of getting our product to as many people as possible. It quickly became apparent that training each Scojo Vision Entrepreneur ourselves would take time, money, and bulky infrastructure. We launched our Franchise Partnership model as a creative solution to accelerate the scale of Scojo Foundation. In this model, we train local organizations with existing networks of health workers, microfinance borrowers, internet kiosk managers, or salespeople to plug our Vision Entrepreneur model into their existing operations. This has allowed us to expand rapidly and with little start-up capital across India and throughout the world.

Looking back to our inception, we must also acknowledge that it has been difficult to sell our product rather than give it away. Yet, we are committed to market-based solutions to alleviate poverty. Programs such as ours create local jobs as well as set up long-term, sustainable distribution channels that enable people to get the tools they need to see and to work. We also believe that when a product is given away for free, people tend to value it less. Theoretically, we could go out and distribute millions of pairs of glasses for free, but we question the impact that would have. We would not be able to sustain ourselves as an organization, our customers would have no way of getting reading glasses in the future, and we would not be able to create employment for our entrepreneurs. Reading glasses are inexpensive, easy to transport, and make a huge difference in people's lives, but getting them to people who need them is a major challenge. We have had to build the distribution channels from scratch to reach the rural poor.

In the beginning, we assumed that training entrepreneurs to sell reading glasses would be an easier task than it was. The lessons we learned in the field are what really helped us progress as an organization. After testing our ideas in the field and learning from the challenges we faced, we determined that the Scojo Foundation recipe for success requires the following key components: a distribution channel to get the product into the market; entrepreneurs in the community to sell the product; a cost-effective, turn-key supply chain; the right staff to motivate entrepreneurs and ensure systems work smoothly; the right marketing and promotions material to make the customers aware of the brand; and finally, the systems to effectively monitor and evaluate performance.

THE NEXT STEPS FOR SCOJO FOUNDATION

A 2007 highlight for Scojo Foundation was when President Clinton featured our work at the Clinton Global Initiative opening session, stating that Scojo Foundation's work is "the sort of thing that the Clinton Global Initiative was designed to do—find ways to create new markets where you can actually empower people by creating a business and solve a big social problem." Dr. Jordan Kassalow was called to the stage with President Clinton to represent Scojo Foundation and its partners in making the commitment to more than triple Scojo Foundation's impact over the next three years. President Clinton has also praised the work of Scojo Foundation on national news programs, naming Scojo Foundation his "favorite commitment this year" on CNBC's *Power Lunch* with Maria Bartiromo. On MSNBC's *Countdown* with Keith Olberman, President Clinton stated that Scojo Foundation "will help hundreds of thousands of people and in the process create a whole new sector of the economy." He also praised Scojo Foundation's work on NBC's *Meet the Press* with Tim Russert, ABC's *This Week* with George Stephanopoulos, and Fox News's *On the Record* with Greta Van Susteren.

Our short-term goal is to execute Scojo Foundation's five-year business plan. This plan outlines our long-term goals and objectives, the resources needed to achieve our objectives, and how we will execute our plans. We have tested and proved our model and are preparing for massive expansion. As of January 2007, we operated in nine countries across South Asia, Africa, and Latin America. Aside from our local networks managed from our offices in Hyderabad, India, and Santa Ana, El Salvador, all our expansion is through our Franchise Partners. In Africa, our pan-Africa arrangement with Population Services International (PSI) is making reading glasses available throughout sub-Saharan Africa. In 2007 we launched our Ghana program. In 2008 we anticipate launching several programs in Latin American countries, including Paraguay and Nicaragua. To date, Scojo Foundation and our partners have supported over 1,000 Vision Entrepreneurs, have collectively sold over 85,000 pairs of reading glasses, and have referred over 80,000 people for comprehensive eye care. We look forward to reaching hundreds of thousands more people in the coming years.

FOUNDERS
Jordan Kassalow

Dr. Kassalow currently serves as Chairman of Scojo Foundation, providing leadership, management, and expertise to its global operations. He was a cofounder of both Scojo Foundation and Scojo Vision, LLC. He is also the founder of the Global Health Policy Program at the Council on Foreign Relations, where he served as an Adjunct Senior Fellow from 1999 to 2004. Prior to his position at the Council, he served as Director of the Onchocerciasis Division at Helen Keller International. He currently serves on the Board of Directors for Lighthouse International and on the Medical Advisory Board of Helen Keller International. The recipient of numerous awards, including the Social Innovator of the Year award from BYU's Marriott School of Management, The Aspen Institute's Henry Crown Fellowship, and a Draper Richards Foundation Fellowship, Dr. Kassalow received his Doctorate of Optometry from the New England College of Optometry and his Masters in Public Health from Johns Hopkins University. In addition to his position at Scojo Foundation, he is currently a partner at the practice of Drs. Farkas, Kassalow, Resnick, and Associates.

Scott Berrie

Scott Berrie serves as President of Scojo Foundation, providing leadership in product development, marketing, and distribution. Mr. Berrie was a cofounder of both Scojo Foundation and Scojo Vision, LLC. Scott Berrie serves as vice president of the Russell Berrie Foundation and trustee with the Shalom Hartman Institute, PAX, and Helen Keller International. Mr. Berrie earned an MBA from New York University's Stern Executive MBA Program. He also earned a Master in International Affairs and a Certificate in Middle Eastern Studies from Columbia University, where he was also a SIPA International Affairs Fellow. He served in the Israel Defence Forces.

Figure 3.1   Vision Entrepreneur Mercedes Queche conducts a vision screening at a sales campaign in Pastores, Guatemala. Courtesy of Scojo Foundation.

ORGANIZATIONAL SNAPSHOT

Organization: Scojo Foundation

Founders: Jordan Kassalow and Scott Berrie

Senior Director: Graham Macmillan

Mission/Description: Scojo Foundation's mission is to reduce poverty and generate opportunity through the sale of affordable eyeglasses and complementary products. Scojo Vision Entrepreneurs are low-income men and women living in rural villages who are trained to conduct vision screenings within their communities, sell affordable reading glasses, and refer those who require advanced eye care to reputable clinics.

Website: www.scojofoundation.org

Address: 12 Desbrosses Street

New York, NY 10013

Phone: 212.375.2599

Fax: 720.228.5188

E-mail: gmacmillan@scojofoundation.org

4

Sustainable Sciences Institute: Developing Scientific Capacity to Address Public Health Needs Worldwide

Josefina Coloma, Eva Harris,
and Martine Zoer

It was the year 1988. Eva Harris was a young, recent graduate in biochemistry from Harvard University. She was set to enter the molecular and cell biology doctoral program at the University of California–Berkeley, with a fellowship from the National Science Foundation, and the next few years of her life appeared to be mapped out. Harris, however, aspired to make her degree meaningful to the world and decided to take a detour (1). Harris, who had been an activist while at Harvard, dreamed of bringing science out of the ivory tower and applying it to real-world problems. The only dilemma was that she had no idea how to accomplish her goal. "When you are a doctor, you have skills that are useful in the rest of the world. But how can you impact others when you are a scientist?" Harris wondered. Although she wasn't sure how, Harris was driven to find out how to make science relevant and significant to the world.

Since she wanted to apply her scientific background where it mattered most, Harris sought opportunities to work in the developing world. Harris looked for and found a sponsor in Tecnica, a now-defunct, Berkeley-based organization that sent technical volunteers, mostly computer scientists, to Nicaragua and South Africa, for two-week stays. Harris, however, wanted to volunteer for a few months and in the field of biology, and no one knew what to do with her. Eventually, she was placed in Managua, the capital city of Nicaragua, with the Ministry of Health (MOH) and at a plasma factory making critical supplies for soldiers at the front. Harris had never been to a developing country, and Nicaragua was not only the second poorest country in the hemisphere but was also in the middle of a war. Roosters ran wild, and power outages and material shortages were an everyday occurrence. Yet despite the situation, people somehow coped with life and embodied an amazing humanitarian spirit in the face of material constraints. Since Harris had been schooled at Harvard and trained in the best laboratories in Paris, Basel, and Boston, she felt totally unprepared to train the Nicaraguans, who had been running their country during a revolution under near-impossible conditions for almost ten years.

Within a few weeks, however, Harris was teaching a daily course in technical English, giving a weekly seminar on biology, troubleshooting a test for endotoxins at the plasma factory, and helping work out a technique for identifying different strains of *Leishmania* based on the migration of proteins in gel. Leishmaniasis is a parasitic disease that is spread by the bite of infected sand flies and causes manifestations ranging from disfiguring skin and mucosal lesions to the fatal destruction of internal organs. It had become a major problem in Nicaragua because soldiers were fighting in the tropical forests in the north of the country, where the disease was prevalent, and then returning to the cities with numerous lesions. Harris worked with her Nicaraguan colleagues to search for a rapid and reliable way to detect and differentiate the strains of *Leishmania* causing the disease in order to trace their spread and determine which patients should be treated with the toxic, heavy-metal therapies needed to kill the parasite.

The three months Harris spent in Nicaragua flew by. The experience was incredibly enriching and life changing. Not only was Harris moved by the urgency of the issues, but she was disturbed that there was so much research and knowledge in the developed world and so little in the developing world. Harris knew that somehow she had to bridge this gap. Meanwhile, she started her doctoral work at Berkeley with the conviction to return to Nicaragua. Prospective dissertation advisers knew that if she joined their labs, it would be under the condition that she would go to Nicaragua each summer to work on her vision of transferring scientific technology. Dr. Jeremy Thorner accepted this bargain, and Harris took on a project in his lab using yeast genetics to study the calcium-binding protein, calmodulin.

The protein assay for leishmaniasis diagnosis with which Harris had been working while in Nicaragua was overly cumbersome and lengthy, so she searched for alternatives. She learned that a researcher at Yale University had developed monoclonal antibodies to *Leishmania* that might work in Nicaragua, so she set up a collaboration and returned the following summer to Nicaragua armed with the antibodies. Unfortunately, the antibody test did not consistently differentiate among the Nicaraguan forms of the parasite. At the same time, Harris had asked her Nicaraguan colleagues what scientific knowledge and techniques they wanted to learn and received the unanimous response of "molecular biology." However, with the rudimentary conditions of the laboratories in Managua, combined with intermittent electricity and running water only two times each week, Harris doubted the feasibility of setting up classical molecular biology experiments. Thus, she found herself faced with an ethical dilemma: when people want to learn something but do not have the resources to carry it out, do you decide not to teach them, or do you teach them anyway, knowing that they will be unable to implement the knowledge? Both the *Leishmania* and molecular biology dilemmas were solved when Harris began working back at Berkeley with Dr. Cristian Orrego, a Chilean-born scientist who had been involved in the early days of the polymerase chain reaction (PCR) and had taught PCR detection of *Leishmania* in Peru. PCR, which at the time had just been invented and made available to researchers in the United States, is a technique in which a specific piece of DNA is multiplied millions of times until enough has accumulated to be visualized using simple detection methods. Harris was elated to find out that, in principle, PCR was straightforward enough so that it could be performed under rudimentary conditions. Orrego taught Harris the technique and helped her plan a five-day lab course in Managua on molecular biology, including an experiment on PCR identification of *Leishmania* parasites (2). Meanwhile, Harris called everyone who would listen looking for support. She managed to secure donations of equipment and supplies from Gibco/BRL, Roche, and Amersham, as well as a $5,000 grant from the New England Biolabs Foundation.

In the summer of 1991, Harris returned to Nicaragua to teach PCR to twenty Nicaraguan scientists. A week before the workshop, she trained her Nicaraguan friend and researcher, Alejandro Belli, in the technique, and together they taught the workshop. They kept things as low-tech as possible. Rather than relying on kits, the participants made their own reagents; instead of using expensive thermocyclers to generate the temperature cycles to heat and chill the samples required for PCR amplification of the DNA target, they manually moved the samples back and forth between water baths at different temperatures. To avoid DNA contamination, they designated separate work and equipment areas for preparation of the PCR reaction mixture, extraction of DNA samples, and performance of PCR amplification, a concept that many laboratories, including Harris's own at UC–Berkeley, still employ today (3).

Despite the fact that there was hardly any running water and only intermittent electricity in the laboratory in Managua, the workshop participants were able to manually amplify *Leishmania* DNA. It was a moment that will live in Harris's mind forever. When the course participants and instructors saw the amplified DNA for the first time, they were stunned and extremely excited, all vying to look through the goggles and get a glimpse of the brilliant DNA bands. That moment was an epiphany for Harris: by understanding the principles of advanced technologies, it was possible to deconstruct and rebuild them under existing conditions anywhere in the developing world (4). By using PCR, they had been able to differentiate strains of *Leishmania* on-site—something that had never been accomplished or dreamed possible in a Nicaraguan laboratory. It was extraordinary to discover that it was actually feasible to demystify and break down this sophisticated technology under rudimentary conditions and apply the findings to local infectious disease problems.

THE AMB/ATT PROGRAM

After the initial success, Harris organized and conducted a second Nicaraguan course in 1992, expanding the application of PCR to detection and typing of *Mycobacterium tuberculosis, Vibrio cholerae*, and malarial parasites, among others.

Also in 1992, while presenting the Nicaraguan experience at a conference in Cuba, she met Josefina Coloma, an Ecuadorian who at the time was completing her graduate studies in microbiology and molecular genetics at UCLA. Coloma was interested in bringing molecular biology skills to her native country, and so they decided to conduct the next workshop in Ecuador. After fifteen years, Coloma and Harris still work closely together both at UC–Berkeley and at the Sustainable Sciences Institute (SSI).

Together, they managed to secure supplies and equipment donations as well as some funding from the American Society for Biochemistry and Molecular Biology. The course, which took place in Quito in 1994, taught twenty Ecuadorian scientists how to use PCR to detect and characterize endemic pathogens, and was a great success. As it turned out, the course was very timely since a cholera epidemic had recently spread from Asia to Peru and Ecuador. As a result of the course, workshop participants started to apply PCR to endemic health problems in their country, including tuberculosis, *Leishmania*, cholera, and dengue virus. The following year, Harris and Coloma returned to Ecuador to teach another workshop that included epidemiology and grant-writing skills in addition to laboratory work.

Things really took off when *Science* magazine published an article about Harris's technology transfer work (1), a novel concept in the early 1990s. Everything snowballed from there. Hundreds of people from all over the world wrote asking for workshops, articles, and presentations. The issues were so urgent and gripping that although Harris completed her dissertation on time and received her PhD in molecular and cell biology in 1993, she ended up canceling her postdoctoral appointment at Stanford University in order to focus on further developing the technology transfer/scientific capacity-building program instead. She felt she had made a commitment to numerous Latin American scientists interested in implementing molecular biological techniques for infectious disease applications in their countries and could not just turn her back on them to continue her scientific career. Dr. Nina Agabian, a parasitologist at the University of California–San Francisco, invited Harris to join her molecular parasitology laboratory and gave her the opportunity to continue to organize more workshops in Latin America, expand the offerings to other countries, and further develop the program.

Encouraged by her success as well as by her mentors and family, Harris created the Applied Molecular Biology/Appropriate Technology Transfer (AMB/ATT) Program in collaboration with her Latin American colleagues. The objective of the program was to adapt modern biomedical technologies to on-site conditions and train local scientists in their use for appropriate application to relevant infectious disease problems. The AMB/ATT Program was a three-phase program consisting of a series of hands-on workshops conducted on-site in countries with limited resources. Phase I facilitated the introduction of molecular techniques for diagnosis and environmental surveillance of locally prevalent infectious diseases; Phase II served to oversee the implementation of these techniques in molecular epidemiological studies and diagnostic programs; and Phase III fostered the use of molecular biology in relevant biomedical research and local public health applications. The basic principle behind the program was to take science to where the problem exists (5). Workshops were conducted entirely in the language of the host country, and instructors included local scientists and participants from previous courses. No previous training was required.

AMB/ATT stressed an inexpensive, do-it-yourself approach to implementing molecular techniques, with an emphasis on having a solid understanding of the procedures and reagents. In addition, it taught simple but effective methods to avoid sample cross-contamination problems, as well as innovative solutions to overcome material constraints. Participants were provided with training in molecular technology, good laboratory practice, and the scientific method. Additionally, participants learned project development and grant-writing skills to aid them in obtaining funding for their projects and administering them independently (6).

The first course in a given country catered to the needs of approximately twenty local scientists, who selected the pathogens to be detected in the workshop based on national infectious disease priorities. The courses began with morning lectures that discussed theoretical aspects of the molecular methodology and the epidemiological relevance of the organism under study. The lectures were open to a larger audience of scientists and students. In afternoon laboratory sessions, participants were divided into small workgroups, each of which executed the techniques discussed that morning. At the end of the Phase I workshop, participants interested in continuing on to Phase II proposed a pilot study applying molecular techniques to their work. Four to five groups of participants selected from the Phase I workshops, plus colleagues from their respective research units, were assembled into teams that designed the pilot study and collected samples for analysis in Phase II, which was conducted approximately one year later.

The Phase II workshops were two weeks long and consisted of two main sections: the first section took place in the laboratory and involved the molecular analysis of the specimens collected in the pilot study; the second section entailed the design of a larger molecular epidemiological study and the development of a proposal for funding. Phase III served to assure the continuity and sustainability of the transfer process through workshops and ongoing collaborations. As part of the follow-up process, continuous communication was maintained between participants and instructors, who acted as informational resources and consultants (6).

One of the program's key objectives was to make the technology as appropriate and low cost as possible. This was accomplished by adapting the equipment and by simplifying the techniques themselves. Adapting technology to existing conditions is vitally important because the on-site infrastructure (including availability of water, electricity, materials, and reagents) varies from site to site and is very different from laboratories in the developed world (6). For example, during pre-course preparations for a workshop in Quito, Ecuador, course instructors were testing the manual amplification of the *Vibrio cholerae* toxin-encoding operon and were increasingly frustrated when all the water baths appeared to be broken and could not reach the temperature needed (92°C or higher) for the denaturation step of PCR. They then realized that at 9,000 feet above sea level, water boils at 89°C, and therefore no water bath in Quito was ever going to reach the desired temperature of 94°C. After some brainstorming, it was decided to add a layer of oil on top of the water bath to approximate a closed system, thus allowing the water to reach a temperature of 92°C and ensuring that the PCR would work (5).

By conducting training courses under conditions that most closely approximate the true working environment of the participating scientists, problem solving is taught, and the possibility of modifying technologies and adapting them to local conditions is demonstrated. Understanding the fundamental principles and technical requirements of scientific methodologies leads to clever adaptations of equipment, the use of alternative techniques, the simplification of protocols, and a reliance on recycling (4). These conditions can foster some of the most ingenious innovations (7). After all, limited access to resources often forces researchers to be creative. Developing-country scientists have learned to improve and use common materials and simple tools instead of more sophisticated ones, thus finding solutions in everyday items, and adapting and converting protocols into low-cost approaches that are useful everywhere. An example of this creativity is the "blenderfuge" invented by Bolivian scientist Nataniel Mamani, which combines a blender, an aluminum bowl, and water-tap adapters to create a microcentrifuge. Another example is his "turntable shaker," which transforms the circular rotation of a record player into a horizontal shaker for the lab (3).

The AMB/ATT Program not only expanded on-site capabilities in less-developed countries to include molecular techniques, but it also fostered the immediate use of these techniques in relevant public health situations. The existence of on-site labs and personnel trained in molecular diagnosis and epidemiology provided immediate readiness to respond to healthcare crises, which is crucial when it comes to the diagnosis and control of infectious diseases outbreaks. An example comes from a Phase II workshop in Quito, Ecuador, where a patient with presumed leishmaniasis was admitted to the hospital at the workshop site. Since the workshop participants were at that very moment testing a number of PCR assays for the detection of *Leishmania* parasites in clinical samples, a biopsy from the patient's lesions was included in the experiment. Results confirmed the presence of *Leishmania* DNA in the patient's lesions and further identified the parasite as belonging to the *Leishmania braziliensis* complex. Interestingly, the classical methods used for immediate analysis of the same sample yielded negative results because of insufficient sensitivity of the techniques, even though the case was clinically and epidemiologically compatible with the diagnosis of leishmaniasis.

AMB/ATT was the formalization of Harris's vision of bringing science to real-world problems. And although the program was much in demand, it was completely virtual. It was Harris along with a group of dedicated volunteer scientists who devoted countless hours to adapting molecular techniques to developing country conditions, preparing protocols and reagents, recycling and washing laboratory supplies, and organizing and teaching workshops, all accomplished while they worked toward their own degrees or at real jobs. Another way to formalize the vision was to consolidate all the information and experiences that Harris had gathered in the first ten years of work in the form of a book. *A Low-Cost Approach to PCR: Appropriate Transfer of Biomolecular Techniques* was published in 1998 by Oxford University Press (3). The book describes Harris's overall approach to technology transfer and scientific capacity building, using PCR as an example; it also serves as a detailed guide to implementing PCR as a practical and inexpensive approach for research and infectious disease diagnosis by developing country scientists.

Although courses were taught in Bolivia, Cuba, Ecuador, Guatemala, and Nicaragua, apart from the occasional grant or donation, there was no funding to continue the program. Then one day in 1997, while Harris was on her way to a workshop in Bolivia, she got a call that changed her life. She had won a MacArthur Fellows Award from the John D. and Catherine T. MacArthur Foundation. Like many others who receive this award, she did not even know she had been nominated until she received the phone call.

THE SUSTAINABLE SCIENCES INSTITUTE: THE EARLY YEARS

The MacArthur Award, which is sometimes nicknamed the "genius award," provided a real boost to the technology transfer program Harris had started almost ten years earlier. It was a public recognition of the importance of the work, and the unrestricted funds provided a means to continue with the initiative in a more formal way. As a result of the award, the Sustainable Sciences Institute (SSI), a nonprofit organization based in San Francisco, CA, was founded in 1998. Harris and her colleagues had envisioned the formation of a nonprofit organization and had even chosen and registered the name in 1995, but until the MacArthur award, no funds had been available to jump-start the organization. In 1998 SSI finally became a reality. Like-minded colleagues, who over the years had contributed to the planning and teaching of workshops, founded SSI with Harris and became members of the original board of directors; they included Alejandro Belli, Christine Rousseau, Guy Roberts, Leïla Smith, Pratima Raghunathan, and Adil Ed Wakil.

Starting a nonprofit organization to carry on the program was the realization of a dream. It was also a lot of work. The board of directors first created a vision as well as a core program. It was their aspiration that the SSI would improve the human condition by the appropriate use of knowledge, science, and technology. As such, SSI's work is based on the premise that global health relies on biomedical scientists and public health workers who can recognize and resolve infectious diseases at the local level. SSI partners with promising researchers in developing countries, offering long-term assistance and mentoring to help them excel in their fields of research and make a difference in the health of their communities. It is SSI's mission to develop scientific research capacity in areas with pressing public health problems. This mission is based on the understanding that developing-country scientists have the ability—and the responsibility—to confront and manage infectious diseases in their own countries, but simply lack the necessary tools.

To work toward this mission, the core Scientific Capacity-Building Program, which is still in place today, was created based on the AMB/ATT model. The program's main purpose is to transfer knowledge and technology to developing-country scientists through in-country workshops, donations of equipment, and small grants for research projects. It is the program's goal to build local capacity to research, diagnose, and control infectious diseases. In the short term, the program enables scientists and public health professionals in the developing world to address issues related to priority infectious diseases. In the long term, the program makes it possible for program participants to improve science education in their countries and to influence informed public health decision making, driving changes in the behavior of those responsible for addressing public health problems. The program has a four-prong approach to capacity building: workshops (both laboratory and scientific writing), small grants, material aid, and networking and consulting.

The laboratory workshops develop participants' laboratory and epidemiological skills and train them in the effective application of these skills to relevant infectious disease problems. The workshops take science to disease-endemic regions so that scientists can adapt techniques and study design to local conditions. Partner countries are selected based primarily on the level of interest of the developing country collaborators, the disease burden, and reliable in-country contacts. All workshops are participatory, hands-on, and conducted in the local language. Trainees include a broad range of scientists and public health professionals, from university faculty and students to Ministry of Health laboratory directors and technicians, to physicians and epidemiologists. To encourage South-South knowledge transfer as well as greater local ownership of the program, resident scientists are incorporated in the planning and teaching process. During each workshop, several participants are trained in SSI's instruction theory and methods. These instructors-in-training take an active role in workshop management and organization, and often go on to teach future training workshops.

The writing workshops develop participants' manuscript- and grant-writing skills in order to broaden their scientific capacity to include additional necessary skills. The manuscript-writing workshops derive from the fact that the scientific community evaluates advancement and stature primarily by the number and quality of research publications a scientist has published in peer-reviewed journals (8). Developing-country scientists are, however, at a disadvantage: they often experience difficulty publishing because of a lack of technical writing skills, guidance in data analysis and manuscript submission processes, and access to scientific journals. The manuscript-writing workshops are designed to provide these scientists with the skills and tools they need to transform existing data into publishable material and increase the likelihood of a manuscript being accepted for publication in a reputable scientific journal. The workshops provide scientific advice, technical writing skills, and one-on-one tutoring from experts in the discipline. At the end of each workshop, each student is expected to have a solid first draft of his or her manuscript. In a similar fashion, grant-writing workshops provide participants with training in research proposal preparation in order to improve their chances of successfully competing for funds.

The small grants program provides follow-up support or seed funds for meritorious research proposals to SSI trainees. The program recognizes the fact that financial support is vital to researchers in underserved areas of the world, where a small amount of money can make a big difference. A few thousand dollars can pay for supplies, the salary of a scientist, and/or cover the cost of a basic epidemiological survey at the community level. The program acknowledges the difference that seed funds can make by awarding small grants to promising scientists who have previously taken part in one or more SSI workshops. All recipients are selected after a rigorous review process during which proposals are evaluated by SSI scientific volunteers worldwide for public health relevance, scientific rigor, feasibility, and budget. Only those proposals with the highest merit receive funding.

The material aid program provides developing country scientists and laboratories with the materials they need to perform research on infectious diseases. SSI has contacts with numerous U.S.-based institutions, companies, and universities that donate materials, supplies, and minimally used equipment or provide deep discounts and/or donations of reagents. The material is then sent to laboratories participating in the training program as well as to collaborators in response to their specific requests. For numerous scientists in resource-poor settings, these donations have been crucial for starting up their laboratories or have allowed them to continue with critical work. For many, SSI's material aid program is the only means to access these goods. Over the years, SSI has donated hundreds of thousands of dollars worth of equipment and material that might have otherwise gone to waste. Equipment supplied includes PCR machines, gel electrophoresis systems, microcentrifuges, power supplies, ovens, incubators, glassware, molecular biology reagents such as enzymes and nucleotides, and other essentials such as pipettors and general laboratory consumables.

A final component of the core Scientific Capacity-Building Program is networking and consulting. This part of the program grew out of SSI's dedication to providing continued support for its trainees. Scientists in developing countries often experience a sense of scientific isolation; to alleviate this situation, SSI serves as a constant resource for technical information and expertise for investigators in the developing world. In addition, SSI believes that in order to make a real and lasting difference in the lives in developing-country scientists, meaningful, far-reaching, and ongoing support from partners in the more-developed countries is needed. The networking and consulting program meets this need by providing the scientists served with mentoring and support for as long as they need it. SSI maintains close contact with all trainees and provides them with scientific advice and information, referrals, information about funding sources, links to online journals and print editions, contacts with networking resources, laboratory protocols, and more. Finally, the program provides networking among scientists locally, regionally, and internationally, and between local researchers and relevant institutions such as the Pan American Health Organization (PAHO), the TDR/WHO, Netropica, the Program for Appropriate Technology in Health (PATH), and the Centers for Diseases Control and Prevention (CDC) to foster dialogue, decrease scientific isolation, increase funding possibilities, and improve concerted efforts in handling outbreaks or epidemics within and across borders.

THE SUSTAINABLE SCIENCES INSTITUTE: A GROWING ORGANIZATION

SSI was founded in 1998 and received 501(c)(3) nonprofit status in 1999. Like any new nonprofit organization, SSI started small and grew steadily each year. During its first year, funding was scarce, and there was no office. That same year, the six-member board of directors held regular meetings, created the bylaws, and hired the first employee: Executive Director Pratima Raghunathan. SSI also held a workshop in La Paz, Bolivia, on dengue, tuberculosis, leishmaniasis, and Chagas disease. The next year, the first annual newsletter was published, the website was launched (www.ssilink.org), an office was rented, a second employee was hired, and two more members joined the board of directors. In addition, SSI held a workshop in Guatemala City, Guatemala, on dengue, tuberculosis, and enteric bacterial diseases and awarded three small grants to two scientists from Colombia and one from Ecuador.

In 2000 SSI established an advisory council, added three more members to the board of directors, and doubled the number of scientific advisors and organizational volunteers. SSI also held successful workshops in Burkina Faso and Venezuela. In 2001 three small grants were funded, workshops were held in Paraguay and Venezuela, a new employee was hired, and SSI moved to a larger office, while the number of volunteers continued to increase. In addition, a lab in Panama was fully equipped, and laboratories in Bolivia, Guatemala, Nicaragua, and Paraguay received shipments of material aid from SSI.

During these early years, SSI was funded through small grants and individual donations. Then in 2002, SSI received a generous grant from the V. Kann Rasmussen Foundation (www.vkrf.org), which allowed SSI to expand its core Scientific Capacity-Building Program. Thanks to the VKRF funds as well as matching funding and other donations, between 2002 and 2007, SSI held a total of twenty-one workshops in Bolivia, Brazil, Colombia, Ecuador, El Salvador, Guatemala, Honduras, Nicaragua, Panama, Paraguay, and Peru. SSI also awarded eleven small grants totaling $100,000 to researchers from Argentina, Bolivia, Brazil, Colombia, Ecuador, Pakistan, and Paraguay.

In 2002 SSI established a new program in Egypt spearheaded by its vice-president, Adil Ed Wakil, focusing on hepatitis C virus (HCV). Egypt has the highest prevalence of hepatitis C in the world, estimated to be approximately 12 percent nationwide (9). Dedicated to sustainable research in the field of hepatitis C, the program fosters collaborations between SSI partners and Egyptian researchers, with the aim of improving Egypt's ability to address the issues associated with this disease. The high infection rate is largely the legacy of treatment campaigns conducted from the 1960s to the early 1980s to control schistosomiasis (a parasitic disease caused by several species of flatworm) among rural populations (10). Because of the high prevalence of hepatitis C in the population, it is still being transmitted at unacceptable rates today through exposures such as dental procedures, injections, folk medicine, household transmission, and blood products (11). Given both the high prevalence and pervasive incidence rate, SSI's hepatitis C program in Egypt is not only necessary but urgent.

Since its inception in 2002, the program has provided local researchers with skills and resources to better combat the hepatitis C epidemic in their country. The program has four areas of in-country focus: (1) a small grants program that provides funding to young scientists who have submitted meritorious proposals on hepatitis research, (2) a fellowship program that fosters interinstitutional collaboration and provides supervised laboratory and epidemiology training for young investigators, (3) an information technology program that helps ensure that relevant peer-reviewed journals are more widely available to academic institutions and their scientists in Egypt, (4) a workshop program that organizes and conducts annual workshops on topics such as immunology, hepatology, writing scientific manuscripts, and preparing grants. The program's first workshop was held in Cairo in 2002; since then, the program has held four more workshops, awarded sixteen grants, and supported seven fellows.

The Technical Training Foundation (TTF) was a founding supporter of SSI and has been a steady and very generous supporter ever since. One of TTF's primary goals is supporting educational endeavors that directly benefit underserved communities and populations nationally and globally. In addition, the foundation supports medical research, particularly related to liver disease and viral hepatitis. The dual role of SSI's program of education and supporting hepatitis research in Egypt has garnered a long-term commitment from TTF, which is enthusiastic about SSI's investment in young Egyptian scientists and interest in expanding both individual and institutional capabilities.

Another exciting development occurred in 2004 when SSI became locally incorporated in Managua, Nicaragua, to administer a three-year, $2.3 million study—the Pediatric Dengue Cohort Study (PDCS)—on the epidemiology and clinical manifestations of dengue in children that paves the way for eventual testing of a safe tetravalent vaccine. Opening a subsidiary office in the country where Harris's work began in 1988 and administering a study of this magnitude has taken SSI's role in the developing world to a new level. Dengue is the most important mosquito-borne viral disease affecting humans, and dengue fever and dengue hemorrhagic fever/dengue shock syndrome have emerged as major public health problems, particularly in Southeast Asia and Latin America. An effective, tetravalent vaccine could dramatically improve the fate of millions of people who are affected by the disease.

Recent studies indicate that by age ten, 90 to 95 percent of children in Managua have been infected with one or more of the four dengue virus serotypes, and up to one in four children in Managua is infected with dengue virus each year (12). The PDCS follows a cohort of 3,700 children aged two to twelve at high risk for dengue in Managua's densely-populated, low- to mid-socioeconomic status District II near the Lago de Managua. The landmark study, a collaboration between the Division of Infectious Diseases at UC–Berkeley, SSI, and the Nicaraguan Ministry of Health (MOH), and supported by the Pediatric Dengue Vaccine Initiative (PDVI), brings together the Nicaraguan laboratory, epidemiology, and clinical sectors in an unprecedented collaboration, building scientific capability and infrastructure to a level previously out of reach. In 2006 the study, which was initially designed for three years, was extended for an additional three years. The study provides detailed and well-documented epidemiological data linked with biologic specimens from a pediatric population in a highly dengue-endemic Latin American setting that are enabling numerous questions about the pathogenesis and epidemiology of dengue to be addressed.

Recently, a parallel project emerged from the highly successful implementation of information and communication technologies (ICTs) in the PDCS (13). This new project, funded initially by TTF, is an entirely local response to the urgent need to overhaul the vaccination and prenatal care system in Nicaragua, and is tailored to help resident scientists and healthcare workers meet this need. Nicaragua's public health system is currently struggling to meet the goal of the Pan American Health Organization for 95 percent vaccination coverage of preventable infectious diseases by 2008, as well as the Millennium Development Goal of a three-quarters reduction in the maternal mortality ratio by 2015 (14, 15). Current efforts at providing vaccine coverage and prenatal care in Managua suffer tremendously from a lack of computerized registries and other inefficiencies. The new project is incorporating a number of technologies to streamline information flow and accessibility, improve the quality of data as well as the quality control procedures that are used, and reduce operational costs in Managua's MOH health centers. As a first step, SSI's informatics team, with direct input from the MOH, designed, refined, and implemented a new informatics tool, the Immunization System Database (SIPAI), to capture data during vaccination campaigns and routine immunizations, and enable real-time analysis. The SIPAI database allows automation of immunization data, generates comprehensive vaccine coverage information, and facilitates immediate decision making that impacts immunization indicators.

In June 2007, the new database was launched, and 100 percent of the health centers in Managua adopted it after a training workshop conducted by SSI and the MOH; version 2 was implemented in October 2007, and routine reporting of immunization indices using SIPAI will soon be mandatory. In addition to the new digital registries at the health centers, new technologies are being piloted in two health centers in Managua with the goal of expansion to the entire health center network in the next few years. These technologies include personal data assistants (PDAs) for registries during vaccination campaigns in the field, unique identifiers for mothers and children to enable immediate access to files via the use of bar codes on vaccination cards, and global positioning devices (GPS) for geo-referencing children's homes to facilitate field visits. The success of this initiative demonstrates the capability of SSI's informatics team to implement information technology (IT) solutions for further improvements to the vaccination and maternal health systems.

Since its inception in 1998, SSI has grown into a medium-sized organization with an annual budget close to $1 million; offices in San Francisco, Managua, and Cairo, Egypt; an eleven-member, highly involved board of directors; and a twelve-member, supportive advisory council. The main office in California has a staff of 6, while the office in Nicaragua employs 25 people and contracts over 100 specialized workers during field operations. As with any nonprofit organization, the organization's reach largely depends on the availability of funding. Although building human capacity is not a priority for most international philanthropies and large donors, SSI has been fortunate to secure enough funding for its programs thanks to the loyal support of various foundations as well as individual donors—although it is indeed a struggle. SSI's fundraising efforts have been boosted by the publicity it has received and continues to receive, as well as by the president's and the vice-president's ongoing and unwavering personal efforts to educate donors and the public about the importance and the impact of SSI's work.

Over the last twenty years, SSI and its precursor AMB/ATT have become world renowned for their pioneering work in scientific capacity building in developing countries. SSI is recognized as a model for technology transfer programs by global health agencies across the country and the world, including the World Health Organization, the Pan American Health Organization, the Organization of American States, the U.S. National Academy of Sciences, the American Association for the Advancement of Science, and the National Science Foundation, and most importantly, by developing country health workers and officials.

PROBLEMS ADDRESSED AND SUCCESSES ACHIEVED

The driving force behind SSI has always been the demand for the organization's work. The first time Harris went to Nicaragua in 1988, she was struck by the lack of resources available to her local peers in terms of equipment, supplies, training, funding, and technical advice. Knowing that the technologies and resources these scientists needed existed—but were unavailable where they were most necessary—inspired her to discover innovative approaches to bridge this gap (16, 17). Developing-country scientists face numerous challenges, from limited material and financial resources to poor physical and communication infrastructures. Because of ever-shrinking economies and national budgets, basic research is a luxury in most developing countries, and many scientists hold several other jobs. The lack of scientific careers, scientific tradition, institutional support, and collaboration within the local scientific community further aggravates the problem, along with the fact that available training is often operational in nature rather than research oriented (18). The importance of scientific research was emphasized by the Global Forum for Health Research report, which states that "strengthening research capacity in developing countries is one of the most effective and sustainable ways of advancing health and development in these countries and of helping correct the 10/90 Gap in health research" (19). The 10/90 Gap refers to the fact that only 5 to 10 percent of all global health research funding is directed to research on health problems that affect 90 percent of the world's population.

And although in recent years, a number of diseases (particularly HIV/AIDS, TB, and malaria) have caught the attention of global funders, the research and diagnoses of many infectious diseases representing a large burden to developing countries around the world (including dengue, leishmaniasis, respiratory, and diarrheal diseases) continue to be severely underfunded. At the same time, infectious diseases are still *the* major cause for morbidity and mortality in the developing world, accounting for half of all deaths, a rate that is 80 percent higher than that in industrialized nations. As a result, there is a defined need in developing countries for local personnel trained to employ modern techniques to detect and study emerging and endemic infectious diseases and design appropriate interventions for their control (20).

Latin America is a good example. Not only are infectious diseases the major cause of morbidity and death in the area, but the prevalence of HIV infection is on the rise. In addition, accelerating urbanization over the past fifty years has led to the appearance of "misery belts" around large cities. These settlements lack basic infrastructure and public services, and are therefore perfect sites for the proliferation of communicable diseases. The lack of capability in national health systems to rapidly and reliably diagnose these diseases only worsens the situation, which is compounded by poor epidemiological and clinical data that cannot be used to devise adequate health strategies and policies. In Latin America, as in the rest of the world, the progress of science varies from one country to the next. And so, despite their proximity and similar cultures, each country has achieved a different level of scientific capacity, with Brazil and Cuba in the lead followed by Argentina, Chile, Colombia, Costa Rica, and Mexico, and trailed by the rest (18).

SSI believes that the problem of infectious diseases requires a global solution because it takes only a day or two for a pathogen to get from one place on the planet to another. SSI is convinced that building scientific capacity in developing countries is necessary if we are to prevent the global spread of infectious diseases. In addition, SSI feels that it is important that all countries, especially those with high burdens of disease, have access to the necessary resources needed to control infectious diseases (17). Unfortunately, much of the work being done to address these issues in the developing world lacks an important component for building long-term effectiveness: researchers and health practitioners who are able to conduct their own research and establish their own priorities. Clearly, "parachute science," in which investigators from developed countries merely collect samples, return home, and publish papers, is of no real use to scientists and citizens in the developing world.

SSI's working premise is that even in low-resource settings, the burden of infectious diseases can be reduced if there are basic resources along with an essential infrastructure that supports the use of low-cost interventions by appropriately trained personnel. Effective disease control is possible but will only become a reality when every nation, regardless of size, location, or wealth, has the capacity to recognize, prevent, and respond to the threats posed by infectious diseases. SSI works to facilitate this process. Since its inception, SSI has served over 1,000 scientists and health professionals from over twenty developing countries. SSI and its precursor program have held forty workshops, awarded more than thirty small grants, and supported seven fellows. In addition, SSI has sent hundreds of thousands of dollars worth of material aid to individual researchers and health centers around the world, and has provided ongoing networking and consulting support to numerous developing-country scientists. And although SSI is proud of the number of people it has served and continues to serve, the organization believes that numbers alone do not capture the true impact and importance of its work. In order to make a real and lasting difference, SSI focuses not only on the quantity of people reached but also on the quality of the interaction. Ultimately the organization's ability to accomplish its mission lies in the success of its collaborators and trainees.

Some successes resulting from SSI's scientific capacity building efforts are as follows:

- In Ecuador, the Instituto Izquieta Perez of the Ministry of Health implemented a new molecular biology laboratory following SSI's guidelines and now uses SSI-taught techniques as part of the national diagnostic system. Implementation of this reference laboratory has boosted the accuracy and speed at which confirmation of clinical diagnosis of dengue occurs and has enabled the diagnosis of other diseases using similar techniques.
- After an unexpected epidemic of dengue virus in Paraguay in 2000, SSI-trained scientists implemented the methods they learned for the rapid detection and characterization of the virus in-country for the first time. Thanks to the subsequent close collaboration between the National University of Asunción and the Ministry of Health, an active surveillance system was established that led to the rapid identification of dengue virus serotypes, mobilization of mosquito control efforts, and containment of outbreaks for several years in a row.
- Only two weeks after SSI-trained Nicaraguan instructors had transferred molecular techniques for rapid diagnosis and typing of dengue in Peru, workshop participants learned about the first-ever outbreak of the disease in the capital city of Lima. The group collected ninety samples and performed the serological and molecular biology tests newly available to them. That same

night they were able to confirm that the outbreak was caused by dengue virus type 3. The next day, the group released the information to health authorities, who as a result, were able to implement immediate control measures.

- SSI has fostered the creation of Centers of Excellence in Managua, Nicaragua; Guayaquil, Ecuador; Medellín, Colombia; Lima, Peru, and Panama City, Panama. Each center has established state-of-the-art laboratories supported by SSI and are now national or regional reference laboratories for research on various infectious diseases.

- In Managua, Nicaragua, where there was once a complete lack of research infrastructure and tradition, after twenty years of collaboration, SSI has helped build public health and research capacity that meets the highest international standards. SSI has also supported community-based programs aimed at the prevention and control of infectious diseases.

- Over the years, participants in SSI training programs have successfully published their work in both local and international peer-reviewed journals, significantly increasing the number of resident researchers that have been able to publish in scientific journals. In addition, most small-grant recipients have published one or more scientific articles as a result of their SSI-funded studies. SSI's manuscript-writing workshops are not only very popular, but at least ten participants have published in peer-reviewed, international journals, and many others have published in local journals as a result. These encouraging results are partly due to the dedication of workshop instructors, who continue to work with the trainees for weeks or even months after the workshops have ended.

- In Egypt, several workshop participants who have attended the grant-writing workshops have used concrete skills learned there to obtain SSI grant proposals to study hepatitis. Scientists attending the manuscript-writing workshops have elevated their publications to internationally recognized journals that are widely read and highly respected. For example, Dr. Mohamed Kohla, a doctor from the prestigious National Liver Institute at Menoufiya University in lower Egypt, who published a review article on the pathogenesis of hepatitis C and coauthored two abstracts presented at the American Association for the Study of Liver Diseases' (AASLD) 2006 conference, based on his participation in an SSI manuscript-writing workshop. He has also written a paper on the lymphocyte phenotype in HCV patients. Three recipients of an SSI small grant have co-authored a paper titled "P53 Mutations in Hepatocellular Carcinoma Patients in Egypt" in the *International Journal of Hygiene and Environmental Health*. Additional small-grant recipients have published their results in acclaimed journals, including *Carcinogenesis*, *Journal of Hepatology*, and *Gut*.

LESSONS LEARNED AND THE ROAD AHEAD

One of the reasons that Harris became a scientist was her attraction to the way the cell works. Harris sees it as a beautiful system that can be used as a model for human society. Within the cell, there is a feedback loop that functions harmoniously as all the elements work together for the greater good of the whole with unprecedented energy conservation. The cell reminds Harris of how the many principles we all dream about in a just human society are being played out in our own bodies (21). As a scientist, she believes she has the responsibility to use her knowledge for the greater good of society. These values are not only the foundation upon which SSI was created, but they continue to inspire the organization's mission.

SSI believes that if we are to foster a truly global scientific culture, mechanisms must be developed that encourage international collaborations. In this era of globalization, it is naïve to believe that infectious disease problems in developing countries do not concern all of us. Mosquitoes, viruses, and pathogens do not adhere to international boundaries. For both humanitarian and utilitarian reasons, we must mobilize our scientific resources to initiate true partnerships that enable global access to scientific knowledge, technology, and products.

Over the years, SSI has learned to be flexible and creative. Its programs adapt to the times and the changing needs of its partners and audience. The manuscript-writing workshops, for example, arose from the need of past trainees who had accumulated and analyzed scientific data and felt ill-equipped to compile the results into coherent manuscripts for dissemination in the scientific world. Similarly, SSI has piloted a bioethics workshop, where participants learn about the ethical dilemmas facing researchers and gain relevant knowledge, enabling them to make decisions and/or influence local decision making regarding ethical issues that affect their research and communities. In addition, to fulfill the evolving needs of researchers and health personnel worldwide, SSI is currently developing new training modules. One of these training modules is a bioinformatics and sequence analysis module that focuses on ways to access available DNA sequences in public domain databases on the Web and on how to use specific programs for sequence and phylogenetic analysis. The module responds to the increased importance of genomics in diagnosis and monitoring of infectious diseases, and to the need for researchers in the developing world to have the tools in hand to track diseases in real time, understand their etiology, and contribute this information to aid in the timely control of epidemics and pandemics.

Another workshop currently under development is a module on information and communication technologies (e.g., PDAs, GIS, barcodes, fingerprint scans, computerized registries, cell phones, voice-over-IP) for application in public health settings. This workshop concept has received great interest for its versatility, including application in clinical trials, optimization of community-based research studies, improvement of immunization efficiency and access to health services, and facilitation of compliance with quality control exigencies (e.g., good clinical practice and good laboratory practice) (13). The workshop module was inspired by SSI's Nicaraguan colleagues, who have successfully implemented low-cost ICTs as part of the PDCS and routine work in the health center, hospital, and virology laboratory in Managua.

One characteristic of Managua is that there are no street addresses. Locals typically give directions like "from where the Pepsi sign was [before the earthquake,

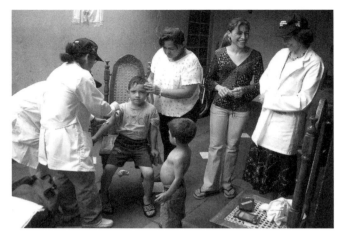

Figure 4.1   Eva Harris (right) with a field team collecting samples from children participating in the pediatric dengue cohort study in Managua, Nicaragua. Courtesy of Alejandro Belli.

which took place in 1972], three blocks up [towards the sunrise, or East]." This makes it challenging to find any location easily. Luckily, high-tech equipment such as GIS, palm pilots, and barcode- and fingerprint-scanning technologies are proving very effective in this environment. These technologies have allowed local researchers to easily locate the nearly 4,000 children enrolled in the PDCS and keep track of their medical records. In addition, using the devices has enhanced the computer literacy and confidence of the health workers trained to use them. For the first time, health workers communicate by e-mail and Skype, and research is conducted on the Internet with the use of PubMed and other reliable search engines. As a spin-off, SSI is now partnering with the Nicaraguan Ministry of Health to help improve national childhood vaccination efficiency and reduce maternal mortality by increasing monitoring and access to prenatal health services.

The Nicaraguan success story illustrates the far-reaching effect of SSI's scientific-capacity building work, where long-term partnerships and ongoing support led to growth at the individual level, which over the years has translated to growth at the institutional level and eventually has impacts on a national level. SSI's overall mission has not changed since the AMB/ATT program was first conceived twenty years ago, but the means by which SSI achieves its goals have evolved over time. Capacity building of human resources in a respectful and culturally appropriate manner is key to the success of SSI's strategy, and the resulting partnerships, collaborations, friendships and trust engendered by the process have created a generation of young researchers and pubic health personnel in developing countries who have increased confidence and commitment to work of the highest quality. This empowerment has led to local researchers taking important initiatives, learning the language necessary

Figure 4.2 Eva Harris (left) in her laboratory at UC–Berkeley with SSI scientific director Maria Elena Peñaranda (center) and SSI executive director Josefina Coloma (right). Courtesy of Jennifer Kyle.

to communicate relevant information to influence their leaders, creating lasting partnerships with researchers around the globe, and participating meaningfully in international projects and collaborations. SSI is thrilled to be a catalyst of change and looks forward to continuing to use science to make a difference around the world.

Acknowledgments

Many thanks to Maria Elena Peñaranda and Kara Nygaard for their excellent editorial assistance, tireless work, and deep commitment to making SSI's mission a success. We are profoundly grateful to the countless volunteers and collaborators the world over who have partnered with SSI to enable science to make a difference in developing countries.

ORGANIZATIONAL SNAPSHOT

Organization: Sustainable Sciences Institute

Founder: Eva Harris

Mission: Established in 1998, Sustainable Sciences Institute (SSI) seeks to improve the human condition by the appropriate use of knowledge, science, and technology. The organization's work is based on the premise that global health relies on biomedical scientists and public health workers who can recognize and resolve infectious diseases at the local level. SSI partners with promising researchers in developing countries, offering long-term assistance and mentoring to help them excel in their fields of research and make a difference in the health of their communities. SSI is in a unique position to respond to the needs of these scientists and health professionals because the organization has built its mission of developing scientific research capacity in areas with public health problems around the understanding that local scientists and health professionals have the ability—and the responsibility—to confront and manage infectious diseases in their countries, but that they lack the necessary tools.

Website: www.ssilink.org

Address: 870 Market Street, Suite 764

San Francisco, CA 94102

Phone: (510) 642-4845

Fax: (510) 642-6350

E-mail: mzoer@ssilink.org

REFERENCES

1. Barinaga, M. 1994. A personal technology transfer effort in DNA diagnostics. *Science* 266:1317–1318.
2. Harris, E., M. López, J. Arévalo, J. Bellatin, A. Belli, J. Moran, and O. Orrego. 1993. Short courses on DNA detection and amplification in Central and South America: The democratization of molecular biology. *Biochem. Educ.* 21:16–22.
3. Harris, E. 1998. *A Low-Cost Approach to PCR: Appropriate Transfer of Biomolecular Techniques.* New York: Oxford University Press.
4. Harris, E. 2004. Scientific capacity building in developing countries. *EMBO Rep.* 5:7–11.
5. Harris, E. 1996. Developing essential scientific capability in countries with limited resources. *Nat. Med.* 2:737–739.
6. Harris, E., A. Belli, and N. Agabian. 1996. Appropriate transfer of molecular technology to Latin America for public health and biomedical sciences. *Biochem. Educ.* 24:3–12.
7. Coloma, M. J., and E. Harris. 2004. Innovative low-cost technologies for biomedical research and diagnosis in developing countries. *BMJ* 329:1160–1162.
8. Coloma, J., and E. Harris. 2005. Open access science: A necessity for global public health. *PLoS Pathogens* 1:99–101.
9. Egyptian Ministry of Health and Population, 1999.
10. Frank, C., M. K. Mohamed, G. T. Strickland, D. Lavanchy, R. R. Arthur, L. S. Magder, T. El Khoby, Y. Abdel-Wahab, E. S. Aly Ohn, W. Anwar, and I. Sallam. 2000. The role of parenteral antischistosomal therapy in the spread of hepatitis C virus in Egypt. *Lancet* 355:887–891.
11. Habib, M., M. K. Mohamed, F. Abdel-Aziz, L. S. Magder, M. Abdel-Hamid, F. Gamil, S. Madkour, N. N. Mikhail, W. Anwar, G. T. Strickland, A. D. Fix, and I. Sallam. 2001.

Hepatitis C virus infection in a community in the Nile Delta: Risk factors for seropositivity. *Hepatology* 33:248–253.

12. Balmaseda, A., S. N. Hammond, Y. Tellez, L. Imhoff, Y. Rodriguez, S. Saborio, J. C. Mercado, L. Perez, E. Videa, E. Almanza, G. Kuan, M. Reyes, L. Saenz, J. J. Amador, and E. Harris. 2006. High seroprevalence of antibodies against dengue virus in a prospective study of schoolchildren in Managua, Nicaragua. *Trop. Med. Int. Health* 11:935–942.

13. Avilés, W., O. Ortega, G. Kuan, J. Coloma, and E. Harris. 2007. Integration of information technologies in clinical studies in Nicaragua. *PLoS Medicine* 4: In press.

14. United Nations. 2002. *Millennium Project, Interim Report of Task Force 4 on Child and Maternal Mortality*.

15. WHO. 2006. Immunization Profile—Nicaragua.

16. Dreifus, C. 2003. A conversation with Eva Harris. *New York Times*, New York, September 30.

17. Harris, E., and M. Tanner. 2000. Health technology transfer. *BMJ* 321:817–820.

18. Coloma, J., and E. Harris. 2002. Science in developing countries: Building partnerships for the future. *Science's Next Wave* September 27.

19. Global Forum for Health Research. 1999. *10/90 Report on Health Research 1999*. World Health Organization, Geneva.

20. WHO. 1999. *Report on Infectious Diseases: Removing Obstacles to Healthy Development*. World Health Organization, Geneva.

21. Harry Kreisler. 2001. Conservations with history: Making science accessible. Interview with Eva Harris. http://globetrotter.berkeley.edu/people/Harris/harris-con0.html.

5

Institute for OneWorld Health: Seeking a Cure for Inequity in Access to Medicines

Victoria Hale

The top five infectious disease killers in the world are HIV/AIDS, tuberculosis, malaria, respiratory infections, and diarrhea. None of these, not even HIV/AIDS, has received sufficient focus by the pharmaceutical industry to meet global health needs. Although these diseases have severe global social and economic consequences, very few effective treatments are available. Further, there are insufficient incentives for industry to invest in developing new safe, affordable, and effective treatments.

Over 60 percent of the world's population lives in the places where these infectious diseases are most prevalent: the tropics. These regions in the middle band around the globe—places such as sub-Saharan Africa, the Indian subcontinent, South East Asia, and parts of Latin America—have high population densities, high poverty rates, and climates that are favorable for insects that transmit disease. Each year, millions of lives are lost to infectious diseases.

Why, in the twenty-first century, is it that in some places people can get medical treatment for nearly any condition, or even for mere complaints, while in other places in the world, millions of children die from diarrhea?

The reason is simple. The therapeutic drugs that exist today are produced by for-profit pharmaceutical companies. These companies operate according to a very strict business model that requires a certain return on investment to shareholders for any project undertaken. Adhering to this business model leads these companies to pursue drugs for wealthy countries, focusing on heart disease, diabetes, cancer, and so-called lifestyle drugs. These targets of opportunity are consistently more appealing than taking on the challenge of treating tropical infectious diseases.

Between 1975 and 1999, out of 1,393 new drugs developed, only 13 were designed to treat tropical diseases. That is less than 1 percent, even though tropical diseases account for more than 90 percent of the worldwide disease burden. As a consequence, fully one-third of the world's population lacks access to essential medicines, and in the poorest regions of Africa and Asia, this figure rises to one-half.

More broadly, only 10 percent of the US$70 billion spent on health research worldwide each year is for research into the health problems that affect 90 percent of the world's population.

The idea behind the Institute of OneWorld Health (iOWH) is to look at this so-called 90/10 gap as evidence not only of past failure, but also of future opportunity. Without question, pharmaceutical companies need to make profits to make drugs. The research that goes into discovery, design, and testing for safety and efficacy is expensive. If we can find ways to redirect back to global health even a fraction of the intellectual property and human resources of the global pharmaceutical community, we can make a real difference. That is our aim.

Today, iOWH has a staff of eighty, in offices in the United States and in India, with the scientific and policy expertise needed to identify new drug opportunities, produce a product development plan, and shepherd drugs through the regulatory approval process. iOWH also has an array of research and development partnerships that work with us to develop a range of products for a variety of diseases. And we have formed the partnerships we need to manufacture and deliver the medicines we produce.[1]

THE BEGINNING: "YOU HAVE ALL THE MONEY"

Back in 2000, I was riding in a taxi and chatting with the driver, an African immigrant. He asked me what I did for a living. I am very proud of the work I do so I was happy to tell him that I am a pharmaceutical scientist. I was taken aback when he responded by breaking out into a fit of laughter. When he finally regained his composure, he remarked with a shake of his head, "You guys have all the money."

All the money, yes. But to what end? His comment crystallized the growing discomfort I had felt at the imbalance of resource allocation that was so evident in my chosen field of work. I recalled another moment of troubling introspection I had experienced not long before, when I was working at the Food and Drug Administration. I came across the fact that up to one in five children in sub-Saharan Africa does not live to see his or her fifth birthday. And each year in the developing world, 10 million people die from neglected diseases, diseases for which no effective treatments exist or are in development.

After my taxicab epiphany, I had an increasingly difficult time keeping these numbers out of my head. The pride I felt in being a pharmaceutical scientist became overwhelmed by feelings of embarrassment at being part of an industry that was not taking full responsibility for the diseases of the world. I thought to myself, if there is anything that I can do personally to change things, how can I not do it?

In further considering the problem, I began to wonder if it might be possible to take the profit imperative out of the drug development equation. Could I create a process for developing drugs, including testing them and getting them approved and manufactured, that would make them as safe and effective as any blockbuster drug, but affordable enough for the poorest of the poor? Is it possible to organize pharmaceutical development around the objective of human impact rather than profitability?

I resigned from my position at Genentech and took two years to travel, reflect, and simply consider the parameters of the challenge. Traveling around the world was an eye-opening experience, helping me better define the questions in my mind and confirming my deep commitment to my pursuit. After a great deal of time and expense, I began to see a way forward.

In July 2000, I founded the Institute for OneWorld Health (iOWH), an entirely new kind of pharmaceutical company.

THE EXPERIMENT: A NONPROFIT PHARMACEUTICAL COMPANY

The pharmaceutical scientists who work at iOWH share a belief that their work can change the world and save lives. Of the many possible paths one could imagine toward this goal, the one we have taken is the development of a sustainable, nonprofit pharmaceutical company focused on neglected diseases.

It is not possible for a nonprofit pharmaceutical company to follow the standard big pharma business model. The big pharma model typically starts with basic innovations, science and discovery in the laboratory, and the exploration of educated hunches.[2] When promising results are identified, they are taken through the lengthy and expensive process of drug formulation and sequential testing in Petri dishes, animals, and humans. Only 1 drug in 10,000 that is discovered actually makes it to clinical trials. Only 1 drug in 10 that makes it to human testing makes it to the market. Compounding the risk, of the few drugs that actually reach the market, 70 percent fail to recoup their R&D investments.

In many cases, drugs are cast aside by standard, for-profit pharmaceutical firms for reasons having nothing to do with their potential to benefit people. For example, some drugs are simply not profitable in any known application. Others may not compete successfully with other known candidates as treatment for a given disease. Still others are discarded because they have unacceptable side effects for the population the drug will treat, even though the side effects may be acceptable for other populations. (For instance, a new antibiotic that causes sleepiness may be unacceptable for people who need to drive or go to work while taking the drug. But for a malaria patient or for a bedridden patient facing certain death from an infectious disease, sleepiness may be a perfectly acceptable side effect.)

iOWH has sought a different path (Figure 5.1). For starters, we do not operate any of our own laboratories. Instead, we have pursued a strategy of networked innovation, with an emphasis on streamlining the traditional process of bringing drugs to market. We streamline in many ways, of which partnership is the most important. We partner with investigators in the public and private sectors to discover new compounds with potential for treating neglected diseases. We partner with for-profit pharmaceutical companies to try to find opportunities to match their castoffs—abandoned, discontinued, or no-longer-profitable drugs—with neglected diseases. And we partner with manufacturers, nongovernmental organizations (NGOs), and

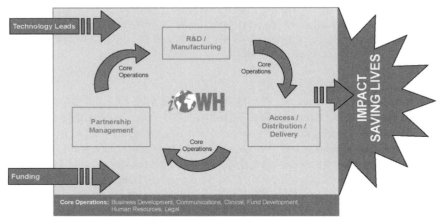

Figure 5.1   The funding model. Courtesy of the Institute for OneWorld Health.

local infrastructure service providers to manufacture drugs and deliver them to patients. Our core operations involve using our R&D experience to coordinate and collaborate with these partners and, most importantly, identifying the technological leads and securing the funding to create—and seize—opportunities to save lives.

We also aim to streamline the clinical trials process wherever possible. This of course does not imply that we cut corners in terms of safety. Rather, if we don't need to do as many trials—perhaps because our drugs do not compete with existing drugs—then we don't. Finding a late-stage drug to take over the finish line enables us to get the most from our investments. Also, when we bring a drug to a developing country's regulatory approval boards, we work with the agency to find the most straightforward path to satisfying the regulatory requirements that will prove safety and efficacy. Ultimately, we still have to do many studies, just as any other pharmaceutical company must do, and these studies can cost tens of millions of dollars.

These costs have been one of the biggest challenges to our model. What replaces profit when you remove it from the equation? We account for success in human terms, and we value each life equally rather than weighting them in terms of ability or willingness to pay. We were working for the same global public health outcomes as philanthropic organizations such as the Bill & Melinda Gates Foundation. We were pioneering a new business model that groups such as the Skoll Foundation and Schwab Foundation were looking to foster. Philanthropic funds would be our main source of revenue, and capital would be put to work to achieve a social return on investment.

But a shared sense of mission alone was not enough to persuade our current partners at the Gates Foundation and elsewhere to support us in the earliest stages of our development. What was required at the outset was a setting that would enhance our prospects for success, enabling us to overcome the scientific, financial, regulatory, and even political hurdles inherent in the development of drugs for neglected diseases. For OneWorld Health, that setting was Bihar, India. The disease was visceral leishmaniasis (VL), also known as "black fever" or kala-azar by those whom it afflicts.

MATCHING PROMISING DRUGS WITH NEGLECTED DISEASES

Paromomycin is an antibiotic developed by Pharmacia (now Pfizer), which discontinued it in the 1970s because it was no longer profitable. This drug floated to the top of our list of drugs to treat neglected diseases because it had such great potential. It had been a very effective and safe antibiotic, so much of the expensive testing had already been completed. Moreover, an African researcher had discovered that paromomycin had a powerful effect on a disease called visceral leishmaniasis, a fatal disease for which safe, effective, and affordable treatment options were urgently needed. Consequently, Pharmacia granted the rights to paromomycin to the World Health Organization (WHO). The WHO had put some efforts into using paromomycin to treat VL but ultimately abandoned the effort.

VL is the second most deadly parasitic disease in the world. It is a devastating affliction. Caused by a parasite spread by a common insect in the tropics called the sand fly, the disease attacks the bone marrow and destroys the body's ability to produce red and white blood cells. This leaves the patient extremely vulnerable to infection. Similar to AIDS patients, those with kala-azar almost always die of a side infection they simply cannot fight.

I visited with patients suffering from kala-azar in Bihar, India, where it is most prevalent, although the disease is also common in Nepal, Bangladesh, the Horn of Africa, and Brazil. This region of India hosts the poorest of people, who have been without adequate nutrition for years of their lives. Those afflicted with the disease are emaciated except for their large bellies, where the parasite hides, enlarging the liver and spleen. Witnessing the consequences of this illness was an experience that marked me indelibly.

In Bihar, a hundred million people are at risk for kala-azar. Approximately 1.5 million people are infected with the disease. There are 500,000 new cases and 300,000 deaths each year. Existing therapies are so expensive that families have been known to put three generations into debt to treat and save a relative. In contrast, the promise of paromomycin was a cure for kala-azar for significantly less money than current available treatments.[3]

Because my staff and I had experience with drug development and the regulatory process in various settings around the world, we entered into the project with full awareness of the obstacles that faced us in seeking to turn paromomycin into a drug for kala-azar, and getting it approved. Among the many obstacles, one had more to do with politics than science: it might be termed the "Constant Gardener" factor. *The Constant Gardener,* a novel by John le Carré, tells the tale of a multinational drug company that took advantage of the political vulnerability of a particular group of people in Africa to test a new drug with known adverse consequences. Precisely because the novel reflects aspects of reality and past experience, Western pharmaceutical companies seeking to test drugs on populations in poor places anywhere in the world are often initially received with suspicion. Lack of trust makes such projects difficult for the for-profit pharmaceutical companies—in some cases, simply infeasible.

We also came to Bihar as outsiders. But we came with a goal not of increasing the value of shares, but of sharing the value of cures. With our public health mission irrevocably encoded into our nonprofit form of organization, we were able to overcome the "Constant Gardener" factor. The trust we cultivated over a period of time allowed us to move forward with our trials even in the challenging rural environments in Bihar.

Reaching our initial goal—conducting clinical trials in Bihar for treatment of kala-azar—took four years. When at last, in 2004, I went to a hospital in India during a trial of our drug, the experience was exciting but also frightening. We had one chance to get this right and show that we could repurpose a drug to treat a disease the world had forgotten. To fail would in some ways be worse than not to have tried at all: potentially, we would discourage future efforts. Seeing patients treated with our drug suddenly sitting up, awake, aware, even hungry, provoked an indescribable feeling of elation.

We submitted the drug to the Indian government for regulatory approval in 2006. In August 2006, Paromomycin IM Injection was approved by the drug controller general of India for the treatment of visceral leishmaniasis (VL), the medical name for kala-azar. The approval of Paromomycin IM Injection came less than three months after the submission of the application for approval, which was prepared by iOWH in collaboration with our partner, Hyderabad-based drug manufacturer Gland Pharma Limited.[4] The drug is expected to be one of several tools for India's National Vector Borne Disease Control Programme (NVBDCP), which aims to rid the country of VL by 2010. We also expect the drug will be used in disease control programs in other leishmaniasis-endemic countries. Our manufacturing partner, Gland Pharma Limited, will make the medicine available at cost—a significantly lower price than currently approved VL therapies.

While we saw the approval of Paromomycin IM Injection for treatment of VL as a sufficient proof-of-concept for a nonprofit pharmaceutical model, the following months brought further validation of our work. In May 2007, the WHO announced the inclusion of Paromomycin IM Injection on their list of essential medicines. Then in June 2007, the *New England Journal of Medicine* published our Phase 3 findings, communicating to a broad audience within the medical community the particulars of the approach we had taken.

THE PHARMACEUTICAL VALUE CHAIN

For all the milestones we reached and the corresponding sense of accomplishment we experienced in 2006, we also ended the year facing a stark reality: it is one thing to develop and manufacture a drug that works, but it is quite another to get that drug to those who need it. As difficult as it is to discover a promising approach and then develop a drug, the final stage of delivering treatment can be the most difficult. Drug distribution must be done by local healthcare workers in local clinics. It involves getting the drug to the right places, storing it safely, and then administering it to people who have been properly diagnosed.

In the case of kala-azar, our strategy of matching an orphaned drug to a neglected disease had worked, but it remained unfinished. As we sought avenues for addressing the challenge of delivery, we began to broaden our thinking about how to approach the challenge of reducing inequities in treatment. It became clear to us that, in order to have our desired impact, we would need to develop the capability to engage at multiple stages along the pharmaceutical value chain.

In the case of paromomycin and VL, we started out in the late stages of research and development with our Phase 3 trials. Then we partnered with Gland Pharma Limited and the International Dispensary Association (IDA) for manufacturing. Last, we developed a plan to distribute and deliver those drugs to the beneficiaries, the people of Bihar. To test our plan, we opened a liaison field office in the city of Patna in Bihar, India, to oversee a Phase 4 pharmacovigilance and access program for the paromomycin treatment, which is administered as a once-a-day injection for twenty-one days. Working with principal investigators who are experts in the treatment of VL and with NGO partners, this Phase 4 program, initiated in November 2007, investigates the safety and efficacy of treatment with Paromomycin IM Injection in progressively more rural areas in Bihar. The first module of the program enrolled approximately 500 patients to provide additional safety data on the treatment.

Over the course of the two-year trial, up to 1,500 additional patients will be included in two subsequent access modules that will extend the network of treatment facilities, providers, and related logistics systems into the most rural areas of Bihar. This is an innovative access model for administering Paromomycin IM Injection that uses an outpatient setting to diagnose and treat impoverished patients and advanced data transmission technologies for pharmacovigilance in the remote areas where VL is endemic.

To deliver drugs to these remote and difficult-to-reach locations, iOWH is seeking to make use of existing infrastructure already put in place by NGOs. For example, there is an existing force of healthcare providers who provide women with prenatal care using a hub and spoke model to carry drugs from a central location to outlying destinations. If we partner with this NGO, we will train the clinicians and rural healthcare providers at local centers in the administration of the drug. The trial is an example of how iOWH extends its partnerships all the way to the village level. Indeed, our work would be nearly impossible without local partners and our in-country presence.

Though establishing a distribution and delivery network is extremely challenging because of the unpredictable nature of these rural areas and the lack of services in them, this step is also the most critical of all those that iOWH takes in terms of its mission to save lives. Beyond the obvious effects of the drugs and their ability to cure patients, the very existence of the drugs can have a ripple effect in a community. It brings hope to family members who no longer face the choice between extreme debt and the loss of a family member. It also brings new knowledge and power to clinicians, who can now diagnose people, knowing that there is an accessible cure to their devastating disease.[5]

Our goal is to refine an effective and transferable access model, enabling us to save lives, bring social change to families and communities, and expand our reach beyond India into other regions burdened by infectious disease. If we are successful, this new product will build demand for new markets along the way. From the manufacturing center in Hyderabad to the bedsides of patients, this drug will create a demand for services to provide transport, delivery, and storage. Local communities become partners with iOWH by providing these services as well as medical care. When a local community becomes healthier both physically and economically, the result can be profound and far-reaching.

In addition to effecting change in rural areas, projects in this part of our value chain (Figure 5.2) also effect positive change in the developed world by

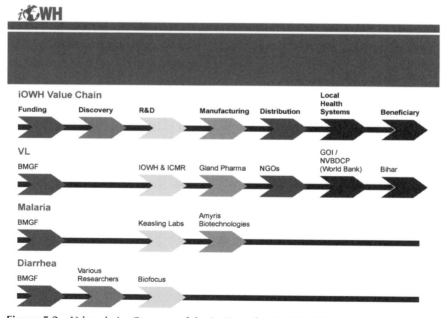

Figure 5.2   Value chain. Courtesy of the Institute for OneWorld Health.

addressing the emerging problem of what we call innovation pileup. There are many innovations coming from scientists and engineers who are developing new tools to prevent diseases and treat patients. But getting these drugs and innovations out of the warehouse and to the patient is often the most challenging part of the problem. When this problem is not tackled, these innovations pile up and become a burden and a disappointment that could, eventually, squelch the creativity of those scientists who invented them. By building channels for these innovations to flow through, iOWH can help prevent innovation pileup.

THE DOORS ARE OPEN

Because we have sought a nonprofit approach to working with innovators to find treatments for neglected diseases, we have observed a change in the attitudes of our for-profit counterparts. In 2000 and 2001, when we first began talking with pharmaceutical companies about our vision for a different approach to drug development, the response to the pitch was skeptical, to say the least. We were asking these companies to surrender to us parcels of hard-won intellectual property. Even if they weren't using the property, the request was bound to meet with considerable resistance—which it did.

Over the past six years, the reception we receive has changed considerably. Pharmaceutical scientists within the conventional drug companies understand the challenge we are seeking to address and, more importantly, can see the value of the approach we propose. Some want to participate in iOWH during a sabbatical or through fellowships. Others offer themselves as resources to help guide us. Even at the corporate level, there is an openness and willingness to talk. We now have access to these companies. They want to know how they can contribute. Although less than a decade ago the doors of collaboration appeared to be shut, today they are open.

The result of this turnaround is that it makes our search for the next matchup of an orphaned drug with a neglected disease that much easier. We have two more in the works already. These new partnerships hold the promise of producing therapies that will cure people afflicted with malaria—the most deadly parasitic disease in the world—and diarrhea.

Our malaria program efforts fall solidly on the manufacturing and distribution links of the value chain. We are focusing on developing semisynthetic artemisinin, a key ingredient in the manufacture of first-line malaria treatments. The project involves a unique collaboration of representatives. OneWorld Health, together with synthetic biology innovator Amyris and leading pharmaceutical company Sanofi-aventis, have created the Artemisinin Project. Its aim is to create a complementary source of non-seasonal, high-quality, and affordable artemisinin to supplement the current botanical supply, thereby enabling millions of people infected with malaria to gain consistent access to lower-cost, life-saving artemisinin-based combination therapies (ACTs). The partnership leverages new technology from Berkeley professor Jay Keasling and Amyris that allows an antimalarial drug precursor, artemisinic acid, to be manufactured using genetically engineered yeast. Keasling and colleagues first described this new technology in the April 12, 2007, issue of the journal *Nature.*[6] Prior to that discovery, only plants produced the compound, making it an expensive and unreliable ingredient for a mass-produced drug.

If it reaches commercial scale, this alternative source of artemisinin would supplement the supply that is currently extracted from the botanical source Sweet Wormwood plant (Artemisia annua) and produce enough artemisinin for ACTs to treat up to 200 million of the more than 500 million estimated individuals who contract malaria each year. This complementary source of supply would improve the availability of high-quality artemisinin derivatives to drug manufacturers and contribute to stabilizing the price of artemisinin-containing antimalarials to benefit patients and payers.

The World Health Organization recommends using ACTs as a first-line treatment for malaria in regions where the usual first-line treatments for malaria are no longer effective because of increasing drug resistance. Malaria is responsible for more than 1 million deaths annually.

The Bill & Melinda Gates Foundation awarded OneWorld Health a five-year grant of $42.6 million in December 2004 to manage the research and development collaboration with Amyris and Dr. Keasling to utilize the techniques of synthetic biology to develop a new technology platform for producing artemisinin and its derivatives.

Our diarrhea program falls at the other end of the value chain. It focuses on discovery. In 2006 the Bill and Melinda Gates Foundation awarded us a US$46 million grant to develop wholly new treatments to complement traditional approaches for fighting diarrhea. Diarrheal diseases are a leading cause of death in children under the age of five worldwide, killing an estimated 2 million children each year. Typically, children die of complications from dehydration. Therapies exist that help rehydrate these children, but no effective therapy exists to stem the loss of fluids in the first place.

Our efforts will focus on developing safe, effective, and affordable new antisecretory drugs that inhibit intestinal fluid loss. These novel antisecretory drugs will be deployed as an adjunct to oral rehydration therapy for the treatment of acute secretory diarrhea,[7] which is responsible for nearly 40 percent of reported cases of diarrheal disease globally. During 2006, the iOWH Diarrheal Disease Program initiated several new collaborations, including one with Bio-Focus DPI, which will apply medicinal chemistry and early-stage drug development expertise to identify new antisecretory drugs, and one with the International Center for Diarrheal Disease Research in Bangladesh (ICDDR,B), which will conduct pre-clinical studies. More recently we have entered into a collaboration with Roche. In this agreement, we will screen compounds from the Roche library to identify a potential new drug for the treatment of diarrheal diseases. (See Figure 5.3.)

Paromomycin	Visceral Leishmaniasis	• A non-profit organization can repurpose, develop and register a new medicine
Semisynthetic Artemisinin	Malaria	• The poorest people deserve the benefit of the most advanced technologies • Expensive biotechnology can be used to reduce drug costs
Anti-secretory drugs	Diarrhea	• New drugs, such as anti-secretories, can be used to improve existing public health tools (i.e. oral rehydration therapy)

Figure 5.3   Proof of concept. Courtesy of the Institute for OneWorld Health.

BUSINESS SUSTAINABILITY: THE MONEY CHALLENGE

The business of creating new drugs is slow and expensive. It involves great diligence and care because of cultural and ethical considerations involved in treating patients with new medicines. We have proven that our model is effective, but not yet that it is sustainable. A critical challenge in our next stage of development will be to transition from exclusive reliance on philanthropic support to a model that combines grant funding with revenues through sales.

With regard to philanthropic gifts and grants, we are increasingly aware of our need to develop a funding pipeline to support our product development at each stage. iOWH could, for instance, invest its funds in identifying good leads for the orphaned drug–neglected disease matchups with the most potential. We would then bring these leads and targets to outside funders that would help fund the development of the drug, and then enter into new partnerships to help manufacture and distribute the drug.

With regard to sales, we have started to consider the applicability of a cross-subsidization strategy: sales of a product to those able to pay could help cover the costs of providing therapies to those unable to do so. Visceral leishmaniasis afflicts almost exclusively the poorest of people, but such is not the case with all neglected diseases. Malaria also affects the middle and upper classes. So does diarrhea. Similarly, a compound could be developed for the same indication in two regions of the world. This so-called dual-market approach has the potential to earn revenue and have public health impact.

Of course, we did not create iOWH to be yet another revenue-maximizing drug company. Our nonprofit model enables us to fulfill our mission to make drugs that are not only safe and effective but also affordable and accessible to all. In order to do this important work far into the future, thus expanding our reach and impact, we must continue to seek innovative ways to grow and sustain the organization.

NEGLECTED NO MORE

The Institute for OneWorld Health is not the cure to global inequities of access to medicines. If it is part of the solution, it will not be because of what we are able to accomplish in isolation. Rather, it will be because others innovate at least as aggressively as we have sought to, by mobilizing resources, forming partnerships, affecting changes in policy, and creating new paradigms that work for the poor, rather than against them.[8]

My own belief, however, is that new technologies, creative organizational structures, and necessary realignments of incentives will be insufficient to bring about such change unless all are combined with one other essential element: moral outrage. When even a single life is wasted for want of a treatment that, if available, could be provided for less than the cost of a box of Band-Aids, we as a global community have failed.

To address this failure will require an effort distributed across the globe, from village clinics to corporate boardrooms—and it will necessitate great humility and compassion. It may begin with the work of organizations such as ours in building awareness and creating new opportunities for action. But it ends only when neglected diseases, and the people they afflict, are neglected no more.

Acknowledgments

I am grateful to Jim Hickman, Ahvie Herskowitz, and Beth Doughterty for their assistance in writing this chapter. This case narrative appeared, accompanied by a case discussion authored by Wesley Yin, in *Innovations*, 2.4 (Fall 2007), as "Seeking a Cure for Inequity in Access to Medicines."

An earlier version of this chapter was published in Innovations: Technology | Governance | Globalization (ISSN 1558-2477, E-SSN 1558-2485), Special Edition for the 2008 Annual Meeting of the World Economic Forum, The Power of Positive Doing, MIT Press, 238 Main Street, Suite 500, Cambridge, MA 02142-1046. © 2007 Tagore LLC. It is reprinted herein with permission.

ORGANIZATIONAL SNAPSHOT

Organization: The Institute for OneWorld Health

Founder/Executive Director: Victoria Hale

Mission: Institute for OneWorld Health develops safe, effective, and affordable new medicines for people with infectious diseases in the developing world. OneWorld Health is a nonprofit pharmaceutical company.

Website: www.oneworldhealth.org

Address: 50 California Street

Suite 500

San Francisco, CA 94111

Phone: 415.421.4700 x 303
Fax: 415.307.7092
E-mail: vhale@oneworldhealth.org

NOTES

1. *Innovations,* World Economic Forum special edition, 106.
2. Davos, 2008.
3. "Seeking a Cure for Inequity in Access to Medicines," *Innovations,* World Economic Forum special edition.
4. *Innovations,* Davos, 2008, p. 111.
5. Ibid.
6. Ro, Paradise, Ouellet, Fisher, Newman, Ndungu, Ho, Eachus, Ham, Kirby, Chang, Withers, Shiba, Sarpong, & Keasling, "Production of the antimalarial drug precursor artemisinic acid in engineered yeast," *Nature* 440 (April 13, 2006), p. 940.
7. Ibid.
8. "Seeking a Cure for Inequity in Access to Medicines."

6

Sustainable Transformation of Communities: The Jamkhed Experience — "We Have Done It Ourselves!"

Shobha R. Arole and Raj S. Arole

Large and diverse, India is a country of paradoxes. In spite of incredible growth in economy and business, 80 percent of the population continues to live on less than $2 a day (Population Reference Bureau, 2007). Women have held the highest political offices in the country, yet a large number of women still hold a low status in society and lack self-esteem. Although part of the world's vanguard in information and computer technology, India still has persistently high rates of infant mortality, maternal mortality, and deaths from chronic and communicable illnesses, with some of the world's worst health indicators, especially for the poor in rural areas and urban slums. Most health professionals, as well as the public, tend to believe that the solutions to India's common health problems lie in well-equipped hospitals and highly specialized personnel who can provide "quality" care.

Against this background, Drs. Rajanikant and Mabelle Arole founded the Comprehensive Rural Health Project (CRHP), a community-based health and development program in Jamkhed, Maharashtra, India. Surmising that health is not limited solely to hospitals and curative services, the Aroles recognized its many other determinants. They believed that economic, environmental, nutritional, and social factors—issues such as the low status of women and the plight of the marginalized—influence health profoundly.

The Aroles founded CRHP in 1970, and since then, it has become an internationally renowned, community-based health and development organization. Over the years, the project has affected and influenced national and international government health policy, nongovernmental organizations (NGOs), faith-based organizations, and businesses engaged in social entrepreneurship. In 1975 the World Health Organization (WHO) published *Health by the People* (Newell, 1975), with a chapter on CRHP. This book was part of the process that led to the WHO/UNICEF conference held in AlmaAta in 1978, resulting in the AlmaAta Declaration on Primary Health Care as the means for providing "Health for All" globally. In 2001 the Schwab Foundation selected the Aroles as outstanding social entrepreneurs for their development of an innovative and sustainable model for health and development.

CRHP currently serves a population of 1.5 million through its primary and secondary health care programs, hospital, and training center. A truly grassroots project, it strives to place health in the people's hands. The Aroles started as pioneers in the field of primary health care, successfully demonstrating a truly sustainable model. As communities and project personnel have interacted to promote lasting change, disease patterns have shifted from primarily communicable diseases to mostly noncommunicable illnesses such as diabetes and hypertension. Both primary and secondary health care continue to be relevant to the issues faced today, and full community participation in the integrated approach to both prevention and cure remains a vital element of the project. With almost four decades of experience, CRHP has established itself as an organization committed to uplifting the poor and marginalized in relevant ways within the communities it serves.

TRANSFORMATION OF INDIVIDUALS AND COMMUNITIES

CRHP has always been about people, community, and transformation. Lalanbai Kadam's story is one example.

> One of CRHP's first village health workers, Lalanbai was born into extreme poverty as a Dalit ("untouchable") in the village of Pimpalgaon. As a child, she often went hungry because her family relied on their landlord's discarded scraps for food. Lalanbai never learned to read and write because her parents could not afford to send her to school. Instead, she was married at age ten and was sent to live with her jealous and violent husband, who forbade her to interact with their neighbors. So intense was his envy that he even tried to kill her by attempting to throw her into the sea. After she became pregnant, Lalanbai was abandoned by her husband and left to raise her young son alone. When he was four, her son became ill with measles, which, according to the traditional beliefs, was caused by a goddess's curse and could only be cured by a divine miracle. Denied food, water, and medicines in hopes of a miracle, his condition worsened and ultimately claimed his life.
>
> After this tragedy, Lalanbai was remarried to an elderly widower, who died soon after their marriage. She then returned to her parents' village to take charge of affairs in her father's home, but because of the stigma of caste and widowhood, Lalanbai was ostracized by her community.
>
> At this time, the leader of her village selected her to receive training at CRHP to become their village health worker (VHW). As an illiterate Dalit woman, Lalanbai was very unsure of her ability to learn and succeed in such a role. But throughout her training, she was treated with respect, working as an equal with women from all caste groups.
>
> When she began her work as a VHW, Lalanbai found that many people were resistant to interacting with a Dalit woman. But the self-confidence she gained through her training at CRHP allowed her to work past these initial

difficulties. As the community began to recognize her skills, they began to see beyond her caste. By sharing her health knowledge, she worked hard to educate her village against the harmful superstitions and traditional practices that had killed her son.

Lalanbai's popularity grew so much that many people wanted her to become the village Sarpanch (leader). The current Sarpanch, afraid that he would lose to her in an election, asked Dr. Mabelle to persuade Lalanbai not to contest the election. Hearing this, Lalanbai laughed and said, "I already rule the hearts of the people of Pimpalgaon. Let him continue to be the Sarpanch! As I have changed, I have changed the world around me, even this backward village of Pimpalgaon, and this is the best reward for me."

In addition to being a leader in her village, Lalanbai has become an invaluable member of the CRHP community. She trains new health workers and serves as an important role model for poor women. She is also part of the training team for visiting health and development professionals and students who come to CRHP's training institute from all over the world. Through her hard work and the training she received at CRHP, Lalanbai went from being a poor and marginalized Dalit woman to a treasured and highly respected member of her community, responsible for transforming the health of her village.

PREPARATION—THE AROLES' EARLY LIFE

Who were the founders and motivators behind this transformation, and where did it all begin?

The son of schoolteachers in a rural area of Maharashtra, Raj Arole grew up understanding the intricacies of village life, including the subtle nuances of the caste system and its undergirding effect on society. At a time when women were hardly literate, his mother managed to become one of a few fully trained female teachers in the region. Amid such progressive values, Raj and all his siblings were well educated, but the real influence in his childhood years was his father. Although he was a teacher, Raj's father spent much of his time helping poor students, providing for others, and generally engaging in social improvement. In this atmosphere, Raj had the opportunities to imbibe social values, realistically understand the socioeconomic setting, and help those less fortunate than himself. This ethos of concern for the poor became deeply etched in his mind.

Raj's determination to become a physician arose when a flood struck his rural hometown of Rahuri. Witnessing the deaths of close friends and neighbors in these bleak and disastrous settings forged his resolve to become a doctor. In Raj's own words, "As a child, I grew up in a village and saw people suffering without a doctor. I myself had bouts of malaria, and the only person to treat me was a paramedic. I remember that my mother had a breast abscess and a simple village woman drained it. When I was twelve, there was a flood bringing with it an epidemic of plague. I saw many of my classmates semiconscious and in agony. That incident became the deciding factor and the real motivation for my desire to become a doctor." Despite the challenges of rural Indian life, Raj set high standards for himself and studied at one of the best medical colleges in India, Christian Medical College, Vellore.

During his time there, Raj met his life partner and wife, Mabelle Immanuel. In contrast with Raj's childhood, Mabelle was sheltered at the theological seminary where her father was a professor; she had very little experience with the harsh reality of rural India. Interestingly enough, Mabelle's father, who had dreamed of becoming a doctor for the poor, had the greatest impact on her throughout childhood. Inspired by his personal aspirations, Mabelle made that dream a reality.

Both Raj and Mabelle grew up in families that instilled in them Christian values and a strong foundation in Christ. Their own personal commitment based on this faith enabled them to commit their lives to serve the poor and marginalized, and have a vision for healthy communities.

Throughout their medical studies, the aspiring doctors never lost sight of the plight of the poor and marginalized; and they met many influential role models. Dr. Paul Brand, a surgeon working with leprosy, emphasized the need to demystify medicine. Much of his research and clinical work took place in small huts or mango groves. The renowned surgeon and physiologist Dr. Somerville also worked to make medicine accessible; he practiced real compassion for his patients, making himself available to them almost anywhere, even under a tree or in the bustling corridors of a hospital, wherever people could see him. Dr. Kutumbiah, a consultant for the president of India, insisted on making clinical diagnoses based on history and physical findings; investigations were used only for confirmation. His accuracy was astounding, especially to those who depended on expensive laboratory procedures. Dr. MacPherson, another physician, donated all of his salary to the welfare of his patients, saving money by eating in one of the cheapest student messes on campus. Such committed and compassionate role models reinforced the core values that inspired Raj and Mabelle to pursue the path that eventually led to the founding of CRHP.

During their internship years, Raj and Mabelle grew closer and quickly realized that they shared the interest, commitment, and zeal to serve the poorest of the poor. In 1960 they married and embarked on their lifelong journey together.

Working in curative-oriented mission hospitals in Maharashtra and Karnataka, they realized something was missing. Although they were providing quality clinical care, they wondered whether their work was really making a difference in the lives of the poor. Their quest to reach the population's most vulnerable members enabled them to be open to change. What was happening to those who did not make it to the hospital, and why were they not coming? What were the reasons for the high rates of maternal and infant mortality in the region?

Raj again shares his experience while at the mission hospital in Vadala:

> Once when I was traveling from Vadala to Salapatupur after finishing a clinic, I suddenly saw a shop with a large crowd around it. I realized that the shopkeeper was seeing patients. There were more patients waiting to see the shopkeeper than even I had seen on that day. I was indignant. After a while, I had a chance to speak to him.

I asked him what he would do if someone had pneumonia, and he said he gave penicillin. Then I asked him what he did for diarrhea, and he said he gave kaolin (a prescription which was used in the 1960s). I began to realize that people in the villages are really interested and willing to learn, and they can take care of simple illnesses. That was the moment at which I developed the idea that people have the capacity to deal with simple yet vital aspects of health.

In search of answers, Raj and Mabelle drove to the villages and held clinics, gaining a basic glimpse into community life and social structure in the villages. Inspired by the American Dr. Hale Cooke, who worked alongside them, they looked deeper into these issues. As Fulbright scholars, the Aroles had the opportunity to complete their medical and surgical residencies in the United States and earn master's degrees in public health at Johns Hopkins University. It was there that they were able to plan a comprehensive, community-based health and development project to be implemented in India. Professor Carl E. Taylor, their mentor at Johns Hopkins, was a source of inspiration and support throughout this process. He introduced his students to different systems of health care and encouraged them to learn from one another. Participants from Johns Hopkins–affiliated projects all over the world opened their eyes to the fact that learning does not only occur in university classrooms but also through village experiences. Knowledge comes not only from the mentor or expert but also from the community.

IN THE BEGINNING IN JAMKHED

Upon their return to India, the Aroles planned to work in a deprived part of Maharashtra, where health care and socioeconomic development were rare and often primitive. At the same time, one of their main objectives was to work in an area of sufficient community interest and willingness on the part of the people to partner and organize for effective change.

Shri Bansi Kothari, a political leader known for his zeal for social work, tracked down the two doctors during their mission to find such a place. Having known Raj and Mabelle even before their sojourn in the United States, he was eager to invite them to a village called Jamkhed, where the community would be receptive to them.

The Aroles traveled remote and often incomplete, dusty roads on their way to meet various village leaders and their communities in the jurisdiction of Jamkhed *taluka* (subdistrict). Drought prone and lacking in socioeconomic development, the Jamkhed area indeed proved to be the right area in which to initiate an innovative approach to health care. The area was truly poverty stricken, with few resources and even fewer public health services.

In the early 1970s, Jamkhed had a population of about 7,000. The village had no running water or electricity, and lacked not just motor vehicles but even a proper road. Surrounding villages and distant urban areas were nearly inaccessible. In this resource-deprived setting, the Aroles decided to set up a low-cost curative care center, and they initiated primary health care programming using a rudimentary understanding of community participation. This meant requesting the community to provide a place to run a clinic as well as adequate quarters to house the staff of the newly inaugurated CRHP. The community responded by providing a rundown veterinary hospital as the clinic site, and the second and third floors of a local merchant's house for lodging. Joining the Aroles was an initial group of ten staff that included the stalwart and faithful ex-army nurse Helenbai (referred to as Akka), nurses, technicians, and paramedical workers. The staff stayed on the second floor. Raj and Mabelle, along with their two children, Ravi and Shobha, age three and ten at the time, lived on the third floor, sheltered only by three walls and a leaking roof.

After the doctors purchased a secondhand Willy's jeep with canvas doors, visits to the surrounding villages became possible. These visits uncovered the many layers of complexity in village social structure. Caste definition, discrimination, and the low status of women played major roles in precluding unity among a community. The practices of centuries etched the traditions of caste and position in the lives of the villagers. The poorest and the most marginalized were not even allowed to attend village meetings, and reaching them meant finding them separately from the general community. Diplomatically holding leader and high-caste meetings before their sessions with the Dalit community produced less bias and more balance in their understanding of the needs of the community as a whole.

As medical professionals, the Aroles assumed that health would be a priority need in the communities. Surprisingly, most villagers identified water, food, and shelter as their biggest concerns, with health much farther down the list. Fully addressing the community's expressed needs became the main thrust of the project, and it was upon these responses that all future success would be built. Poor rainfall resulting in the lack of water for agriculture and domestic use was a major issue. OXFAM and other agencies partnered to provide tube wells in nearly thirty villages, effectively providing clean drinking water for the masses.

This one intervention had several far-reaching implications. Safe drinking water decreased the incidence of waterborne diseases and illnesses such as diarrhea, hepatitis, cholera, and typhoid. Furthermore, the tube wells were strategically placed in the low-caste sections of each village. This forced those from the higher castes to draw water in the low-caste areas. Mobility and intermingling of the caste groups was one of the first ways in which the rigid structure of the caste system began to deteriorate.

Nutrition programs for children also increased flexibility among the castes. Children, who would normally sit according to their caste designation, now were subtly rearranged according to shirt color, outfit, or some other neutral designation. Simple interventions such as these brought about distinct and very important social change.

The Aroles' immediate response to the felt needs of the community left a deep impact in villages with a long history of exploitation. Most villagers found it difficult to believe that the CRHP team harbored no ulterior motive. Their commitment to and genuine interest in the needs of the rural poor built a relationship of mutual trust and an authentic understanding of community participation. But this did not happen overnight. Making regular and consistent contact with the villages, listening to the people, and facilitating appropriate interventions, all with patience and a sense of humor, were essential in order to move forward and maintain that trust.

Raj and Mabelle, as medical doctors, were effectively able to address the curative needs of the people. This capability was significant, and their competence and professional skills became well known and much praised. As the large backlog of pressing medical problems in the population gradually eased, the Aroles' credibility as physicians as well as the community's receptivity to preventive and promotive health care increased significantly. The organization of large-scale medical and surgical camps for hundreds of people also did much toward achieving this goal.

Before the end of the second year in Jamkhed, a Marwadi (business community) family generously donated five acres of land to build more permanent facilities—a hospital for CRHP and housing for its staff. This site became CRHP's official campus, and over the last three decades, seven more acres have been added to the compound.

FLEXIBILITY AND INNOVATION—LEARNING FROM THE PEOPLE

Initially, CRHP placed an auxiliary nurse midwife (ANM) in each village to take care of common health problems—maternal and child health, family planning, tuberculosis treatment and control—through daily home visits and clinics. But after a year-long trial period, the ANMs had not effected significant changes in public health or social conditions. Uncovering the reasons for the failure of this model enabled the Aroles to learn a great deal from this experience. The ANMs, largely from urban backgrounds, did not belong to the villages. They did not speak the villagers' colloquial Marathi, nor did they feel comfortable living among them. They did not know the families or feel the same concern for the people as did those who were native to the communities. Most of the ANMs were young, unmarried women who felt awkward and timid when visiting homes and discussing delicate matters such as family planning.

This apparent failure proved to be a stepping stone to an innovation, a revolutionary concept in the field of public health and community development. While discussing possibilities for alternatives with the communities, the Aroles toyed with the idea of training illiterate women from the villages to deal with common health problems. Both the villagers and the Aroles thought it was worth a try. A woman working with CRHP, Mrs. Joshi, liaised with the community. Adept at grassroots promotion of family planning, she, along with local community members, chose a number of women to be trained as village health workers (VHWs). The project's openness and flexibility to try this new idea led to an incredible impact on health during the following years.

The health worker training brought women of different castes from CRHP project villages to Jamkhed for two weeks to engage in health education sessions and personal development. For these illiterate women who had never left their homes or villages, the experience was new and shocking. They were used to veiling their heads with saris and identifying themselves only by caste or village or husband; for many, this was the first time they were introduced by their own names and acknowledged as individuals. It was also the first time in their lives that their daily activities were not controlled or dictated by men, either fathers or husbands. But the greatest challenge came in crossing the boundaries of caste. Cooking and eating food together, sharing rooms—these new and tradition-breaking ideas were initially difficult to comprehend. They wondered how they would survive at CRHP and normalize these new concepts.

Drs. Raj and Mabelle tactfully allayed their fears. Taking the women to the medical lab, the doctors drew each woman's blood and asked each woman to identify the samples according to caste. They were unable to do so. They could not differentiate their chest X-rays either, able to identify neither their own nor those of other castes. The ideas finally began to make sense. Reassured that the training would be beneficial, the women continued learning with greater enthusiasm.

Those first weeks, however, were still difficult, filled with self-doubt and apprehension. One of the VHWs-in-training, Salubai, relates her experience:

> I was chosen to come to the classes. I was extremely afraid and wondered what would happen to me. I could not speak, and my mouth went dry. One of my colleagues, Lalanbai, had encouraged me to come. After the first visit to the center, I decided I wouldn't go again. But Lalanbai encouraged me, and slowly the doctors and staff encouraged me. There were still times when I wasn't sure of myself, but in time I gained confidence.

From those first two weeks of trainings through the present, CRHP has promoted personal development—instilling and building self-confidence, self-worth, faith, and values—in addition to nurturing a well-rounded understanding of important health and social issues. These foci set the cornerstones for the success of the VHW training. Today the VHWs continue to visit CRHP for weekly, on-going training and group interaction from noon each Tuesday to late afternoon on Wednesday.

VHWs — AGENTS OF TRANSFORMATION

The first twenty VHWs concentrated on particular priority health areas in their respective villages. These included maternal and child health (MCH), family planning, tuberculosis, leprosy, and waterborne illnesses. Working as part-time volunteers, these women would visit families and disseminate health knowledge throughout their communities. In return, CRHP provided support as the women initiated income-generating activities to improve the conditions of their families. But the VHWs name the tremendous pride and satisfaction from engaging in community development and improving their neighbors' health as their greatest reward. Village members, transcending prejudice and mistrust, bestow profuse praise and respect on their VHWs, regardless of caste. This development is truly remarkable in a society so deeply entrenched in age-old traditions and practices. As a recognized and respected part of a health team that included doctors, nurses, and paramedical workers, the VHWs gained significant credibility and further improved their standing as health experts and valuable community members.

Rural India, riddled with superstitions, fear, and skepticism of science, was in no way an easy place to practice modern medicine in the earlier decades of the project. Blaming many illnesses on curses and the wrath of gods, villagers often turned to magic and local Indian shamans and faith healers. The traditional practices of old women were followed without question or understanding. Much of the time, these practices and beliefs were harmful, contributing to high rates of infant, child, and maternal mortality. Changing the practices and beliefs of so many generations was an immense challenge. By providing quality curative care and medical services, the Aroles had convinced the villagers of their investment in the communities' felt needs and their desire to eliminate suffering. Raj and Mabelle realized that lasting and sustainable changes in health could occur only if adequate time and energy were given to demystify health knowledge and set it back in the people's hands, as through the VHWs. Innovative and culturally appropriate, the Aroles showed that illiterate women could use health knowledge and practices responsibly to transform the health of communities. It is the VHWs, in fact, who significantly improved health indicators and changed people's quality of life.

Improvement in health depends not on curative services but in changing knowledge, attitudes, and practices about illness and health. This change was not achieved through traditional Western medical education practices of hierarchical teaching and condescension. Rather, the initial years saw the health team listening to villagers and deciphering their beliefs and practices. Taking time to understand local attitudes facilitated the relevant introduction of alternative scientific knowledge, impressively effecting changes in health and social practices.

The VHWs were skilled at sharing local proverbs, stories, examples, and metaphors to relate new concepts in understandable ways. As their health knowledge improved, they were able to create analogies between daily life events and scientific explanations for problems such as diarrhea, malnutrition, and disease. For example, unwatered plants quickly perish; children, too, can die of dehydration and need water as plants do to sustain life. Another example relates to a common folk tale that an infant needs to cross seven bridges. The VHWs developed flashcards depicting the building blocks for a strong bridge in the first year of life, among them things such as immunization, nutrition, and clean drinking water.

THE INNOVATIVE HEALTH SYSTEM — DEVELOPING
THE POTENTIAL OF PEOPLE

The CRHP health program uses a modular and interactive three-tier referral system. At the grassroots level are the village health worker and community organizations such as the Mahila Mandals (women's groups) and Tarun Shetkari Mandals (men's groups). At the project level lies the training center and a forty-bed hospital, providing low-cost, secondary care with round-the-clock emergency, medical, surgical, pediatrics, and ob/gyn. care. The mobile health team, consisting of nurses, paramedical workers, social workers, and occasionally a doctor, provides the intermediary link.

The staff of CRHP has greatly contributed to the success of this model. Their flexibility, openness to new ideas, and willingness to work at any time have enabled the project to move forward and adapt to changing health and social conditions. Although salaries are meager, the high levels of satisfaction and motivation have kept most of the staff at the project for over thirty years, even after retirement. Many of them have likewise been transformed and actualized in ways they would once have thought unimaginable. Such change is reflected in the life of Mr. Moses Guram.

Moses originally comes from Andhra Pradesh, a state on India's eastern coast. His family was poor, and there was never enough to eat. As a young boy, he left home in search of a job and ended up in the city of Pune, 1,300 km away, with a job as a helper at Spicer College. He came to Jamkhed with the college team to help build the health center. After the building was finished, Moses wanted to stay; he had fallen in love with a young cook. He had only four years of formal schooling, but he had a strong physique, so he was given the job of night watchman. An industrious fellow, Moses helped the motor mechanics and also spent his time observing the X-ray technician and electrician. Since every worker is expected to share knowledge and skill with those who show interest, Moses soon learned how to operate the generator and understand electrical circuits. As he showed aptitude and interest, he acquired new skills. He went to Jaipur to learn how to make the Jaipur foot from the famous orthopedic surgeon, Dr. P. K. Sethi, who had developed a simple, low-cost prosthetic leg appropriate for the Indian lifestyle. Today, Moses is in charge of the workshop that manufactures artificial limbs, calipers, and other equipment for physically handicapped persons. He has traveled with a CRHP team to Liberia and Angola, and men from these countries have come to Jamkhed to learn from him.

He reflects: "I was trusted, and knowledge was with me. I was nobody; today people call me 'doctor.' Many doctors and professionals take my advice. I have been associated with the manufacture of over 17,000 artificial limbs and calipers that were provided to needy people in the state of Maharashtra. Civic clubs organize camps; they invite me with the team to manufacture limbs. I see my picture appear in the newspapers. You cannot imagine the joy I get. Twenty-four hours a day I keep thinking of how to improve the prosthesis. How can I make the caliper simple and light enough that a small child can use it? I have a dozen young men, whom I have trained, working with me. I share all the knowledge I have with them and encourage them to be like me. My brothers and sisters are working in the Middle East and have often called me to join them. I tell them, 'Money cannot buy the joy that I have in my work!'"

With his wealth of experience and knowledge of the project, and as a native speaker of Telugu, Moses has become an essential part of the training team, working as an interpreter for hundreds of people coming from all over Andhra Pradesh—village health workers, auxiliary nurse midwives, and project managers, who regularly come to Jamkhed through the state government's Society for the Elimination of Rural Poverty (SERP) collaboration with CRHP.

VILLAGE TRANSFORMATION BY THE PEOPLE

In many of the villages, forming men's groups called farmers' clubs proved easier in the highly patriarchal societies that made access to women difficult. Community groups are organized around the self-interests of the people. The men wanted to learn ways to improve agriculture and the care of their animals. Then, they began to recognize the interrelationships among health, nutrition, agriculture, economics, and eventually even women's status. With this understanding, men slowly began to allow their wives to participate in Mahila Mandals, also organized around the self-interests of these women. Slowly, these groups gained momentum and, as they strengthened, addressed such issues as health, income generation, and social practices.

The organization of participatory community groups and the impact of VHWs created a synergy that transformed the landscape for health and society in all project villages. Concerted community efforts at integration through the breaking of caste barriers and the improvement of women's status were essential for making Health for All a reality.

The experience of transformation spread to other villages by the people themselves, and thus primary health care became a movement in our area, encompassing 250 villages (300,000 people) within twenty years.

An example from the village of Ghodegaon is instructive in demonstrating the dramatic change that has occurred since the project initiated its work there. Ghodegaon was one of the first villages to invite CRHP to work with it. A group discussion held in 1991 recounted the changes that had occurred in Ghodegaon, with reflections on the brutality and injustices of the past (Arole and Arole, 1994, 2003).

Shahaji Patil, a local farmer and member of a farmers' club, described his experience with positive transformation. "It was only twenty years ago [1971] that Ghodegaon was one of the poorest villages in this area. The hills were bare, and the fields barren. Every year the monsoon rain swept away the topsoil, leaving us the dry, parched earth full of gullies and eroded land. Few of us had enough water to cultivate the land. The social workers of CRHP understood that we could not have good health unless we had good agriculture. They helped us to come together. We forgot our caste differences and our social status. All of us, rich and poor, joined together, and we terraced and leveled the land. We built twenty-three dams and dug forty irrigation wells. We planted over 200,000 trees on the hillside and on our farms. We prevailed on the Government to give land to those who did not have any. Everyone in the village has land today. We got together and with CRHP's help brought those barren lands under cultivation and so have enough food to feed all our children. There is no need to go out of the village in search of food."

For the previous fifteen years, Angadrao Gavhale, a Dalit, had been Sarpanch of Ghodegaon. He said, "Twenty years ago, we Dalits could not come to the center of the village. As a child, I could not go anywhere near the temple. Now I have built my house close to the temple. Yes, many changes have taken place. My family was landless, but today I have land and irrigated fields. I have planted an orchard and raised a plant nursery. Some of the Dalits now own choice land in the valley. Our children are healthy, and all the girls and boys in my community go to school. We all have land and have built good homes. Formerly we were made to live outside the village in thatched huts separated by a wall from the main village."

A high caste man interrupted, "Yes, today we all from different castes are sitting together, drinking tea and eating snacks. Traditionally we did not socialize with the low caste; rather, we who are twice born (high caste) have exploited the poor for centuries. We made them work day and night on our farms and often paid them with leftover food and grain. We would boycott them if they did not obey our orders."

"We Dalits would be simmering with anger and would take revenge in our own way. We used to poison your prize bullocks and cows," replied Angadrao.

Shahaji responded, "Then we punished you by burning your huts."

Then they all laughed together, remembering their actions; and in a more serious vein, Shahaji said, "Yes, the high caste often behaved like animals and treated the Dalits and other low castes in an unjust way. Now we have learned how to behave like human beings. Yes, we have our differences, but we have learned to respect and appreciate each other."

Shahaji continued, "Years of drought had left us frustrated. Every year half the young people of the village would migrate for a few months to sugarcane factories to keep their families from starving. Poverty and frustration led to drinking and gambling. There were twelve illegal breweries and a few gambling dens in the village. Anyone who came to Ghodegaon would see drunken brawls. People from surrounding villages also came to join in the drinking and have their luck with cards. It was a common sight to see men lazing around in the front square of the village.

"Added to this misery was sickness. Children were emaciated; many had swollen limbs and potbellies. Many children died before they reached school age, and women died in childbirth because there was no doctor around. Well-to-do people went to the doctor in Jamkhed, but the poor depended on the *devrushis* (magicians). Then we heard that a doctor and his wife had come to Jamkhed to work in the villages. We invited them to Ghodegaon."

Yamunabai Kulkarni, the village health worker, animatedly spoke about herself and her experiences. "Twenty years ago it was unheard of for a

Brahmin woman like me to sit with men or socialize with Dalit women. As a woman, I was confined to my home, and sometimes I worked on our ancestral farm. Now I am free and serving the entire village as a health volunteer. In the beginning, it was difficult for me to visit Dalit women and especially to deliver their babies. I have been a VHW since 1974. I have never been to school. I look after the health of the mothers and children. I have conducted over 550 [by 2007 over 800] deliveries and have not lost a single mother during this time. This village has about 250 couples, and 150 of them practice family planning. Many women have undergone sterilization, and some take oral contraceptives. I visit all the families in my village and follow up the children.

"Ghodegaon was a different village before I became a VHW. Most adults suffered from guinea worm infection. We still have scars of this infestation on our ankles, knees, and backs. Now it is no longer a problem. We were superstitious and thought that most diseases were curses of a goddess. There used to be repeated epidemics of cholera. We used to sacrifice goats and chickens to appease the particular goddess. Cholera did not disappear. Now since I became a VHW, cholera is no more. Every year ten to fifteen children used to die in the village; now hardly a single baby dies."

One village woman said of Yamunabai, "Doctors only give medicine when people are sick. Yamunabai is more than a doctor to us. She has taught us simple home remedies for day-to-day illnesses like coughs, fever, and diarrhea. But more than that, she teaches us how to keep from falling sick."

"My friend here had leprosy," said Kisanrao Sole, pointing to the man sitting next to him. "He lives next to me. We drove him out of the village because he had leprosy, but now we are not afraid of leprosy. He lives in the village again, and Yamunabai treats him like any other patient. In fact, all thirty-five of our leprosy patients are almost cured by Yamunabai. Some of them are active in the village. Their children are also married and settled in life."

Angadrao, the Sarpanch, talked about Yamunabai: "Ghodegaon people are healthy because of Yamunabai. She is very enthusiastic about her training and her work. One day she was returning to Ghodegaon from Jamkhed. It was raining hard, and the stream was flooded. With a baby in her arms, she was trying to cross the swollen stream, and she slipped and fell into the water. Both mother [Yamunabai] and baby were swept away by the strong current. A couple of men rescued them. They scolded her for leaving the house in the rain and endangering her own life and that of the baby. She replied, 'My training has saved many lives in my village. For the sake of the village, I am willing to take the risk.'"

Shahaji concluded, "We villagers have worked together, improved our farms and farm animals. This has ensured adequate and nutritious food. Clean water and sanitation have eliminated many illnesses. The whole village worked toward the removal of caste differences and have learned to treat women and girls as equals of men. We can proudly say that Health for All has become a reality in Ghodegaon. CRHP has shown us the way, and we have learned to work together for the betterment of our village. Now we do not need to depend on the Aroles or CRHP. As we continue to develop, we are not alone; scores of villages around Ghodegaon are taking part in this movement. Each village develops at its own pace, as some take more advantage of their new-found knowledge, and some do not."

Ghodegaon today is a model of sustainable health and development in action. The links between health and other spheres of life underscore the priorities in making Health for All a reality. Ghodegaon so impressed government and administrative leaders that it was recognized as an "ideal village" and awarded a cash prize to further develop services and infrastructure. Although there are many examples of successful development in villages like Ghodegaon, each has its own character and unique story to tell. Existing at varying stages of health and development, villages progress at different speeds, and they develop interventions and use the programs that best suit their own needs.

While Ghodegaon's farmers' club was involved and active, in Kusadgaon it was the women's groups that played a greater role in advancing community health and socioeconomic development. Kusadgaon's vivacious and enthusiastic VHW, Sashikala, motivated the formation of a strong women's group. This group not only improved the health of their families and community, but it also organized a broom-making business, which was a great benefit to their economic well-being. The women's grasp of multisectoral relationships and interdependence brought not only tangible improvements in the health indicators of their community but also a significantly improved quality of life.

SUSTAINABILITY AND GLOBALIZATION

Throughout the 1980s and 1990s, the majority of CRHP's work centered on community participation and development. Eventually, the older project villages became self-reliant enough to manage community-based programs with little supervision and assistance from CRHP.

In 1989 a new project was developed in the tribal area of Bhandardara, six hours from Jamkhed. The purpose of this project was to demonstrate that grassroots workers, along with the help of a few social workers, paramedical workers, and volunteers from villages from the Jamkhed area, could promote primary health care in a different context and even without a hospital and infrastructure. This experience enabled the people to realize that healthcare can be provided by the people themselves, through spreading knowledge and changing harmful attitudes and practices.

From 1990 to 1992, Raj and Mabelle were visiting professors of international health at Johns Hopkins University, Baltimore. There, they shared their experiences with students and colleagues. This time in the United States, and later in Italy as Rockefeller Fellows, also enabled them to write *Jamkhed: A Comprehensive Rural Health Project* (Arole and Arole, 1994, 2003).

The three-year period during which Raj and Mabelle were abroad tested the sustainability of the project. With clinical experience gained in Bihar and the Himalayas of Uttar Pradesh, daughter Shobha, also a physician, was well prepared to assume the responsibilities of the hospital; she gradually moved into her current role as associate director of CRHP. Throughout this transition period, the staff remained steadfast and supportive of the project's leadership and mission.

Beyond mere sustainability of its work, the organization took on a new role as a model project for global health and development.

In 1993 Raj returned to Jamkhed and continued the work with Shobha. Mabelle stayed on in the United States as health and welfare consultant for the United Methodist Church. During her three years in this role, she collaborated with Cathie Lyons and Nora Boots to promote community-based primary health care (CBPHC) in a number of countries throughout Latin America and Africa. This attracted a large number of international participants to the primary health and development courses taking place at CRHP's training center in Jamkhed.

Mabelle was invited to serve as UNICEF's health and nutrition advisor in South Asia, a position she held from 1996 to 1999. Through this appointment, she was able to influence governments and policies, particularly in the area of women's and children's health. She traveled extensively throughout South Asia, inviting those she met to visit Jamkhed for a firsthand look at primary health care. During this time she also wrote two books: *Voices of South Asian Women* (Arole, 1995), on the plight of women in South Asia, and one on the impact of the religions of South Asia on women's and children's rights.

As Shobha took the reins in clinical work and provided assistance in training at Jamkhed, Raj directed his full attention to the trainings and development of the project through collaboration with various government officials. Mabelle returned at intervals to help with training. All three shared administrative responsibilities and encouraged the staff to be conscientious in their community work. Since 2005, son Ravi also has taken on responsibilities.

The Jamkhed Institute for Training and Research in Community Health and Population was established in 1993, with the support of DFID and Tearfund in the United Kingdom. Many visitors had suggested the creation of a formal training center in order to spread the Jamkhed model more effectively throughout the world. The initial diploma course included three months (now two months) in residence, with a two-week refresher after six to eight months in the field. Besides this course, electives, internships, and a one-month residential course for international medical, public health, and allied health students are held every year. In addition, short, custom-tailored courses for NGOs and government agencies are organized regularly. In order to cater to the needs of various groups, the curriculum is flexible, although the emphasis on comprehensive and holistic approaches to health is consistent. Incorporating practical approaches and field exposure, this initiative realized the goal of a community-based health and development training program.

Since its inception, over 20,000 participants (villagers, project managers, policy makers, medical professionals, social and development workers, etc.) from across South Asia and from nearly 100 other countries have received training at CRHP. In the early 1980s, CRHP trained 2,000 VHWs for the government of Jamkhed's district of Ahmednagar. The governments of various states such as Andhra Pradesh and the tribal districts of Maharashtra are now implementing the Jamkhed model on a large scale. Similar projects, incorporating the concepts of comprehensive primary health care, are working in various parts of India and Nepal. On an international level, people have taken back the knowledge, skills, inspiration, and hope they learned at Jamkhed and applied them to the diverse situations and circumstances facing their own communities. Governments, NGOs, and faith-based and private-sector groups have likewise been impacted by CRHP. Its holistic health approach, both grounded and concrete, establishes it as a global model for sustainable health and development.

With the sad passing of Dr. Mabelle in 1999, Drs. Raj and Shobha and other CRHP staff have increased their involvement in training for primary health care, global health and development, personal development, and leadership skills. The majority of practical learning comes from the personal experience of CRHP's staff, village health workers, and community members, who are in unique positions to serve as teachers and role models. This learning, in addition to the lessons from each other's backgrounds and experiences, brings about a personal transformation in the students who come to Jamkhed. These highly motivated students are capable of truly serving their communities in a far-reaching and sustainable manner.

One such student is Mr. Ramesh Khadka. Ramesh, a dental assistant from Nepal, was greatly interested in working in primary health care. After resigning from hospital-based work, he started a project known as Share and Care in Nepal, despite minimal financial security. A year later, his wife joined him, and with his team, he worked in the hill villages of Nepal. Applying the principles of comprehensive CBPHC and the Jamkhed model, his project became very successful. He also shared his experiences with other organizations, such as Future Generations in Arunachal Pradesh. Share and Care continues to send staff members to Jamkhed for training.

Along with Mrs. Nora Boots, the health coordinator for Latin America of the United Methodist Church, Mabelle had visited various countries in order to help set up and train groups. A few years later, Shobha, along with a colleague, Ms. Kate Landuyt, was able to evaluate a number of these projects, particularly in Brazil and Bolivia. The success of an indigenous woman with only primary school education and no knowledge of Spanish was one of the inspiring highlights of this visit. Living in a remote and hilly part of Bolivia, this woman had managed to transform the health of her community to such an extent that her work was televised. She had spent three months in Jamkhed's diploma course, during which time she had presented an impressively lucid and practical action plan that surpassed those of the more professionally experienced and educated classmates. A satellite-training center, directed by Ms. Lu Garcia, has now been developed in Latin America, and a number of Latin American projects advised by CRHP have become very successful in both urban and remote rural areas.

Similar projects have been attempted in parts of Africa, but frequent political instability and constant conflict have stymied most efforts at CBPHC. In one of the positive programs undertaken in war-torn areas of Sierra Leone, Congo, and Angola, a team from Jamkhed taught local people to make artificial lower limb prostheses for landmine victims and other amputees. A group from Africa visited Jamkhed to learn the techniques for making these devices. More than 1,000 prosthetic limbs have been provided through these teaching programs.

MABELLE, IN MEMORIAM

The year 1999 was a difficult one at CRHP. Mabelle was bravely battling a viral heart disease, and she passed away that September. In her memory, a women's rehabilitation center was established at CRHP's farm for victims of violence and stigmatized conditions. There, women living with HIV/AIDS, women with leprosy, widows, and women abused and forsaken by their husbands have a chance to transform and regenerate their lives through income generation, counseling, personal development, and medical care. Along with sustainable farming skills, they learn about management, livelihood, health, and development so that they are able to be empowered, independent, fully functioning persons. Through it all, the residents of this center are part of a supportive and caring social environment.

The farm manager, Ratna, is a victim of HIV/AIDS. Barely clinging to life when she came to the rehabilitation center, Ratna is now a radiant and vibrant young woman who has become a model example of what can be achieved with inner strength and a caring environment. Below is a brief account of her life.

Ratnamala Jaganath Chavan is a young, HIV-positive woman who, through the help of CRHP and the rehabilitation program on the farm, has been able to live a productive and fulfilling life despite her HIV status. Ratna contracted the virus from her husband. Soon after the birth of their child, Ratna's husband became ill, complaining of stomach pains and fever. Despite much expensive medical treatment, his health did not improve, and he died after four months. Ratna's eleven-month-old son also became sick and died soon after. Ratna herself was ill with a continuous fever, but she was not aware that she was HIV positive.

After the death of her son, Ratna attended a health seminar in Mahijalgaon, CRHP's subcenter, where she met Monica, a social worker, who recommended that she visit Jamkhed and meet Dr. Arole. The doctor listened to Ratna's story, examined her, and agreed to provide her with treatment at no cost. She went to live and work on the Khadkat farm, starting at first with light work in the plant nursery. As she continued with therapy, she became healthier, through love and caring, nutrition, and early treatment of infections, and was able to start doing more active work.

Ratna is currently receiving antiretroviral treatment through CRHP's AIDS program, which helps to control her disease and keep her healthy. Although only twenty-five years old, she is now one of the farm's most able and effective supervisors, helping to manage the workers and coordinate activities in the dairy, fields, and animal farms while assisting with various training programs. Ratna occasionally speaks to groups of high-risk or HIV-positive women about ways to become empowered and take protective measures.

Ratna explains, "Now I am happy and keep myself busy in my work. I think my life is meaningful, and I help and comfort other girls working with me here." Today Ratna is energetic and bright, epitomizing a person who lives an abundant and well-integrated life.

PRINCIPLES OF COMMUNITY-BASED PRIMARY HEALTH CARE

There are certain principles derived from the work of CRHP that have a world-wide application, particularly for those interested in sustainable approaches to health and development. The ideals of equity, integration, and empowerment each carry a unique significance that captures the essence of comprehensive, community-based primary health care.

Equity enables all people, particularly the poor and marginalized, to have appropriate health care. This may entail house visits to meet the needs of those most marginalized by social divisions and discrimination on the basis of caste, religion, or disease status. Rather than thinking of health only in terms of medical care and hospitals, equity includes a community-based approach that focuses on the family.

Integration exists in various forms. The Comprehensive Rural Health Project is named this because it is truly comprehensive. Integration in healthcare combines prevention, promotion, cure, and rehabilitation, all of which are provided either at the grassroots level, with backup or referral to the health center. The integration of biomedical science with alternative health systems—particularly herbal, acupressure, and homeopathy—is employed when appropriate. Alternative therapies are applied only where there is adequate data or experience supporting their efficacy. Emphasizing that health does not exist in isolation, a third type of integration involves the multisectoral coordination of development activities. CRHP also incorporates integration in service provision, addressing together pregnancy, under-five care, leprosy, tuberculosis, family planning, and more, all according to the needs of the people.

Health depends on far more than science and pathogens, hospitals and doctors—socioeconomic change, education and empowerment (particularly of women), agriculture, nutrition, environment, and sanitation all play crucial roles. Indeed, the social determinants of health often have the greatest impact upon individuals, families, and communities. In the same way that varied external factors comprise health, the synergy of mind, body, and spirit into a coordinated and complete whole acknowledges that human beings are more than the simple assembly of various systems. Health is a state of harmonious well-being, both personal and social. The promotion of holistic health through the incorporation of the arts, spirituality, and other humanistic perspectives further supports the principle of integration.

Equity and integration are incomplete without the idea of empowerment. Empowerment means equipping individuals with the knowledge, skills, and personal development that will enable them to function to their fullest potential in society. In India's rural areas and urban slums, the voiceless women and children, Dalits and tribals lack opportunities to rise from their state of marginalization. Helpless and bereft of dignity, they are not enabled to choose or decide, and consequently have little power of self-determination. Many do not even have enough food and suffer daily from injustices and inequalities, especially in healthcare and education. Empowerment of the marginalized is about gaining the dignity to live life as human beings endowed with spiritual worth and intrinsic value, free to make decisions and obtain the knowledge to escape the superstitions and harmful beliefs that dominate their lives. When this happens, they become positive instruments of change in their homes and communities, realizing the dream of Health for All in its broadest sense. To achieve this, empowerment must be contextualized by value systems that are constructive to the family and the society.

The preceding examples reflect the way that the success of the work at Jamkhed lies in the realistic and practical application of these principles of equity, integration, and empowerment.

LESSONS LEARNED

Some of the lessons learned by Drs. Raj and Mabelle over the first twenty years follow, in their own words (Arole and Arole, 1974, 2003):

> People are the key actors in health. Over 80% of disease prevention depends on individual and community action. It is important to recognize that, even in conditions of poverty, the sharing of scientific knowledge combined with the coping experience of people can bring about positive health.
>
> We professionals have to change our attitudes and need to share our knowledge in a way that poor people and the least educated can understand and make their own choices according to their needs. The knowledge should be shared in such a way that people are liberated and empowered with the ability to assess, analyze and act according to their needs and resources. Often our health education is oppressive and dictatorial without reference to people's needs, resources, abilities and social circumstances.
>
> Planning health programs needs to have flexibility. We started out with a project plan where Auxiliary Nurse Midwives were the primary health care workers, but the village people thought otherwise and felt that a person from their own community should be chosen. Our project responded accordingly by shifting to the village health worker model.
>
> We had planned from the very beginning to spend 70% of our time in preventive services. But in order to prove our credibility and develop rapport, we had to modify this plan.
>
> Primary health care cannot stand alone; it needs the support of the health system. The VHW's credibility depends upon the training and support she gets from doctors and nurses. A good referral system therefore needs to be in place.
>
> Health professionals need to recognize that non-medical interventions, such as safe drinking water, sanitation, good nutrition and caring practices, have a far

greater impact on health than what professionals alone can provide. To achieve good health, it is also necessary to acknowledge and address socioeconomic issues, like the status of women and Dalits.

FUTURE DIRECTIONS

Through the work of Raj and Mabelle Arole, their daughter, Shobha, and son, Ravi, the organization has scaled up dramatically since the 1970s when it was just a small project trying out an experimental, community-oriented model.

Although there has been much achieved in primary health care, there is still much more to be accomplished. Shifts in disease patterns are gradually moving the focus from malnutrition and curable communicable illnesses (tuberculosis, leprosy, malaria, diarrhea) to congenital problems in children and manageable, noncommunicable diseases in adults, such as diabetes, heart disease, hypertension, and now mental health. Primary health care is a dynamic process, and a community-based approach can and must be applied to these conditions as well. The VHWs already know how to take blood pressures, check sugar levels in urine, and screen for some types of cancer, and they are learning about mental illness.

The support system of the secondary care hospital is improving. A new, fifty-bed hospital is currently being constructed (completed in April 2008), not to be an ivory tower but to cater more effectively to the current needs of the poor and marginalized while providing services for those seeking more specialized medical care. Since medicine is an art and not just a science, social factors, clinical examinations, and the patient-physician relationship are emphasized. The promotion of holistic health in its widest and broadest sense is the hospital's aim.

Today, Dr. Raj Arole is an NGO representative and consultant to the National Rural Health Mission (NRHM), chaired by India's prime minister. The NRHM has incorporated a number of elements developed in Jamkhed, including village health workers and community groups, and it is developing a nationwide plan for implementing this strategy throughout rural India. NRHM's ultimate goal is to bring development and improvements in health care to the 70 percent of Indians who live in rural areas.

The work of CRHP has had far-reaching implications and will continue to do so in the future. The project's pioneering work in this field has contributed to the widespread practice of Jamkhed's principles now, more than thirty-seven years later. There is a real need to spread holistic health and sustainable development while improving our environment to renew the rich resources that our Creator has given us. In a time of disorder, destruction, and violence, community-based health care, development, and environmental conservation are keys to restoring a fragile earth. The more holistic our approach, the more we will be able to see the restoration of peace and unity in ourselves, our families, our communities, and the environment that nurtures our social units.

QUESTIONS AND ANSWERS WITH THE AROLES

The following are views on various issues and discussions of pertinent questions with Dr. Raj Arole and Dr. Shobha Arole:

• *What were the initial sources of funding and further funding?*

When we were in the United States in the 1960s, we spoke to various people. At a convention of the Disciples of Christ in Indiana, there was a man who said, "We don't know you well, but in faith we give you $20,000." In the 1970s this seemed like a large amount of money, and indeed it could achieve much in the poverty stricken setting of rural India. Another church gave money to set up a clinic and a place for us to stay. Eventually the project collected a startup budget of $50,000. Once in Jamkhed, we tried to raise money by charging basic patient fees from those who could afford to pay, while providing charity care for the truly poor. Thirty percent of the money eventually came from the clinical work. Gradually, as more contacts were made, most donations started coming from personal contacts and later from churches and funding agencies in Europe and North America.

• *How much financial sustainability is there now?*

About 60 percent of our expenses are covered by patient fees and training tuitions. We are also developing various income-generating farm programs. At the same time, it is important to note that total financial stability is an ideal that may not be realistic when serving the destitute poor. There are very few organizations working with the poor and marginalized that can be truly self-sufficient without shifting their focus more toward the well off rather than the poor. Therefore, a certain amount of outside funding is needed for operating costs and new program startup costs.

• *What kinds of measures are used to determine "success"?*

There are a number of health parameters that are determined quantitatively, such as maternal mortality rate, infant mortality rate, immunization coverage, percentage of safe deliveries, and the prevalence of various diseases. In addition, there are parameters that measure socioeconomic development. Women's empowerment can be measured by the way women assume responsibility and their status both in the family and the community. Many of these parameters are measured through qualitative studies. The beneficiaries in CRHP's project villages also carry out periodic surveys with staff to monitor progress in terms of health and socioeconomic development.

In training programs, one examines how trainees are influencing their own communities in health and socioeconomic development. Further indicators examine how state and central governments apply the CRHP principles in providing health care to poor and marginalized groups nationwide.

• *What was the tipping point to move from concept to reality?*

CRHP was among the very first organizations in the world to use and train illiterate women as health workers. From the experience of the first twenty VHWs, understanding how much they could learn and how effective they were in their communities in providing care and health education showed that these capable women were the key to the transformation of their villages. They drastically improved the health of women and children, and they brought about a significant reduction in communicable and chronic illnesses. Through their assistance, this concept was spread to other villages. This approach now works through different NGOs and government agencies in many states of India and many countries of Africa, Latin America, and Asia, and it has become an accepted international norm.

The CRHP model is really based on prevention and promotion of holistic health, as compared to solely curative care. For example, in China the barefoot doctors were high school graduates who basically did curative work. In contrast, the VHWs are illiterate women and volunteers, who continue to work in a comprehensive way on a large scale.

• *How are obstacles and opportunities met creatively?*

A massive famine in the 1970s presented CRHP with an opportunity to conduct relief activities, child nutrition programs, immunizations, and massive health education in the communities. These efforts were based not just on giving people some help, but rather they were founded on immense community involvement, which was one of the first steps in developing community participation. This also provided a good opportunity to show that health and development are two sides of the same coin. There was a need for water for agriculture, and therefore environmental improvements, such as afforestation and watershed development, were also introduced. Social justice issues were dealt with, and therefore through these efforts what seemed to be setbacks turned out to be opportunities for primary health and development.

• *How do you create original solutions?*

By living with the people, sharing their life, and studying how they cope. CRHP has always kept the focus on the poorest sections of each community, realizing what we can do for them and what they can do for themselves. This focusing helps us to find universal solutions to common health and social problems. Being open to new ideas requires courage, but at the same time, we need to be critical of commercialized medical solutions.

- *How can you scale up?*

Working continuously and accompanying rural communities for the past thirty-seven years gives confidence to people and helps suggest solutions to the bureaucracy and those political leaders who are well intentioned and striving to achieve real change at the grassroots. Engaging in practical and continuous dialogue with people and, at the same time, refining the understanding of the poor as well as understanding the reality of poverty and the limited knowledge of people help us to scale up. We acknowledge that development is a dynamic, continual, and long-term process that will take years of effort. However, given adequate and appropriate support during the formative years of a project, the community can assume an ever-increasing role and responsibility for sustaining local health and development programs, with a gradual decrease in the involvement of the NGO.

- *Where does your inspiration come from?*

Inspiration for the Aroles and much of the staff has come from universal spiritual values and a deep-seated faith in following the example of Christ.

- *What direction do you see for the future?*

Convinced that health and development are inseparable, we will strive to conduct more development work, especially for marginalized groups and forsaken women, in the areas of environment, agriculture, health, and the development of healthy families through a holistic strategy. We will continue to use a comprehensive approach to health and development, and promote physical, economic, mental, social, and spiritual well-being for individuals, families, and communities. Holistically combining community development, health, and environmental issues to build interdependent public health ecosystems on both micro and macro scales is an alternative way to achieve peace and wholeness in communities throughout the world.

IN CLOSING

Engage in constant dialogue with the people, not working merely for them but also with and among them. Although the government bears ultimate responsibility, we need to help people see what individuals and communities can do. Only then will you be able to see how the government programs and schemes can multiply with your efforts. Do not make programs and people, regardless of low income level, totally dependent on the government, but rather encourage self-reliance and unity.

APPENDIX

Table 6.1   Comprehensive Rural Health Project (CRHP), Jamkhed, India. Changes in
Health Indicators (1971–2006)

Year	1971	1976	1986	1996	1999	2004	2004 India	2006
Infant Mortality Rate	176	52	49	26	26	24	62	24
Crude Birth Rate	40	34	28	20	20	18.6	23.9	14.8
Maternal Health								
• Antenatal Care	.5%	80%	82%	96%	87%	100%	64%	100%
• Safe Delivery	<0.5%	74%	83%	98%	98%	100%	43%	100%
• Family Planning	<1.0%	38%	60%	60%	60%	68%	41%	65%
Children under 5								
• Immun.	0.5%	81%	91%	92%	99%	83%	70%	87%
(DPT, polio)								
• Malnutrition	40%	30%	30%	5%	5%	<5%	47%	<1%
(wt for age)								
Chronic Diseases								
• Leprosy	4	2	1	0.1	<0.1	1.7	0.24	1.9
(prev./1000)								
• TB (prev./1000)	18	15	11	6.0	4.0	0.5	4.1	1.2

Courtesy of Shobha and Raj Arole.

Table 6.2   Overview of CRHP Activities (1970–2006)

TB patients treated	9,621
Leprosy patients treated and rehabilitated	5,089
Artificial limbs and calipers provided	17,222
Tube wells for safe drinking water	198
Plant nurseries–villages	203
Land leveled (hectares)	10,433
Irrigation wells dug	523
Check dams	223
Houses built for poor people	283
Women involved in credit program	6,064
Training skill formation (tailoring, weaving, fishing, agriculture, dryer)	1,859
Training in community-based health (since 1983) (grassroots workers, policy makers, project managers, health and development professionals and students, etc.)	
• Persons from India	17,661
• Persons from other countries	1,911

Courtesy of Shobha and Raj Arole.

ORGANIZATIONAL SNAPSHOT

Organization: Jamkhed (aka Comprehensive Rural Health Project—CRHP)

Founders: Shobha Arole, Raj Arole

Mission/Description: The Comprehensive Rural Health Project (CRHP) was started to provide health care to rural communities. It developed a comprehensive, community-based primary health care (CBPHC) approach. CRHP is located at Jamkhed, which is located far from any city and is typically rural, drought prone, and poverty stricken. One of the main aims of the project is to reach the poorest and most marginalized and to improve their health. With values of compassion, justice, respect, and trust, the CRHP at Jamkhed works to empower people, families, and communities, regardless of caste, race or religion, through integrated efforts in health and development.

Website: http://www.jamkhed.org/

Address: Comprehensive Rural Health Project

Jamkhed, Dist. Ahmednagar

Maharashtra–413 201

India

Phone: +91.2421.221322

Fax: +91.2421.222892

E-mail: crhp@jamkhed.org

REFERENCES

Arole, M. (1995). *Voices of South Asian Women.* Kathmandu: UNICEF, South Asia Office.

Arole, M., and Arole, R. (1994, 2003). *Jamkhed: A Comprehensive Rural Health Project.* Jamkhed, India: CRHP.

Newell, K. (Ed.) (1975). *Health by the People.* Geneva: World Health Organization.

Population and Economic Development Linkages, 2007 Data Sheet. (2007). Washington, DC: Population Reference Bureau.

BIBLIOGRAPHY
Books

Arole, M. (1995). *Voices of South Asian Women.* Kathmandu: UNICEF, South Asia Office.

Arole, M., and Arole, R. (1994, 2003). *Jamkhed: A Comprehensive Rural Health Project.* Jamkhed, India: CRHP.

Husale, D. (2003). *Mukta* (life stories of Village Health Workers in Marathi; English translation in process). Jamkhed, India: CRHP.

Chapters

Arole, M. (2002). "The Comprehensive Rural Health Project in Jamkhed, India." In Rohde, J. and Wyon, J. (Ed.). *Community-Based Health Care* (pp. 47–60). Boston: Management Sciences for Health.

Arole, M., and Arole, R. (1975). "A Comprehensive Rural Health Project in Jamkhed (India)." In Newell, K. (Ed.). *Health by the People* (pp. 70–90). Geneva: World Health Organization.

Arole, M., and Arole, R. (2002). "Jamkhed, India: The Evolution of a World Training Center." In Taylor-Ide, D. and Taylor, C., *Just and Lasting Change* (pp. 150–160). Baltimore: Johns Hopkins University Press.

Arole, R. (1993). "The Comprehensive Rural Health Project, Jamkhed." In Antia, N. and Bhatia, K. (Ed.). *People's Health in People's Hands: A Model for Panchayati Raj* (pp. 125–140). Bombay: Foundation for Research in Community Health.

Arole, R., Fuller, B., and Deutschmann, P. (2005). "Community Development as a Strategy for Promoting Mental Health: Lessons from Rural India." In Herrman, H., Saxena, S., and Moodie, R. (Ed.). *Promoting Mental Health* (pp. 243–251). Geneva: World Health Organization.

Articles

Arole, S., Arole, R., Premkumar, R., Murray, M., and Saunderson, P. (2002). "Social stigma: A comparative qualitative study of integrated and vertical care approach to leprosy." *Leprosy Review* (73): 186–196.

Arole, S., Premkumar, R., Arole, R., Mehandale, S., Risbud, A., and Paranjape, R. (2005). "Prevalence of HIV infection in pregnant women in remote rural areas of Maharashtra State, India." *Tropical Doctor* (35): 111–112.

Kermode, M., Herrman, H., Arole, R., White, J., Premkumar, R., and Patel, V. (2007). "Empowerment of women and mental health promotion: a qualitative study in rural Maharashtra, India." *BMC Public Health* (7): 225.

McCord, C., Arole, R., Arole, S., and Premkumar, R. (2001). "Efficient and effective emergency obstetric care in a rural community where most deliveries are at home." *International Journal of Gynecology and Obstetrics* (75): 297–307.

Research

Chitnis, Ketan. (2005). "Communication for empowerment and participatory development: A social change model in Jamkhed, India." PhD dissertation, University of Ohio.

Nossal Institute, University of Melbourne, Australia, in partnership with CRHP (2007–2008). "To assess mental health literacy among CRHP project villages and develop a mental health training program for village health workers."

Yan, Jennifer Pui Jan. (2005). "Empowerment of adolescent girls: The Jamkhed experience." Master's thesis, Department of International Health, Melbourne University, Australia.

Prizes and Awards

1979   Ramon Magsaysay Award for Community Leadership (Asian "Nobel" prize)

1985   Honorary Doctorate for Public Service, Gettysburg College, Pennsylvania, USA

1988	NCIH Award for Service in International Health, Washington, DC, USA
1990	Padma Bhushan National Award for Social Service (Raj)
2001	Schwab Foundation for Social Entrepreneurs Award, Geneva, Switzerland
2004	Dr. Babasaheb Ambedkar Dalit Mitra Award for work among backward classes (Raj)
2005	Mother Teresa Memorial National Award for Social Justice (Raj)
2006	Zee TV Astitwa for Outstanding Woman in Health Care (Shobha)

7

International Center for Equal Healthcare Access: Defeating the Developing World's Dependence on Perpetual Western Charity in the Field of Healthcare

Marie Charles

Dedicated to Maximilian and Antonia Marie

When the International Center for Equal Healthcare Access (ICEHA) was founded on November 21, 2001, the world's attention was focused on a need for funding and the availability of affordable, low-cost drug treatments as solutions to the AIDS pandemic that was ravaging the developing world. Understandably, the field of "Global Health" was not yet well developed at that time, and few in the West had any experience implementing "access to anti-AIDS medication" programs, with millions of dollars in backing, only to realize that entire healthcare systems in the developing world were almost nonexistent. The most pertinent question for me became one of how we can build these critical systems in a sustainable, effective, empowering way without taking years to accomplish the end result?

What initially started as a very small pilot program in Vietnam and Cambodia has since spread its wings rapidly across countries and continents. Working in countries as diverse as Nepal, Vietnam, Cambodia, South Africa, Lesotho, Burundi, Rwanda, Ethiopia, Suriname, Kiribati, Zimbabwe, and Zambia, ICEHA is deploying over 6,500 aggregate person-years of high-quality, professional medical expertise from doctors and nurses in the Western world to their colleagues in the developing world, saving hundreds of thousands of lives.

Out of great vision, passion, and ultimate persistence, ICEHA grew into the "global leader in clinical skills rapid transfer to emerging nations," an international nonprofit organization with offices at present in London, New York, and Stellenbosch.

IMMEDIATE AND SUSTAINABLE IMPACT

The sustainability and defined scope of ICEHA's endeavors can best be highlighted using the example of a clinic in Vietnam that has become "mentored out."[1] Binh Thanh clinic is located in Ho Chi Minh City, one of the areas with the highest HIV prevalence rate in Vietnam. Only in March 2005 was funding made available to provide anti-AIDS medications to AIDS patients through the Vietnamese public sector. In collaboration with the Provincial Health Authorities and Family Health International, Binh Thanh OPC became the first outpatient AIDS clinic. Given the high level of stigma associated with being HIV positive in Vietnam, the clinic opened in March 2005 without publicity. At the time of opening, the Vietnamese healthcare providers at Binh Thanh clinic had received a two-week didactic training course in AIDS care and were told to start providing patients with AIDS care and treatment. Of course, it is quite a different matter to be told how to do a spinal tap for crypto-meningitis than to have the confidence and practical skills to carry out the procedure. Hence, to get the clinic personnel up to speed and institute the necessary operational systems, ICEHA was asked to send its volunteer clinical mentors to Binh Thanh OPC during the initial period of introduction of AIDS care and treatment in the clinic. In this country where HIV-infected patients typically go into hiding, Binh Thanh OPC had 200 patients in HIV care within six weeks of opening, 600 patients in AIDS care with more than 1,000 patient visits another six weeks later; and three months after that, 1,200 patients were in AIDS care, with the clinic personnel having started to provide leadership to clinics in the surrounding areas. At that point, ICEHA pulled back as quality control procedures showed that our local colleagues were providing the best AIDS care possible within the existing resource limitations. Therefore, the clinic was, in our parlance, "mentored out." Thirty-two local healthcare providers had been given practical clinical expertise by seven clinical mentors over a period of six months. Following ICEHA's pullback, the clinic continued to flourish. By March 2006, the patient population had grown to 1,500, and the local government relocated the clinic to a larger space. Binh Thanh OPC clinic remains a model of excellence in the region and is being copied throughout the country with the assistance of ICEHA's clinical mentors.

In addition, an unintentional result of our clinical mentoring activities turned out to be the effect on local healthcare workers of being exposed to passionate colleagues and of being given the skills to provide the best care possible. By the time the clinic became mentored out—and this is true in all clinics where we are asked to deploy ICEHA clinical mentors—the clinic staff walked around as if they owned the clinic: they were proud and passionate to work there, having seen their standing in their communities rise as word about the quality of their services had spread. This was quite a different picture from the staff's attitude when we initially arrived, an attitude that had been rooted in the high level of stigma associated with caring for AIDS patients.

WHAT WAS THE TRIGGER?

Ten years ago, a Western infectious disease physician landed in Rwanda, confident, hopeful, and with a supply of antiretroviral medications (ARVs) for 100 AIDS patients in his suitcase. His assignment was to set up an AIDS research program in this country stricken by AIDS. The infectious diseases clinic looked good by local standards, desolate by ours. Clinic personnel were delighted to see him and appreciative of the medication supply, while patients in dire need of AIDS care were lined up outside the clinic walls, looking gaunt, the sparkle of life gone from their eyes.

Rather quickly, however, did he realize that unless he, as a Western healthcare provider, was going to put these patients on the ARV medications he had carried with him, they would not be receiving the treatments they so urgently needed. The Rwandan physicians looked at the bottles of pills with a mix of horror, puzzlement, and excited anticipation. They had participated in a two-week, didactic training course on AIDS care, but that had been only theory. And what is the value of theory in real life anyhow? When an AIDS patient entered their small office, they would continue to be highly reluctant to give him any physical examination, or touch him for that matter, still afraid that they might perhaps "catch AIDS" that way. As for these various interesting-looking pills, their questions came quickly: "What are they?" "How would one use those?" Along similar lines, the operational systems needed for AIDS care were close to nonexistent in the clinic. Nurses were not keeping patient records, nor were patient flow systems set up, a situation that resulted in waiting lines of more than 500 patients on Monday with none on Tuesday. Lab tests were, of course, not available, and neither were proper dispensing procedures at the pharmacy in residence.

A phone call to the employer of the Western physician followed. "No, he couldn't come home in a week. He couldn't just leave the medications in the clinic; there was no infrastructure for AIDS care, no operational systems, no practical medical expertise. The AIDS research program would not be started on time. Indeed, he would need several months to set up the care delivery system that would ultimately get the medications from his suitcase into the patients in a clinically justified way. If not, a worse epidemic—a resistant one—could be created."[2]

The employer of that physician was the International Therapy Evaluation Center (IATEC) at the University of Amsterdam. And the chief operating officer of IATEC was Dr. Marie Charles.

As a Belgian physician with a master's degree in international affairs from Columbia University, I had been offered the position of COO in the late 1990s after having lived in Indonesia and Malaysia for several years. At that time, IATEC was a multimillion-dollar, university-based research center that conducted clinical research in HIV and AIDS across the developing world. But despite the fact that we were well funded and able to bring antiretroviral medications into the African clinic settings which universally lacked both AIDS care and treatment, the lack of adequate healthcare infrastructures was an impediment to the rapid implementation of our clinical research programs, and hence by inference, to any level of AIDS care delivery.

A year into my job, the UNAIDS-brokered Accelerated Access Initiative (AAI) was announced. Under AAI, five large pharmaceutical multinationals had agreed to provide antiretroviral medications "at cost" to selected developing countries in an attempt to help stem the AIDS pandemic. It was quite clear to all of us that, while most certainly reduced drug costs were an absolutely necessary step, unless one were to set up the critical delivery systems necessary for AIDS care, no amount of increased international donor funding or a reduction in drug costs would benefit the patients on the ground. Indeed, months after AAI was announced in a high-profile fashion and as the initiative failed to show much immediate increase in numbers of patients receiving treatment, one could sense the public opinion starting to turn against the possibility that antiretroviral medications could be given to patients in resource-poor settings because of the "resource poverty" aspect of these developing countries. We knew well that the lack of resources did not prohibit the delivery of antiretroviral medications to those who needed them. Our HIV clinical research was indeed carried out successfully, and HIV clinical research is quite a bit more complicated than AIDS care. The turn the public opinion was starting to take was scary, and it needed to be corrected urgently.

Hence, over the summer of 2000, after many controversial discussions in my own home after work, I managed to convince two colleagues to co-found a separate nonprofit organization with me called PharmAccess International. We had no budget, no employees, no logo, and no website, but we had a great vision of what needed to be done in terms of proving that a lack of patients on treatment in the developing world despite lower drug costs, was an issue of undeveloped or absent healthcare systems, and not one of medications that were too complicated for resource-poor settings. In our search for clinics with existing operational systems, we approached Heineken Breweries. Although Heineken's corporate medical insurance scheme did not cover AIDS care and treatment at that time, each of its nine subsidiaries throughout Africa had well-established clinic facilities, trained medical staff, laboratories, and pharmacies. In the end, it took one of the two other co-founders, Richard Hoetelmans, and me nine months of meetings at senior corporate levels; analyses ranging from the clinical protocols to be used to economics, public relations, and negotiations with pharmaceutical companies; and countless evenings and weekends of background work before I received a call on July 21, 2001, that Heineken's corporate board had decided to include AIDS care and treatment in the medical insurance scheme for its employees. It was a multimillion-dollar implementation contract. Within six weeks, we had the first employees of Heineken on ARV treatment in Rwanda and Burundi, the pilot countries. Heineken Breweries had become the first multinational corporation to provide AIDS care and treatment to its workforce. Many have since followed in Heineken's footsteps.

However, just weeks before this landmark phone call in July 2001, I had been relocated back to Manhattan and was faced with the question of how to run an organization I had co-founded from an ocean away. It had been one thing to handle conference calls with Heineken's management in Amsterdam at 3 a.m. in New York; it was another to manage employees and programs for years to come from a distance. Declining the suggestion by my co-founder colleagues that I run the business development side from Manhattan, I decided to resign from the board and as managing director of PharmAccess International. The remaining directors compensated me financially for the time I had spent in successfully building the organization, a gesture that would later prove vital in ICEHA's startup phase. In addition, I inherited the U.S. corporate entity, which had not yet been put into operations. Richard Hoetelmans resigned for personal reasons a few weeks after I left, leaving only one of three original co-founders ultimately in charge.

My vision in setting up the Dutch nonprofit had always been one where we would initially target the private sector to put AIDS patients on antiretroviral treatment quickly, but from there, we would build the bridge into the public sector where the largest number of AIDS patients were and still are. Building the bridge into the public sector would have entailed leveraging various resources from the private sector, including financial, operational, clinical facilities, and so on, in order to build up the public healthcare sector to such an extent that AIDS care and treatment could be provided easily there, too. Realizing that the Dutch nonprofit organization had a very different vision upon my leaving, I decided to found yet another nonprofit organization, the International Center for Equal Healthcare Access (ICEHA) to focus solely on building healthcare capacity in public healthcare systems across the developing world, leveraging the enormous untapped human capital resource called "clinical expertise" so abundantly available in the West.

ICEHA's initial focus would be infectious diseases and AIDS, without precluding an expansion into other fields of medicine at a later date. Robin Lewis, PhD, associate dean at the School of International and Public Affairs (SIPA) at Columbia University in New York, had been following my career path from afar and joined the board of directors of ICEHA from the onset. Briefly thereafter, we were joined by Brian Boyle, MD, JD, assistant professor of infectious diseases at Cornell Weill Medical College in Manhattan and internationally recognized for his HIV expertise. From the beginning, both of them intrinsically understood the need for ICEHA's existence and were willing to do whatever it would take to help the organization achieve its mission and vision. ICEHA began operations on November 21, 2001. Similar to my previous entrepreneurial experience, here too did we have a great vision for filling a need that no one else addressed, a long name, a few directors, no employees, and no funding at all.

Within days, Robin Lewis asked me to give a two-hour seminar on ICEHA and its underlying philosophy to a group of Southeast Asian fellows who were in residence at Columbia University. I had only a business card at that time. Little did I realize then how vitally important this early seminar would turn out to be for ICEHA's future. Indeed, a few weeks thereafter, I received a Christmas card from Hanoi, signed by a certain Professor Trinh Ngoc Trinh, a name that did not sound familiar. Since I travel frequently and meet countless people around the world whose names unfortunately tend to blend together after a while, I politely sent a Christmas card back only to receive, by return mail, a beautifully written, one page proposal containing a highly detailed account of how ICEHA's proposed activities could greatly help improve the healthcare system in Vietnam, especially in light of the important role healthcare professionals play in the prevention of HIV transmission. The proposal was signed by the same Professor Trinh, director of the Highland Education Development Organization (HEDO). While I could not locate his name or his organization on Google, and despite the fact that we did not have any funding for ICEHA at that time, I decided to use some of the limited savings from my previous venture for an exploratory trip to Vietnam, a country I had never visited before.

When I arrived in Hanoi on a foggy Saturday afternoon in March 2002, all I knew was that someone by the name of Trinh Ngoc Trinh would fetch me at my hotel the next morning at 6 a.m. and that we would drive together to Langson Province for meetings with the Provincial Health Authorities and the People's Party Committee. In addition to being the director of HEDO, Professor Trinh turned out to be professor emeritus in education and a national hero for his outstanding contributions during the Vietnamese-French war. HEDO has been in existence for more than fifteen years and is a Vietnamese nongovernmental organization (NGO) that implements programs to improve the livelihoods, health, and education levels of the ethnic minorities in the highlands of Vietnam. Langson Province is a stunningly beautiful highland province of approximately 750,000 people on the border with China. Located on major trucking and tourist routes, its HIV prevalence rate was higher than that of surrounding provinces. At some point during the six-hour

Figure 7.1   ICEHA Vietnam-Lao Cai Province. Courtesy of ICEHA.

early morning drive, Professor Trinh informed me that Professor Do Nguyen Phuong, Vietnam's minister of health at the time, had sent me his welcome wishes and apologized for not being able to meet in person given that he was in Laos on that day. I accepted the welcome with a smile, understanding that a lot of politics were happening behind screens I had yet to discover existed.

After an exquisite lunch in a hawker-stall restaurant, I was brought to an official meeting hall in a French colonial style building that housed the offices of the Provincial Health Authorities. The setting was surreal: French colonial architecture with bright bougainvilleas climbing the walls, heavy wooden French doors half ajar offering a peek of the sky where monsoon-like thunder clouds were rapidly stacking up, and the meeting room inside looking as though a top Chinese interior decorator had his dream fulfilled with all of its gold- and red-colored trimmings. Six hours and forty Vietnamese teacups later, HEDO, myself, and three representatives of the Provincial Health Department and the People's Party Committee agreed that a three-way collaboration would be the best method for building local healthcare capacity and clinical skills appropriate for the looming fight against HIV. At no point in time had I been asked for material resources or financial support. The only requests I had received were for clinical skills and expertise.

The days following were spent in a myriad of visits and meetings at the provincial hospital, various district hospitals, and village clinics, allowing me to get a sense of the healthcare structure in the province. Once back in Hanoi, HEDO arranged visits with people they thought would be influential in turning the proposed collaboration into a success. Figuring that Vietnam was their country, that they had invited me, and that the success of the program would be as much their responsibility as my own, I merely followed their lead, a tactic we use to this day at ICEHA.

On the final evening before flying back to New York, Professor Trinh asked me whether I would mind stopping by the house of the minister of health on our way to dinner. Despite the fact that this was an unannounced visit in a country where foreign visitors and high-level government officials do not exactly mingle informally, Professor Trinh and I ended up joining Professor Do Nguyen Phuong and his family at the dinner table. A soft-spoken, brilliant man and an extraordinary leader, the ten minutes during which Professor Phuong questioned me about the proposed collaboration and ICEHA's activities culminated in an official government approval, a fact that would only become clear to me during the years that followed as government officials changed appointments, and program approvals of other NGOs were revoked, while ICEHA has yet to have a straw put in front of its feet to this day. All we continue to be asked for is a faster expansion and scale-up within the country.

Although it was as obvious to me then, as it is now, that the extraordinary wealth of human capital in clinical skills and capabilities so abundant in the West is what many countries in the developing world really want to help them build their own human resource capacity, ICEHA was not able to attract donor funding easily. We were in an ironic dilemma of being a startup organization without a track record or brand name recognition, addressing an issue—the lack of critical healthcare systems and healthcare capacity—that donors at that time did not consider to be an issue, and proposing to fix the issue by using a method most had never heard of (namely, the rapid transfer of clinical skills through mentoring), and yet, we did have a product that the developing world not only needed but clearly wanted. It seemed to me that there was—and to this day remains—a significant disconnect between what "the West" perceives to be the issues in need of being addressed through international development versus what developing countries know they need, and the ways in which these countries think that it can be delivered most effectively inside their borders.

However, while the average Western donor did not understand or value "capacity building" at the onset, our message right away resonated as well with colleagues in the medical profession as it did in the developing world. As word of what I was proposing to do with ICEHA spread, the number of qualified colleagues who contacted me with offers to help rose exponentially. The vast majority of them had more than ten years highly specialized clinical expertise, had reached the pinnacle of their medical careers, and had extensive family lives—all of which meant that, even though they could not easily give up their lives in the West to work overseas for a few years, they were passionate about wanting to make a personal contribution in the fight against the AIDS pandemic, and they were also able to make some time available, pro bono. The one thing they needed was an opportunity overseas, defined in time, space, and content, where they could make an impact the very second they arrived, put systems in place that would stay in place after their assignment was completed, see the situation change as their assignment progressed, and upon their return, know that everything they had done was there to stay. Initially, only physicians contacted me, but soon thereafter nurses joined, later on followed by pharmacists and lab technicians. In the early stages, almost all offers to become involved came from within the United States. However, over the years, we have reached a point where we are now sourcing expert healthcare workers from over fourteen countries. As such, we opened up a European office in London in April 2006 to more adequately and efficiently channel the European applicants through our vetting and matching system prior to sending them on assignments.

Unfortunately, the funding hurdle meant that I would need to keep on tapping into the small amount of personal savings that I had received from my Dutch nonprofit. It also meant that I would need to ask our colleagues not only to work as volunteers but also to cover their own expenses while overseas until we had proven the need for ICEHA's existence and the basic program model, both a necessity to attract funding. Given that the Vietnamese had invited us into their country with open arms and given that they understood exactly what we were all about, we decided to do the proof-of-concept with them. Although the concept phase would take almost twenty months to be completed, this was the first real step for ICEHA in becoming the "global leader in clinical skills rapid transfer to emerging nations." As an after-the-fact note, I ended up receiving the National

Medal of Honor from the Vietnamese president, Mr. Nguyen Minh Triet, at the opening of the National Assembly in Hanoi in June 2007. The National Medal of Honor was given for global leadership in sustainable healthcare development in emerging nations and specifically for ICEHA's impact on the Vietnamese healthcare system.

SYSTEM BUILDING THROUGH RAPID SKILL TRANSFER—THE PROGRAM MODEL

ICEHA's program model is one of system building through rapid skill transfer and empowerment. The model is underpinned by a co-investment scheme whereby the majority of the funds needed are being provided by the recipient developing countries themselves.

Twenty months is a long time for a proof-of-concept trial. The timing was mainly a result of having to build the organization on a shoestring, against the prevailing public opinion of how international development aid should be delivered, and of being in part self-funded, in part funded with the help of $50,000 from a few corporate donors in 2002 and 2003. The proof-of-concept was not focused on the co-investment structure for which ICEHA would later become so well known; rather, it focused on proving that healthcare capacity and healthcare systems can be built rapidly, in a very cost-effective way, using volunteer experts for a minimum of six weeks. At the very moment of the proof-of-concept period coming to a successful close, we had $1 left in our corporate bank account on December 31, 2003. Although we did not have any employee responsibilities or liabilities at that point, I had still cut it quite close, and two directors of the board resigned very shortly thereafter, leaving Brian, Robin, the treasurer, and myself to continue, all of us as committed as ever. Fortuitously, ICEHA received its first large corporate foundation grant in January 2004. At last, the organization was in a position to structure its program model, provide the required quality control, and start off on its path of growth that would ultimately lead it to expand into twelve countries across Africa, Asia, and Latin America by December 2007.

ICEHA operates in a small niche and specialized format. What it provides to the developing world is very specifically "practical clinical expertise adjusted for resource limited settings." Even then, we only agree to make ICEHA's resources available when a range of criteria have been met by the countries requesting ICEHA's assistance. A typical example of how this works is highlighted by a recent experience: A few weeks ago, a delegation of the Ministry of Health of Congo Brazzaville came to meet me in London. They arrived in the morning, leaving London again that same evening. The delegation included the Director General of the Ministry of Health, the Senior Advisor on HIV/AIDS to the Minister of Health, the Head of the National HIV/AIDS scale-up program in the country, and the Technical Advisor in HIV/AIDS to the Ministry of Health. This high-level delegation of four had arrived with the signature power of the Minister of Health. We had not worked with Congo Brazzaville before and had not had lengthy program discussions with anyone in that country. However, in the months leading up to our meeting in London, that government had designed its national scale-up plan for tackling the AIDS epidemic in their country. Through hearsay or word-of-mouth from colleagues in neighboring countries, ICEHA had been brought to their attention, and due diligence on us had been completed before a meeting was requested in person. Over the course of three hours, the high-level delegation explained the contents and design of their national plan, the structure of the healthcare system, and the potential role ICEHA clinical mentors could have in helping their country achieve its goal of providing access to AIDS care and treatment for all who need it. The local healthcare workers had already received classroom HIV/AIDS training courses, but this didactic knowledge did not give them the confidence to provide the actual care, nor did it teach them how to set up the necessary operational systems in the clinics such as the keeping of patient records, the organization of clinic flow, universal precaution procedures, referral systems for complex cases, and so on. At the end of the three hours, I was asked whether we might consider giving their request for multidisciplinary teams of ICEHA clinical mentors top priority. Timing for implementation was determined at the meeting to be as soon as possible. The example of Congo Brazzaville is almost a perfect textbook example for how ICEHA's clinical mentoring model tends to spread across the developing world.

The level of misconception about AIDS care on the part of healthcare workers in the developing world cannot be underestimated. It reaches deep with possible detrimental ramifications. To date, we continue to run into situations where healthcare workers who have just started putting patients on antiretroviral medications turn to us, excited about the progress these patients seem to be making, yet at the same time wondering how long they should keep the patients on the medication before they can send patients home given that they do look so much better. At that moment, we know that the entire basis for AIDS care and treatment was somehow not understood by the treating healthcare worker even though he or she did have classroom training. Indeed, the antiretroviral medications do turn AIDS into the equivalent of a chronic disease—provided the patients take the prescribed regimen diligently for the rest of their lives, and provided resistance to the therapy does not occur. However, if patients take the medications on and off, or for short periods of time, or split the dosages with their family members, or any number of scenarios along these lines, the AIDS virus becomes resistant to the existing therapy and a much worse epidemic than the current one will be in the making.

In another country, and this example, too, continues to be found across the developing world, we were in the infectious disease ward when a late-stage AIDS patient was wheeled in by his family, only to be brushed off to an empty bed with the wave of a hand by the clinic staff member. Eventually, the attending physician agreed to do a physical examination. He took out his stethoscope, and put the ends of the instrument in his ears while dropping its head onto the skin of the patient from almost five inches above, making sure that at no point in time his fin-ger tips actually touched this patient. It turned out that he indeed had been told of the ways in which HIV transmits (skin contact not being one of the possibili-ties), but that having been told is one thing while believing it fully and acting on that belief is yet another. Only gradually, after seeing the ICEHA clinical mentors give proper physical examinations to admitted AIDS patients during their clinical mentoring assignments, did this physician in question come to trust the fact that he, too, could safely touch the AIDS patients.

Upon exiting the infectious disease ward, we were startled to see a disposable syringe lying outside on the windowsill next to a bottle with alcohol in a hospital where the nursing staff had been properly instructed that needles are a one-time deal and are not to be used from one patient to the next. Theory is obviously not translating into practice. The reuse of unsterilized needles from one patient to the next has been highlighted increasingly by the World Health Organization (WHO) over the past few years. In a neighboring hospital, needles were obviously dis-carded regularly because we found them lying in heaps on the ground next to the hospital building. In addition to the children playing in the heaps, street vendors, too, would regularly gather to find the needles, repackage them, and sell them in their street stalls or on the markets.

None of these issues, and countless others that this chapter does not allow enough space for, are too difficult to be rectified or too cumbersome. The most effective way to remedy the gap between theoretical knowledge and practical expertise is to provide local healthcare workers who have received didactic training with some form of a safety net while they are applying the acquired medical theory in clinic practice.

We only stumbled on the clinical mentoring model through reflection and out-of-the-box thinking, having had prior experiences with ineffective, large-scale classroom training courses for which Western faculty were flown into a developing country to "teach" local colleagues how to provide AIDS care even though they themselves had little knowledge of the resource-poor settings from which the audience came. The courses were extraordinarily expensive, and knowl-edge retention rates hovered around 10 percent three months after the course; the percentage of actual application of the acquired knowledge in the developing-country clinics was even less. The competing practice of training foreign physicians by flying them from the developing world to the West for six months so that they could receive training in Western hospitals did not fare much better, both in terms of high cost and in terms of lack of efficacy in teaching these physicians how to provide AIDS care to their patients back home.

ICEHA's signature clinical mentoring model is rooted in the medical training we received ourselves and in the realization of what made us learn how to provide patient care. Most certainly, didactic lectures in an auditorium gave us the theoretical understanding of medicine but not the competence or confidence to actually care for patients. The lectures were necessary but not sufficient: their theory had to be turned into practical expertise during the subsequent years of residency, years during which we saw patients with a more senior physician looking over our shoulders, providing a safety net in case we needed guidance.

For every clinic ICEHA has sent its clinical mentors to, we have found that it takes anywhere from three to five months of continuous clinical mentoring for a clinic to become "mentored out." "Mentored out" is a state in which our local colleagues are providing the best care they can within the existing resource limitations of their clinics. Once a clinic has become mentored out, ICEHA clinical mentors pull out, leaving in place a structure that works, is sustainable, and is there to stay, bearing fruit for many years to come. The aspect of "continuous" clinical mentoring for three to five months is rather important. One does not change attitudes or build operational systems in a lasting fashion in only a few weeks, even though many overseas assignments offered through other organizations allow for two-week stints in foreign locations. Personally, I believe that two-week assignments resemble a practice of medical tourism or provide an opportunity to put a bandage on a situation and on a single patient, but do not provide a lasting remedy or a system for thousands of patients. Given that ICEHA clinical mentors can commit to participating for six weeks on a pro bono basis, but not for three to five months, we achieve the continuous coverage needed by sending consecutive ICEHA clinical mentors to the same clinic, thereby guaranteeing that the impact of the clinical mentors is lasting, sustainable, and optimal.

The kind of clinical mentors ICEHA sends to each respective clinic is entirely dependent on the job at hand. For instance in Lesotho, a country with the world's third highest HIV prevalence rate at 23 percent and only a handful of physicians present, the Ministry of Health decreed that nurses in the village clinics would be the ones administering first-line AIDS care and treatment. The Lesotho nurses had been given a ten-day didactic training course in Maseru, following which they were sent back to their clinics and tasked with providing AIDS care. To help them bridge the gap between the lectures and actual work, ICEHA clinical mentors were requested through the Clinton Foundation HIV/AIDS Initiative (CHAI) to provide coaching to the local nursing staff in the very clinics where they were working. Because the local staff members to be mentored were nurses, ICEHA sent nurse clinical mentors. Other countries, such as Congo Brazzaville, request ICEHA clinical mentors in teams of five, including a physician, nurse, counselor, pharmacist, and lab technician, given that their national scale-up plan calls for AIDS care to be delivered with a multidisciplinary team approach.

The practical clinical expertise ICEHA provides to the developing world is based on what is needed locally; it is provided in such a way that it does not artificially re-create Western healthcare delivery since that would be utterly unsustainable. Therefore, all clinical mentoring is provided within the national HIV care and treatment guidelines of a specific country, taking into consideration the limitations of resources in the various settings. Indeed it would be a futile exercise to have ICEHA clinical mentors coach local colleagues on the interpretation of MRI scans when no such machine exists in that country; at the same time, teaching local clinic staff how to use the basic X-ray machine that had been so generously donated by an international charity twenty-four months ago and is sitting idle in a corner because no one knows how to operate it, can make the difference between life and death for some patients.

Once a decision has been made by ICEHA to agree to a request for clinical mentors from a new country, a local partner is chosen to handle all local logistics and help assure quality control. At no point will one see ICEHA's logo embossed on the door of a company car, or above the entrance of a well-designed office in the developing world. Our discrete policy to instead and deliberately work through a local partner has led in many cases to the program being perceived as "a local initiative with local ownership," rather than as another international development project. Beyond the philosophical meaning, this policy also has practical implications for the implementation of the program. Not only would it be very cumbersome for ICEHA staff to arrange for a local translator in the Mekong Delta from our offices in New York or London, ICEHA's method of clinical mentoring is also quite different from what people in the developing world have come to expect of international aid groups. Indeed the common assumption of what foreign healthcare workers will be doing has led us to the discovery that it is not sufficient to prepare ICEHA clinical mentors in great detail before sending them on a mentoring assignment; it is equally important that the healthcare workers in the receiving clinics are prepared and understand that the ICEHA clinical mentors are not there to take over the jobs and responsibilities of

Figure 7.2   ICEHA Nepal—Seti Clinic in Dhangadhi. Courtesy of ICEHA.

local clinic staff. The ICEHA clinical mentors will only exponentially increase the clinical competency of local colleagues who can optimize the care they themselves provide as a result. This specified role of ICEHA clinical mentors is diametrically opposed to the direct care delivery most international NGOs in the healthcare field focus on, a practice that perpetuates developing-world dependence on Western aid and charity in the field of healthcare. It takes solid preparation of the staff in the receiving clinics in order to make them understand the difference.

The list of ICEHA in-country partners continues to grow, but so far they include World Health Organization (WHO), Highland Education Development Organization (HEDO), National Center for HIV, Dermatology and STD (NCHADS), Family Health International (FHI), Care International, COVAB, HealthNet TPO, Right to Care, Foundation for Professional Development, Project Support Association, CHAI, and Network of People Living with HIV/AIDS Nepal (NAP+N).

An Unorthodox Funding Model: Co-Investment

As mentioned above, ICEHA was set up without seed funding and the initial years of 2002 and 2003, during which we completed the proof-of-concept were very hard indeed. If it had not been for my ability to work full-time without a salary, it would have been an impossible exercise.

So, while we were fundraising in the first eighteen months with limited success, it became quite clear almost from the onset that it would be one thing for us to raise funding in the West to cover the costs of recruiting the clinical mentors, of screening them for their qualifications and personality, of preparing them adequately, of ensuring that they were matched to the appropriate clinic, and of managing them throughout their field assignment. It would be another thing entirely to fundraise additionally for all costs associated with the actual placement of the clinical mentors in the developing world for minimum periods of six weeks. Although the ICEHA clinical mentors contribute their time and skills on a pro bono basis, all reasonable trip expenses are covered. Given that the developing countries themselves approach us with the line "what ICEHA provides [practical clinical expertise] is exactly what we need and want," I decided that it would be more efficient to come up with some kind of cost-sharing arrangement both sides could live with and which would fall in line with ICEHA's philosophy of empowerment.

To date, the co-investment deal that has worked for all sides is one where ICEHA does not charge the developing countries for any of the costs ICEHA incurs in screening and preparing the clinical mentors. ICEHA finds its own private, individual, and corporate donors to cover that side of the equation. At the same time, the developing countries are required to cover all in-country implementation costs that occur as a result of the clinical mentoring activities. These costs include basic room and board, local transport, economy class plane ticket, and other necessary expenses. One could say that each developing country pays for the cost of skill transfer within its own borders. The fact that both sides contribute financially is offset tremendously by the value of the in-kind contribution of the clinical mentors, who participate on a pro bono basis. Indeed, if funding from any source would have had to cover Western salaries for clinical mentors while on assignment, one would need to put a serious question mark to the value and the cost-effectiveness of any such program. As a net effect of the co-investment approach, for every $2,000 of Western funding, an additional $6,000 to $8,000 in funding is released by a source within a developing country itself, both of which are offset by a value ranging between $12,000 and $28,000 per clinical mentor per assignment.

Loyal and Visionary Donors, Committed to Curing the Dependence of the Developing World on Charity, Rather Than Simply Feeding That Dependence

Sometimes people ask me why it took so long for ICEHA to build a stable donor base. Having reflected on the question, the answer is one not limited to ICEHA but is applicable to anyone running one step ahead of what is considered to be cutting edge. It naturally takes a little while for any entrepreneur to find a way to effectively communicate an unorthodox message to others who are used to thinking in a conventional way; at the same time, it also takes a while to find those donors who are sophisticated and farsighted enough to understand the value of actually building complete systems that will result in millions of smiling children a few years down the road as opposed to one smiling face today, which might not even be alive to be smiling tomorrow.

Over the years, ICEHA funders in the West have included generous private individuals, many of whom know our clinical mentors personally or professionally. These and others believe in the system-building model as strongly as we do and see the immediate value of their investment to the extent that some of them, having committed to raising a specific amount from friends and colleagues, have taken out personal bank loans when a commitment could not be filled by their pool of friends alone.

The vast majority of the funding, however, comes through a small group of extremely insightful and loyal visionary corporate donors. Over the years, these have included the J&J Foundation, Tibotec Corporation, Rufford Foundation, William A. Haseltine Foundation for Medical Sciences and the Arts, Gilead Foundation, Elton John AIDS Foundation, Bristol-Myers Squibb Foundation, St. Stephen's AIDS Trust, American Foundation for AIDS Research (AmFAR), Merck Foundation, and International Finance Corporation. In-country implementation costs have been covered by a variety of in-country funding mechanisms, including through the WHO, the Global Fund for Malaria, TB and AIDS, DFID, USAID, and PEPFAR, as well as various local branches of multinational corporations. In the end, the origin of the in-country funding is not as important as is the fact that the funding needed locally is already available within the country in question.

Our Western funders, both individuals and corporate, are an extraordinary and dedicated group, with many of them having contributed month after month, year after year, excited to see the organization grow and realizing its tremendous impact. The pivotal factor in dealing with any donor has been personal contact and engagement: one person within a foundation who decides to champion our cause by helping us through the application process, or who decides to contact colleagues in fellow foundations, alerting them to ICEHA's value proposition, which frequently results in those foundations inviting us to submit grant proposals. The same is true at the individual level, where we have seen the most extraordinary gestures of generosity. These individuals tend to have met us personally; tend to know one of our clinical mentors and send in the donation in his or her honor; or tend to be a past, present, or future clinical mentor who is so taken by the model that he or she becomes a perpetual donor. Past clinical mentors have held concerts for us, donating all proceeds, or have referred wealthy patients to us when asked what their favorite charity is. Most recently, we were even adopted as "favorite charity of the year" by the Stop AIDS student group at Newcastle University in the UK. Without all these funders, we could not be doing what we do so well: saving lives and building the systems that free developing countries from their dependence on Western charity and aid in the field of healthcare.

Quality Control, Monitoring, and Evaluation

I personally think that much of the international donor funding is being spent all too frivolously on monitoring and evaluation (M&E) methods "McKinsey Style," whereby the M&E component itself becomes a flourishing industry even more so than the impact of the program it is supposed to be measuring. Nevertheless, a certain level of M&E is most definitely necessary to show that one's activities are indeed having the impact they are intended to. As such, the quality control ICEHA uses is quite strict yet optimized to show exactly what needs to be shown, namely the impact of clinical mentoring on setting up sustainable healthcare systems and—as a result—the impact on saving lives of patients, not one time, but for decades to come.

The quality control of ICEHA's programs encompasses both quantitative as well as qualitative measures. At the beginning and upon completion of their assignments, ICEHA clinical mentors complete a pre- and postassessment questionnaire regarding the clinic systems and care provided. These are not judgment questionnaires but rather objective measurements of what is happening in the clinic over time. All data collected are entered into an SPSS database, and trends are analyzed on a per-clinic and a per-country basis.

In addition, each clinical mentor has to submit, on a weekly basis, a brief report of activities, either via e-mail or in transcribed teleconferences with ICEHA staff. These weekly reports in freestyle format cover anything relevant to the experience. They serve multiple purposes, but one of their main benefits is that they indicate at which stage the ICEHA clinical mentor has built a relationship of trust with local counterparts to the extent that these counterparts will accept the practical skills the mentor is attempting to impart. Clinical mentoring does not work if the foreign clinical mentor is perceived as a "Western professor who will tell the local healthcare workers how to deliver care." Clinical mentoring does work when it is perceived as an exchange of expertise between two sides that are equals in terms of social standing within their own societies. It works when there is an underlying basis of trust and mutual respect. How can we tell that this is happening? Pretty much across all countries and clinics where ICEHA clinical mentors have ventured, it has taken ten days to two weeks before we receive a report stating something along these lines: "You will never believe what happened today, but Dr. XYZ pulled me aside and asked whether I might be willing, in my spare time, to also provide clinical coaching to his colleagues in the other clinic where he works, but which is not on the list to receive clinical mentors . . ." When we receive an e-mail like this, it shows us that the underlying basis of trust and mutual respect has been built, and we know that the effectiveness of the clinical mentoring can increase exponentially from that point onward. In the meantime, although we receive feedback from the ICEHA clinical mentors on a weekly basis, our in-country partner is in contact with the clinic personnel to ensure that any issues arising from their end are addressed, and to double-check that the activities of each clinical mentor are appropriate for the clinic setting and the existing resource limitations.

The final piece of quality control is a final trip report, which is an extensive document that discusses all activities the clinical mentor undertook during his/her field assignment, every issue that was encountered plus measures taken to remedy the issue, the status of the clinic upon leaving, and a recommendation as to whether further clinical mentoring is needed or whether the clinic might be mentored out. The report is submitted to ICEHA and shared with ICEHA's in-country partner; it follows a predetermined, fixed outline and is written in such a way that it can be sent on to the minister of health of the respective country when appropriate and in the interest of the country's healthcare system. If the clinic is set to receive additional clinical mentors, this report is also shared with them to ensure that they know the baseline from which they are supposed to start.

As for the quality control on the clinical mentor side—namely how mentors perceive their experience with ICEHA—the best indicator is the rate of return of our clinical mentors: almost 30 percent of them participate again within twelve to eighteen months of their first assignment, with many having participated four or five times as of this writing. We also have several ICEHA clinical mentors who have found their assignments so rewarding that they have temporarily left their careers in the West either to take on permanent teaching positions in the country of their field assignment or to become perpetual ICEHA clinical mentors, going from one field assignment to the next. Regardless of how many are repeat volunteer clinical mentors, 99 percent of our clinical mentors call us within two weeks of their return back home with the words "thank you so very much—this was the most extraordinary experience of my personal and professional life."

WHO ARE THE ICEHA CLINICAL MENTORS?

All of us are quite fortunate to have been born in the West and to have been given extraordinary educations with brilliant careers as a result. However, there comes a point in life when these brilliant careers reach the pinnacle of their success, and when we start looking outside of them for additional opportunities where we, as individuals, can have a greater impact, often much beyond what we can have in our own clinic settings. At the same time, we do not want to forgo our brilliant careers, and we usually also have family lives that would prohibit us from moving overseas for any lengthy period of time. Ideally, we would like to be given an opportunity defined in time, place, and content where we can make a significant impact, see the systems change with our own eyes, and know that these now optimized systems will remain in place once we return to our own home life. And that is where ICEHA comes in.

While ICEHA uses a minimum requirement of three years of clinical expertise beyond residency, a large proportion of healthcare professionals applying have more than ten years of specialized clinical expertise. They come from a wide variety of backgrounds: physicians, physician assistants, nurse practitioners, nurses, social workers, pharmacists, and lab technicians; they also come from a wide variety of clinics and hospitals, including academic, community based, public, and private practice. Most recently the pool of volunteer ICEHA clinical mentors available for the six-week minimum commitment has surpassed the 700 mark. In total they represent more than 7,500 aggregate person-years of clinical expertise on offer to the developing world.

Recruitment, Screening, and Preparation of ICEHA Clinical Mentors

In the early years of ICEHA, prospective candidates contacted me as word about ICEHA spread through the grapevine. However, once we had the proper financial resources and were experiencing the exponential increase in demand for our clinical mentors from overseas, we put a solid recruitment structure in place where word-of-mouth referrals are still a significant player, but where recruitment goes much beyond that. ICEHA clinical mentors are recruited at every venue they might possibly be found congregating, from their clinics to national and international conferences, from small seminar discussions about the potential for individual impact to continuing medical education (CME) courses.

The recruitment itself has two components, one impersonal (through magazine advertisements or Internet search engines) and one personal. If I were to have to pick one method over the other, I would say that the personal recruitment method is the *conditio* sine qua non. Many of our colleagues with tremendous expertise to share, who would be great clinical mentors, are sitting on the fence, attracted to the idea but unsure whether they should make the leap of faith. An ad in a newspaper or on the Web will pique their interest but will not be sufficient to make them submit an application to become a clinical mentor. The in-person interaction with ICEHA staff at various venues, as well as personal referrals from colleagues, helps them decide to turn their dream into reality. Personally, I think that it is a comfort-zone issue, one in which they learn from the personal contact that they will be taken care of and managed well throughout the process, and not just put on a plane to a desolate faraway place without further contact.

Once prospective candidates submit applications to become ICEHA clinical mentors, we subject them to a rigorous screening and selection process, much beyond their clinical capabilities or paper résumé with references. Prior experience in the developing world is a plus but not a must, given that our model is quite different than that of other organizations, and we have found that often our most flexible and best clinical mentors have been those without prior preconceived notions about what it will be like, notions they developed during their experiences with other organizations.

The success of the field assignment will depend as much on an applicant's clinical expertise as it does on personality. Being a clinical mentor is not for everyone. Over the years, we have turned away some well-known professors from various academic institutions because they, while being respected professors in their own right, did not have the personality or ability to interact with their local colleagues in a way that clinical mentors need to be able to do: as colleagues on the same professional level with neither side being more of an expert. Individual personalities are also important from a cultural perspective. There are cultural differences across all continents on this planet, and methods of social interaction that work in Europe do not necessarily go over well in the United States, or vice-versa as we all well know. Similarly so, not all personalities are suitable for Asian cultures, and neither are all of them appropriate for African settings.

Given that it would be very contrived and inadequate to attempt to assess personality and character of applicants through a paper résumé or an Internet-based questionnaire, we require instead that all ICEHA clinical mentors attend a mandatory, two-day preparation course held regularly in New York, London, Sydney, or Stellenbosch for qualified applicants from those regions. These preparation courses are the main selection tool, allowing us to observe the interaction between candidates in group discussions as well as to assess an applicant's personality on an individual level. The courses also prepare the attendees for what is awaiting them as ICEHA clinical mentors, how they will need to leave Western-specific clinical knowledge at home while learning to think inside country-specific guidelines and resource limitations, how they might use creativity and out-of-the-box thinking to ensure that their practical clinical expertise can be transferred onto their local colleagues without putting these same local colleagues in a position where they feel as though they are being treated as students.

The courses are well received, with several attendees having commented over the years how they have gone overseas with other organizations in the past, including with the U.S. government, but how no one has ever set them down to make them reflect and understand what it will take to be successful in these settings.

Mentors are initially slightly surprised and sometimes even uncomfortable at being told to forget their Western habits and resource-rich wisdom the very moment their plane takes off for their assignment. However, one of the reasons why ICEHA clinical mentors end up valuing their overseas experience so highly is because it brings them back in touch with the basic reasons why they went into medical or nursing school in the first place, reasons grounded in a passion to care for patients at a human level, to use clinical skills and human interaction to make a diagnosis, and to cure the sick rather than being directed by printed lab values on a computer sheet.

Once the clinical mentor candidates have passed the screening tests and preparation course, ICEHA staff contractually engages and matches them to available positions in the developing world not only according to their availability, skill levels, and the needs of the receiving clinics, but also according to their personalities. The contract is needed to formalize the assignment given that they are not embarking on a relaxing vacation but on a job with responsibilities, albeit without pay.

So far the screening and preparation process has worked very well, and the percentage of failed placements—as defined either by a clinical mentor returning home early or by a clinic asking a clinical mentor to leave—has been limited to only 1 percent. In contrast, the percentage of return volunteer clinical mentors hovers around the 30 percent mark.

A NONHIERARCHICAL ORGANIZATION
OF PASSIONATE ENTREPRENEURS

ICEHA prides itself on being a nonhierarchical, non-bureaucratic organization. I am an entrepreneur and a strong believer in the fact that when one empowers carefully selected people, they will live up to the task at hand and passionately run with the responsibility given to them. This is true not only for ICEHA's clinical mentors and for our colleagues in the developing world, but also for ICEHA's extraordinarily gifted and dedicated staff. To date, every staff member, with only one exception, has first contributed to the organization as an operational volunteer. This means that they are given significant responsibility within the organization's operations but work under a volunteer contract, without compensation, financial or otherwise. This practice allows both sides to experience in real life whether there is a mutually beneficial match. ICEHA has benefited tremendously from dedicated operational volunteers from the very beginning, with Kathy Reniers, Emy McCord Schwimmer, Cassandra Doll, and Ruchi Rastogi among the very first ones to help me refine the model and pull the proof-of-concept off the ground.

ICEHA's first paid employee came about in an unconventional fashion. During the academic year 2002–03, Columbia University SIPA gave me a team of seven graduate students whom I asked to conduct due diligence background research for ICEHA's possible entry into Cambodia. Columbia's commitment was solid, and SIPA covered the costs for field visits of the entire team to Cambodia so that their research would be anchored in reality. Upon graduation, all students stayed in touch, showing up en masse at ICEHA's fundraisers, referring colleagues, and providing other connections. There was one who remained in closer touch: an exceptional young woman named Katie Graves-Abe. A daughter of diplomats, Katie had moved around the globe throughout her upbringing. She had lived in the West as well as in places as remote as Democratic Republic of the Congo and had taken to ICEHA's model like a fish to water. Upon graduation, Katie had accepted a job with another foundation but continued to help ICEHA as a volunteer during her spare time. Nine months later, she called me, asking if I might let her know when I would have an employee position within ICEHA. Timing was fortuitous: a few weeks prior, we had received our first grant allowing us to cover recruitment processes, and while funding was fully allocated to all activities to be done, I thought we could pull $25,000 into a salary package for our first employee. Ultimately, how can one build an organization, for profit or nonprofit alike, if one is not willing to invest in people with talent? Realizing, however, that Katie was earning significantly more in her other job, I mentioned that I did not think our package was a fair proposition, but it was all I had. Within twenty-four hours she accepted, taking the jump. From the very beginning, she had significant responsibilities as the person behind ICEHA's selection process, and her responsibilities have only increased exponentially over the years.

The way Katie became involved is mirrored by all ICEHA staff, both employees and volunteers. ICEHA remains an organization based on values such as passion, integrity, loyalty, honesty, and empowerment; it is an organization where every staff person has to be an entrepreneur in his or her own right, passionately fighting for ICEHA's vision.

FACTORS FOR SUCCESS

The factors underpinning ICEHA's success are multiple, but if I needed to summarize them in one line, it would come down to this: empower people and ask them to take responsibility. Empowerment in ICEHA happens at various levels: empowerment of our local colleagues in the developing world, whereby we give them the practical clinical expertise, which allows them to take responsibility for their patients; empowerment of governments in the developing world, whereby we do not decide for them what they need and when, but rather they decide that for themselves (and, as a result, help pay for it); empowerment of the ICEHA clinical mentors, who are given the local framework within which they need to provide the clinical mentoring and yet have to rely on their own creativity and initiative to make it work; and empowerment of ICEHA's staff, whereby every staff person, employee and operational volunteer alike, is given the target goal of what they have to achieve, but is empowered and supported to do what it takes to get there.

The specific characteristics that constitute ICEHA's success are more expansive than a one liner, however. They include

1. System building and system change
2. Sustainability
3. A simple model highly defined in content and parameters
4. Micromanagement of ICEHA clinical mentors; the "personal touch" in selection, preparation, matching, and management
5. Financial co-investment
6. Immediate impact
7. Local responsibility
8. Effectiveness and cost-effectiveness of ICEHA interventions
9. Leverage of resources
10. Scale and replication within countries and across continents

THE FUTURE: SCALE AND GROWTH

ICEHA's future is one of scale and vast expansion. ICEHA's sustainable model and immediate impact are proven and solid. However, what is even more important, it is not us sitting in New York or London deciding that what ICEHA has on offer is what the developing world will want; rather, it is the developing world approaching us, not with requests for material assistance but instead with requests for our ICEHA clinical mentors and the practical clinical expertise they can impart on their local colleagues.

Over the next five years, ICEHA will grow its pool of volunteer clinical mentors from more than 700 to 2,000, while its deployment programs will aim to add four to six new countries each year without necessarily leaving any of the existing countries prematurely. In addition, ICEHA will be expanding its clinical mentoring model beyond HIV/AIDS to include other fields of medicine, such as primary care, internal medicine, emergency medicine, and OB/GYN. The expansion into other fields of medicine is mainly due to requests by countries that have seen the clinical mentoring model work beautifully and sustainably for HIV/AIDS. As a result of this expansion, ICEHA's impact on healthcare systems in the developing world will scale exponentially, impacting millions of lives across the globe, not one time but forever to come.

In order to meet the challenge of such scale and exponential growth, ICEHA will need to add a long-term quality to its funding base, which, to date, still runs on a year-to-year basis, as is true for many nonprofits. At the same time, a year-to-year funding basis would never be acceptable in the for-profit industry because no organizational long-term strategy can be implemented in this way. Obtaining funding that can cover multiyear costs will allow the organization to successfully build and execute its vision of scale like an unstoppable space rocket.

SUMMARY

ICEHA's model is not about one-way, endless charity; rather, the model is one of ultimate system change, empowerment, high leverage, scale, replication, sustainability, immediate impact, and innovation.

Although ICEHA is using this model to build healthcare capacity in the developing world, the same model could be used in other fields, including education in schools, management capacity in government offices, and economic development. All it would take is someone who is very passionate about the cause using the obvious solution we have developed, and putting him or herself 150 percent behind it, 150 percent of the time. Ultimately, this is ICEHA's story.

ICEHA did start as a dream and a strong conviction that the way in which international development was tackling the AIDS pandemic was incomplete and misguided. But in the end, if not for the passion, commitment, and dedication of all of ICEHA's clinical mentors who forgo a Western income for six weeks at a time in order to impart their knowledge to their colleagues in the developing world as a human capital transfer, if not for ICEHA's dedicated staff, all of whom started as operational volunteers working after-hours while being employed elsewhere, and all of whom end up working passionately more than seventy-hour work-weeks as employees, if not for our loyal and visionary donors, and if not for the solid support of ICEHA's board members and countless friends and colleagues who often ventured out on a personal limb to help me get ICEHA off the ground but prefer to remain quietly behind the scenes, I really would still be dreaming my dream to this day.

That would have been a great pity. The results have been extraordinary so far; the scale-up is an even greater promise.

ORGANIZATIONAL SNAPSHOT

Organization: International Center for Equal Healthcare Access (ICEHA)

Founder and Executive Director: Marie Charles

Mission/Description: ICEHA is a nonprofit organization of physicians and nurses who volunteer their medical expertise to developing countries in order to equip the local healthcare professionals with the skills needed to take care of their own patients within existing resource limitations.

Website: www.iceha.org

Address: 101 West 23rd Street

Suite 179

New York, NY 10011

Phone: 847-232-9885

E-mail: mcharles@iceha.org

NOTES

1. Excerpt from personal correspondence, FAQs ICEHA (www.iceha.org).
2. Marie Charles, "Perspectives from the International Center for Equal Healthcare Access: Improving HIV care in Western countries: Lessons learned in the developing world." *Medscape* (October 25, 2005). Available at http://www.medscape.com/viewarticle/514563.

8

Flying Doctors of America

Allan Gathercoal, Teresa
Bartrum, and Myron Panchuk

If you just happened to be a pilot and had $700, where would you go? What would you do? Most of us would probably fly to the Caribbean for a bit of rest and relaxation, or perhaps to Manhattan to go to dinner and a Broadway play. In 1990 Allan Gathercoal took his faith in God and the goodness of others, combined that with the $700 dollars, and took off on a "wing and a prayer," to fly this organization's first medical/dental mission to the garbage dumps outside Mexico City. He remembered the saying "Find a need and fill it, find a hurt and heal it" and used that as the runway for creating a unique, but desperately needed, organization know today as Flying Doctors of America.

Not aligned with any religious or denominational group, this nonprofit organization has flown over 160 humanitarian missions and provided medical services for over 130,000 persons in need in Mexico, Central America, South America, the Caribbean, India, China, Mongolia, Vietnam, Thailand, and parts of the African continent.

Flying Doctors of America has grown into a collaborative effort of medical and non-medical professionals who volunteer their talents and time to reach out and assist the world's poorest of the poor. By traveling to remote destinations and serving the most desperate populations, Flying Doctors of America lives by the spirit of one of the greatest humanitarians of all time, Mother Teresa of Calcutta. As she gave hope to the hopeless, this group does so also by visiting those who live in the darkness of poverty and by healing the sick and disabled.

BACKGROUND

Allan Gathercoal is a Christian humanitarian, who sought to put "feet on his faith." His graduate studies in psychology and theology and his personal belief system have been incorporated into a dynamic and ongoing synthesis of theory and

Figure 8.1   Flying Doctors of America medical team in Salta, Argentina. Courtesy of Allan Gathercoal.

praxis that actualizes the core teachings of the Christian gospels. Allan's vision for the Flying Doctors of America is rooted in his own soul-searching that critiques the church as being solely concerned with its own finances, operations, and dogmatic correctness. Institutional self-absorption can only be remedied through an authentic Christian praxis of compassion and care. As he began to look at the church with a critical eye, he discovered that too little is given for the care of the downtrodden, widows, orphans, and of the oppressed and poor. In 1989 he began to conceive of a movement that would liberate both the doctor and the patient by inviting physicians and dentists of the United States in medical missions to travel as a medical team to developing countries and work among those living in abject poverty. In such a manner, the core spiritual values of Christ's teaching and ministry find expression in improving the lives of the disenfranchised.

Through research done at Virginia Tech, Allan discovered that the majority of physicians and dentists (99 percent) never leave the confines of their offices in America to help the world's poor. He contacted scores of physicians and dentists and asked them what stopped them from giving back to those in need; their consistent concerns were time, management of mission, and cost. How would they get to where they are going, and who would help them get there and how much would it cost them in time and money? This motivated Allan to formulate the concept of

Flying Doctors of America, with the purpose of creating short-term, affordable/tax deductible, and professionally managed medical missions. Doctors would only have to volunteer one or two weeks of their time, cover personal out-of-pocket costs—and Flying Doctors of America would do the rest.

With Flying Doctors, everybody wins. The medical and non-medical volunteers miss only a few days of work and go on the adventure of a lifetime. Support volunteers serve as translators, team leaders, photographers, and healthcare assistants. The individual or corporate sponsors get tax benefits plus the knowledge that they are making a real difference in the world. And most of all, those in need receive first-rate medical care.

As the result of much soul-searching, brainstorming, and research, Flying Doctors of America was launched in 1990, with the express purpose of bringing hope and healing to the world's poor. Allan's mission was to fulfill the intent of Christ's teachings: to love the least of my brothers and sisters in this world. For Allan Gathercoal, love is not just a noun, but a verb. This understanding of love demands action and an ongoing engagement in the world that has fueled Flying Doctors of America since its inception.

An effective innovator and entrepreneur, Allan Gathercoal has worked as a church growth minister, started up new churches, and designed educational programs in California. He has earned masters degrees in psychology and theology and a doctorate from Columbia Theological Seminary. President and founder of Medical Mercy Missions, Inc., Allan promotes interfaith dialogue, and in 1996 he received the Vision of Race Unity Award. While these credentials are impressive, the most outstanding attribute Allan possesses is his passion to help those in desperate need.

MISSIONS

In circling the globe for the last seventeen years, the work of Flying Doctors of America has reached as far as Africa, India, and China. Currently, about 80 percent of the work focus is in Central America, South America, and the Caribbean. However, efforts are being made to expand beyond these regions, and new fields of assistance are being explored.

Missions are ranked on a three-level system. Each level becomes more physically arduous for the volunteers. Most anyone, for example, most anyone can go on a Level 1 mission. For such missions, volunteers are housed in a hostel or hotel. They also have access to showers, flush toilets, and good food. From their places of residence, volunteers are transported to and from the clinics and hospitals where they are assigned to serve.

Level 2 missions are more demanding. These missions take volunteers further out into rural communities. Typically, there is no electricity, and churches or schools serve as makeshift clinics. At times, volunteers sleep on cots in the mayor's house or in the church itself, and do not have such amenities as hot shower and flush toilets.

Level 3 missions are the most arduous and physically demanding. Volunteers travel to their assignments in the most remote areas of the world by hiking, on horseback, or by dug out canoe. They sleep in tents, dig their own toilets, and wash by taking sponge baths or simply jumping into a local river or lake. Volunteers for Level 3 missions must meet criteria established for physically fitness, emotional health, and the skills needed to serve indigenous peoples. The geographic areas served by Level 3 missions are the Amazon, the high Andes Mountains, and the plains of Mongolia.

Occasionally, there is a fourth level that occurs during times of conflict and serves the needs of war-torn areas and refugee camps. These missions are not advertised or promoted on the Flying Doctors of America's website. Those selected for these special Level 4 missions have been with Flying Doctors of America for some time and have served on multiple missions. They must be capable of enduring overwhelming stress and be in great physical shape. Most volunteers for these critical missions have military backgrounds and are very athletic. These missions are rare and may occur only every few years.

The goal of each mission is to fulfill three critical areas of concern: (1) provide immediate medical and dental intervention and care, (2) establish reciprocity and cooperation with local providers, and (3) analyze the greater needs of the community. As intervention becomes established and the local population is being attended to, local healthcare providers are engaged in building a relationship of mutual cooperation and respect with their American colleagues. As members of Flying Doctors of America begin to educate their host community on everything from dental to personal hygiene, they are also being reciprocally educated by the indigenous medical community. This mutuality encourages the sharing of information and the acquisition of a working knowledge of pressing health needs; quite often, it facilitates dialogue with the public health officials in that country.

Allan is concerned that some individuals erroneously think they have the authority to resolve the medical healthcare needs of foreign countries. The missions of Flying Doctors of America are opportunities to serve as liaisons between the targeted community and the resources available in that country. In such a manner Allan's concept of the Flying Doctors' job is to accomplish its immediate mission and to empower the local population. It is the job of the volunteers to remain sensitive to the traditions and customs of local groups and their way of life.

The work of Flying Doctors of America volunteers is to empower local communities in engaging their governments to create change. For example, citizens may not even know that their government has a program that could make more water available. Local activists make contact with nongovernmental organizations (NGOs) that specialize in creating new sources of water such as building new wells. By addressing and accommodating the pressing infrastructure needs of the local community, volunteers will attempt to establish the contacts needed to find the means and the resources to resolve these concerns.

Flying Doctors of America has a database in excess of 16,000 volunteers. Over 10,000 of these volunteers are doctors and dentists, and about 4,000 are pharmacists, nurses, and general volunteers. An average surgical team consists of six to eight volunteers, while a primary dental or medical team consists of approximately sixteen volunteers.

FLYING DOCTORS OF AMERICA: CONCEPT TO REALITY

In fulfilling the call to provide medical assistance to the world's needy, Flying Doctors of America has been transformed from an organization based on Christian practice to an interfaith humanitarian organization—one that embraces religious, racial, and multicultural diversity. The objective has always been to bring hope and healing to the world's poor as Mother Teresa did. By traveling to some of the most remote regions of the globe, volunteers have experienced the challenge of adventure in high-risk areas. This has been characterized by some as a way of embracing their own "inner Indiana Jones." It has been Allan's experience that if you challenge physicians with adventure as well as care and medical relief work, most will respond enthusiastically and be eager for the challenge. They will go and take care of the poor, and also enjoy the adventure of having done so. An additional benefit is to come home and tell your buddies about it over a cup of coffee. Fortunately, there continues to be a positive response on behalf of the medical and dental communities. After all, there would be no medical missions without them.

Allan Gathercoal is himself a model of personal growth and transformation. In many ways, his spiritual life has been an alchemical process from transforming "lead into gold." As a Minister and committed Christian, he has walked a path of personal individuation that has taken him from accepting the status quo through the soul-searching of doubt and questioning. An expansive intellectual foundation in theology and psychology, melded with his commitment to developing dynamic leadership skills, has taken him to a new horizon of possibilities and social engagement. When he encountered the barriers of organizational lethargy, he surpassed them with the prophetic vision of the organization he founded. Christ's message to build the kingdom of God in this world did not fall upon deaf ears. It led Allan to understand and appreciate the synergy of God and man's co-creative activity in building a new and better world. In meeting and working not only with Mother Teresa but also with Hindus, Muslims, Jews, and peoples of all faiths and spiritualities, he has come to understand his path of personal growth and individuation to be a witness to the boundless love of the infinitely divine in the lives of all men and women.

Allan Gathercoal engages his thousands of volunteers in a similar process of personal growth and transformation by inviting them to find "release" from the confines of offices, the slavery of schedules, and the rat race of routines. A cognitive shift begins to take place, and the volunteer begins to identify the leadenness in his or her life and to embrace new potential. For many, this means taking stock and doing some needed soul-searching, which leads to actualizing greater potential and interest in the welfare of others. There is no doubt that this alchemical process has changed not only Allan's perspective on life, but has touched the lives of his volunteers as well.

FUNDING

There is an old adage that says, "No money, no mission." Unfortunately, even the charitable work of nonprofit groups needs to be funded. Allan funded the first mission himself. To get this fledgling organization off the ground and keep it "flying," financial resources needed to be found.

Allan first received funding by simply asking. He admits that there is no other way than going out as a supplicant. You hit the pavement, start visiting your colleagues, and pitch them your idea. Depending upon whether or not the person sees the benefits of a donation, the response will be either positive or negative. All organizations are faced with the hard reality that financial appeals are difficult and time consuming.

Acquiring funding from foundations can be cumbersome. Allan expressed his frustration with endless paperwork and the need to jump through endless hoops. This kind of legwork requires so much time and energy that the big NGOs such as the American Cancer Society actually employ dedicated staff that do nothing but write grant proposals. Successful management of the fundraising task demands commitment and a strong belief in the vision of the organization. But it can be done.

OVERCOMING OBSTACLES

Flying Doctors of America has experienced numerous growing pains as it continues to enhance its organizational viability. Through the years, flexibility in program development and an effective analysis of costs and needs has tweaked and fine-tuned this group's ability to serve the needs of the world's poor. Critical focus has been given to three important aspects of its operations: (1) maintaining a fleet of planes, (2) providing for warehouse and storage space, and (3) developing an ongoing working relationship with other humanitarian organizations.

Initially, Flying Doctors of America had its own planes. However, by the mid 90's it was decided that it would be more cost effective to sell off most of the fleet and take advantage of commercial flights. This radical reduction in the costs of fleet ownership and maintenance opened up Allan's eye to taking a look at the question of warehouses and storage.

An organization that is regularly engaged in medical missions needs easy and quick access to equipment, supplies, and pharmaceuticals. In this situation, Allan benefited from his cost-cutting decision to sell his fleet of planes. The warehouses and storage facilities that Flying Doctors owned were also sold. Excessive cost and the timing of medical missions were cited as the reasons for making this decision. Not only was the actual ownership of warehouse space costly, but there was also the added concern that the donated pharmaceutical products would exceed their expiration dates. Perhaps developing a model of partnering with other groups would be the wisest approach in successfully alleviating these growing concerns.

One example is the partnership developed with Medical Assistance Programs. The sole purpose of this group is to collect donations of medications and equipment. Since Medical Assistance Programs already does the footwork of networking with pharmaceutical and equipment providers, there is no need for Flying Doctors to duplicate these efforts. There is also no need to be concerned with storage or the potential hassle of disposing of expired medications.

In facing these and other barriers and obstacles, Allan Gathercoal's perseverance and innate ability to adapt renewed his vision for Flying Doctors, and he sought out other humanitarian agencies with areas of specialized interest with which to partner. Cooperation and reciprocity are key concepts for successfully attaining goals in the twenty-first century. This is true not only for the business world, but also for advocates and agents of change in a world of health inequality.

MISSION EXAMPLES: BOLIVIA AND PERU

In August 2007, Flying Doctors of America took a group of doctors on a mission to a women's prison in La Paz, Bolivia. The team consisted primarily of twelve medical and dental volunteers, but also included nurse practitioners, chiropractors, and support personnel. Colonel Victor Conde Salcedo, general director of penitentiary services (Direct General del Servicio Penitenciario) provided team members with photo IDs that allowed them access to the prisons of Bolivia as officially recognized medical and dental providers.

Flying Doctors of America is the first non-Bolivian NGO to visit women's prisons in this country. Since most of the imprisoned women are poor and homeless, their children stay and live with them. At each of the prisons, Flying Doctors of America volunteers were able to set up makeshift clinics with a focus on general medical needs, pediatrics, and gynecology. Team members were housed in a local hotel and transported on a daily basis by van.

Roseanne Carroll and her husband, Dr. Scott Carroll, were volunteers for the Bolivian Women's Prison Mission. This was their third mission with Flying Doctors of America. They prefer missions in more exotic locales so that they can traverse jungles and endure more physically demanding conditions. The Carrolls mentioned that Allan finds the best drivers who plan out the best transportation routes for traveling through remote regions. This gives the volunteers a needed sense of security and the knowledge that they are taken care of very well. Despite living for a few days with little to no technology and at times coming home with gastrointestinal problems, the Carrolls both expressed deep gratitude for the profound experience they had as volunteers. Words do not suffice in describing the well of feelings and thoughts experienced during the mission work.

A common theme mentioned by the Carrolls, and echoed in interviews with other volunteers, was the oneness of all humans in a world of great diversity. They find that in reaching across cultures and the barriers of language, customs, and religious traditions, their participation in the missions of Flying Doctors of America has benefited them perhaps even more than the recipients of their care. They also feel very fortunate to be able to share these experiences with each other. Otherwise, the fear of not being able to grasp the full impact of this experience would be difficult to process. The missions have really put life into a new perspective for them, especially when they discovered that most Bolivians live on a one dollar a day.

Roseanne and Scott recounted their last day in the women's prison. Roseanne was able to participate in distributing reading glasses to the inmates. The inmates quickly formed a line and tried to secure the best spots they could while still attending to their duties. Roseanne noticed a woman who was crying hysterically. She soon found out that the woman had to finish her chores before she would be able to stand in line to receive a pair of glasses, and she feared they would all be gone before she was able to get in line. This upset her horribly, for she dearly wanted a pair of glasses to improve her eyesight. Roseanne assured this woman that a pair would be saved for her. The relief she saw in this woman's face melted her soul. Roseanne said she could never ask for a greater reward than knowing the impact this two-minute encounter had on this woman's life. On the last day at the prison, the team saw over 500 patients, which included women and children.

Dr. Carroll also recalled an event on a mission to Peru that touched him deeply. He remembers waiting for their canoes to arrive on the banks of a small village. For some reason, there was a delay, and the team found themselves with time on their hands. Within ten minutes, the team had set up a makeshift clinic and was able to see the entire village before their canoes arrived. He recalls how good he felt in being able to assist another group of people. The gratitude they expressed to Dr. Carroll and his team was overwhelming.

CURRENT DIRECTION

Flying Doctors of America is always exploring new concepts and ideas in medical practice, such as the use of herbal medicines and homeopathic cures. Flying Doctors of America board members have been impressed with the positive results of current research in these areas and would like to dedicate resources in promoting this new approach. For example, researchers have discovered a berry in the Amazon that shows promising results in curing certain types of cancers. Homeopathic and natural medicines are a new area of investigation that embraces a holistic approach to the treatment of illness.

After a number of years of operation, Flying Doctors of America has added physical therapy teams to their missions by inviting orthopedic doctors, chiropractors, physical therapists, and massage therapists to participate. Recognizing that many of the individuals they treat suffer from skeletal and muscular deterioration because of strenuous physical labor, the decision to address this issue by incorporating physical therapy teams has been a godsend to many.

At least four times a year, the board of directors of Flying Doctors of America meets for brainstorming sessions in which a critical look is taken at their entire operating philosophy. One unique aspect of Flying Doctors of America is that each director is required to lead a mission every two years. This time spent out in the field is refreshing and helps board members come up with new ideas and concepts. Flying Doctors of America also encourages its members to think outside of the box, and see what is going on with other NGOs and in other places in the world. By not restricting their own vision, they just keep pushing the envelope.

In keeping with Peter Drucker's idea that an organization needs to totally reinvent itself every seven years to be successful, Flying Doctors of America continually works at enhancing its original mission and purpose. Flying Doctors of America continues to revise itself in the hopes of providing the world with better medical care. This is their prime objective.

FUTURE DIRECTION

Flying Doctors is also looking at integrating its work with that of environmental groups concerned with developing medicines and treatments originating in such places as the Amazon. An eco-friendly philosophy that values the role of indigenous peoples and their contributions to the healing arts is a means not only of valuing the medical practices of native cultures, but also a way of protecting the Amazon region itself.

Al Gore's documentary, *An Inconvenient Truth,* has been a source of great inspiration for Flying Doctors of America. By expanding their direction with an ecological focus, an emphasis on protection of the environment and natural resources will assist in bringing an improved quality of life for those served by Flying Doctors of America.

IF I ONLY KNEW THEN . . .

Although Allan completed inquiries into what would entice physicians to volunteer, he wished he had investigated other NGOs that were working in the same or similar areas of service. After Flying Doctors of America had been in practice, Allan discovered two or three major organizations engaged in similar nonprofit endeavors. He realized that much initial trial and error could have been avoided had he expanded his researched from the very start. Allan recommends that when creating new organizations, it is crucial to seriously evaluate your plans. Take a look not only at what other NGOs are doing, but also consider how their concepts can make a difference and how their organizations are being successful.

Another key element that Allan wished he had spent more time considering is funding. A motto on Allan's desk reads "there is no mission without margin."

Regarding money, people give to groups they know, believe in, and that benefit them. This knowledge would have made fundraising a lot easier.

ALLAN'S MENTORS

Allan has had a score of mentors. He attributes his passion for caring and giving to Mother Teresa because he witnessed her putting these values into practice. Dr. William Pannell, Senior Professor of Preaching at Fuller Theological Seminary, challenged Allan theoretically. Dr. Walter Brugeman from Columbia Theological Seminary also challenged him to be a practitioner of rhetorical criticism and "live the text of the prophets." These are just two of the many whom Allan cites as having influenced him.

Some of the best have been on his board of directors. These have been individuals who have constantly enhanced Allan's values and challenged him as to how the organization was going to realize those values. Allan believes that individuals do not begin think outside their paradigms unless they have people who challenge them. He thinks that people basically live by the law of inertia, and they stay at rest until they are pushed by an outside force that makes them more active and engaged.

Allan's final piece of advice to others is to "Just Do It!" You are going to learn as you do it. The best teacher is experience. Do your initial research, but after that, "Go for It!" You do not want to be one of the millions who say over and over, "I was going to." Just go out there and do it. Allan admits that there will be critics and there will be failures, but you are also going to have your victories. You are going to have that deep satisfaction of knowing that you made a difference!

FLYING DOCTORS OF AMERICA BOARD OF DIRECTORS

Michael Altman. Michael has been a volunteer since 1990 and has served on the board of directors of Flying Doctors of America since 1991. He has been on several medical missions and currently serves as a team leader. As a CPA for twenty-six years, Michael currently runs a financial advisory practice with Ameriprise Financial. He served as vice-chairman of the Cobb County Republican Party in 2005–07 and treasurer in 2004–05. He was appointed by the governor to serve as chairman of the Georgia Commission on the Holocaust.

Ed Atwell, MD. Dr. Atwell, a graduate of the University of Maryland School of Medicine, completed his internship and residency in orthopedic surgery at the Medical College of Georgia, followed by a sports medicine fellowship. Now in private practice in Cartersville, GA, he is also an active pilot and has served several terms as the president of the Cartersville Pilots Association. Dr. Atwell has served on the Flying Doctors of America board of directors since 2003 and has been chairman since 2005. He says, "The practice of medicine has been extremely rewarding and fulfilling to me. Leading and participating in medical missions allows me to give back some of these blessings."

Allan M. Gathercoal, DD, MTh, MA. Allan is the president/founder of Flying Doctors of America, which he founded in 1990. He travels the globe, but his second home is in Latin America. He has been the team leader on more than 140 medical/dental missions. Allan is an ordained minister and holds a doctorate from Columbia Theological Seminary. He is a private pilot and an aficionado of adventure sports. He was born in England.

Allen Hord, MD. Dr. Hord is a physician at the Piedmont Hospital (Atlanta, GA) where he specializes in pain management. He maintains an adjunct appointment as clinical associate professor of anesthesiology at Emory University School of Medicine in Atlanta, GA. Dr. Hord is certified by the American Board of Anesthesiology and was awarded a Certificate of Added Qualifications in Pain Management. Dr. Hord is also certified by the American Board of Pain Medicine. In 2004 he was once again voted to the list of Best Doctors in America.

Kayreen Jeter, RN, BSN. Kayreen is a registered nurse with primary experience in adult health and has been an intensive care nurse for nineteen years. During this time, she has also worked for a cardiothoracic surgical group for six years and managed an ICU for two years. Her primary area of expertise is ICU bedside nursing for cardiothoracic surgery patients.

FLYING DOCTORS OF AMERICA BOARD OF ADVISORS

Héctor Guillermo Vilar Rey, JD. Dr. Guillermo is the director general for the Gobierno de la Provincia de Salta. He is an accomplished lawyer (professor of law) and is fluent in Spanish and English. He represents his country and the Provincia de Salta throughout the world. He has recently traveled to the United States, Canada, Chile, Bolivia, Paraguay, Brazil, Uruguay, Spain, England, Turkey, Israel, and Egypt. He was born in Salta, Argentina.

Dan Bailey. Dan owns a website design and marketing business (danbailey.com) and has been working with Flying Doctors of America updating the organization's website and marketing efforts via e-mail since 2005. A native of Atlanta, GA, and former police officer, Dan has been in the computer technology industry since 1990.

Sherman Wade. A graduate of Saint Norbert College in Green Bay and the University of Wisconsin–Milwaukee Graduate School, Sherman served four years as a captain in the U.S. Army and the last 35 years in the trade show business. Since retiring in 2002, he has been a marketing consultant to trade show organizers and the managing partner of a real estate investment company. Very active in the community, Sherman has served on the board of directors of Atlanta Children's Shelter, the Atlanta Chapter of the Leukemia & Lymphoma Society, and presently on the board of the Atlanta

Track Club. He has been on Flying Doctors missions to Mongolia, Peru, and Bolivia and joined the board of directors in 2002.

ORGANIZATIONAL SNAPSHOT

Organization: Flying Doctors of America

Founder: Allan Gathercoal

Mission/Description: For more than eighteen years, Flying Doctors of America has been bringing together physicians, dentists, nurses, chiropractors, other health professionals, and non-medical support volunteers to care for people who otherwise would never receive professional medical care. The organization runs short-term medical/dental missions to the rural regions of the developing world. They operate under the "Mother Teresa Principle," focusing on the poorest of the poor who live in conditions that are difficult for most Americans to imagine.

Website: www.Fdoamerica.org

Address: 15 Medical Drive

Cartersville, GA 30121

Phone: (770) 386-5221

E-mail: FDOAmerica@aol.com

9

Caring for Torture Survivors: The Marjorie Kovler Center

Mary Fabri, Marianne Joyce,
Mary Black, and Mario González

The Marjorie Kovler Center for the Treatment of Survivors of Torture, a program of Heartland Alliance for Human Needs & Human Rights, commemorated twenty years of providing comprehensive services to torture survivors in October 2007. Since 1987, the Marjorie Kovler Center has worked with more than 1,500 survivors of torture from seventy-four different countries in Africa, Latin America, the Middle East, Asia, and Eastern Europe.

Torture is the deliberate infliction of severe physical or psychological pain carried out by anyone acting in an official capacity for the purposes of extracting a confession, punishment, intimidation, or discrimination. Torture exerts control over people and communities to create a cycle of fear, intimidation, and alienation.

Survivors of torture often suffer from complex posttraumatic stress that manifests as anxiety, distrust, depression, flashbacks, intrusive memories of the traumatic event, concentration and memory problems, and a range of physical symptoms. Disempowerment of individuals and communities is the goal of torture. The goal of treatment, therefore, is to empower survivors to use their strengths and reclaim personal integrity and a sense of control in their lives. The Marjorie Kovler Center helps survivors restore trust in others and reestablish a sense of community.

This chapter will provide a brief history of the torture rehabilitation field and the development of the Marjorie Kovler Center, with its unique model of providing quality care to torture survivors using and managing pro bono professional services. The philosophy and model of care created by the center's staff and Executive Clinical Committee will be discussed through an examination of the political and cultural dynamics of torture, and its impact on individuals and communities. An overview of the center's current demographics will also be provided.

THE CHICAGO IMMIGRANT AND REFUGEE EXPERIENCE

Chicago has a long history as a port of entry for immigrants seeking to improve their lives. In 1888 the Travelers Aid Society was founded to assist young people entering the city. Two years later, activist Jane Addams founded the Hull House and was quickly providing social services to more than 1,000 individuals a week. Addams worked for legislation to protect immigrants from exploitation, limit the working hours of women, mandate schooling for children, recognize labor unions, and provide for industrial safety. In 1908 Grace Abbott, a beneficiary of Hull House's services, became the first director the Immigrants' Protective League, which combined direct service and advocacy for broader social reforms for immigrants.

Travelers Aid and the Immigrants' Protective League merged to form Travelers Aid of Metropolitan Chicago in 1967. With funding assistance from the United Way, the two organizations served travelers, immigrants, prisoners, and others living in destitution. In 1980 these two organizations legally incorporated to form Travelers and Immigrants Aid (TIA), now named Heartland Alliance for Human Needs & Human Rights. With a social justice perspective and a vision to expand services, the newly hired president, Rev. Dr. Sid Mohn, reinvigorated TIA's mission to serve the poor and most vulnerable.

The influx of refugees from Southeast Asia to the United States as the result of the Vietnam War began in 1975 and impacted refugee resettlement services and policies. In 1978 the Illinois Department of Mental Health in collaboration with the Illinois state refugee coordinator, Dr. Edwin Silverman, conducted a Community Forum on Asian mental health concerns that brought together community leaders and mental health professionals. The meeting led to the development of Asian Human Services to serve the mental health needs of the pan-Asian community in Chicago.

The Refugee Act of 1980 created the Federal Refugee Resettlement Program to diversify and provide for the effective resettlement of refugees. This was followed by a Refugee Mental Health Initiative by the Office of Refugee Resettlement, which provided funding to the Department of Mental Health in various states to develop culturally specific services for different refugee populations. In Chicago, these events resulted in Travelers and Immigrants Aid developing a refugee mental health program in 1982, which used bilingual refugee staff to assist identified refugees with mental health problems. The bilingual staff provided social services in the community and interpreted for psychiatrists conducting evaluations and monitoring medications. It was not long before the bilingual staff recognized that some refugees were torture survivors.

A RESPONSE TO TORTURE

The United Nations General Assembly adopted and proclaimed the Universal Declaration of Human Rights on December 10, 1948. Article 5 states, "No one shall be subjected to torture or to cruel, inhuman or degrading treatment or punishment." In 1961 Amnesty International was founded and began advocating for prisoners of conscience who were being detained and were enduring cruel and inhumane treatment. In 1972 Amnesty International launched a worldwide campaign for the abolition of torture. The growing human rights movement provided a foundation for the development of the torture rehabilitation movement worldwide.

In 1979 members of a Danish medical group obtained permission to admit and examine torture victims at Copenhagen University Hospital in Denmark. Three years later, in 1982, Dr. Inge Genefke founded the Rehabilitation and Research Centre for Torture Victims (RCT) in Copenhagen as an independent institution with its own premises.

The Canadian Centre for Victims of Torture was founded by several Toronto doctors, lawyers, and social service professionals, many of whom were associated with Amnesty International. They had begun to recognize torture victims, many of whom were seeking refugee status in Canada, in their practices as early as 1977. This group of professionals recognized the need for specialized services for the social, health, and legal problems faced by this particular group.

In the United States, a similar process was also taking place. In 1978 Dr. David Kinzie, a psychiatrist at the Oregon Health Sciences University, began a small program to treat traumatized refugees coming to Oregon after the Vietnam War. Dr. José Quiroga, a physician who fled Chile after the coup that overthrew President Allende, and Ana Deutsch, a marriage and family therapist who had escaped with her family from the "Dirty Wars" in Argentina, began seeing torture victims in 1980 at the Venice Family Clinic in Southern California. This collaboration eventually led to the development of the Program for Torture Victims in Los Angeles. On the East Coast, Dr. Richard Mollica, a psychiatrist, co-founded the Harvard Program in Refugee Trauma with Jim Lavelle, a social worker. In the Midwest, Minnesota governor Rudy Perpich worked with the local human rights community to found the Center for Victims of Torture in May 1985 in Minneapolis-St. Paul.

Attorneys, physicians, psychologists, and other service providers were becoming aware of the growing numbers of torture survivors living in the metropolitan Chicago area. Thousands of Southeast Asians were resettled in the aftermath of the Vietnam War and Cambodian genocide. The migration of undocumented Central Americans fleeing civil conflicts in their homelands, especially from El Salvador and Guatemala, resulted in the migration of thousands of undocumented refugees. Torture-affected individuals and families began presenting in legal clinics, medical settings, and social service agencies.

Service providers were not alone in their growing awareness of the special needs of survivors of torture. The Sanctuary Movement was formed to develop a network of faith-based shelters for Central Americans fleeing the civil wars in their homelands. The Wellington Avenue United Church of Christ in Chicago was the second church in the country to declare sanctuary, housing Salvadoran and Guatemalan families in 1982. Eventually, area churches and synagogues formed the Chicago Metropolitan Sanctuary Alliance. During 1983 and 1984, the Chicago Religious Task Force on Central America relocated Salvadoran and Guatemalan refugees by establishing an "underground railroad" from Arizona to Chicago. Also in 1984, Amnesty International launched its second Campaign against Torture. The Wellington Avenue Church was a meeting place for concerned Chicagoans. It was in this sanctuary community that TIA's president, Dr. Mohn, met Chicago attorney Craig Mousin. The meeting resulted in a collaboration that eventually led to the development of the Midwest Immigrant Rights Center (MIRC) in 1985 as a program of Travelers and Immigrants Aid. MIRC (now grown into the National Immigrant Justice Center, or NIJC) became a network of pro bono attorneys trained to represent asylum seekers who would otherwise not have access to legal representation.

Physicians and psychologists in Chicago also became engaged in the issue. Dr. Robert Kirschner, a forensic pathologist at the Cook County Medical Examiners Office, began working on the examination of remains found in Argentina in 1985. This and other experiences gave him expertise in forensic documentation of human rights abuses. Concurrently, Dr. Irene Martínez, a physician at the then Cook County Hospital (now John Stroger, Jr. Hospital) and a survivor of torture from Argentina's "Dirty Wars," began identifying torture survivors in the emergency room at the hospital. As a Spanish-speaker, she was frequently referred patients from Central America. "I thought they were torture survivors because they reminded me of me," she stated.

Martínez was a former Amnesty International prisoner of conscience and activist, coming to the United States in 1981 after her release from detention in Argentina. She first made her way to Los Angeles, California, where she met Dr. Quiroga and Ana Deutsch, then providing treatment for torture survivors at the Venice Family Clinic. It was from this encounter that Martínez learned that the feelings she had been experiencing since her release had a name: posttraumatic stress disorder (PTSD). She shared that this information helped her realize she was not losing her mind. It made her think that other torture survivors might also benefit from having a better understanding of the psychological consequences of torture.

In July 1983, Dr. Martínez began her residency in internal medicine at Cook County Hospital in Chicago. She gave a presentation titled "Psychology and Human Rights Abuses" at the Illinois Psychologists Association's (IPA) annual meeting in November 1986, which led to conversations in December of that year between psychologists from the IPA and health providers from Cook County Hospital interested in providing services to torture survivors.

It was a natural development for Chicago's Travelers and Immigrants Aid (now Heartland Alliance), which already had developed a refugee mental health program, to house a torture treatment center. Dr. Edwin Silverman, chief of the Bureau of Immigrant and Refugee Services, Illinois Department of Human Services, and long-time advocate for refugee concerns, met with Dr. Sid Mohn, president of Travelers and Immigrants Aid to discuss the need for a center in Chicago to serve torture survivors. Drs. Kirschner and Martínez began providing valuable documentation for MIRC attorneys representing Central American asylum seekers.

Initial discussions about providing health services, including mental health and social assistance, began with Sister Sheila Lyne, president and chief executive officer of Mercy Hospital & Medical Center. In February 1987 a formal meeting occurred that included representatives of key organizations: Sister Sheila Lyne of Mercy Hospital; Steven Miles, MD, from the University of Chicago's Center for Clinical Medical Ethics; Dr. Sid Mohn, president of Travelers and Immigrants Aid; Thomas Hollon, PhD, and Susana Schlesinger, PhD, from the Illinois Psychological Association; and Robert Kirschner, MD and Irene Martínez, MD, from the Cook County health system. The idea of a Chicago center specializing in the treatment of survivors of torture had the support of people and organizations that could make it a reality. They agreed to carry out the following initiatives by the end of 1987:

1. The director of the Refugee Mental Health Program at TIA was psychologist Dr. Antonio Martínez. With funding from the Bureau of Refugee and Immigrant Services of the Illinois Department of Human Services, his position was restructured to provide him with time to help establish a model of care for a torture treatment center in Chicago to be housed under the auspices of Travelers and Immigrants Aid; he would later become the center's first director.
2. Dr. Steven Miles agreed to have the Center for Clinical Ethics host a conference at the University of Chicago on the treatment of survivors of torture. This conference would bring together the leaders in the field, including Barbara Chester from the Center for Victims of Torture in Minneapolis, MN; Dr. David Kinzie from the Intercultural Psychiatry Program, Oregon Health & Science University, Portland, Oregon; Dr. Irene Martínez, physician at Cook County Hospital in Chicago and a survivor of Argentina's "Dirty War"; Dr. Richard Mollica of the Harvard Program in Refugee Trauma at Massachusetts General Hospital; Dr. Elena Nightingale, one of the editors of the recently published *The Breaking of Bodies and Minds: Torture, Psychiatric Abuse and the Health Professions* (W.H. Freeman, 1985); and Dr. Glenn Randall, coauthor of *Serving Survivors of Torture* (American Association for the Advancement of Science, 1991).
3. Dr. Irene Martínez spoke at a Social Issues Section–sponsored presentation at the 1987 Illinois Psychological Association's annual meeting to identify other interested psychologists. Her presentation was titled "Treatment and Needs of Victims of Torture and Their Families."
4. Mercy Hospital committed to providing medical services to ten identified torture survivors, including physical and dental care as well as psychiatric services.

The collaborative and multidisciplinary spirit of this group was essential to the creation of a torture treatment center in Chicago. It reflected a synergism that would be contagious as the planned events took place throughout 1987.

During this time, Chicago philanthropist Peter Kovler had read about the Rehabilitation and Research Centre for Torture Victims in Copenhagen. Through the Blum-Kovler Foundation, Peter Kovler initiated funding in the amount of $75,000 that helped launch the financial reality for the Chicago-based torture treatment program in November 1988. The foundation's only request was to name the Center after Kovler's mother, Marjorie—thus began the Marjorie Kovler Center for the Treatment of Survivors of Torture.

The multidisciplinary working group met several times throughout the year and followed through successfully with their commitments: Dr. Antonio Martínez was named director of the Marjorie Kovler Center. He attended the conference at the University of Chicago where he announced the intent to recruit volunteers interested in providing services to torture survivors, who would be screened and referred by the newly formed Marjorie Kovler Center. A piece of paper was passed around for potential volunteers to list their contact information. A list of fifty names was compiled, and the interested individuals were invited to the first meeting of clinical volunteers on February 20, 1988.

PROVIDING SERVICES FOR TORTURE SURVIVORS

The Marjorie Kovler Center for the Treatment of Survivors of Torture was located in the diverse Uptown neighborhood of Chicago, where many new immigrants and refugees initially settle. Nestled on the third floor of a building that housed multiple refugee assistance programs, the Marjorie Kovler Center had two office spaces and three staff members. Dr. Antonio Martínez divided his time between the Refugee Mental Health Program and the Marjorie Kovler Center, providing administrative coordination. The additional staff included a full-time clinical supervisor and a half-time case manager. A staff triad of administration, clinical work, and case management/volunteer coordination provided the structure, which allowed pro bono professionals and other volunteers to contribute services. The first year's budget was approximately $80,000 for staff salaries, rent, and other direct costs. Within the first four months, thirty-two individuals were accepted as clients at the Marjorie Kovler Center. The caseload included torture survivors from Vietnam, Cambodia, Guatemala, El Salvador, Mexico, Chile, Peru, Iran, and Iraq. By the end of the calendar year, the client numbers reached seventy-four, and Ethiopia and Honduras had been added to the country of origin list.

A core group of twelve pro bono therapists emerged from the outreach efforts and became the Executive Clinical Committee. The twelve clinicians provided guidance and consultation to the staff of the Marjorie Kovler Center in developing a clinical model of care using pro bono professionals. The committee started to meet once a month for one hour to discuss program challenges such as screening and coordinating volunteers. A three-hour multidisciplinary meeting followed and provided volunteers an opportunity to discuss cases in a supportive, confidential setting. This monthly, four-hour time slot became integral to developing a cohesive volunteer model of care for torture survivors.

Torture treatment was a relatively new field, and most of the volunteers had no practical experience in treating torture survivors. A multidisciplinary and comprehensive approach evolved.

CASE STUDY

Understanding the political and cultural context of torture survivors' experiences became an essential part of providing appropriate treatment. Most of the pro bono clinicians had experience working with trauma, but not torture; experience working in therapeutic dyads, not triads that integrated an interpreter; and experience with different economic classes, but not necessarily different worldviews. Learning to be sensitive to the consequences of officially sanctioned torture, developing a communication rhythm with an interpreter, and being open to the consideration of different ways of understanding the world presented challenges to Western-trained clinicians providing psychotherapy to indigenous and other individuals from the non-Western world.

An example that illustrates these challenges involved a clinical psychologist working with an unaccompanied minor from Central America. Maria (not her real name) had made her way to Chicago via the Sanctuary Movement. While living with a family who had agreed to provide for her needs as an adolescent, she was referred to the Marjorie Kovler Center for behaviors that included lying and hoarding food. Her trauma history included being orphaned as an infant when her parents were disappeared. She was raised by an older woman, who was taking care of many children orphaned by the civil conflict in their country. Maria also survived her village being bombed, and her own abduction and rape by soldiers. After giving birth to a child as the result of the rape, Maria worked in the city and sent the money she earned to the woman who had raised her and was now raising her child. After several harassing encounters with the military, Maria fled to the United States, fearing the harassment would escalate into more abuse. Her crossing as an undocumented minor assisted by the Sanctuary Movement provided her with some assurance of refuge once she arrived safely in Chicago.

Maria was fifteen years old when a family who agreed to provide her with basic needs and education received her. This was a difficult transition, however, and was fraught with many miscommunications and misunderstandings. Identifying and understanding these issues was a primary task of individual psychotherapy.

Maria was of indigenous descent, had a second grade education, and had been raised in a rural village where, she described, everyone contributed to the well-being of the community. Her description of the woman who raised her and other orphans was that she was her *abuela*, or grandmother, and that the other children were her brothers and sisters. Maria also described having several different pseudonyms and indicated that using different names was part of survival when meeting strangers. She described learning as a child that it was not safe to trust people she did not know. The political context of civil war and the cultural and linguistic worldview of *campesino* life, in addition to Maria's multiple traumatic experiences, were all essential components for the therapist to understand. The use of a Spanish-speaking interpreter to assist the therapy process was a challenge for Maria, since Spanish was her second language; for the therapist, who needed to rely on the interpreter to be the conduit of communication; and for the interpreter, who had to ensure accurate representation of what was being said. All the participants were unfamiliar with these conditions of psychotherapy. There was a huge learning curve to be mastered.

Creating a safe environment became the first task of therapy. Maria's grandmother had been a significant figure in Maria's life, and she missed her very much. At her own initiation, Maria performed a ceremony where she used her indigenous belief system to call upon her grandmother to be "present" during the sessions. The blending of psychotherapy with an indigenous practice provided a cross-cultural blending of healing strategies. Fortified by the felt sense of her grandmother, Maria was able to talk about her multiple traumas in a psychotherapeutic context. Additionally, Maria found family therapy sessions an important component of her treatment, stating, "They are my family now and need to know what is happening in my life."

Maria regularly brought forth her deep connections to her community and her *abuela,* and placed her own experiences in the context of a collective experience. Center staff and volunteers recognized what the collective experience brought to Maria's reservoir of strength and resilience. The case manager, volunteers, and other service providers worked in a collective spirit, closely coordinating with the therapist to address needs that affected Maria's daily life. Maria needed medical attention for contractures secondary to scarring from napalm burns, English as a Second Language classes, intensive support during multiple housing transitions, employment assistance, and referral for legal assistance. Recruiting pro bono providers as needs arose, accompanying Maria to appointments in the community, and responding to crises was also a collaborative effort sustained for a decade. By sharing who she was with us, Maria unwittingly led our center into a deeper sense of collective responsibility, action, and joy. Maria remains engaged with the center's services, activities, and the same helping professionals after seventeen years, reflecting her resilience, independence, and connectedness.

A CLINICAL MODEL FOR TORTURE TREATMENT

The Marjorie Kovler Center's clinical model developed with special attention to three areas: (1) understanding the dynamics of torture and its psychological effects, (2) grounding treatment in a political context, and (3) adapting treatment to varying cultural concepts about torture and mental health. Initially, our knowledge of torture and its effects was limited to the kinds of trauma we were accustomed to seeing in our professional practices. Only by listening carefully to survivors—to their stories and their feedback—and reflecting with colleagues over time did we begin to understand how we could best offer assistance as a program. Treatment constantly interacts with the dynamics of torture and its political and cultural contexts. As illustrated in Maria's story, we continue to rely on the client/survivor as expert on issues related to her own experience and as the ultimate arbiter of a treatment's success.

Dynamics of Torture

The most immediate aspects of our clients' initial presentation are the palpable feelings of vulnerability and mistrust. Whether a person's gaze is cast downward and words are spare, or eyes look fearfully to you, silently pleading for respite from pain, nonverbal expressions communicate volumes about past experiences and present needs. We wanted to communicate safety and trust to survivors. To do this effectively, we knew we had to first understand the survivors' core experiences of torture. Humiliation, threat of death, unpredictability, and complete powerlessness pervade torture. The intentional application of extreme physical pain accompanied by interrogation was also destructive to language that might describe it (Scarry, 1985). The depth of trauma was degrees of intensity beyond what most clinicians had previously encountered and treated, so we read and discussed what was available on the subject as we began meeting with new clients and listening carefully.

Social Conditions

Literature from Latin America, both clinical and autobiographical, illustrated the specific context of torture for many of our first clients. It underscored the strategic, systematic way torture was used to exert power and silence dissent. Jacobo Timmerman wrote not only of the shocking brutality to which he and others were subject in Argentina, but his narrative also provided insight into methods and psychological aspects of perpetrators in a torturing hierarchy (Timmerman, 1981). Regimes combined isolation with extreme brutality for maximum, long-term impact. It seemed clear that a central objective of perpetrators was to convince the victims that no one would believe their stories, even if they survived to tell them, leaving survivors with an enormous and unjust burden of guilt and shame. Dictatorial regimes had effective propaganda machines to generate myths about the threat dissidents constituted. Regimes tried to marginalize individuals, diminish the influence their voices could have on others, and stigmatize their families. Many regimes were able to convince sectors of civil society to collude with the idea that a political or social group could be regarded as almost subhuman, a "torturable class" of people (Conroy, 2000, p. 27). Learning about these realities helped us understand clients who avoided telling their stories or disclosing significant details about their experience of torture and persecution. We were also challenged to believe the unbelievable.

The conditions present for systematic terror often included collaborating institutional elements, such as clergy allied with dictatorships and other professionals, such as physicians and psychologists, lending credibility to inhuman methods of enforcing state control (Lifton, 2004; Scarry, 1985). Understanding this nuanced aspect of some torture experiences helped us to be sensitive to clients hesitant to seek needed treatment, and to modify how we were accustomed to conduct medical and psychological evaluations. We became more conscious that we might be perceived as authority figures and adjusted our style and workspace to convey warmth and safety. Accommodating the need for a slower pace—a first session dedicated solely to helping the client feel more at ease, explanations for reasons why questions were asked or actions taken, and reassurances that survivors were not obligated to comply with any request we might make—we proceeded with increasing awareness. The knowledge and reality that "helping" professionals collaborated with torturers also brought staff and volunteers closer to understanding that the capacity to torture could be present in all of us, however distressing the idea.

Political Asylum

These powerful psychological themes of guilt, shame, and silence had legal ramifications once a survivor had arrived safely in this country (Bogner, 2007). Many survivors avoided talking about their experiences to prevent the onset of painful, intrusive memories and to attempt to forget, however elusive the wish. In the early years, many did not apply for political asylum out of fear of retraumatization or fear of retaliation against their families at home. In 1996 Congress passed the Illegal Immigration Reform and Immigrant Responsibility Act, which profoundly restricted protection for asylum seekers by requiring expedited filing of asylum applications (McAndrews, 2002). Torture survivors were suddenly compelled to enter a retraumatizing, unpredictable legal process before they had an opportunity to stabilize their lives. There is an inherent and frightening power differential in the asylum process, increasingly adverse and accusatory. Here, the burden of proof is on the asylum seeker, who needs to produce documents to support the claim. In their home countries, however, the focus is on evading immediate danger to survival. Those who manage to flee are able to do so because a support network mobilizes on their behalf, often paying bribes to help them escape captivity, obtaining false documents if necessary, choosing the destination, and making travel arrangements. Most never imagine having to prove they were tortured, as if living through it and carrying the emotional and physical pain were not proof enough.

The psychological pressure to prepare for the asylum process often overwhelms survivors, and the discretionary nature of decisions can be devastating. Therapeutic support is critical as a client constructs a written narrative testimony of his or her persecution. Center staff and volunteers have responded to these legal imperatives with treatments that emphasize symptom management, coordination of constant efforts to provide medical and psychological forensic documentation of torture, and the finding of resources to assist clients in chronic economic instability. Asylum applicants are not eligible for any government assistance and often have prolonged waits for work authorization. Documenting the effects of torture is a labor-intensive process for a volunteer organization, but when survivors are granted asylum, there are tremendous concrete and symbolic gains. Asylum represents a crucial step toward security and family reunification, as well as a milestone in the treatment stage of safety (Herman, 1992). Twenty years later, the legal process continues to present challenges to the treatment team—intensified by heightened suspicion of asylum seekers since September 11, 2001, and increased discretionary powers for immigration judges (REAL ID Act, 2005).

Strength in Community

The legal pressures, profound trauma, and often disabling physical and psychological symptoms facing survivors led the Marjorie Kovler Center to a collaborative, multidisciplinary treatment approach. As much for our own benefit as for the clients', a collective approach would provide peer support for intense trauma work and help us form a community of support and healing. The systemic use of torture to destroy real or perceived threats to power can result in a strong disincentive on the part of survivors and their communities to organize, take action, or voice dissent. Informed by the survivor's experience of isolation and helplessness, we hoped to recreate a sense of community. By first helping a survivor to connect with his or her innate strength and resilience, and then helping the survivor connect with our community, we were offering ours as a bridge to others.

The political context of torture, systematic in its disempowerment, permeated our understanding of empowerment as a core objective of treatment and our belief that effective treatment should extend beyond the individual (Bronfenbrenner, 1979). Offering assistance to increase English language proficiency (ESL classes and volunteer tutors), to obtain training and employment (occupational therapist), to address causes of physical pain (nurses, doctors, dentists, physical therapists, acupuncturists, massage therapists), to engage in expressive therapies (art, dance, movement), or to attend a cooking group or free cultural event are center services that complement individual psychotherapies. Reduced symptoms of insomnia, depression, and anxiety, along with participation in activities beyond the therapeutic dyad, signal an increasing sense of agency and a change from the core dynamics of torture.

Sharing Power

The dynamics of power exist simultaneously at personal, interactional, organizational, and structural levels (Wolf, 1999). Our objective to encourage empowerment influenced our organizational layers (after increased funding in 2000 from the Torture Victims Relief Act) and methods of service delivery—from administrative to clinical, intake evaluation to case management model, and interactions with clients around health and material needs. A balance of power and awareness of choices is critical to the effectiveness of services and the quality of our relationship with survivors. Empowerment may initially manifest in a choice to accept or decline a particular recommendation in the Initial Treatment Plan. Over time, however, many clients have recovered their voices of dissent and have spoken to the media, lobbied officials in Washington, D.C., established activist organizations, and filed civil lawsuits against torturers who reside in this country. The center has been uniquely engaged at these broad levels of empowerment: supporting Torture Abolition and Survivors' Support Coalition International (TASSC), founded and run by survivors; inviting collaboration with a client advisory board; working with torture survivors who pursue justice through civil cases supported by the Center for Justice and Accountability (CJA) by providing psychological evaluations and support; and promoting clarity and consistency in our mission so that the Marjorie Kovler Center is easily identified with our model and strong public stance against the use of torture.

Importance of Relationship

Torture is a relational trauma and a political act, using a range of techniques intentionally applied by another human being for maximum humiliation and harm. One of its central aims is to undermine a person's ability to form healthy relationships. The psychological imprint of the survivor's forced relationship with a cruel and unpredictable authority confounds subsequent relationships. For survivors, the prospect of entering a relationship is anxiety provoking and potentially retraumatizing. Relationships are often avoided in early stages of recovery. For example, survivors may hesitate to come to the center after being referred by someone or may spend their days alone in their rooms, avoiding interaction with roommates or potential encounters outside the home. To the extent that any situation or relationship begins to reconstitute elements of the torture experience (i.e., a sensory piece of the present that resembles the traumatic past), a survivor will feel increasingly vulnerable and respond accordingly (e.g., shut down emotionally, show signs of central nervous system hyperarousal, have a flashback, avoid repeating the experience). Survivors who have disclosed painful details of their torture to a therapist or attorney may avoid coming to the next appointment.

To engage survivors in treatment, the center's staff and volunteers knew they would have to earn trust in clear and intentional steps. Although retraumatization is unavoidable, minimizing it is a philosophical and operational tenet for our center. All team members are mindful of incorporating choices in their interactions with survivors: to slow the pace, to not disclose a detail until ready, to sit facing the provider or not, and to accept medication or not. Clear information and descriptions of the process help shape realistic expectations. Providing choices becomes a therapeutic intervention whose effect is to convey sensitivity to their vulnerability, gradually instill trust and safety in the relationship, and restore confidence in the survivor's own inherent ability to heal.

Survivors suffered profound betrayal in the context of a human relationship and often have needs for transparency beyond conventional clinical boundaries. They often challenge clinicians to respond to questions about our political views or stance on U.S. support for or involvement with their country's military. Having been exposed to the worst of humanity, survivors often wondered why we were doing this work, suspicious of our motives. To respond in the classical ways in which we are trained would risk retraumatizing or alienating our clients. Instead, it has been essential to demonstrate solidarity with survivors and the movements for social change with which they have typically been associated. In the center's early days, the clinical committee, struggling to respond in ways sensitive to the dynamics of torture, would openly discuss these issues. A model of therapeutic accompaniment developed to provide reassurance for the existential dilemma of trusting people again and to recognize the pervasiveness of retraumatizing experiences in survivors' daily lives.

Therapeutic Accompaniment

The practice of accompaniment challenges traditional ideas of clinical boundaries (Fabri, 2001). Often, professional boundaries are defined by meeting in an office for a set amount of time. In working cross-culturally, we have found that to engage survivors who come from countries and cultures with limited if any knowledge of the Western mental health model, it is necessary to make adjustments and modifications to conventional frameworks. This may include, but is not limited to, a physician conducting a forensic medical examination in a non-medical setting, a psychotherapist accompanying a survivor who was raped as part of her torture to a medical examination, or a case manager driving and staying with a client through her dental appointment. It may also involve therapy in a client's home. The guiding principle determining how and when to adjust conventional boundaries is found in answering these questions: Is this therapeutic for the survivor? Will it enhance engagement in treatment? Does it promote greater safety and trust? We have learned boundaries are internalized, and professional roles can be maintained in any physical environment.

A Therapeutic Partnership

The Therapeutic Partnership is a model of psychotherapy using interpreters to meet the needs of cross-cultural mental health. Using the empowerment model that permeated the philosophy of care of the Marjorie Kovler Center, the expertise of each participant—survivor, interpreter, and clinician—was acknowledged as an essential component of the therapy process. A collaborative methodology was promoted: the therapist was viewed as providing expertise on the psychological consequences of severe trauma, such as torture, and strategies for recovery; the survivor was an expert in what trauma had occurred and its expression within his or her own cultural, linguistic, and political context; and the interpreter was the conduit for communication, an expert in the languages spoken by the therapist and survivor. There were also times when the interpreter provided more than language interpretation. When the interpreter was from the survivor's homeland, he or she was also a cultural broker, often translating the meaning of behaviors and expressions in ways that promoted deeper under-standing of the communication. Additionally, the interpreter at times was an advocate for either the survivor or the therapist, assisting the other in grasping the full meaning of what was needed or being expressed. The therapeutic triad became a therapeutic partnership and reflected respect and trust, necessary ingredients for psychotherapy.

Spiritual Support

Another vital component developed by Eva Sullivan-Knopf, an early case manager at the Marjorie Kovler Center, was the Irene Pastoral Counseling Program, Irene designating "peace" in the Greek tradition. With a background in ministry, Eva recognized the importance of spirituality in a survivor's life and worldview. The Irene component essentially was organized around offering pas-toral counseling to Marjorie Kovler clients. The volunteers and consultants to the program represented many faiths, including Buddhism, Christianity, Islam, and Judaism. Eva continued to consult with volunteers even after she left for a church ministry. Many of the volunteers continued this service, but the Irene component itself eventually diminished over the years without on-staff leader-ship. The legacy, however, continues with ongoing links to communities of faith, particularly the Chicago Theological Union and local mosques, churches, and temples that provide spiritual support to clients and consultation to staff and volunteers.

POLITICAL CONTEXT OF TORTURE

The first clients at the center were predominantly Latin American and Southeast Asian; therefore, it was imperative that we as a program understood the sociopo-litical history and current policies of United States' involvement in those hemi-spheres. Basic questions such as how the economic and political interests of the United States interacted with the power structures of each country could have implications for treatment. One had to be able to distinguish between official reports of the "communist reign of terror" in Central America and reports from a union organizer from Guatemala or catechist from El Salvador who was system-atically targeted for torture, disappearance, and assassination (President Ronald Reagan televised speech, 1984). Staff and volunteers had to demonstrate they were not antagonistic to the opinions or activities that led to the client's persecution. Our program also had to reassure clients we did not have government ties and would protect confidentiality.

A sociological framework that explained the relationship between war, oppression, and mental health was especially useful to elucidate the psychological and spiritual effects of the wars in Central America on communities (Martin-Baró, 1994). The concept of our own liberation being tied to others' liberation was not only consistent with the guiding philosophy of liberation movements prevalent in Latin America at the time, but it was also useful to shift the inherent power differential in a treatment relationship to a more equitable balance. One therapist remembers her Guatemalan clients sharing in greater depth after they saw her marching in a protest against U.S. policies in Guatemala. Many volunteers were drawn to the center's work, appalled by knowledge that torture was prevalent and either overtly or covertly supported by our government. Learning that survivors were in Chicago in substantial numbers, they hoped they might contribute in some small way to a survivor's recovery and begin to wedge into systems perpetuating the practice of torture. This continues to be a central motive for our volunteers twenty years later.

As staff and volunteers listened for the first time and then repeatedly to stories of gross human rights violations, we looked to each other and to those we trusted for points of reference. We experienced shifts in our worldviews and episodic vicarious trauma, as in nightmares and symptoms of anxiety or depression that had not been present prior to the work. We also came to question the impact of our work as long as torture persisted with impunity all over the world. Acknowledging the presence of social phenomena such as denial and dissociation in our own society (including friends and family) compelled us to break the cycle of social denial by action and by speaking out in solidarity with our clients (Herman, 1992). The U.S. government's participation in torture is now widely known. The photos and national debate dealt a psychological blow to many clients who do not have the luxury of debating the issue in abstract terms. We have continued standing with our clients to oppose the use of torture of any kind against any human being.

EFFECTS ON FAMILIES

The Marjorie Kovler Center adopted the United Nations definition of torture: "Any act by which severe pain or suffering, whether physical or mental, is intentionally inflicted on a person for such purposes as obtaining from him or a third person information or a confession, punishing him for an act he or a third person has committed or is suspected of having committed, or intimidating or coercing him or a third person, or for any reason based on discrimination of any kind, when such pain or suffering is inflicted by or at the instigation of or with the consent or acquiescence of a public official or other person acting in an official capacity" (UN Convention). The Mothers of the Plaza de Mayo, from Argentina, taught us about the suffering of family members of the disappeared. Just as torture is an oppressive tool applied systemically, the center's clinical committee recognized the corresponding need to systemically treat the effects of torture in the family. Some children felt they must keep secrets about their mother's, father's, or sibling's torture or disappearance to shield the family from stigma in the community or further persecution from authorities. In many countries, there are substantial threats to families and risk of persecution once a member flees the country. Many family members have witnessed extreme violence in their communities and are traumatized, even though they themselves were not tortured.

The center's staff and volunteers understand our clients' symptoms and behaviors in relation to their experience of torture—as normal reactions to abnormal circumstances rather than pathology. This approach brings solidarity into the clinical framework and incorporates a political consciousness into our conceptualization of PTSD and its treatment. PTSD is a common, albeit imperfect, diagnosis to describe symptoms survivors frequently experience once they survive torture. Although assisting clients to decrease the frequency or intensity of these symptoms is essential to the recovery process, the center also values the long view on treatment. When a survivor recovers his or her voice, this is a political act of demonstrating to the torturing regime that they failed to silence or incapacitate the survivor. For example, although clients who bring lawsuits against torturers enter a public, prolonged, and emotionally taxing process, they have reported significant therapeutic gains from confronting the perpetrators in a federal courtroom where juries have ruled in the survivor's favor. The survivor as plaintiff often pursues this line of justice to honor the memory of so many who did not survive, reclaiming the path of social justice begun long before their persecution. Many clients, even after their lives are more stable and secure, continue to exercise power in meaningful ways. Accompanying clients in their goal to reclaim justice is a rich and complex process. Many of us who know and work with survivors have ourselves been transformed by their experiences of profound social engagement.

CULTURAL CONTEXT OF TREATMENT

Many of our early clients from Latin America and Southeast Asia came from cultures that valued the collective over the individual. They expressed themselves in the collective "we" and had always lived with extended family before fleeing their country. We considered the importance of the survivor's role in family and community, and brought clinical intervention into those dimensions. Long-term group work with both Cambodian women and Guatemalan exiles also involved seeking assistance from the community to help reframe cultural concepts and incorporating expressive therapies to facilitate the therapeutic process and engage the wider community.

CASE STUDY: CAMBODIAN WOMEN'S GROUP

The Cambodian women who had been tortured and raped by soldiers of the Khmer Rouge understood their experience in the context of karma, a Buddhist concept of cause and effect that asserts one's past actions are the cause of present circumstances. The women felt deeply responsible for their own suffering and believed it was directly related to terrible acts committed in past lives. Furthermore, they did not want to talk about it. Pat Robin, a volunteer psychologist, sought consultation from the center's then director, Antonio Martínez. Together, they invited cultural experts to help them overcome these obstacles to treatment. One was an academic who met with the clinical committee and offered to reframe the women's interpretation of karma. Rather than having had past lives as terrible people, they were likely to have been diligent caregivers in their communities, which explained why they needed to allow others to care for them in this lifetime.

A Buddhist monk in the community was consulted about how to work with the women when they did not wish to talk about their trauma in Western fashion. He shared a parable about the need to follow the river as it bends, suggesting that clinicians needed to adapt to the group's inclinations even if it meant forging a new path. The group eventually worked with a local dancer/choreographer Jan Erkert to create "Turn Her White with Stones," a dance piece where the women were able to incorporate their stories and traditional rituals into the choreography and finally into a dance, which was performed by an Erkert Company dancer at Columbia College. The women's group also collaborated with a drama therapist to produce a theatrical piece on their survival and resilience under the Khmer Rouge. The women created a dark, narrow maze through which individuals, escorted by the women, entered the theater. They led the audience members to their seats in this way to convey a sense of the fear and confusion the women had felt in refugee camps. With attention to movement and narrative, the women collectively faced and re-shaped traumatic memory with a greater sense of control, and they also were able to illustrate their stories to a wide community audience. This acknowledgement of their experience was very meaningful to them.

CASE STUDY: GUATEMALAN GROUP

Mario González, a Guatemalan psychotherapist and long-standing staff member, who understood the political culture of resistance and mistrust, organized a Guatemalan group of men and women in the late 1980s and later worked together with Antonio Martínez as co-facilitator of the group. Beginning in a church basement, the group later rotated meeting in each member's home, a step that drew members together as well as helped them feel safe. Trust and security were fleeting for Guatemalans in that period when the approval rate for political asylum was less than 1 percent (INS *Year-book*, 1984) and the U.S. government was funding the brutal dictatorship. The early goals were to break the isolation members were experiencing and to rebuild the sense of community they had lost in exile. The group received support from the larger community, including Casa Guatemala and Su Casa, a Catholic Worker house. Group meetings were always followed by informal social gatherings in spirited Guatemalan fashion. The group transitioned from previous discussions of traumatic material to lighter conversation in a relaxed setting, nourished by the presence of children, spouses, friends, music, dance, and traditional food.

In 1990 group members expressed concern about their children dealing with the effects of trauma, loss, and dislocation. New volunteers were recruited to meet with the children while the parents met in a separate room. This new group incorporated therapeutic activities to support the children's identity as Guatemalan as well as help them cope with the challenging transitions to life in a large North American city. As children of survivors, the young group members carried their own suffering. The group members developed a distinct role in the community, where they contributed to the cultural and political activities through traditional Maya dance, theater, and art; they named themselves Konojel Junam (All Together). They also worked with Jan Erkert and performed a piece of their own design, "Jornadas de Esperanza" (Journeys of Hope) to a full house at the Harold Washington Library.

After several years of meeting together and moving through distinct stages, the adult group focused on an oral history project to bring validation to their experiences and raise awareness about the human rights situation in Guatemala. The group had collected testimonies of members in the form of life narratives rather than focusing solely on traumatic events. They received funding for one year from the Illinois Humanities Council to present a series of public presentations they named "Twelve Parallel Lives." Each narrative represented a sector of Guatemalan civil society targeted by the repression. The series of presentations, which took place in public spaces such as the Chicago Cultural Center, universities, and bookstores, included an introduction, reading of one narrative by someone other than the author, discussion facilitated by a center volunteer with questions from the audience, and closing with a marimba and traditional dance by Konojel Junam. A community arts group created a series of paintings and prints inspired by the narratives and donated the image used on the flyer. The Guatemalan community actively participated and donated traditional food. Community support and validation was meaningful to the group, and Chicagoans benefited from the opportunity to learn directly and personally about the human rights situation in Guatemala.

INNOVATIONS

This section introduces ways in which the center's program has and continues to evolve to meet the needs of our clients. Whether challenged by changes in funding, demographics, or shifts in immigration policy, the center remains committed to develop and test creative responses.

A Community Organization

The Marjorie Kovler Center developed an individualized approach to treatment that is nonhierarchical, noninstitutional, and nongovernmental, and its organizational structure mirrored this approach. The internal structure and spirit of the center's organization of staff and volunteers remains basically horizontal. Everyone, from interns to senior directors, is encouraged to contribute ideas and opinions, make coffee, wash dishes, and mop up when necessary. Clear and direct communication is valued over chain-of-command style. Our clients tend to be hypersensitive to the power dynamics of human behavior—an open, warm community serving tea or coffee to all visitors encourages a return visit and the chance to form bonds of trust and friendship. There is no mistaking how much we have learned and still have to learn from survivors—about forming community, engaging in social action, courageously speaking out against injustice, enduring the losses, and sharing the victories together.

Recent Funding and Growth of the Torture Treatment Program

From 1987 to 2000, the center relied on numerous grants beginning with the initial grant from the Blum-Kovler Foundation that launched the Marjorie Kovler Center. This foundation has continued to support the center's work with an annual donation. Additional sources of funding have included local (e.g., Michael Reese Trust Fund) and national foundations (e.g., Rosenberg Fund for Children) as well as individual donors. Functioning on a small budget that provided two full-time and one half-time staff, the center has depended on volunteers in providing services. Maintaining consistent funding was an ongoing struggle and required administrative coordination of grant writing and reporting. In the mid-1990s, the Marjorie Kovler Center applied for and received funding from the United Nations Voluntary Fund for Victims of Torture. This additional resource has helped fund a staff position that conducts intake assessments.

Minnesota Senators Dave Durenberger and the late Paul Wellstone, a Republican and a Democrat, first introduced the Torture Victims Relief Act (TVRA) in 1994. Enacted in 1998, the TVRA had strong bipartisan support in both the House and the Senate. In 2000, the first year of appropriated funds that implemented the TVRA, the Office of Refugee Resettlement in the Administration for Children and Families awarded four-year grants to seventeen organizations.

The Marjorie Kovler Center was one of the grantees in 2000 and has continued to receive funding through the Torture Victims Relief Act. This meant that almost overnight the center staff increased from three to nine. A stronger infrastructure to support the volunteer network was a direct outgrowth of this funding, and the capacity to provide services to torture survivors doubled within twelve months.

Current Case Management and Community-Building Efforts

Case management and volunteer coordination were essential components of the initial design of the center. The growth in 2000 allowed for case management to build a team (two full-time staff and two full-time volunteers). They have built a unique model of service provision, linking client needs with skilled volunteers. Rather than a traditional case management model, whereby each is responsible for coordinating services for a set caseload of clients, the model follows a trans-disciplinary approach. As such, roles and responsibilities for each service (e.g., coordination of health appointments, forensic exams, ESL tutoring, special events) are rotated, resulting in greater knowledge of services and resources by the team and greater accessibility for clients.

Nurturing Familiar Occupations: Farms and Bees

Historically, the Marjorie Kovler Center has been committed to community building, and case management supports this through organized trips and activities. The case management team solicits free tickets and coordinates client groups to attend local cultural events, many relating to the clients' culture and others expanding exposure to local resources. Community building expanded beyond the Chicago city limits when a volunteer, Tom Spaulding, invited the center's clients and staff to visit a rural farm, Angelic Organics. Here, clients had the opportunity to participate in farm tasks and specialized workshops. The farm held special meaning for clients who reconnected with positive experiences and memories from their home countries. As a Guatemalan woman shared, "You can see many farms, but none invite you in. Here you feel at home."

After trips to the farm, clients expressed the wish to return. This inspired the development of a local urban farming project where clients could use their agricultural skills and experience connection with the earth in their own neighborhood. With staff support and resources from the Angelic Organics Learning Center, the center began collaborations with the Chicago Waldorf School, and clients have been planting and tending their organic garden located only two blocks away. This urban farm project also promoted the development of a rooftop apiary at the center, with honeybees as the "livestock." Clients have the opportunity to harvest honey and tend to the bees—an occupation familiar to many— under the guidance of volunteer, Mirsad Spahovic, who was a beekeeper for twenty years in his native Bosnia.

Nourishing Universal Rituals: International Cooking Group

Vegetable produce from the garden and honey from the roof are used every other week by the international cooking group. At each group meeting, a client oversees preparation of a meal from his or her home country, and group members follow the client's lead, pitching in with chopping, sautéing, and seasoning, culminating with sitting down to share and enjoy a delicious meal. Participation in familiar occupations and engagement in universal rituals have served to support rebuilding of community, evidenced by high turnout and sustained membership in these groups.

Dignified Work

Vocational assessment of a survivor's skills is another aspect of joint case management and occupational therapy services offered at the center. An Occupational History assessment is conducted when a client is referred to occupational therapy (OT). This assessment considers the interests, skills, and strengths of the client in the home country as well as adaptation to the new environment. OT services are primarily concerned with how the sequelae of torture, displacement, and acculturation affect a survivor's ability to perform meaningful occupational roles in the domains of self-care, leisure, and work within challenging environments that systemically restrict occupational opportunities. The new environments confronted by refugees and asylum seekers often foster "occupational deprivation," which prevents access to potential opportunities and inhibits the essential need for belonging (F. Kronenberg, N. Pollard, 2005; G. Whiteford, 2005). The most predominant environmental obstacles identified by clients in the OT assessment include (1) barriers to employment, such as long waits for work authorization, lack of readily available jobs, difficulty transferring existing skills, and limited access to further education; (2) isolation, including lack of social opportunities that feel safe and culturally comfortable as well as homesickness; and (3) diminished status secondary to the loss of occupational roles, for example, in the role as family provider, parent, or community leader. The occupational therapist works closely with case managers who assist with specific vocational tasks, including creating a résumé, filling out job applications, practicing for interviews, and obtaining educational equivalencies.

The paucity of culturally familiar social opportunities and opportunities for enhancing skills is addressed through group activity interventions such as community outings, the international cooking group, urban farming groups, and links to appropriate community resources. These services, designed to meet needs that clients identify, demonstrate that engagement in positive experiences offers a means for clients to use their skills and capacity to create safe connections and communities. These have taught us that engagement in meaningful experiences can be transformative.

CURRENT DEMOGRAPHICS

The Marjorie Kovler Center has sought to transform programming and services in response to survivors' needs and systemic environmental changes. The demographics of countries represented have shifted dramatically over the past twenty years. The number of survivors receiving services at the Marjorie Kovler Center has also steadily increased with each year. Tables 9.1 through 9.4 indicate the current demographics of survivors receiving services at the center, referral sources, and volunteer valuations.

Table 9.1   Participant Demographic Information for Fiscal Year 2007

		Age	No.	%	World region (nationality):		
Persons served: 330		0–10	5	1%	Africa	209	63%
Female	164 (50%)	11–20	23	7%	Latin America	50	15%
Male	166 (50%)	21–30	89	27%	Asia	35	11%
Survivor status:		31–40	117	35%	Europe	15	5%
Torture survivors	284 (86%)	41–50	61	18%	Middle East	14	4%
Family members	46 (14%)	51–60	30	9%	North America	5	2%
		61–70	7	2%			

Source: 2007 Annual Report, Marjorie Kovler Center of Heartland Alliance.

CONCLUSION

As demographics shift in response to worldwide conflicts, the lessons learned about providing a healing environment for survivors of torture continue. A remarkable journey has been undertaken in Chicago through the work of the Marjorie Kovler Center. This chapter shared snapshots of the journey and provided insights into the necessary social conscience and community effort that go into creating a response to a social illness such as torture. The journey is bittersweet. We are happy and saddened by our twenty-year efforts to assist survivors of torture in rebuilding their lives. It is our sincere wish to close our doors one day because our services are no longer needed—that torture is no longer practiced in the world we share.

Table 9.2   Nationalities Served in Fiscal Year 2007 (total 53)

Afghanistan	1	Eritrea	19	Nigeria	2
Albania	6	Ethiopia	15	Pakistan	2
Angola	4	Guatemala	27	Rwanda	3
Benin	1	Guinea	5	Senegal	1
Bosnia-Herzegovina	5	Haiti	4	Sierra Leone	1
Bulgaria	1	Honduras	1	Somalia	5
Burkina Faso	2	India	1	Sri Lanka	1
Burundi	2	Indonesia	1	Sudan	8
Cambodia	1	Iran	2	Thailand	1
Cameroon	33	Iraq	3	Tibet	1
Chad	5	Kenya	4	Togo	43
Chile	1	Kosovo	3	Tunisia	4
Colombia	9	Liberia	7	Turkey	4
Congo	13	Malawi	2	Uganda	11
Congo (DRC)	24	Mauritania	3	United States	5
Cote d'Ivoire	2	Mexico	1	Vietnam	15
Ecuador	6	Mongolia	1	Zimbabwe	2
El Salvador	5	Nepal	1	Total	53

Source: 2007 Annual Report, Marjorie Kovler Center of Heartland Alliance.

Table 9.3   Referral Sources in Fiscal Year 2007

Source of Referrals	Oct. 2006–Sept. 2007
Mutual Aid Associations	8
Ethnic/Religious Communities	38
Hospitals/Clinics	3
Lawyers/NIJC	43
Other	8
TOTAL	**100**

Source: Year-end Data Report, Marjorie Kovler Center of Heartland Alliance.

BIOGRAPHIES

Rev. Dr. Sid Mohn is president of Heartland Alliance for Human Needs & Human Rights, a service-based human rights organization focused on investments and solutions to help the most poor and vulnerable in our society succeed. He joined the organization in 1980, and also serves as president of its three partners: Heartland Housing, Heartland Health Outreach, and Heartland Human Care Services. Prior to his tenure at Heartland Alliance, he held positions with the Chicago Urban League, the Kane/DeKalb Counties Employment and Training Consortium, International Documentation, and La Casa Center. Dr. Mohn is a graduate of Temple University, received his Master of Divinity from the School of Theology at Claremont, California, and his doctorate from McCormick Theological Seminary in Chicago. He is a United Church of Christ clergyperson and a member of the Order of Ecumenical Franciscans. Dr. Mohn is past chair of the board of directors of the National Immigration Forum and is a member of the board of directors of International Social Services U.S. Committee for Refugees, Chicago Commission on Human Relations, and Global Chicago.

Rev. Craig Mousin has been the university ombudsperson at DePaul University since 2001. He received his BS *cum laude* from Johns Hopkins University, his JD with honors from the University of Illinois, and his MDiv from Chicago

Table 9.4   Volunteer Hours and Valuation in Fiscal Year 2006

Volunteers	Hours	Rate	Value
Amate and Mennonite Volunteers	4,800	$12	$57,600
Counseling by trainees	1,904	$50	$95,200
Clinical professionals	1,588	$100	$158,800
Interpreters	219	$40	$8,760
Case Management volunteers	810	$10	$8,100
Total	9,231		$328,460

Source: 2007 Annual Report, Marjorie Kovler Center of Heartland Alliance.

Theological Seminary. He joined the College of Law faculty in 1990, and served as the executive director of the Center for Church/State Studies until 2003, and co-director from 2004–07. He is an associate editor of the center's publication, *Religious Organizations in the United States: A Study of Identity, Liberty and the Law* (Carolina Academic Press, 2006). He co-founded and continues to co-direct the center's Interfaith Family Mediation Program. He has taught in DePaul's School for New Learning, the Religious Studies Department, the College of Liberal Arts and Sciences, and in DePaul's Peace Minor program. He has also taught immigration law and policy as an adjunct law professor at the University of Illinois College of Law. Rev. Mousin began practicing labor law at Seyfarth, Shaw, Fairweather & Geraldson in 1978. In 1984 he founded and directed the Midwest Immigrant Rights Center, a provider of legal assistance to refugees, which has since become the National Immigrant Justice Center. He also directed legal services for Travelers & Immigrants Aid between 1986 and 1990. He helped found DePaul College of Law's Asylum and Immigration Legal Clinic. Rev. Mousin was ordained by the United Church of Christ in 1989. He has served as an associate pastor at Wellington Avenue U.C.C. and was a founding pastor of the DePaul Ecumenical Gathering (1996–2001). Rev. Mousin is the secretary of the board of trustees of the Chicago Theological Seminary. In addition, he is member of the leadership council of the National Immigrant Justice Center and the Immigration Project of Downstate Illinois. Both provide legal services to immigrants and refugees. He previously served on the Illinois Equal Justice Project of the Chicago and Illinois State Bar associations.

Edwin Silverman, PhD, received his bachelor's degree from Purdue University and his doctorate from Northwestern University. He has been employed by the State of Illinois since 1973. From 1976 until 1997, he administered the Illinois Refugee Resettlement Program, which became part of the Illinois Department of Public Aid in 1980. In 1997 the program became part of the Illinois Department of Human Services, and he continues to administer it as the chief of the Bureau of Refugee & Immigrant Services. He has actively participated in the development of program and policy at the federal level, and contributed to the drafting of the Refugee Act. He is president emeritus and active on the executive board for SCORR, the national affiliation of State Coordinators of Refugee Resettlement. He has received awards from the federal government, the United Nations High Commissioner for Refugees (UNHCR), and various community groups for his contributions to the area of refugee resettlement. He also received the assistant secretary's Public Service Award from DHHS and was one of five national recipients in 1995 of the American Society for Public Administration's National Public Service Award.

Thomas Hollon, PhD, received his doctorate in clinical psychology in 1955 from Catholic University and earned the Diplomate in Clinical Psychology from the American Board of Professional Psychology in 1961. Dr. Hollon served on the staff of Rockford Memorial Hospital, on the boards of the Rock River Valley Mental Health Association and the Shelter Care Ministries (serving the homeless mentally ill), and on the faculties of DePaul University and the University of

Illinois College of Medicine. He served as president of the Illinois Psychological Association, chair of its Social Issues Section, and its representative to the council of the American Psychological Association. On a pro bono basis, Dr. Hollon served as chair of the Citizens Advisory Council of Illinois Mental Health Region 1-A and of the Winnebago County Health Planning Committee; president of the local chapter of United Cerebral Palsy; and member of the Illinois Human Rights Authority, the Suicide Prevention Council, the Health Professional Network of Amnesty International, and the Psychologists for Social Responsibility. Finally, Dr. Hollon was central to organizing the national Conference on Victims of Torture at the University of Chicago in 1987, co-sponsored by the IPA, Cook County Hospital, and Amnesty International. He then led the way the following year to the establishment of the Marjorie Kovler Center for the Treatment of Survivors of Torture under the aegis of Travelers & Immigrants Aid and IPA, and he served for the center's first eight years as a volunteer therapist and the chair of its Executive Clinical Committee.

Susana Jiménez Schlesinger, PhD, is a clinical psychologist who earned her doctorate in counseling psychology from Loyola University in 1983. She taught at Loyola University, the Institute for Christian Ministries at the University of San Diego, Central YMCA College, and the National College of Education in Evanston, IL. She served as a consulting psychologist with the Head Start Program, Enhanced Family Childcare Homes Program of El Valor, and the Boys & Girls Clubs of Chicago, and continues her longstanding private practice. She served as chair of the Social Responsibility Section for the Illinois Psychological Association from 1994–97 and is presently chair of their Peer Assistance Committee and liaison for Ethnic/Minority Issues. She also represents the IPA on the Coalition of Illinois Counselor Organizations Steering Committee for the Prevention of Violence in Schools. She volunteered as a Spanish-speaking psychologist at the John Garfield School's Family Enrichment Program. Finally, she was a founding member of the Marjorie Kovler Center, served on its Executive Clinical Committee, and was a pro bono bilingual psychotherapist.

Irene Martínez, MD, is an internist at John Stroger, Jr. Hospital of Cook County in the Division of General Medicine and is a member of the Preventive Medicine Section. A native of Córdoba, Argentina, she graduated from medical school in 1980. Dr. Martínez was a *desaparecida*/political prisoner during Argentina's "Dirty War." She was an Amnesty International prisoner of conscience and moved to the United States after she was released from prison. In the mid-1980s, Dr. Martínez became an advocate for torture survivors, recognizing their special needs from her own experiences. She was one of the founding members of the Marjorie Kovler Center of Heartland Alliance in Chicago, where she continues to contribute her expertise. She strongly encourages the practice of artistic expression to be part of the healing process and disease prevention. Dr. Martínez enjoys painting, writing, dancing, and caring for her daughter

Sr. Sheila Lyne, RSM, is president and chief executive officer of Mercy Hospital & Medical Center, Chicago's first hospital. Sister Sheila holds a master degree in psychiatric nursing from St. Xavier University and an MBA from the University of Chicago. Sr. Sheila's association with Mercy dates back to 1958 when she was a student nurse. In 1970 Sister Sheila was appointed director of Mercy's Diagnostic and Treatment Center. She was promoted from this position to assistant vice president and director of human resources. As vice president, Sister Sheila honed her skills and solidified her role as a leader within the organization. She was named acting president in October 1976 and president in February 1977. In 1991, she was appointed commissioner of the Chicago Department of Public Health. She was the first woman to hold the position as well as the first non-physician. Since her return to Mercy in December 2000, Sr. Sheila has focused on the development and expansion of Mercy programs and services that respond to the growing communities surrounding the hospital. Sister Sheila is a member of the Sisters of Mercy of the Americas, Regional Community of Chicago, and currently serves on the board of St. Xavier University.

Steven Miles, MD, is professor of medicine at the University of Minnesota Medical School in Minneapolis and is on the faculty of the university's Center for Bioethics. He is board certified in internal medicine and geriatrics, and teaches and practices at the University of Minnesota. Previously, he was assistant professor of medicine and associate director of the Center for Clinical Medical Ethics at the University of Chicago, 1986–89. He has taught in many countries and has served as medical director for the American Refugee Committee for twenty-five years, which has included service as chief medical officer for 45,000 refugees on the Thai-Cambodian border and projects in Sudan, Croatia, Bosnia-Herzogovina, Indonesia, and on the Thai-Burmese border. He has published three books, more than twenty chapters, and 120 peer-reviewed articles on medical ethics, human rights, tropical medicine, end of life care, and geriatric health care.

Antonio Martínez, PhD, is a clinical psychologist and co-founder of the Marjorie Kovler Center, serving as its director for the first seven years. Dr. Martínez earned a PhD in clinical psychology and critical theory, at the University of Massachusetts–Amherst, a masters degree in community social psychology at the University of Puerto Rico–Rio Piedras, and a BA in general studies concentrating in psychology and anthropology at the University of Puerto Rico–Rio Piedras. Presently, he works with the Ambulatory Health Services of Cook County at the Dr. Jorge Prieto Family Health Center in Chicago. Dr. Martínez is also regular trainer for the International Office of Immigration and Naturalization Services Asylum Division at the Federal Law Enforcement Center in Glencoe, GA. He has addressed the chief justices of the Immigration and Naturalization Service at their national annual conference regarding issues of torture and credibility. Dr. Martínez has lectured about trauma and the severe consequences of abuse and torture in the United States, Mexico, Guatemala, Costa Rica, Panama, Puerto Rico, Chile, Argentina, London, and Nepal, and Colombia. He also provided expert testimony for the People's Law Office representing four survivors of police torture in Chicago under Commander Burge. He received several awards recognizing his work in the area of trauma induced by torture, including the Norma Jean Collins Award, the

Chicago Community Trust Fellowship, and the UNESCO Chair for Peace. He had the honor of being a consultant to actress Glenn Close in her Toni Award performance as Paulina, a torture survivor, in the Broadway play *Death and the Maiden*. He is an advocate of a systemic and developmental model for the accompaniment of survivors of torture. His philosophy of treatment was published by the Universidad Pontificia Javeriana and the Center Terres des Homes, Italia, Centro de Acompañamiento y Atención Psicosocial Terres des Hommes Colombia, Bogota 2004, "Modelo de solidaridad de atención a los sobrevivientes de tortura."

Fertile Soil

This life-giving soil,
On which the sower plows
One furrow after another
Terrace upon terrace
Carefully spreading seeds
With the sole purpose
Of creating a garden teeming with hope,
Watered with her children's tears,
Making her womb a more fertile place.

In this soil,
The seasons of the year are lived daily.
In autumn,
Fallen branches gently gathered
Are carried as fertilizer to the garden,
And in the gentle silence of the night,
Our hearts' anguish is softened.
When winter arrives,
And suffering's cold overtakes us,
The warm embrace and the sower's own suffering lift us.
With spring we see
The rebirth of life,
A restlessness revealed,
And a great desire to smell the scent
Of newness, of beauty and of what has been lost.
And beneath the summer's burning sun
Arises the steep slope of loneliness.
Each somber and bitter step
Accompanied by exile and torture
But soothed by mother earth's lifeblood.

On this soil,
When the tempest, the thunders, the forests' lament
Overpower the depth of your being
Snatching your breath and your reason for living,
Someone is ever present to remind you

Of the dance of the winds over the rivers,
Of the joyous and colorful song of the birds,
And of the shining rainbow
Revealing her brightness after the storm.

This fertile soil
Is indeed nurtured with love,
Her sowers keeping ignited
The eternal flame of unconditional commitment,
Defying the silence of a dark day,
Knowing that with the coming of the dawn
They will see the sun rise and,
With the delicate touch of the dew,
Will bring forth the sweet fragrance
of solidarity, respect and mutual understanding.

Beautiful soil, thank you.
For upon entering your space
The dawn springs up in us,
Though perhaps for only a moment,
And from your womb sprout
Peace, goodness, warmth, compassion.
For the fruit of your harvest is love.
Thank you, sowers,
For your difficult and steadfast work.
Graced by your dedication and affection,
From this soil we taste the sweetest of all nectars.

     Matilde De la Sierra
     Chicago, IL
     August 25, 2007

     Dedicated to Kovler Center
     On its twentieth anniversary

Tierra Fértil

Esta tierra productiva,
en donde el sembrador hace un surco y otro surco,
tablón tras tablón esparciendo las semillas cuidadosamente;
con el único propósito de construir una huerta llena de esperanza.
Es una tierra regada con el llanto de sus hijos;
llanto que hace de su vientre un lugar más fecundo.

Esta tierra en donde las estaciones del año
se viven a diario.
En el otoño,
las ramas caídas recogidas gentilmente
son llevadas al huerto para que sirvan de abono,

y en el silencio de la noche
el dolor de nuestros corazones se hace suave.
Cuando el invierno llega,
y el frío del sufrir se apodera de nosotros,
el abrazo cálido y el mismo sufrir del sembrador nos levanta.
Con la primavera,
vemos el renacer de la vida,
con una inquietud descubierta,
con un gran deseo de sentir el aroma de lo nuevo,
de lo bello, de lo perdido.
Y bajo el candente sol del verano,
se sube la cuesta de la soledad,
con paso sordo y amargo,
acompañado por el destierro y la tortura;
pero atenuado por la sangre vital de la madre tierra.

En esta tierra;
cuando la tempestad, los truenos, el lamento de los bosques
dominan lo más profundo de tu ser,
siempre existe alguien que te recuerda
de la danza de los vientos sobre los rios,
del canto alegre y vívido de los pájaros,
y el arco iris reluciente que deja ver
su brillantez después de la tormenta.

Esta tierra fértil realmente está tratada con amor.
Sus sembradores mantienen encendida
la llama perenne de entrega incondicional;
desafiando el silencio de un día obscuro
a sabiendas que a la espera de la madrugada
se vislumbrará la salida del sol y,
junto al roce delicado del rocío,
traerán el perfume de la solidaridad,
el respeto y la mutua comprensión.

Tierra bella, gracias.
Porque al entrar en tu espacio nace en nosotros,
aunque sea por un instante, la aurora,
porque de tu vientre germinan
la paz, la bondad, la cordialidad, la compasión;
porque el fruto de tu cosecha es el amor.
Gracias sembradores
por su trabajo arduo y continuo.
Porque por su dedicación y cariño,
de esta tierra se obtienen los mejores néctares.

Matilde De la Sierra
Chicago, IL
Agosto 25, 2007

Dedicado a Kovler Center
Por su 20mo aniversario
(Reprinted with permission.)

ORGANIZATIONAL SNAPSHOT

Organization: Marjorie Kovler Center

Founder/Executive Director: Mary Fabri

Mission/Description: The Kovler Center provides comprehensive, community-based services in which survivors work together with staff and volunteers to identify needs and overcome obstacles to healing. Services include mental health (individual or group psychotherapy, counseling, psychiatric services, and a range of culturally appropriate services on-site in the community), health care (primary health care and specialized medical treatment by medical professionals specifically trained to work with torture survivors), case management (access to community resources, including tutoring, ESL, food, transportation, special events), interpretation and translation (bridging cultural and linguistic barriers in medical, mental health, and community settings), and legal referral (referral and collaboration with immigration attorneys and organizations).

Website: http://www.heartlandalliance.org/kovler/index.html

Address: The Marjorie Kovler Center of Heartland Alliance

1331 West Albion

Chicago, IL 60626

Phone: 773.751.4045

Fax: 773.381.4073

E-mail: MFabri@heartlandalliance.org

REFERENCES

Bogner, D., Herlihy, J., & Brewin, C. R. (2007). Impact of sexual violence on disclosure during home office interviews. *British Journal of Psychiatry, 191*(2), 75–81.

Bronfenbrenner, U. (1979). *The ecology of human development.* Cambridge: Harvard University Press.

Conroy, J. (2001). *Unspeakable acts, ordinary people: The dynamics of torture.* New York: Alfred A. Knopf.

Emergency Supplemental Appropriations Act for Defense, the Global War on Terror, and Tsunami Relief, 2005. Public Law 109-13, 109th Congress (May 11, 2005). Retrieved October 9, 2007, from http://www.epic.org/privacy/id_cards/real_id_act.pdf.

Fabri, M. (2001). Reconstructing safety: Adjustments to the therapeutic frame in the treatment of survivors of political torture. *Professional Psychology: Research & Practice, 32*(5), 452–457.

Herman, J. L. (1992). *Trauma and recovery.* New York: Basic Books.

Immigration and Naturalization Service. (1984). *Statistical yearbook* (Table 3.3, p. 77). Washington DC: U.S. Government Printing Office.

Kronenberg, F., Pollard, N. (2005). Overcoming occupational apartheid: A preliminary exploration of the political nature of occupational therapy. In F. Kronenberg, S. Algado, N. Pollard (Eds.). *Occupational therapy without borders: Learning from the spirit of survivors* (pp. 58–86). New York: Elsevier.

Lifton, R. J. (2004). Doctors and torture. *New England Journal of Medicine, 351*(5), 415–416.

McAndrews, R. K. (2002). Asylum Law Reform. *New England Journal of International & Comparative Law, 8:*1, pp. 103–124.

Martin-Baró, I. (1994). *Writings for a liberation psychology* (A. Aron, S. Corne, eds.). Cambridge: Harvard University Press.

National Immigrant Justice Center (n.d.). *National immigrant justice center: Home.* Retrieved October 7, 2007, from http://www.immigrantjustice.org/.

Office of the United High Commissioner for Human Rights (December 10, 1984). *United Nations Convention against torture and other cruel, inhuman or degrading treatment or punishment.* Retrieved October 7, 2007, from http://www.ohchr.org/english/law/cat.htm.

Reagan, R. (May 9, 1984). Televised speech, Retrieved October 1, 2007, from http://www.pbs.org/wgbh/amex/reagan/timeline/index_4.html.

Scarry, E. (1985). *The body in pain: The making and unmaking of the world.* New York: Oxford University Press.

Timmerman, J. (1981). *Prisoner without a name, cell without a number.* New York: Alfred A. Knopf.

Whiteford, G. (2005). Understanding the occupational deprivation of refugees: A case study from Kosovo. *Canadian Journal of Occupational Therapy, 72*(2), 78–88.

Wolf, E. R. (1999). *Envisioning power: Ideologies of dominance and crisis.* Berkeley: University of California Press.

10

International Center on Responses to Catastrophes

Stevan Weine

For the past fifteen years, I have conducted a program of services research concerning understanding and helping with the psychosocial needs of families impacted by the global catastrophes of war and forced migration. Since 2002, I have also led efforts at the University of Illinois–Chicago's International Center on Responses to Catastrophes, to build an academic context for interdisciplinary approaches to services research concerning contemporary global catastrophes. This chapter describes this research and reflects on key aspects of the work including family resilience, community collaboration, services, cultural theory, and ethnography.

NEED FOR BROADER PERSPECTIVES

Diffuse are the workings of violence and power.

—W. G. Sebald (2003)

When I talk with those who have survived war and have become refugees or forced migrants, they tell me about the crushing problems they have encountered, which may include combat, siege, imprisonment, murders, atrocities, poverty, loss of their homes and communities, separation from family, loss of opportunities, health problems, and social and cultural isolation. But often enough, they also express hopes for the future, which are often focused on the young. We all wish we could provide them with what they need to improve their lives, be it better housing, jobs, schools, or neighborhoods, or just help them make it through a lonesome day.

One thing that can be done to help is research. Research is a way of rigorously documenting these people's experiences and systematically trying to understand how to offer effective help, perhaps through psychosocial interventions. We do this work because they deserve it, and because we believe the knowledge gained through research can make a difference in the helping efforts that either are, or could be, offered. Research with families impacted by war and forced migration is especially needed given the complexity of their situations, the intractability of some of the difficulties that they face, and the varied ways they manage to survive.

For the past fifteen years, I have been committed to helping families impacted by war and forced migration both through providing community-based services and through conducting investigations that better clarify how psychosocial interventions might be useful in addressing some of the difficulties that these families and we prioritize. I decided to do both service provision and research having encountered too many situations where the intent to do good through services has not resulted in demonstrable benefit to those in need. I am also acutely aware that when academics conduct investigations with no apparent links to efforts to help, this may also be problematic. At best, the efforts at service provision and services research operate synergistically: helping and learning can go hand in hand.

What bothers me is that even if I can do this research, it by no means guarantees that policymakers and programs in governments and nongovernmental organizations (NGOs) will pay attention. So one chooses to do investigations that seem to have a reasonable chance of convincing decision makers to help affected families and communities. Sometimes I want to respond by studying every catastrophe that crosses my path; however, it would be foolish to try to do that. Thus, I have worked at being more disciplined, approaching catastrophes by conducting what may be called a program of services research.

In conducting services research with families impacted by war and forced migration, one key challenge has been to set a broad interdisciplinary framework for this work that adequately addresses people coming from different geographical regions and cultures, out of different war and forced-migration experiences, and thus facing different mental and physical health problems, with different needs, strengths, and meanings. After having variously used the terms war, torture, refugee, genocide, migrant, poverty, and pandemic to define each situation, we have often used the term "catastrophes" as a reasonable framing device for the work that we have been doing. Catastrophes refer to wide-scale events, including human-made conflicts, pandemics, and natural disasters, which result in massive destruction, losses, and distress. Our work has focused primarily on human-made events, often related to war. Furthermore, since many of these events take place in global environments that involve cross-border and cross-cultural processes, we have sometimes used the term "global catastrophes."

Global catastrophes present a complex array of experiences and outcomes that emanate from events of mass violence, deprivation, displacement, and disease that are associated with long-term social instability. Global catastrophes exact grave tolls on individuals, families, communities, and societies. The variety of responses to such tragic events that exist in assortments of services, policies, and practices are too often fragmented, short term, and not supportive of local communities and cultures.

I came to the issue of global catastrophes from the trauma mental health field. It was through my experience leading the efforts to write International Trauma Training Guidelines for the International Society for Traumatic Stress Studies in the late 1990s that I saw just how wed the trauma mental health field has been to individual, psychopathological, and cognitive models. Through the consensus guidelines we developed (Weine et al., 2002), we hoped to change the attitudes and behaviors of professional experts who conduct international trauma trainings by encouraging them to adapt approaches that were more contextually broad. Our success was at best mixed, I believe, in part because the trauma mental health field has had so few constructs and methods to work at levels other than the individual, the psychopathological, and the cognitive. This impacted my research career by making me further commit to a services research approach, which emphasized other levels of focus for services and research, especially family, community, culture, and resilience. To learn more about these areas, I had to go outside the refugee trauma literature to learn from other literatures such as those of prevention, public health, community psychology, and family therapy.

I have seen evidence, not only from the trauma mental health field, that investigations of catastrophes are too often approached within one sector, or from the perspective of a single discipline. Additionally, there is little empirical knowledge that attempts to understand the processes of vulnerability and resilience at the levels of families, communities, cultures, systems, and societies. Research into these experiences requires innovative perspectives that regard catastrophes as part of broader public health, social, cultural, and political crises. For governments and NGOs to develop and implement more effective helping efforts, I believe these dimensions must be better comprehended.

I recognize that the term catastrophe is not without its disadvantages. In the era of 9/11 and Hurricane Katrina, when catastrophes appear regularly on the mass media, the term catastrophe has come to be associated with events that are deeply concentrated in time and require emergency and short-term responses. When I use catastrophes, I do not mean to imply any such restrictions in time or scope. Indeed, many catastrophes are prolonged, as are their ongoing and evolving consequences for individuals, families, communities, and societies, requiring long-term responses. Although there still exists some unease around the use of this term, we have found that it has been productive in building an interdisciplinary space in academic medicine within which it was possible to build knowledge that informs multisectoral helping efforts for families impacted by war and forced migration.

A PROGRAM OF RESEARCH

For the past fifteen years, I have led a program of services research designed to help families and communities that have endured several different types of global catastrophes. This program began at the time of ethnic cleansing in Bosnia-Herzegovina in 1992, with a focus on the issue of mental health services for

Bosnian refugees in the United States, and extended into mental health services issues in post-conflict countries of Bosnia-Herzegovina and Kosovo. Beginning in 2001, this program of research expanded to focus on HIV/AIDS in predominately Muslim postwar societies (Kosovo and Tajikistan) because we found this was a priority public health issue that was not being comprehensively addressed or investigated. It has also expanded to focus on teenage refugees and their families from African countries, including Liberia and Burundi, now in the United States. To date, this work has been supported by multiple funders, including Yale University, the University of Illinois–Chicago (UIC), the State of Illinois Department of Human Services, the Ministry of Health of Kosovo, the U.S. Civilian Research & Development Foundation, several private foundations, and four grants from the U.S. National Institute of Mental Health (NIMH).

The overall intent of this program of research has been to (1) conduct studies that scientifically elucidate the basis for helping families impacted by war and forced migration through psychosocial interventions; (2) conduct investigations informed by social sciences and cultural theory of the social and cultural processes shaping families' services experiences; (3) advocate for interdisciplinary research efforts that bridge intervention and cultural realms so as to more adequately address the real-world problems of families impacted by war and forced migration; and (4) assist service organizations in developing programs and policies that are better attuned to the psychosocial needs of families impacted by war and forced migration.

INTERNATIONAL CENTER ON RESPONSES TO CATASTROPHES

Services research concerning families impacted by war and forced migration cannot occur without a proper research environment that provides research infrastructure, collaborators, consultation, training, supervision, mentoring, and resources. This type of research environment has been built through establishing a university-based center. The International Center on Responses to Catastrophes (ICORC) at UIC was established in 2002 in order to advance scholarship and services in this area of contemporary importance for the city of Chicago and the world.

ICORC is a cross-campus unit organized through the Department of Psychiatry and the Office of the Vice Chancellor of Research. Its primary mission is to promote interdisciplinary research and scholarship that contributes to improved helping efforts for those affected by catastrophes. The center is highly interdisciplinary in its approach, with university faculty from collaborating departments and colleges representing mental health and health services, humanities, and social sciences. Vital to the center's work is building domestic and global collaborations with academic, advocacy, and services organizations. ICORC activities have three core realms of focus:

- **Documentary:** to document the human experiencing of global catastrophes through literary and multi-media approaches

- **Ethnographic:** to analyze the cultural and social dimensions of global catastrophes through ethnographic inquiries
- **Intervention:** to conduct innovative, family-focused, and community-based services research on the mental health consequences of global catastrophes

In fulfilling its mission, ICORC

- Conducts interdisciplinary, collaborative and original research on responses to global catastrophes
- Serves as a venue for regular scholarly dialogue on topics central to the documentation and improvement of responses to global catastrophes
- Promotes partnership and collaboration within UIC, as well as with other organizations and institutions conducting research and interventions in this area
- Prepares the next generation of scholars, scientists, documentarians, and policy makers through interdisciplinary education and training

In a subsequent section, I will provide summary descriptions of some of the projects that ICORC has undertaken thus far in fulfillment of this mission. Here, I want to highlight that although I am the author of this text, none of this work that constitutes the program of services research was or could be done alone. It has required many kinds of partnerships with interdisciplinary academics (from other health professions, the humanities, and social sciences), with community leaders, parent advocates, students, and trainees. Many, but not all, of their names are included as co-authors in the publications listed in the references. We think of ICORC as a place where conversations and collaborations that usually do not occur can take place. I have found it to be a helpful, although not uncomplicated, structure within which to work. For example, there is the ongoing concern of how to provide interdisciplinary training and mentoring to beginning investigators who come from different backgrounds and disciplines.

Lest I give the impression that institutional arrangements are the only necessary elements to building a program of services research, allow me to mention a few words about how I became a services researcher. In 2006, when I was asked to speak at a roundtable of community psychologists, the organizer, Professor Ed Trickett of the UIC Department of Psychology, asked me to explain how I became a services researcher focused on these types of global catastrophes. The story that I told emphasized the role of mentoring. As much as I have imagined myself to be treading new paths, I have always known that as a researcher, I depended greatly upon others to help me reach destinations. Even the very things that we call "paths" and "destinations" need to be invented before they can be realized. You need to know that there is a place for you. You have to be able to see that place and the way that will get you there. You have to hope that you can make it. Just seeing or hoping is not enough. You need to actually do things to get there: talk a different talk or walk a different walk. I know that I could not have done any of these things on my own. Over the past twenty-five years, I have had many mentors. I found them in when I was in college, at medical school, completing a psychiatry residency, and serving as a faculty member. These mentors have included poet Allen Ginsberg, psychologist Daniel Levinson, psychiatrist Ivan Pavkovic, family scientist Suzanne Feetham, medical anthropologist Norma Ware, and ethnographer and rhetorician Ralph Cintron. Without my multiple and distinct mentors, I would never have been in a position to conduct a program of services research.

RESEARCH PROJECTS

A program of research is a series of research projects, each building on the ones before and aiming toward a focused understanding of several priority concerns. What follows are descriptions of some of those projects, arranged geographically and chronologically, with the key themes that have organized this work. Although I will not mention all of the names of my collaborators in this overview, it is important to again note that none of these projects were conducted alone. All required scientific and community collaborations in order to succeed.

Bosnian and Kosovar Refugees in the United States

Treatment and Services Studies

I came to services research on refugee and migrant families via posttraumatic stress syndrome (PTSD) research (Weine et al., 1995(a); Weine et al 1995(b)), treatment research, and ethnographic and cultural studies. The treatment studies provided preliminary evidence that both Selective Serotonin Reuptake Inhibitors (Smajkic et al., 2001) and testimony psychotherapy may lead to improvements in PTSD and depressive symptoms, and to improvements in functioning, among refugee adults (Weine et al., 1998). However, what was just as notable was how many refugees chose not to participate in treatment at all or, having received effective treatments, decided to drop out. This fact led us to conduct several studies of refugee mental health services, including a study of access (Weine et al., 2000) and an investigation of the roles of providers' attitudes and approaches in the delivery of effective mental health services for refugees (Weine et al., 2001). This last effort revealed that among service providers, there was substantial misinformation and stigma concerning mental health symptoms of refugees and treatment for those symptoms. It also revealed that providers were not doing enough to educate individual clients, family members, or community members about the effects of trauma on individual and family mental health.

We engaged in extensive ethnographic- and humanities-based studies of Bosnian survivors and their narratives. An ethnographic study of a Bosnian refugee family provided a close, detailed portrayal and analysis of how one refugee family used its own strengths and resources to heal and adjust (Weine et al., 1997). I also pursued book-length studies that focused on the narrative dimensions of survivors and refugees. My first book investigated the Bosnian cultural value of *merhamet,* a self and group concept associated with multiethnic co-existence (Weine, 1999). A second book examined cases and theory concerning the use of survivors' testimonies across several historical contexts and service sectors, drawing upon Mikhail Bakhtin's theory of the dialogic narrative (Weine, 2006). A third book, *Our City of Refuge: Teens, War, and Freedom,* tells the story of teenage refugees from Bosnia-Herzegovina in the city of Chicago (Weine, under review).

Intervention Research with Migrants and Refugees

Insights derived from the aforementioned studies gave us an empirical basis to try to help refugees through focusing on helping their families. This led to developing a family intervention with narrative methods that aimed to improve access to mental health services and other sources of support. The Prevention and Access Intervention for Families (PAIF) was conducted with Bosnian refugee families in Chicago from 1998–2003 by a collaborative, multidisciplinary services research team at UIC (Weine, 1998). This NIMH-funded study investigated a Coffee and Families Education and Support Group (CAFES), which was a time-limited, multiple-family education and support group for Bosnian families. This condition was compared with a control group that received no such intervention. A group of survivors with PTSD and their families were randomly assigned to receive either the intervention or the control condition. Longitudinal assessments occurred every six months for eighteen months to document effects over time postintervention. Results showed that the CAFES multiple-family group was effective (1) in engagement (73%) and retention (Weine et al., 2005(b)); (2) as an access intervention in the overall sample (longitudinal increases in the number of mental health visits [$p < .005$]; both depression [$p < .003$] and family communication [$p < .0159$] enhanced the group's access effect) (Weine et al., in press (b)); and (3) as a preventive intervention (with increased social support in subsamples of males, urban families, and the more highly traumatized) (Weine et al., 2004). Youth CAFES was an adaptation of CAFES to more specifically focus on the needs of teen refugees in Chicago that has been qualitatively studied (Weine et al., 2006). Tea and Families Education and Support (TAFES) was an NIMH-funded adaptation of the CAFES intervention for newly arrived Kosovar refugees in Chicago. The results showed increases in social support and psychiatric service use among participating families (Weine et al., 2003). In sum, these CAFES studies demonstrated that multiple-family groups with families postwar may be effective in increasing networking, knowledge, and communication, and to a lesser extent support. It showed that further investigation of multiple-family groups postwar is warranted, especially research focused on youth.

Joining Multiple-Family Groups

To improve the engagement strategies of preventive interventions for refugee families, this NIMH-funded study used mixed methods to investigate family factors and processes involved in engaging Bosnian refugees in multiple-family support and education groups (Weine, 2001). Refugee families that joined multiple-family groups were distinguished from families that did not in terms of differences in quantitative factors. Families that engaged had previously experienced statistically significant more transitions, more traumas, and more difficulties in adjustment.

Family processes that may be related to multivariate analysis of these quantitative factors in relation to engagement and retention were specified through qualitative investigation (Weine et al., 2005(b)). The findings indicated that engagement may be related not only to factual characteristics of families, but also to family members' perceptions about strategies for responding to adversities. Families that engaged had concerns about traumatic memories that persisted despite avoidant behaviors. However, what they perceived as more of a problem were concerns regarding maintaining the family, supporting their children, and rebuilding their social life. This study underlined the importance of a focus upon engagement in conducting multiple-family groups with families that have experienced adversities related to political violence. Engagement strategies for multiple-family groups should correspond with the underlying family factors and processes by which refugee families manage transitions, traumas, and adjustment difficulties.

Kosovo

Kosovar Family Professional Education Collaborative

In May 2000, the Kosovar Professional Education Collaborative (KFPEC) was founded by Dr. Ferid Agani of the University of Prishtina, Dr. John Rolland of the University of Chicago, and myself (Rolland & Weine, 2000). The KFPEC aimed to support and enhance the family work of Kosovar mental health professionals and to design and implement family-oriented mental health services in Kosovo. The KFPEC chose to build family services centered on a psychoeducational, multiple-family group program for severe mental illness. The KFPEC's work was at the core of the mental health policy of the Kosovar Ministry of Health and its seven regionally based community mental health centers. The objective of one study was to describe the effects of a psychoeducational, multiple-family group program for families of people with severe mental illness in postwar Kosovo (Weine et al., 2005(c)). The subjects were thirty families of people with severe mental illnesses living in two cities in Kosovo. All subjects participated in multiple-family groups and received home visits. The program documented medication compliance, number of psychiatric hospitalizations, family mental health services use, and several other characteristics for the year prior to the groups and the first year of the groups. The families attended an average of 5.5 (out of 7) meetings, and 93 percent of these families attended 4 or more meetings. Comparing the year of the group intervention with the year prior to the intervention, there were multiple significant changes, including decreased hospitalization (p < .0001); increased medication compliance (p < .0001); increased use of combined oral and depot medications (p < .0003); increased family members' use of mental health services (p < .0143). We also conducted ethnographic interviewing and observations with Kosovar and international providers and policymakers (Cintron & Weine, 2004; Weine, Agani, & Cintron, 2003; Weine et al., 2003) and with Kosovar adolescents, family members, and community members regarding HIV/AIDS (Weine et al., 2004). The KFPEC program also provided training for mental health professionals, led to policy change in the Ministry of Health, and resulted in successful dissemination of the multiple-family group program to five other community mental health centers. In addition, KFPEC has a many-year track record in providing contextually sensitive and culturally competent expert training and consultation on building family resilience–based mental health services in Kosovo.

Kosovar Attitudes on Drugs and HIV/AIDS (KADAH)

To specify the sociocultural issues impacting HIV prevention, our team conducted a multi-sited ethnography of illegal drugs and HIV/AIDS in Kosovo that included participant-observation initiatives in schools, community and service sites, and households, and in-depth interviews with Kosovar adolescents and families (Weine et al., 2004). This study specified the opportunities and obstacles for addressing HIV risk behavior associated with families' "practical knowledge" (Scott, 1998). Several forms of families' practical knowledge among parents and youth were identified, labeled, and defined through analysis of field notes and interview transcripts. For example, for Kosovar youth and parents, HIV/AIDS was "not a big problem" compared with the political, economic, social, and cultural crises. Kosovar youth saw HIV/AIDS risks from the vantage point of the "new reality" and its problems of "boredom" and the "cooler" lifestyle. Kosovar parents regarded HIV/AIDS as a "contemporary disease" that "assaults Kosovar tradition." They feared "losing the youth." Other selected sociocultural variables and their impact on key intervention realms were specified. For example, in showing how HIV is being storied by youth and families, it raised the question of how an intervention script should frame HIV/AIDS as a moral discourse. This study identified multiple key sociocultural variables that impacted youth and family behaviors as well as HIV prevention. KADAH also established a functioning interdisciplinary research team that demonstrated the feasibility of conducting ethnographic research concerning HIV/AIDS in Kosovo.

Preliminary Adaptation of KFARY

We developed an intervention, called Kosovar Families Addressing Risks in Youth (KFARY), which is an eight-session, multiple-family group that improves family support and diminishes youth prerisk and risk behaviors for thirteen to sixteen year olds at elevated risk. Seven sessions of multiple-family group interventions, a first version of the KFARY intervention manual, was collaboratively written by the KFARY Kosovar and American investigators by incorporating elements of CAFES, CHAMP (McKay et al., 2000), and Be Proud! Be Responsible! (Jemmott, Jemmott, & Fong, 1998). Then the KFARY manual was "prepiloted" in Kosovo using ethnographic methods designed to analyze evidence regarding the intervention's feasibility and acceptability in the Kosovar context. Specifically, we conducted a session by session run-through over five days with a group of Kosovar families that included fourteen-to-sixteen-year-old children. For each session, the KFARY ethnographic fieldworker took notes of group sessions, as well as of the one-hour daily family feedback sessions and one-hour debriefings of the KFARY facilitators.

This process generated field notes that were then analyzed to yield select session-by-session findings. Several overall conclusions were that (1) families enthusiastically endorsed the KFARY groups as demonstrated in their full attendance and in their statements (e.g., "I didn't imagine that I'd work with my son"); (2) the group will likely be more effective if it targets a subgroup of adolescents at elevated risk, such as those with school problems; (3) engagement and retention will increase for girls and women if babysitting is provided so that they do not have to stay home with younger kids; and (4) some key terms and scripts need to be adapted so as to have appropriate meanings for Kosovars, such as "self-respect," "shame," and "family strengths." On the basis of this evidence, a second version of the KFARY manual was collaboratively written. In sum, prepilot evidence suggests that KFARY is feasible and acceptable to Kosovar youth and families. We are presently seeking funding for a wider implementation and evaluation of the KFARY HIV/AIDS preventive intervention.

Tajikistan

Formation of Collaboration between American and Tajik Researchers

In 2004 I met Dr. Mahbat Bahromov, a physician and public health official from Tajikistan, who was at the time completing a master's degree in international health policy from Brandeis University. We traveled to Tajikistan and secured research permission from government authorities, identified a team of Tajik investigators, conducted site visits, and expanded the collaborative dialogue. Dr. Bahromov was awarded a Muskie Fellowship that allowed him to spend three months with the UIC research team to receive further training in qualitative data analysis and HIV/AIDS prevention research. He then returned to Tajikistan where he became employed in the Tajikistan HIV/AIDS Center as the HIV/AIDS coordinator of the National Coordinating Committee to Fight and Prevent HIV/AIDS, TB, and Malaria in Tajikistan. Dr. Bahromov and I formed a collaboration between ICORC/UIC and the Tajikistan HIV/AIDS Center to focus on the issue of Tajik migrants and HIV/AIDS. Between 2005 and the present, I visited Tajikistan and Moscow multiple times. Several collaborative pilot studies were conducted, including the following two pilot studies.

Pilot Ethnographic Study of Married Male Migrants

This pilot study aimed to preliminarily characterize married male migrants' HIV/AIDS risk and protective knowledge, attitudes, and behaviors, as well as key contextual factors that would likely impede or facilitate a preventive intervention (Weine et al., in press (a)). This was a collaborative, multi-sited ethnography in Moscow that included minimally structured interviews with sixteen subjects and focus groups with a total of fourteen subjects. All invited subjects agreed to participate.

The results suggested that many Tajik male migrant workers in Moscow were having unprotected sex with commercial sex workers. Although some of the migrants had basic knowledge about HIV, the migrants' ability to protect themselves from acquiring HIV is compromised by harsh living and working conditions as a consequence of being unprotected by law in Russia. The migrant workers' experience of being unprotected appears to diminish their self-efficacy in ways that would likely also impede efforts at HIV prevention. For instance, it appears to interfere with their assessment of HIV risk. Tajik male migrant workers in Moscow also have important sources of religious, community, and family support that may facilitate targeted HIV prevention interventions. One example is the value of being the provider and protector of the family. To respond to HIV/AIDS risks amongst Tajik male migrant workers in Moscow, preventive interventions are needed that take into account their harsh living and working conditions and that mobilize existing sources of religious, community, and family support. Further study is needed to more comprehensively characterize HIV/AIDS risk and protective knowledge, attitudes, and behaviors, as well as key contextual factors that would likely impede or facilitate a preventive intervention. These results call for further systematic study of the relationships between masculine norms and HIV risk and preventive behavior. The issues of polygamy, socioeconomic independence, and risk awareness should also be points of focus.

Ethnography, survey research, and intervention development is presently being conducted through the support of the U.S. Civilian Research & Development Foundation. For example, we are collaboratively developing and piloting an intervention for men to be conducted on the four-day train ride from Dushanbe to Moscow.

Pilot Ethnographic Study of Wives of Migrants

This study aimed to examine the experiences of the wives of migrant workers in Moscow and to characterize their HIV/AIDS risk and protective knowledge, attitudes, and behaviors (Weine et al., 2005a). This was a collaborative ethnography in Dushanbe that included minimally structured interviews with twenty wives of migrant workers currently working in Moscow. No person refused to be interviewed. The results documented the wives' concerns over their husbands' safety and health in Moscow, and the many difficulties of wives living without husbands in Tajikistan. Wives give tacit acceptance to their husbands' sexual infidelity in Moscow. In a male-dominated society, gender norms limit wives' abilities to protect themselves or their husbands. The wives had limited awareness of HIV as well as limited ability to speak about sexual activity, HIV/AIDS, and condoms, or to request HIV testing. Wives do not use condoms with their husbands and have no choice but to depend upon the husband's role as protector. Wives turn to their in-laws or to their "circle of friends" for support, but seldom do these relationships focus on HIV/AIDS.

To respond to HIV/AIDS risks among the wives of Tajik male migrant workers in Moscow, preventive interventions should consider enhancing knowledge among wives and seeking feasible ways to empower wives to talk with their husbands about HIV/AIDS risks and protection. We are presently collaboratively developing and piloting a preventive intervention with women from the circles of friends to be conducted through the community-based poly-clinics.

Refugee Youth in the United States

HOMES for Refugee Youth

To address the concerns of refugee adolescents who come from other countries to Chicago, ICORC started Houses of Memories and Expectations (HOMES). In the summer of 2004 and 2005, HOMES recruited fifteen Chicago high school students who were refugees from Afghanistan, Somalia, Sudan, Liberia, Ethiopia, Iraq, Bosnia-Herzegovina, Kosovo, India, Nigeria, and Congo. Visiting artists introduced the teens to writing and photography, and guided them in exploring themes of home, family, war, migration, identity, and the future. The teens explored Uptown neighborhoods, wrote stories, and took photographs. Nerina Muzurovic (a former adolescent refugee) and I assisted them with applying to college and helped them practice writing college essays. The teens built "houses of memories and expectations" that had a gallery exhibition and together compiled a "visual ethnography" of refuge that was published (Weine, 2004). The HOMES experience showed that creative arts offer potentially useful modalities for engaging and helping teen refugees. HOMES demonstrated that many of the central concerns of Bosnian refugee adolescents were also shared by other refugee adolescents, including trauma-related suffering, access to services, educational challenges, and family support. However, HOMES also showed that adolescents and their families from non-Western cultures have markedly different expectations regarding services and adolescence itself. HOMES demonstrated that it was possible to engage youth and families from new refugee communities and to form a productive group of adolescents from multiple cultural groups.

A Services Approach to Preventive Mental Health for Adolescent Refugees

This three-year ethnographic study, presently being conducted, in collaboration with Dr. Norma Ware of Harvard University, aims to develop contextual knowledge on (a) family and ecological resources that protect against mental health problems for at-risk refugee adolescents and (b) the service sectors working with this population (Weine & Ware, 2007). This knowledge will serve two purposes, one substantive and the other, methodological. Substantively, study results will inform the subsequent development of a preventive intervention for two African refugee groups. Methodologically, it will shed light on the nature and scope of ethnographic study needed for intervention development with new refugee populations. This study is guided by family eco-developmental theory; theories of resilience, trauma, and migration; and a services approach. The specific aims are to (1) examine, over time, the experiences of at-risk Liberian and Burundian refugee adolescents so as to characterize the family and ecological protective resources that may be enhanced by preventive services; (2) examine the service sectors working with these groups to reveal how service structure, processes of care, and practitioner knowledge and perceptions promise to facilitate or impede preventive interventions; and (3) conduct a meta-analysis of the study data and methods to clarify the type and extent of ethnographic study needed for intervention development with new refugees. This study collects data on refugee youth and families in Illinois and Massachusetts. Thus far, we have conducted observations and begun interviews with adolescents and families. The results of this ethnography will be documented as papers to elaborate new models for preventive interventions with newly arrived refugee teenagers as well as one or more actual interventions that can be collaboratively piloted and evaluated in the communities where the refugees live.

Key Themes of Our Approach to Services Research

Several key themes define our approach to researching with families impacted by war and forced migration related to global catastrophes. These include family resilience, community collaboration, services, cultural theory, and ethnographic methods.

Family Resilience

The family is arguably the most important life context for survivors of human-made global catastrophes given that most have suffered severe losses to their connections to community and society. The results of our studies have detailed the struggles of families where multiple traumas and losses interacted with parental distress, social and economic difficulties, and cultural transition. Along with the stories of struggle, evidence of strength and resilience also emerged. The analytic findings from several studies have demonstrated a number of family resources that appeared to help shield youth, for example, from mental health and behavioral problems. These included (1) family communication about difficult issues including trauma and mental health concerns, (2) parental monitoring and supervision of youth, (3) family emphasis on education, (4) parental school involvement, (5) conversion of the cultural capital of youth, and (6) parent advocacy for youth. Much of our family intervention work is based upon family strength and resilience approaches (Walsh, 1998). For example, CAFES tried to enhance existing family strengths such as family togetherness. Because families do not function in isolation, our conceptualization of families also encompasses ecological protective resources such are those involving the school and community. Thus, we use family eco-developmental theory, which envisions family members in the context of a family system that interacts with larger social systems (Szapocznik & Coatsworth, 1999). Our focus on the resources that exist in the family also has led to a focus on preventive interventions that may enhance these resources and reduce negative outcomes. One constant issue of concern is that the family is defined very differently in varying sociocultural contexts, which means that family-focused interventions must always take into account these differences and not impose a definition of the family that does not fit.

Community Collaboration

Our research is informed by a community-based, participatory research approach where community members, persons affected by the conditions under study, and other key community stakeholders are partners in each phase of the work from conception to dissemination of results. Key community-based, participatory research (CBPR) principles that we follow include (1) building on cultural and community strengths (e.g., family values); (2) co-learning among all community and research partners; (3) shared decision making; (4) commitment to application of findings with goal of improving health by taking action, including social change; and (5) mutual ownership of the research process and products (Israel, Schulz, Parker, & Becker, 1998; Schulz, Krieger, & Galea, 2002). We believe that a CBPR approach is necessary to address the specific mental and physical health challenges in refugee, migrant, and traumatized communities. Most important is giving families, youth, schools, and community leaders a real say in the development and implementation of interventions. Also essential is fostering collaborations with community, health, mental health, educational, and religious institutions. Thus, a CBPR approach should (1) make the voices of families impacted by war and forced migration heard and relevant to services and science; (2) increase the confidence and competence of community-based providers, educators, and leaders; and (3) build a learning system that keeps knowledge flowing and communication open between these communities, organizations, and researchers.

Services

Our research approach also prioritizes service sectors, which refer to an array of different organizations and groups, both community and clinical, whose work aims to address the needs facing families impacted by war and forced migration.

We are interested in the different types of interventions that services provide for families impacted by war and forced migration, including both clinical and preventative interventions. We continually ask ourselves the core question that underlies services research: what works for whom, under what conditions, and toward what ends? (Hohmann & Shear, 2002). Because refugees, forced migrants, and other traumatized persons often do not have access to or may not seek traditional mental health services, we are especially interested in preventive and innovative intervention approaches. Our approach further focuses on showing how service structures, processes of care, and practitioner knowledge and perceptions can facilitate or impede effective interventions for families impacted by war and forced migration. We believe that it is essential to build empirical knowledge in this area if we are to be able to deliver effective psychosocial interventions to families impacted by war and forced migration in real-world settings.

Cultural Theory

Our approach incorporates cultural theory that offers a more contextual and nuanced view of the cultural changes relating to trauma and migration than current psychological formulations may do. For example, we have used the concept of "cultural capital," derived by Bourdieu (1977, 1998), to analyze the social integration of immigrant youth in French schools. Cultural capital is defined as the meanings, knowledge, customs, achievements, and outlooks that are related to a person's social positions. This has led to an interest in the processes of converting cultural capital that can be observed and documented in refugee and migrants, especially in youth. It is common for social science researchers to use cultural theory to critique institutions and practices. What is unique about our program of research is that we seek to integrate this commitment to cultural theory–based inquires with a commitment to making better interventions. Thus, the objective is to promote deeper cultural understanding and also to promote better interventions. We do not believe that these are incompatible goals. Our experience has demonstrated that service providers and organizations, although sometimes reluctant to subject their work to rigorous cultural critique, have in several instances identified the benefits of having learned to adapt their methods to better fit with the particular cultural situations of families impacted by war and forced migration.

Ethnographic Methods

Our research uses ethnographic methods because they offer an appropriate way to address the challenges facing research being conducted in socially and culturally diverse settings. For example, one challenge is the lack of basic knowledge of what cultural norms matter for youth in predominately Muslim societies and how those norms impact HIV prevention. A second challenge is the lack of scientific knowledge about the process of adapting interventions. Our chances of meeting these challenges are increased by choosing ethnographic methods (Weine & Ware, 2007). Certain core principles guide most ethnographic research, especially (1) an iterative process, in which data are analyzed as they accumulate, and the resulting insights and questions subsequently are investigated as part of a single data collection effort; (2) collection of data over an extended period of time, often years; (3) immersion in the field setting and collection of data through observations; (4) the use of informants, that is, people living in the setting who teach researchers about the phenomenon under study; and (5) a purposeful sampling strategy that involves selecting as informants those from whom we are likely to be able to learn most about the phenomenon under study. Ethnographic methods offer ways of analyzing the impact of culture and context upon experience, and the processes of change (Weine, Ware, & Lezic, 2004). Ethnographic methods have been productively used to complement quantitative research methods and in intervention development and evaluation (Hohmann & Shear, 2002).

TRAINING TOMORROW'S RESEARCHERS

In June 2006, I sat in Buenos Aires for coffee with Dr. Derrick Silove, a leading researcher in refugee mental health from the University of New South Wales in Sydney, Australia (Silove, 1999). Derrick told me he fears that many of today's established researcher programs in refugee mental health may not survive beyond their leaders, and that their leaders' expertise may not be adequately transferred to the next generation. I told Derrick that this critique could certainly apply to me, and that I was especially concerned about how to train the next generation of interdisciplinary researchers focused on psychosocial interventions with refugees and other traumatized populations. Although over the past fifteen years I have mentored many beginning investigators who have been involved in writing papers, getting grants, traveling abroad, and providing services, I know I could be doing more. My own experience receiving mentoring tells me that to conduct high-quality research on traumatized populations requires more than a small dose of mentoring and research experience. It requires a continuous and concerted effort of mentoring, supervision, and research opportunities with capable interdisciplinary mentors.

A few U.S. academic centers have federally supported programs that offer some research training in topics that include a focus on refugees. These include the Harvard Program in Refugee Trauma, University of Chicago Program in Culture and Mental Health Behavior, and the Tulane-Xavier Minority Training in International Health. However, there are not many U.S. investigators conducting high-quality clinical or preventive research concerning families impacted by war and forced migration, and that includes few who are in position to provide specialized mentorship to beginning clinical investigators.

Most mental health professionals and health professionals who are working with refugees do so as practitioners. They may have a wealth of information and practical experience, but they have few opportunities for obtaining high-quality research training and mentoring by more advanced researchers. Few beginning clinical investigators have opportunities to learn and conduct research with families impacted by war and forced migration. Yet many students, trainees, and junior faculty are highly interested in conducting research that helps develop evidence-based interventions for the large numbers worldwide who have been impacted by human-made and natural catastrophes. We have attempted to respond to these needs through ICORC, where we have created opportunities for beginning investigators to conduct research on families impacted by war and forced migration. However, I believe Derrick Silove's concerns are correct, and that there is more those of us in the field could do to make possible the kind of mentoring that beginning investigators need in order to ensure their continuing ability to build research knowledge and services on behalf of families impacted by war, forced migration, and other global catastrophes.

ORGANIZATIONAL SNAPSHOT

Organization: International Center for Responses to Catastrophes

Founder and Executive Director: Stevan Weine, MD

Mission/Description: The primary mission of the International Center for Responses to Catastrophes (ICORC) is to promote multidisciplinary research and scholarship that contributes to improved helping efforts for those affected by catastrophes. The center, at University of Illinois–Chicago (UIC), is highly multidisciplinary in approach, with university faculty from collaborating departments and colleges representing mental health and health services, humanities, and social sciences. Vital to the center's work is building national and international collaborations with academic, advocacy, and services organizations.

Address: University of Illinois, College of Medicine, Department of Psychiatry 1601 W. Taylor Street, Fifth Floor, Chicago IL 60612

Phone: (312) 355-5407

Fax: (312) 996-7658

E-mail: smweine@uic.edu

REFERENCES

Bourdieu, P. (1998). *Practical reason: On the theory of action*. Stanford, CA: Stanford University Press.

Bourdieu, P. (1977). Cultural reproduction and social reproduction. In J. Karabel & A. H. Halsey. (Eds.). *Power and ideology in education* (pp. 487–510). Oxford, England: Oxford University Press.

Cintron, R., Weine, S. M., & Agani, F. (2004). Exporting democracy. *Boston Review*.

Hohmann, A., & Shear, K. (2002). Community-based intervention research: Coping with the "noise" of real life in study design. *American Journal of Psychiatry, 159,* 201–207.

Israel, B. A., Schulz, A. J., Parker, E. A., & Becker, A. B. (1998). Review of community-based research: Assessing partnership approaches to improve public health. *Annual Review of Public Health, 19,* 173–202.

Jemmott, J. B., Jemmott, L. S., & Fong, G. T. (1998). Abstinence and safer sex HIV risk reduction interventions for African American Adolescents. *Journal of the American Medical Association, 270,* 1529–1536.

McKay, M., Baptiste, D., Coleman, D., Madison, S., McKinney, L., Paikoff, R., & CHAMP Collaborative Board. (2000). Preventing HIV risk exposure in urban communities: The CHAMP family program. In W. Pequegnat & J. Szapocznik. (Eds.). *Working with families in the era of HIV/AIDS* (pp. 67–88). California: Sage.

Rolland, J., & Weine, S. M. (2000). Kosovar Family Professional Educational Collaborative. *American Family Therapy Academy Newsletter, 79,* 34–36.

Schulz, A., Krieger, J., & Galea, S. (2002). Addressing social determinants of health: Community-based participatory approaches to research and practice. *Health Education and Behavior, 29*(3), 287–295.

Scott, J. (1998). *Seeing like a state.* New Haven and London: Yale University Press.

Sebald, W. G. (2003). *After nature.* New York: Modern Library Paperbacks, 105.

Silove, D. (1999). The psychological effects of torture, mass human rights violations, and refugee trauma: Toward an integrated conceptual framework. *Journal of Nervous and Mental Disease, 187*(4), 200.

Smajkic, A., Weine, S. M., Bijedic, Z., Boskailo, E., Lewis, J., & Pavkovic, I. (2001). Sertraline, Paroxetine and Venlafaxine in refugee post traumatic stress disorder with depression symptoms. *Journal of Traumatic Stress, 14*(3), 445–452.

Szapocznik, J., & Coatsworth, J. D. (1999). An eco-developmental framework for organizing risk and protection for drug abuse: A developmental model of risk and protection. In M. Glantz & C. R. Hartel. (Eds.), *Drug Abuse: Origins and Interventions* (pp. 331–366). Washington, DC: American Psychological Association.

Walsh, F. (1998). *Strengthening family resilience.* New York and London: Guilford Press.

Weine, S. M. (1998). *A prevention and access intervention for survivor families.* (RO1 MH59573-01). Washington, DC: National Institute of Mental Health.

Weine, S. M. (1999). *When history is a nightmare: Lives and memories of ethnic cleansing in Bosnia-Herzegovina.* New Brunswick and London: Rutgers University Press.

Weine, S. M. (2001). *Services based research with refugee families.* (K01 MH02048-01) Washington, DC: National Institute of Mental Health.

Weine, S. M. (2004). *HOMES exhibition book.* Chicago, IL: International Center on Responses to Catastrophes.

Weine, S. M. (2006). *Testimony after catastrophe: Narrating the traumas of political violence.* Evanston, IL: Northwestern University Press.

Weine, S. M., Agani, F., & Cintron, R. (2003). International and local discourses on the public mental health crisis in post-war Kosovo. *Bulletin of the Royal Institute of Interfaith Studies, 5*(1).

Weine, S. M., Agani, F., Cintron, R., Dresden, E., & Griffith, V. (2003). Lessons of Kosovo on humanitarian intervention. *Social Analysis, Forum series, First World Peoples, Consultancy and Anthropology* (pp. 33–42). New York: Berghan Books.

Weine, S. M., Bahromov, M., Brisson, A., & Mizroev, A. (2005a). *HIV and male migrant workers in Tajikistan: Risks for the family.* Poster presented at the NIMH International

Conference on the Role of Families in Preventing and Adapting to HIV/AIDS, New York.

Weine, S. M., Bahromov, M., Brisson, A., & Mizroev, A. (2008). Unprotected Tajik migrant workers in Moscow at risk for HIV/AIDS. *Journal of Immigrant and Minority Health.* (Available online at http://www.springerlink.com/content/m62g2849385x5537/?p= 0d5359bd71a64bbdb3b9c8354f25b372&pi=3.)

Weine, S. M., Becker, D. F., McGlashan, T. H., Laub, D., Lazrove, S., Vojvoda, D., & Hyman, L. (1995a). Psychiatric consequences of ethnic cleansing: Clinical assessments and trauma testimonies of newly resettled Bosnian refugees. *American Journal of Psychiatry, 152*(4), 536–542.

Weine, S. M., Becker, D., McGlashan, T., Vojvoda, D., Hartman, S., & Robbins, J. (1995b). Adolescent survivors of "ethnic cleansing": Notes on the first year in America. *Journal of the Academy of Child and Adolescent Psychiatry, 34*(9), 1153–1159.

Weine, S. M., Cintron, R., Brisson, A., Agani, F., Berxulli, D., Arenliu, A., Landau-Stanton, J., & Ware, N. (2004). *Families' practical knowledge of preventing HIV/AIDS risk behaviors in post-war Kosovo.* Poster Presented at the NIMH Conference on the Role of Families in Preventing and Adapting to HIV/AIDS. Atlanta, GA, July 2004.

Weine, S. M., Danieli, Y., Silove, D., van Ommeren, M., Fairbank, J., & Saul, J.(2002) Guidelines for international training in mental health and psychosocial interventions for trauma exposed populations in clinical and community settings. *Psychiatry, 65*(2), 156–164.

Weine, S. M., Feetham, S., Kulauzovic, Y., Besic, S., Lezic, A., Mujagic, A., Muzurovic, J., Spahovic, D., Rolland, J., Sclove, S., & Pavkovic, S. (2008). A multiple-family group access intervention for refugee families with PTSD. *Journal of Marital and Family Therapy, 34*(2), 149–164.

Weine, S. M., Feetham, S., Kulauzovic, Y., Besic, S., Lezic, A., Mujagic, A., Muzurovic, J., Spahovic, D., Zhubi, M., Rolland, J., & Pavkovic, I. (2004). Family interventions in a services research framework with refugee communities. In K. Miller & L. Rasco. (Eds.). *From clinic to community: Ecological approaches to refugee mental health* (pp. 263–294). Mahwah, NJ: Lawrence Erlbaum.

Weine, S. M., Knafl, K., Feetham, S., Kulauzovic, Y., Besic, S., Lezic, A., Mujagic, A., Muzurovic, J., Spahovic, D., & Pavkovic, I. (2005b). A mixed-methods study of refugee families engaging in multi-family groups. *Family Relations, 54*, 558–568.

Weine, S. M., Kuc, E., Dzudza, E., Razzano, L., & Pavkovic, I. (2001). PTSD among Bosnian refugees: A survey of providers' knowledge, attitudes and service patterns. *Journal of Community Mental Health, 37*(3), 261–271.

Weine, S. M., Kulauzovic, Y., Besic, S., Lezic, A., Mujagic, A., Muzurovic, J., Spahovic, D., Feetham, S., Knafl, K., & Pavkovic, I. (2006). A family beliefs framework for developing socially and culturally specific preventive interventions for refugee families and youth. *American Journal of Orthopsychiatry, 76*(1), 1–9.

Weine, S. M., Kulenovic, T., Dzubur, A., Pavkovic, I., & Gibbons, R. (1998). Testimony psychotherapy in Bosnian refugees: A pilot study. *American Journal of Psychiatry, 155*, 1720–1726.

Weine, S. M., Muzurovic, N., Kulauzovic, Y., Besic, S, Lezic, A., Mujagic, A., Muzurovic, J., Spahovic, D., Feetham, S., Ware, N., Knafl, K., & Pavkovic, I., (2004). Family consequences of political violence in refugee families. *Family Process, 43*, 147–160.

Weine, S. M., Pavkovic, I., Agani, F., Jukic, V., Ceric, I. (2006). Mental health reformer and assisting psychiatric leaders in post-war countries. In G. Reyes. (Ed.). *International disaster psychology* (pp. 65–84). Westport, CT: Praeger.

Weine, S. M., Raijna, D., Kulauzovic, Y., Zhubi, M., Huseni, D., Delisi, M., Feetham, S., Mermelstein, R., & Pavkovic I. (2006). Development and implementation of CAFES and TAFES: Family interventions for refugee families from Bosnia and Kosovo. In G. Reyes. (Ed.). *International disaster psychology* (pp. 37–64). New York: Praeger.

Weine, S. M., Raijna, D., Kulauzovic, Y., Zhubi, M., Huseni, D., Delisi, M., Feetham, S., Mermelstein, R., & Pavkovic, I. (2003). The TAFES multi-family group intervention for Kosovar refugees: A descriptive study. *Journal of Nervous and Mental Diseases, 191*(2), 100–107.

Weine, S. M., Razzano, L., Miller, K., Brkic, N., Ramic, A., Smajkic, A., Bijedic, Z., Boskailo, E., Mermelstein, R., & Pavkovic, I. (2000). Profiling the trauma related symptoms of Bosnian refugees who have not sought mental health services. *Journal of Nervous and Mental Diseases, 188*(7), 416–421.

Weine, S. M., Ukshini, S., Griffith, J., Agani, F., Pulleyblank Coffey, E., Ulaj, J., Becker, C., Ajeti, L., Elliot, M., Alidemaj-Sereqi, V., Landau, J., Asllani, M., Mango, M., Pavkovic, I., Bunjaku, A., Rolland, J., Çala, G., Saul, J., Makolli, S., Sluzki, C., Statovci, S., & Weingarten, K. (2005c). A family approach to severe mental illness in post-war Kosovo. *Psychiatry, 68*(1), 17–28.

Weine, S. M., Vojvoda, D., Hartman, S., & Hyman, L. (1997). A family survives genocide. *Psychiatry*, 60, 24–39.

Weine, S. M., & Ware, N. (2007). A services approach to preventive mental health for adolescent refugees. (1 R01 MH076118-01A2) Washington, DC: National Institute of Mental Health.

Weine, S. M., Ware, N., & Lezic, A. (2004). An ethnographic study of converting cultural capital in teen refugees and their families from Bosnia-Herzegovina. *Psychiatric Services, 55*, 923–927.

11

International Trauma Studies Program

Jack Saul

The International Trauma Studies Program (ITSP) is a training and research institute committed to enhancing the natural resilience and coping capacities in individuals, families, and communities that have endured and/or are threatened by traumatic events resulting from domestic and political violence, war, and natural disaster. ITSP pursues its mission through providing professional training, implementing and evaluating innovative community-based initiatives, offering technical assistance to international organizations, and helping to build a global learning community in the areas of trauma, mental health, and human rights.

Dr. Soeren Buus Jensen of Copenhagen and I founded the International Trauma Studies Program in 1998. It is one of the few trauma programs committed not only to training professionals who serve survivors of all forms of traumatic events, but also to developing and evaluating family and community-oriented mental health and psychosocial services for survivors of massive trauma and loss. To best serve this population, it has been the mission of ITSP to advance the scientific understanding of the impact of catastrophic events on individuals, families, communities, and societies at large, as well as the corresponding pathways to recovery and resilience.

Since its inception, ITSP has provided intensive, one-year (two-semester) training to more than 300 practitioners, who over the last ten years have developed numerous training programs, research projects, and clinical and psychosocial initiatives for populations of survivors in more than thirty countries. First established as an interdisciplinary program based at New York University (NYU) School of Medicine, ITSP now runs as an independent 501(c)(3) nonprofit organization affiliated with the Columbia University's Mailman School of Public Health, where I am currently an assistant professor of clinical population and family health.

HISTORICAL OVERVIEW
Background

The International Trauma Studies Program grew initially out of the Bellevue/ NYU Program for Survivors of Torture, which I co-founded in 1995. The Bellevue program was established as a medical and mental health service for torture survivors. In developing a treatment philosophy, the program took a strengths-based approach. It regarded survivors as having resources and assets that have enabled them to survive their victimization; thus, the aim of treatment was seen as enhancing their re-empowerment. We recognized the necessity of using a culturally sensitive approach with clients, which drew on their own cultural and religious resources for healing from the effects of severe human rights abuses. In addition to intensive individual, group, and family psychotherapy, we focused on symptom reduction, assistance with social difficulties, and networking with community organizations. The rationale was that if the survivors were supported and given relief from immediate symptoms, they could mobilize their natural, inherent capacities for healing and coping. We saw the process of recovery from the trauma of torture as progressing in stages: from the sense of unpredictable danger to reliable safety, from dissociated trauma to acknowledged memory, and from stigmatized isolation to restored social connection.

Within the first two years of its development, the Bellevue program provided needed medical and mental health services to scores of torture survivors from over forty countries. As the program developed, there was a growing awareness of the need to develop a broader range of services for this population in metropolitan New York City. At the time, it was estimated that there were over 400,000 torture survivors living in the United States, with between 70,000 and 90,000 survivors living in the New York City area alone. Most of these survivors had already resided in the area for years with their families, living in immigrant enclaves, and likely had never received specialized services for the long-term affects of any severe traumatization they may have experienced. There was a need to develop programs outside the hospital setting in the communities in which the refugees resided, programs that could offer alternative psychosocial services to populations from cultures that were not always open to or could not benefit from Western forms of psychotherapeutic intervention. For example, a support group of Tibetan refugees seen at the clinic wanted help in setting up their own nonprofit organization so they themselves could assist other Tibetan refugees with the myriad of social and economic challenges to adapting to life in New York. But the requirement of the hospital was that these refugees were to be diagnosed and treated for a mental health disorder in group or individual therapy.

In the context of a growing need for a more comprehensive psychosocial approach to assisting refugee survivors of torture, as well as the need for more intensive training of staff and interns at the hospital in working with severely traumatized survivors of human rights violations, we began to look at the need to create opportunities for advanced training at NYU. It was then that I met Soeren

Buus Jensen, a psychiatrist from Denmark, who had spent the previous three years (1994–96) working with the World Health Organization (WHO) in the former Yugoslavia during the war. He was the WHO program manager for mental health services and later the head of the overall Humanitarian Aid Program for WHO during the war (SR/special representative). Among his initiatives were the implementation of regional trauma-training programs for Bosnian, Croatian, Serbian, and Macedonian mental health practitioners who were providing services for traumatized victims during the war, while they themselves were suffering from some of the same traumatic experiences and reactions. The so-called regional model provided training in thirteen different regions for thirty to thirty-two professionals (mainly psychiatrists and psychologists) through a one-year course.

In some areas such as Mostar, Bosnia, practitioners were brought together under United Nations' protection for joint training workshops. Dr. Jensen conducted the intensive training courses called PPT (Posttraumatic Therapy), which included didactic training in trauma theory and intervention, case supervision, and experiential work in supervised groups on how the practitioners could take care of themselves and prevent burnout while doing such emotionally demanding work. The training model was developed based on previous experiences gained from his training programs in Denmark and further inspired by his encounter with the Chilean Human Rights movement (1989–93).

Dr. Jensen developed a network of international advisors on trauma training for a nongovernmental organization (NGO) he created called the International University Center for Mental Health and Human Rights, and was meeting with experts from around the world to learn about trauma-training programs. To his surprise, as he toured Europe and the United States, he found very few training programs. Jensen and I decided to develop an intensive trauma-training program at NYU similar to that run during the Yugoslavian war.

Phase One: 1998–2001

Initial financial support to develop the ITSP was provided through a curricular development challenge grant from NYU's Provost Office. The goal was to create an interschool and interdepartmental program at the university that could provide postgraduate training as well as act as a catalyst for the development of academic courses in the study and treatment of psychosocial trauma. The nature and content of the training program was influenced from the beginning by our clinical and research experience with survivors of political violence—torture, war, state terrorism, and genocide. I had been a research assistant for Professor Hillel Klein, MD, from Hadassah Medical School and director of the Jerusalem Center for the Study of Psychosocial Trauma and Holocaust. Klein, a practicing psychoanalyst and Holocaust survivor, had done pioneering work on the impact of massive trauma and loss on individuals, families, and society, and had been a proponent in the early 1980s of shifting attention in the trauma field from a focus on the pathology of trauma to the understanding of the intra-psychic, familial, social, and cultural resources that were important in Holocaust survivors' return to living productive lives—that is, their process of adaptation and revival (Klein, 2003).

Prior to his work in the former Yugoslavia, Jensen had done research with survivors of state terrorism in Chile, where he became interested in the uses of testimony to promote the process of healing. As recalled in *Trauma and Healing under State Terrorism* (Agger and Jensen, 1993), psychologists in Chile found that survivors who had given testimonies, in the context of creating documentary evidence for later war crimes trials of those who had carried out torture and disappearances from the Pinochet era, were found to have improved mental health compared to those who had not given testimony and were still waiting in line to do so. Based on this work and what they saw as the importance of survivors having a purposeful context in which to construct a coherent narrative of their experience, Agger and Jensen developed a method of testimony therapy with refugee survivors of torture living in Denmark (Agger and Jensen, 1990).

Jensen brought to the curriculum the human rights framework from South America, referred to by the acronym DITE—documentation, investigation, therapy, and evaluation. The mental health and human rights perspective advocated a position of therapeutic non-neutrality in working with victims of human rights violations: it was important in this work to establish an alliance in condemning the inhumane practices suffered by the victim.

The training program began at NYU in the fall of 1998 with over forty students participating in the course in two separate tracks: one was a more intensive track was for clinicians and the other, requiring fewer hours, was oriented toward community-based practices and open to practitioners other than mental health professionals (e.g., lawyers, community activists, youth workers, managers of NGOs, United Nations personnel, and artists). The program revolved around workshops run by visiting faculty who were at the forefront of the trauma field, and leaders at the International Society for Traumatic Stress Studies (ISTSS), the most prominent organization promoting research and clinical practice in work with trauma survivors. The format of the training was divided into didactic work on trauma theory and intervention, case studies, and self-care. Students worked in small groups to discuss cases, engage in role-play and other experiential learning methods, and discuss the impact of the work on themselves as well as strategies for self-care. In the tradition of the Yugoslavian training program, students were required to carry out a project in order to complete the program. These projects ranged from workshops, to small clinical studies, to the development of citywide advocacy activities for trauma survivors. Three students teamed up the first year to create a program honoring survivors of torture on the UN day commemorating survivors.

The development of the ITSP training program was enhanced by its participation in the International Society for Traumatic Stress Studies Task Force on International Training, co-led by Drs. Stevan Weine and Yael Danieli (2003). The goal was the development of guidelines for training in mental health and psychosocial response in international contexts. At the time, there were tensions in the field of trauma response. There was a critique of mental health professionals streaming into war zones and post-conflict settings to offer Western-oriented therapeutic techniques and concepts for trauma treatment, but ignoring the political, economic, social, and cultural contexts and hierarchy of needs of the recipient populations. This set of guidelines was one of the inputs for the development of recent guidelines on mental health and psychosocial response by the Inter-Agency Standing Committee's recent report titled "IASC Guidelines on Mental Health and Psychosocial Support in Emergency Settings" (IASC, 2007).

Community-Based Services for Survivors of Torture

ITSP pursued its commitment to community-oriented work with survivors of torture and refugee trauma by establishing a nonprofit called Refuge, which established an alliance with other three other organizations assisting torture survivors in the New York area—Solace/Safe Horizon; Doctors of the World, USA; and the Cross Cultural Counseling Center of the International Institute of New Jersey (IINJ)—to form the Metro Area Support for Survivors of Torture Consortium (MASST). The MASST Consortium, under the leadership of the Solace/Safe Horizon director Ernest Duff, received a Torture Victims Relief Act (TVRA) grant from the U.S. Office of Refugee Resettlement, and over the six years of TVRA funding support, the MASST Consortium developed a range of services for over 2,000 survivors of torture and their family members. Services included information and practical assistance; support for families and youth; referrals for legal, medical, and social services; educational and vocational development; individual, family, and group counseling; community development and capacity building; community arts and cultural programming; and medical and mental health evaluations for political asylum.

Refuge's role in the consortium was the provision of technical assistance to Solace/Safe Horizon and IINJ on the development of family-oriented clinical services, training of clinicians and community workers, and the development of a network of mental health professionals that provided pro bono therapeutic services to survivors of torture and their families. In 2000, Refuge became a member of the National Consortium of Torture Treatment Programs with the other members of the MASST Consortium.

From the Clinic to the Stage

One innovative project developed by Refuge in its work with refugee communities was Theater Arts Against Political Violence. The project was developed by Steven Reisner, a psychoanalyst and former actor and theater director; Robert Gourp, a theater director; and myself as the producer. In working with torture survivors, it became increasingly apparent that many of them desired a public forum to speak out about the injustices they had endured in their country of origin—and the injustices that were still taking place. Many had been student leaders and political activists before coming to live in exile in New York City. There is a lot of emphasis about working with the individual or family in the privacy of the therapy office, where what is said does not leave the office, but work that is done privately can leave out the political dimension. We began to see that there was a value in creating a public forum where survivors could speak about their experiences, and we felt there was a necessity to work in a fashion that created a nonhierarchical exchange with survivors.

The program had its origin at Bellevue Hospital in a project with the then U.S. Department of Immigration and Naturalization Services to train asylum offices in methods of sensitively interviewing applicants who were severely traumatized. One thing we did was to hire a theater group and trained the actors to play traumatized refugees—something quite counterintuitive for actors who rarely had knowledge of such human rights violations in their own lives. The asylum officers would role-play interviews with the actors, and we would freeze the action to speak about what was happening during each interview.

After the training, the theater group expressed an interest in creating a play about the issue of human rights violations—and the collective responsibility we all share in relation to these violations. The theater group began to explore themes related to political violence and the refugee experience. Because this experience was foreign to most of the actors, despite the actors being a culturally diverse group, they began to invite refugees who had been political prisoners to meet with the theater group to talk about their experience, and eventually to engage in a collaboration with the director and actors to create a performance based on the survivors' experience and creative input.

We found that the refugees felt honored to have the opportunity to speak with artists about their lives. For many, it was first time they had been asked by Americans about their experience. We brought Tibetans, Guatemalans, Africans, and eventually a group of Chileans to meet with the theater group. These Chileans had been living in the Bronx for over fifteen years and had rarely spoken to Americans about their experience. The Chileans were very appreciative that we were offering them a space to tell their stories and then to have their stories represented theatrically. We started a collaborative process in which the Chilean survivors spoke about their experiences during the Pinochet era, their imprisonments and experiences of oppression and torture, and the actors engaged them in a dialogue. Then the theater group would go to work improvisationally on the material and bring back scenes to the survivors, who would critique the work and make recommendations: "You portrayed the pain effectively, but what we didn't see were the moments of humanity, warmth, and humor that was so important to us when we were in prison." The theater work opened up a dialogue among survivors, actors, and mental health professionals that had not been anticipated.

The Theater Arts Against Political Violence performed at Tibet House in New York City during an event to honor torture survivors. By that time, the group of Chileans had begun to engage in conversations about their experiences as political activists and prisoners with members of their own families and community, and with other Latin American communities in New York. Two months later, they took the raw, unedited video of the theater work and the performance to Chile on their first visit in fifteen years. There, they met with other activists and theater groups to share their work. The theater work became part of an opening of communication within families and communities, and in the transnational community to which they belonged. In 2000 Theater Arts Against Political Violence was invited to collaborate with the International Organization for Migration on a project that integrated theater approaches in the training of psychosocial counselors in Kosovo. The project culminated in the production of a theater piece performed at the National Theater in Prishtina, Kosovo (Reisner, 2003).

Internationally Based Training and Services

In 2000 ITSP became a partner in the development of family- and community-oriented mental health services in postwar Kosovo. In May of that year, a collaborative team effort between American and Albanian Kosovar mental health professionals was initiated to address the enormous psychosocial and mental health needs of the Kosovar population following the end of the war in 1999. The project, called the Kosovar Family Professional Education Collaborative (KFPEC), was co-sponsored by the University of Illinois–Chicago (UIC), the University of Chicago, the American Family Therapy Academy, the International Trauma Studies Program at NYU, and the University of Prishtina. The Albanian Kosovar team based in the Department of Psychiatry and Neurology at the University of Prishtina Medical School decided to develop a strengths-based mental health orientation in their hospital and emerging community mental health system. They decided to draw on existing resources in the Albanian Kosovar community to promote recovery after the period of oppression and war, as well as to address other public mental health concerns.

In the aftermath of the war in Kosovo in 1999, the Albanian Kosovar society was faced with having to build a mental health system while at the same time having to contend with widespread experiences of loss, violence, and forced geographical displacement. The Serbian authorities had permitted very few formal health or mental health services in the previous ten years, and most mental health and social services for Albanian Kosovars had been provided by a parallel system of professionals and paraprofessionals who worked underground, usually without pay. A few mental health practitioners had been able to continue their education and provide services at University Hospital in Prishtina. This small group of psychiatrists, psychologists, and nurses took responsibility for building a mental health system and providing services to a large number of families in need. During the war, most of the Albanian Kosovar mental health professionals had fled the country. Many had lived in refugee camps and had faced serious danger, as well as the loss of family members and friends.

One of the innovative projects initiated after the war by Albanian Kosovar mental health professionals was the development of mobile teams. These teams went to some of the villages to work with families that had suffered major losses during the massacres that had been perpetrated on hundreds of villages in Kosovo. It is estimated that over 10,000 Albanian Kosovars had been murdered.

The American and Albanian Kosovar group visited one of the small villages, where they had been working with a number of families. Slovia was a village where Albanian and Serbian Kosovars had lived together for decades. It was a small agricultural village of 2,000 people some thirty miles southwest of the capitol, Prishtina. One evening in May 1999, Serbian military forces entered the village. They sent a group of Serbians from the village to identify the male Albanian leaders there. The next day, Serbian forces entered the village, took males from the houses, and shot them, often in front of their families. One group of villagers managed to escape the village but were later caught and slaughtered. The violence lasted throughout the day. Bodies were buried in mass graves just outside the village. Days later, the Serbian forces returned to the village, and in an attempt to remove the evidence of their atrocities, dug up the corpses, placed them on trucks, and departed the area. On a hill above the village, half the graves of the fifty-eight people who had been massacred were empty. It was not likely that the bodies would ever be retrieved. For many families, their grief at losing up to five members of their families was compounded by their not having the bodies available for a proper funeral according to Muslim tradition (Saul, Ukshini, et al., 2003).

One of the consequences of the massacre was that with the death of the younger, stronger men of these families, the elders, often elderly women, had to take an active role in leading their extended families of widows and children. The Kosovar mental health professionals who had begun to work with these families took an approach that explored their sources of strength and resilience. During this initial phase of work with families, the Kosovar professionals were very interested in developing a mental health expertise based on strengthening family and community resilience.

The KFPEC received funding in 2001 to develop a services-based training program aimed at developing psychoeducational groups for families of the severely mentally ill. This five-year project successfully led to the development of teams at each of the regional community mental health centers in Kosovo. In December 2006, the program became integrated into the Kosovo's health system (Pulleybank-Coffee, Griffith, et al., 2006).

During this time, ITSP also worked with the Center for War, Peace and the News Media in implementing a diversity training program with Serbian and Albanian Kosovar media professionals. The program brought over forty media professionals together in Prishtina for a two-week training in investigative journalism, which included a two-day module on trauma reactions as well as strategies for interviewing victims of violence, addressing the journalists' own traumatic stress reactions, and developing methods of self-care. The groups came together to work on a collaborative project on the families of the missing in each ethnic group.

During this first phase in the development of ITSP, a number of principles emerged. First, there was a shift from focusing exclusively on training in individually oriented clinical approaches to treating trauma survivors, to emphasizing the strengthening of the natural support systems of family and community. We learned from our work in the community with survivors in New York, with survivors in the context of theater, in the development of individual and collective narratives, in Kosovo, and through our international training faculty. By the end of the three years, we were bringing in approaches that derived from specializing with working with trauma survivors, or working with populations in non-Western contexts; in addition, we were questioning the efficacy of mental health approaches to trauma response in Western contexts as well. This realization and critique was further crystallized as we experienced the events of September 11, 2001, in our neighborhood (where ITSP faculty lived and worked) and were faced with responding as professionals and as residents to one of the hardest-hit populations. By that time, we had trained more than 100 mental health and allied professionals in our nine-month training program in trauma theory and intervention. Many of those trained at ITSP filled the ranks of directors and managers of newly funded projects to work with the victims of 9/11 in hospitals, community mental health centers, and schools.

Phase Two: 2001–2004

Before September 11, 2001, I could not anticipate that I would soon be bringing our professional expertise into my own home, my children's school, and my local community. I live in downtown Manhattan and my children—ages five and eight at the time of the terrorist attacks—attended a public school two blocks from the World Trade Center site. It was in my children's school that I began to work with other community members to address the needs of children, adults, and families as a community.

A reversal took place: I was now the "local" and began to experience myself what my international colleagues had told me about post-disaster situations elsewhere: the ever-present print, radio, and television journalists chasing after the story; international relief organizations arriving on the scene and interviewing local professionals to inform their own funding applications; the missionaries and outreach workers offering support; and the influx of trauma and grief counselors and body therapists of all kinds. Downtown Manhattan had become a spiritual and therapeutic supermarket. At the same time, the local population was engaged in numerous activities to assist others, yet their efforts to promote recovery, much as in international contexts, were undervalued and received very little direct financial support. The capacity of local mental health professionals in the community, as well as organizations that had been working all along to assist youth and address other community problems, were often ignored (Saul, 2007).

We anticipated, based on our international experience, that there would be an influx of researchers and clinicians focusing exclusively on the symptoms and treatment of posttraumatic stress disorder (PTSD). And in fact, quite quickly, a great deal of funding was directed toward training mental health professionals to treat individuals suffering from PTSD; at the same time, the grassroots efforts of professionals, community organizations, and community members addressing the ongoing needs of those around them only rarely gained the attention of private funders, relief organizations, and government agencies. We thus made a decision to focus our energies on developing both a community project in lower Manhattan and a disaster response training program that would bring to the New York mental health community the family and community approaches to trauma and disaster based on a resilience framework.

Downtown Community Resource Center

The week that the fourth year of our program started, our students could not pass the checkpoints in Lower Manhattan to get to class. Many of us living downtown had been directly affected, escaping from the falling buildings and the debris storms, and having to evacuate our homes for a period of time. But the class went on, and we added an emergency symposium for New York mental health professionals on trauma response with a presentation by Dr. Jensen, who had arrived in New York City that week to open the ITSP course.

In order to address the needs of children and families in lower Manhattan, I joined a group of parents, some of who were mental health professionals, who teamed up to create family support committees in the schools. These school communities were on the west side of downtown Manhattan, just next to the World Trade Center site in the neighborhoods of Tribeca and Battery Park City. These communities comprised children, teachers, parents, residents, and workers who had experienced the greatest physical exposure to the events of 9/11: the deaths of friends and family members, direct threats to their own lives, emergency evacuations from workplaces and schools, physical danger from the debris storms, displacement from their home and businesses, and environmental contamination. With all of New Yorkers, they also faced a series of subsequent events, including the plane crash in the borough of Queens, going to war in Afghanistan and Iraq, the anthrax contamination, and numerous threats accompanied by heightened terrorist alerts.

The family support programs formed a coalition across school communities to share ideas about how to address the emotional consequence of the events of 9/11 among children and parents. The initial approach of the New York City Board of Education to address the needs of children affected by these events had focused on screening them for PTSD and offering therapeutic services to those who were identified as having difficulties. As mentioned earlier, not only was very little attention paid to the impact of these events on teachers and parents, but neither group was asked for input regarding the children's evaluations. Moreover, although the mental health of children became the focus of the school system's efforts, there was initially no place for parents to discuss their own concerns as a group. To tackle this, the family support committees developed community forums where parents, teachers, and school staff from the downtown elementary schools could come together to address emerging concerns. ITSP's community-based work was supported and enhanced by the participation of Dr. Claude Chemtob, a child psychologist and disaster specialist, who moderated the community forums and advocated for the project with local funders. The community approach we used was based on the work of Dr. Judith Landau, a child and community psychiatrist, whose Link Model of Community Resilience became the inspiration for our work to promote recovery by engaging and supporting community members in their efforts to promote recovery (Landau and Saul, 2004).

During one of the forums, a needs assessment was conducted, and members of the school community established as a priority creating a public space or resource center where community members could come together and share ideas, projects, resources, and their combined creativity. This center was to have the following goals:

- To recognize and strengthen existing skills, resources and resilience in the community
- To enhance connectedness in families, neighborhoods, organizations, and occupational groups
- To promote mental and physical wellness in youth, adults, and families
- To create forums for public discourse and the expression of the multiplicity of community voices, viewpoints, and histories

We received funding from the New York Times Foundation to start a community resource center, and then worked with the Federal Emergency Management Agency (FEMA) Project Liberty for a contract to establish a resource center in the community that could support the efforts of community members and offer them stipends and administrative support to conduct programs. On a voluntary basis, many people living in lower Manhattan were already developing a variety of activities for children and families. The goal of the funding would be to support these activities, promote sustainability of these projects, and prevent burnout. Refuge was eventually awarded a substantial contract from FEMA to develop a demonstration project promoting community resilience through community engagement.

Through the resource center, community members were able to engage residents and workers beyond the school community to develop a number of projects for youth and families. Two projects focused on promoting public discourse about the challenges and ways of coping with the impact of 9/11: a community video narrative archive and a theater project based on the oral histories of community members. Developed by downtown residents, the archive housed a diversity of community voices and experiences, and made the stories of downtown life available on the Web and in public places in the area. It became a site where people could hear others' stories and gather to share and record their individual or family stories. The theater project was an adaptation of the previous work of Theater

Arts Against Political Violence in its use of performance as a way of bringing together community members, artists, mental health professionals, and others in a collaborative mode for exploring, expressing, and representing experience as well as providing a public space for groups to reflect on that experience. The project involved the development of an ensemble of professional actors who collected community stories from group interviews following 9/11 and transformed them, through improvisation, into a theatrical performance. Ironically titled "Everything's Back to Normal in New York City: Below Canal—A Work in Progress," the piece was performed in the community, followed by discussions among the actors and the audience. During each subsequent performance, the ensemble incorporated the community's reactions from the one before. As the work progressed, it followed and interacted with the shifting experience of people living and working in Lower Manhattan. The theater project was envisioned as an ongoing catalyst for community conversation during the coming year. Other projects initiated by community members and supported by the resource center included a community-based disaster preparedness and response initiative that has produced a published manual; a community website; peer support programs, including one for artists and one for journalists directly affected by the terrorist attacks; and a Samba rhythm school for teenagers throughout New York City.

The work of the resource center reinforced our view that by tapping into community competencies and resilience after major traumatic events, professionals

Figure 11.1   Scene from "Everything's Back to Normal in New York City," performed in the fall of 2003. Photo courtesy of Jack Saul.

could best foster mental health. What we saw in the aftermath of September 11, 2001, in New York City is that a comprehensive approach that endorses connectedness and enhances resources at the levels of the individual, family, and community most likely will have the best chance of promoting a lasting recovery.

Disaster Response Workshop Series

Within a week after the 9/11 terrorist attacks, ITSP initiated a series of workshops for professionals on disaster and trauma treatment. Experts in the field either volunteered or taught for very low fees, and donations for the training were used to support community projects in Lower Manhattan. The workshops broadly focused on individual, family, and community resilience perspectives. From September 2001–May 2003, over 3,000 professionals attended the workshop series. One unique aspect of the training was bringing in the experience of international presenters who had experience working in contexts dealing with the aftermath of violence and terrorism, including Palestinian and Israeli mental health professionals and colleagues from Kosovo, Africa, and Latin America. Nancy Baron presented a workshop titled "Turning the Tide? Working with Violence Affected Families and Communities from the Field in Africa." The workshop reversed the usual expectation of knowledge transmission and examined the relevance of using helping models from developing countries with long-standing conflict in the work with communities in New York City. It examined comprehensive, community-based psychosocial and mental health interventions developed in Uganda, Sudan, and Burundi to assist populations affected by violence. These interventions build on the natural strengths of the traditional African society, empowering families and communities to manage members' psychosocial concerns.

One of the most important things we attempted was to address the gap between those specializing in developing and researching evidence-based approaches to trauma treatment, and those who had been working with families and communities that had suffered trauma. Judith Landau and I helped organized plenaries during the next year at the annual conferences of both the American Family Therapy Academy in New York City and the International Family Therapy Association in Istanbul. These conferences brought together prominent practitioners from the field of trauma treatment with family therapists and international practitioners. Bridging these two fields was incorporated into the mission of ITSP and has since shaped the development of its curriculum, with the participation of prominent family therapists and systemic theorists who have been working with families that had suffered from child abuse, domestic violence, poverty, homelessness, and political violence.

Phase Three: 2004–2007

The next phase in ITSP's development was characterized by an intensified focus on international training, development, and evaluation of family and community resilience approaches with survivors of torture and refugee trauma in

New York City. We also applied principles of community engagement and resilience to the development of supportive learning communities among current students and alumni of our training program. During this phase, we were responsive to the needs of organizations that were turning to us for help in facilitating staff welfare programs.

One of the strengths of the program was the increasing linkage between training and fieldwork in communities. Scholarships to the training program have been given each year to community activists from the former Yugoslavia, West Africa, Cambodia, and Latin America, who are developing programs for refugee populations in New York. As part of the training on community interventions, community leaders are often invited to class to engage in simulated community forums. Here, they are trained collaboratively with students in conducting needs assessments, enhancing community leadership and capacity, program development, and evaluation.

By the beginning of the third phase of its development, ITSP had gained recognition as an organization with expertise in family and community approaches with traumatized populations. Members of our faculty were invited to give numerous international presentations, as well as host international visitors interested in learning more about the community-oriented work carried out in Lower Manhattan. Presentations and connections were made with organizations in the Middle East, including Iran, Jordan, Pakistan, Turkey, and Egypt. Throughout this phase, we received numerous requests from universities and NGOs for assistance in the development of a similar comprehensive trauma-training program.

As our 9/11 work was winding down, and with numerous trauma-training programs and trauma centers having been developed in New York since 9/11, we were able to turn our attention back to working with communities that had suffered from the devastations of war and forced migration, and to begin to further develop international collaborations for training. In our work with New York refugee populations, we increasingly focused on addressing the needs of survivors of torture and refugee trauma. Our program, Refuge, continued to receive funding as part of the MASST Consortium with three other organizations. Our role had shifted over the years from providing training and technical assistance to refugee mental health professionals at our collaborating organizations to collaborative work with refugee communities in which there were high numbers of survivors of torture and other traumatic human rights abuses. In 2002 we initiated a partnership with leaders of the West African community in Staten Island.

Following a community forum and needs assessment, we began working with community "links," or change agents, to address the most pressing needs of this primarily Liberian and Sierra Leonean population (Landau, 2007). The leaders of this emerging community organization decided it would be best to operate as a project under the auspices of our nonprofit, Refuge. The first priority was to establish a community space that was geographically accessible to refugees living in the housing projects in the Parkhill neighborhood of Staten Island. The housing management donated a space that was converted into a community drop-in center and named African Refuge. The links understood that many members of this community of over 4,000 refugees living in close proximity had not taken advantage of available health and social services. Under the leadership of Mr. Jacob Massaquoi, a torture survivor himself, who had managed to escape the civil wars in Liberia and gain political asylum in the United States, African Refuge began offering basic social services and acted as a much-needed bridge between community members and provider organizations. The center grew, organically responding to expressed needs of the refugees coming to the center, providing immigration assistance, access to health insurance and health care, job and educational counseling, computer education and access, informational forums, and case-work services. The strategy was to offer needed services to whoever came in to the center and ask for only a minimum of information from this highly suspicious population of refugees. They were not only dealing with the emotional aftermath of the war, and the loss of family members, home and property, but also the challenges of now living in one of the most impoverished and crime-ridden neighborhoods of New York City.

A number of collaborative arts projects were implemented at Africa Refuge. One such project was *Coming Home,* an arts initiative that used photography and film to connect older Liberians in the Diaspora with friends and family at home. A group of eight elders in Staten Island, NY, came together over the course of two months to create messages for the project coordinator, Serena Chaudhry, to carry to friends and family in Liberia. Then Ms. Chaudhry delivered the messages, filmed responses, and returned them to the Staten Island community. *Coming Home* culminated in a multimedia exhibit in December 2006 at the Snug Harbor Cultural Center on Staten Island. The exhibit featured stories, photos, and films taken by the elders and their friends, families, and allies.

The mission of African Refuge was to find successful ways of delivering services to survivors of torture and war. Within two years, Mr. Massaquoi and his small group of community volunteers had managed to provide services and referrals for close to 600 community members. A survey of those attending the center for services found that over 80 percent of the adult participants had experienced the recent wars, and close to 50 percent of them reported personal experiences of having been tortured. With the success of the program, the housing management in Parkhill offered African Refuge another space to create a youth and family center.

By 2007 African Refuge had created a collaborative, after-school tutoring program in partnership with the International Rescue Committee and was establishing a Youth Task Force in Staten Island to address the growing needs of African refugee youth and strategies to reduce tensions between these youth and other ethnic groups. With the establishment of the Liberian Truth and Reconciliation Commission's Diaspora statement-taking program, African Refuge became an implementing partner with this commission, under the leadership of Minnesota Advocates for Human Rights, in providing outreach, community sensitization, and psychosocial follow-up for statement givers. Responding to the need to promote improved intergroup relations and collaboration as essential ingredients in the African refugees' adaptation to life in the United States, African Refuge widened its scope to address the needs of anyone from the neighborhood in need of services. ITSP would continue to provide technical assistance and capacity building in order to promote African Refuge as an African-focused torture and refugee psychosocial program.

The year 2007 also saw the development of ITSP's first field-based training program in Arua, Uganda, under the leadership of ITSP's director of international training, Dr. Nancy Baron. The program was a response to the need to provide training in the development of psychosocial programs in developing countries as well as offer a train-the–trainer course. The site in Uganda could accommodate students from the United States and Europe as well as provide training for psychosocial staff working for NGOs in Africa and the Middle East.

As we enter our tenth year, ITSP has refined its mission to continue to research family and community resilience approaches with populations that have endured massive trauma and loss, and to build the capacity of a diverse group of professionals involved in this work on a national and international level. Over the past ten years, ITSP has developed an audio-visual library of over 600 hours of workshops, and is now pursuing the technology to make these resources, as well as current education activities, available to international groups requesting assistance and partnership in developing similar programs in their countries.

The International Trauma Studies Program has also initiated an annual multidisciplinary conference in trauma studies for the general public. A conference in 2007, titled "Narratives of Suffering and Transformation," brought together professionals and students from the fields of psychology, psycho-analysis, anthropology, literary and performance studies, human rights and law, journalism, and the arts to examine current constructions of social trauma and the War in Iraq.

WHAT HAS MADE ITSP DISTINCT?

ITSP's distinct contribution to the field of trauma, mental health, and psychosocial response has been largely shaped by three factors: our focus on working with survivors of political violence from a systemic approach, our location in New York City, and our firsthand experience as responders to the World Trade Center attacks.

Many of us at ITSP have come to trauma work with a theoretical perspective grounded in a family systems approach, as well as experience working with survivors of political violence. This has, from the beginning, led us to attend to the social and political dimensions of traumatic suffering and, in particular, to the social contexts in which people recover or are vulnerable to exploitation. Two members of our faculty, Esther Perel and Steven Reisner, both children of survivors of the Nazi Holocaust, have brought an invaluable perspective to the program based on their firsthand knowledge of survivor families and communities, as well as their experience working in theater. Other faculty and advisors—Soeren Buus Jensen, Judith Landau, Nancy Baron, Nancy Wallace, and Donna Gaffney—

have had extensive international mental health and human rights experience in diverse cultures, which has reinforced a comprehensive approach that includes interventions with populations at multiple levels of the individual, family, community, and society at large.

As the program has developed in New York City, we have benefited from resources and opportunities that have strengthened our international and multidisciplinary perspectives, including the presence of the United Nations, international humanitarian and human rights organizations, academic institutions, and the city itself as a center for media and the arts. New York City as an international crossroads has enabled ITSP to have ongoing exchanges with visiting scholars, practitioners, and students. The large and diverse immigrant population in New York City naturally challenges professionals working with diverse populations to articulate the cultural meanings, biases, and values underlying their work.

Since we have been have working on the development of international mental health and psychosocial response during the past decade, our firsthand experience as a local population of residents and professionals dealing with the impact of 9/11 has provided invaluable experience of the challenges in doing this work. Even though our experience in New York was markedly different from the experiences of those in developing countries, where resources and systems of mental health care are almost nonexistent, there were some similar difficulties. We witnessed some of the same problems seen elsewhere in emergency response, such as the difficulties of coordination, responding to the needs of local populations, and the challenges of collaborative engagement with communities in developing systems of care. We saw the limits of U.S. national approaches to disaster and terrorism preparedness and response, and the conflicts of interest that are created when disaster response is outsourced to profit-oriented companies. This experience has strengthened our advocacy for both top-down and grassroots approaches to disaster preparedness and response.

ORGANIZATIONAL CHALLENGES

The greatest organizational challenge faced by ITSP as a small nonprofit organization has been making the choice to pursue only funding for research and program development that fits our mission. We have had many opportunities to pursue available funding in the trauma field, which focuses on the predominant scientific discourse, privileges symptom reduction, and tends to ignore the social and political environment of the affected populations. These avenues of revenue, while plentiful, would take us in a different direction than we believe is needed, so in the face of underfunding, we have chosen to find independent, creative solutions. Just as in most places in the world where populations are recovering from disasters, we have had to be innovative and to rely on the goodwill of volunteers. Many senior professionals have devoted a great deal of volunteer time to our community psychosocial and arts projects. The lack of resources has also reinforced the need to engage survivors themselves as equal partners in the project of healing.

This approach has enabled us to do pilot work that now informs current research proposals. Because of the focus on our work, we have also become a resource for an international network of professionals in the mental health field that has been developing culturally sensitive family- and community-based approaches to trauma work.

Another challenge we face is finding adequate funding for community-based organizations. This is illustrated in the current work we are doing with the West African refugee community where we are developing a task force to strengthen the capacity of the community to address the needs of their youth. Funding for this type of service is usually directed to large organizations, while very little funding goes where it is needed most: directly to community-based organizations. As a result of this situation, the large organizations outside the community have the financial resources to do the work but do not have access to the local population. The community-based organizations, who are more in tune with the needs of the community members and have the greater ability to engage them in seeking services, have access but insufficient resources to provide these services themselves. As we have learned, when a community-based organization such as African Refuge engages the community, the demand for services often stretches the organization beyond its resources. At the same time, the large provider organizations with funding look to the community organizations for help in referring clients to them, but are usually unable to fund the community organizations for this very time-consuming outreach work. The community organizations, consequently, often feel ethically compelled to provide unreimbursed outreach services to the large organizations, which depletes the smaller organization's resources. We end up having to advocate for the community organizations so that their capacity is not undermined by the larger provider organizations.

Over the years, our training program has relied on the contributions of senior professionals who have not been available to become part of an ongoing core group for the organization because of competing commitments. For the most part, it has not been financially possible to fund such professionals to be available on an ongoing basis. Instead, we have been supporting the development of an alumni community that can contribute to the development of the organization as well as provide voluntary support and consultation for the organization's activities. Still, there is need for administrative support to help maintain the program and provide a structure for continued education, project support, and referral for clinical services and workshops.

FUTURE DIRECTIONS

Over the past ten years, the upsurge in interest in the psychosocial and mental health consequences to people who have suffered traumatic events has led to numerous training and intervention programs. These programs have been directed at the effects of torture, war, natural disasters, and the consequences of individual, familial, and communal violence. Experience and evidence has shown that there are few trained professionals capable of mounting an effective response to these situations. Experts rushing in from other countries frequently lack an understanding of the language, culture, and political context of the countries to whose needs they are responding, and their programs frequently are not integrated into existing response structures. These efforts, hastily organized, provide short-term interventions that leave people without support for their long-term needs.

In response to the ongoing training needs, the International Trauma Studies Program is currently in the process of refining its goals for the future. Based on a review of current research in the field, the documentation of hundreds of hours of workshop presentations and discussions, and a body of clinical and community data collected in both our international and local work as well as through conversations with our network of faculty and program participants, a number of observations have emerged as starting points for our future direction.

First, as we have seen in international responses to catastrophes in recent years, Western mental health perspectives and efforts often have suffered from an arrogance and a lack of self-criticism and openness that have led to ineffective and economically wasteful efforts worldwide, and in many cases, have been damaging because they have undermined local capacities and ways of coping with traumatic events. Fortunately, there has been an emerging consensus about core principles that should guide future international work, as well as a set of best practices, recently published in the IASC Guidelines on Mental Health and Psychosocial Support in Emergency Settings (IASC, 2007). The core principles of this work include the promotion of human rights and equity, maximizing the participation of local populations in humanitarian response, doing no harm, building on available resources and capacities, integrating support systems, and developing a multilayered set of complimentary supports that meets the needs of diverse groups. What we have advocated in New York in response to local mental health needs (such as work with refugees and response to the World Trade Center attacks) has been to learn from international expertise in dealing with catastrophe. This view has been further reinforced through exposure to numerous international programs as well as experience in the field. We are in the process of making available through our website (www.itspnyc.org) training resources that can be accessed by international practitioners. There is currently a need for more research and development of evidence-based practices that focus on collaborative or participatory models of working with families and communities.

Another observation that has been important in defining our future direction is that promotion of psychosocial well-being is a process that in many contexts must be addressed in relation to the needs within a community to promote justice, reconciliation, and broader social development. One of the current challenges in our field is how we might develop participatory approaches in post-conflict settings that are culturally and contextually appropriate. How do we engage with local communities so that they can develop their own solutions to redress past grievances and promote individual and collective healing? How can we address the larger social, political, and economic causes of suffering as an integral part of advancing psychosocial well-being. And what are the human resources and sources of resilience that may promote processes of coexistence between previously conflicted groups? These are some of the questions that will be central to future training and research initiatives at ITSP.

A third observation that has already informed our work, as well as our training program, is that what may be the most effective tool in building capacity to address the needs of populations dealing with catastrophe is the development of supportive helper communities. ITSP has already engaged in a process of convening alumni groups and creating online communities of professionals and community workers in need of support and educational resources to enhance their work. We envision, during the next year, developing a global classroom that can bring professionals together from different countries for workshops and ongoing consultation, supervision, and peer support.

ORGANIZATIONAL SNAPSHOT

Organization: International Trauma Studies Program

Founder/Executive Director: Jack Saul

Mission/Description: The_International Trauma Studies Program (ITSP) perspective is that recent natural and human-made catastrophes have highlighted the need for a multidisciplinary approach to the study, treatment, and prevention of trauma-related suffering. ITSP is now a training and research program affiliated with Columbia University's Mailman School of Public Health. The program has been enriched by the participation of a diverse student body, ranging from mental health professionals, healthcare providers, attorneys, and human rights advocates to journalists and media professionals, academicians, oral historians, and artists. Students and professionals are given the opportunity to develop and share innovative approaches to address the psychosocial needs of trauma survivors, their families, and their communities. ITSP offers a dynamic combination of academic studies, research, and practical experience working with trauma survivors in New York City, the United States, and abroad.

Website: http://www.itspnyc.org/

Address: International Trauma Studies

c/o Jack Saul, Ph.D.

245 Fifth Avenue, Suite 2205

New York, NY 10016

Phone: 212-889-8117

Fax: 212-889-8117

E-mail: jacksaul@mac.com

REFERENCES

Agger, I., & Jensen, S. B. (1990). Testimony as ritual and evidence in psychotherapy for political refugees. *Journal of Traumatic Stress, 3*(1), 115–130.

Agger, I., and Jensen, S. B. (1993). *Trauma and healing under state terrorism.* London: Zed Books.

Baron, N., Jensen, S. B., & de Jong, J. T. V. M. (2002). Mental health of refugees and internally displaced people. In J. Fairbanks, M. Friedman, J. de Jong, B. Green, & S. Solomon. (Eds.). *Guidelines for psychosocial policy and practice in social and humanitarian crises* (pp. 243–270). New York: Report to the United Nations.

Fullilove, M., & Saul, J. (2006). Rebuilding communities post-disaster: Lessons from 9/11. In Y. Neria, R. Gross, R. Marshall, & E. Susser. (Eds.). *September 11, 2001: Treatment, research and public mental health in the wake of a terrorist attack* (pp. 164–177). Cambridge: Cambridge University Press.

Inter-Agency Standing Committee (2007). *IASC Guidelines on mental health and psychosocial support in emergency settings.* Geneva: IASC.

Klein, H. (2003) *Survival and trials of revival: Psychodynamic studies of Holocaust survivors and their families in Israel and the diaspora.* Posthumous manuscript.

Landau, J. (2007). Enhancing resilience: Families and communities as agents for change. *Family Process, 46*(3), 351–365.

Landau, J., & Saul, J. (2004). Facilitating family and community resilience in response to major disaster. In F. Walsh & M. McGoldrick. (Eds.). *Living beyond loss.* New York: Norton.

Pulleyblank-Coffey, E., Griffith, J, & Ulaj, J. (2006). The first community mental health center in Kosovo. In A. Lightburn & P. Session. (Eds.), *Handbook of community-based clinical practice* (pp. 514–528). New York: Oxford University Press.

Reisner, S. *Private trauma/public drama: Theater as a response to international political violence, In* SF Online, 2.1 (Summer, 2003) (http://www.barnard.columbia.edu/sfonline/ps/reisner.htm).

Saul, J. (1999). Working with survivors of torture and political violence in New York City. *Zeitschrift für Politische Psychologie, 7*(1–2), 221–232.

Saul, J. (2007). Promoting community resilience in lower Manhattan after September 11, 2001 [monograph]. *American Family Therapy Academy: Systemic Responses to Disaster; Stories of the Aftermath of Hurricane Katrina,* Winter 2007, 69–75.

Saul, J., Ukshini, S., Blyta, A., & Statovci, S. (2003). Strength-based treatment of trauma in the aging: An Albanian Kosovar case study. In J. Ronch & J. Goldfield. (Eds.). *Mental wellness in aging: Strength based approaches* (pp. 299–314). London: Health Professions Press.

Weine, S., Danieli, Y., Silove, D., Van Ommeren, M., Fairbank, J., Saul, J. (2002). Guidelines for international training in mental health and psychosocial interventions for trauma-exposed populations in clinical and community settings. *Psychiatry: Interpersonal and Biological Processes,* 65(2), 156–164.

BIBLIOGRAPHY
Media Articles about Our Work

Barry, E. (2007, October 31). Seeking hidden accounts of atrocity. Retrieved from *New York Times* website. June 4, 2008, http://www.nytimes.com/2007/10/31/nyregion/31reconcile.html?_r=1&n=Top/Reference/Times%20Topics/People/B/Barry,%20Ellen&oref=slogin.

Cohen, P. (1999, May 8). The study of trauma graduates at last. Retrieved from *New York Times* website. June 4, 2008, http://query.nytimes.com/gst/fullpage.html?res=9A05 E0DD1F3CF93BA35756C0A96F958260.

Riccardi, S. (2001, August 3). Where journalism strokes ethnic hostility. Retrieved September 24, 2003, from the University of Washington, Dart Center for Trauma and Journalism website, www.dartcenter.org.

Rosenberg, T. (1997, December 28) To hell and back. Retrieved from *New York Times* website, June 4, 2008, http://query.nytimes.com/gst/fullpage.html?res=9807E5DC123EF93 BA15751C1A961958260.

Saul, J. (2002, September 11). 2 pillars are crucial to helping children adjust. *New York Times,* p. 17.

Schmitt, E. (1997, December 21). Asylum agents learn to assess tales of torture. *New York Times*, p. A1.

Waters, R. (2004, November/December). The citizen therapist: Making a difference in the wider world. Surviving disaster: Jack Saul believes communities are the antidote for trauma. *Psychotherapy Networker,* pp. 40–41.

Video and Performance

Saul, J. (producer), & Ray, J. (director). (2002). *A partnership for kids: Post 9/11 coping strategies for the school community* [video]. New York: International Trauma Studies Program, NYU.

Saul, J. (producer), & Reisner, S. (director). (2000). *Head soup: The work of Theater Arts Against Political Violence* [theatrical production]. New York: Refuge.

Saul, J. (producer), & Gampel, A. (director). (2003). *Everything's back to normal in New York City: Below Canal, a work in progress* [theatrical production]. New York: Downtown Community Resource Center, International Trauma Studies Program, NYU.

Websites

African Refuge. www.africanresilience.org.

Coming Home: Connecting Older Liberians in the Diaspora with Family and Friends Back Home. www.itspnyc.org/african_refuge/cominghome.html.

International Trauma Studies Program. www.itspnyc.org.

Theater Arts Against Political Violence. www.itspnyc.org/theater_arts_against.html.

12

Center for Health, Intervention, and Prevention

Jeffrey D. Fisher

The Center for Health, Intervention, and Prevention (CHIP) is based at the University of Connecticut (UConn) in Storrs, Connecticut. Since its inception, CHIP has created new scientific knowledge in the areas of health behavior (understanding how and why people behave as they do with respect to their health) and health behavior change (understanding how to change individuals' unhealthy behavior to embrace more healthy alternatives). This knowledge is used by CHIP to design, implement, and evaluate practical interventions to change unhealthy behaviors (e.g., sexual and drug use behaviors that can transmit HIV) in populations at risk for poor health and even death. Worldwide, many such populations are impoverished and disenfranchised, experience serious health disparities, and are urgently in need of interventions to help protect them from poor health. CHIP designs its interventions with substantial input from behavioral scientists, from those who will receive the interventions, and from those who will implement them (J. Fisher, Cornman, Norton, & Fisher, 2006). Its interventions are theory based, cost-effective, and designed to be widely disseminated to large numbers of individuals to maximize the interventions' impact on seemingly intractable health problems. Work at CHIP helps to advance health promotion science and practice at the national and international levels.

CHIP started as the University of Connecticut AIDS Risk Reduction Project (ARRP) in 1985, in an attempt to respond to the emerging international HIV pandemic. Since the early 1980s, HIV has killed approximately 27.1 million people worldwide (UNAIDS, 2007) and remains today an extremely serious global health threat. In CHIP's early years as ARRP, its research was focused entirely on increasing HIV prevention behaviors in populations at risk. It was essentially the work of two brothers, Jeff and Bill Fisher. My brother Bill and I were born on the same day three years apart. We shared birthday parties as children and experienced sibling rivalry growing up. We both went to graduate school in social psychology at Purdue

University, overlapping in our studies by one year. I became a professor at the University of Connecticut, and Bill became a professor at the University of Western Ontario. Our early HIV prevention research was funded by a single grant from the U.S. National Institute of Mental Health (NIMH), and we were assisted in our work by a few staff members.

We had grown up in the 1960s (a "curse" in that we felt a need to do something to try to "change the world"), and both of us had become disaffected with some of the focus of social psychology, the field in which we had received our doctorates. Although social psychology had the theoretical insights, methodologies, and statistical procedures to make important contributions to the solution of critical social and health problems, it tended to eschew such activities. In stark contrast, from our early days as graduate students, our orientation, nurtured by our mentor, Dr. Donn Byrne, had been to apply social psychological theories and experimental methods to address "real world" problems.

We both had done early theoretical and applied work on human sexuality with Byrne, and had worked together and even jointly published a study on condom purchasing behavior while in graduate school (W. Fisher, Fisher, & Byrne, 1977). However, until the start of the HIV epidemic, the preponderance of my early career work had been on recipient reactions to help (e.g., exploring what types of help spawn the greatest subsequent self-help efforts by recipients), and most of Bill's had been on pregnancy prevention and on the effects of sexual stimuli on human behavior. After about ten post-PhD years researching different areas, we began working together again early in the HIV epidemic on human sexual behavior—and especially on how to change HIV risk behavior. This work ultimately led to the creation of CHIP.

I had been a professor at the University of Connecticut for over twenty years when CHIP began with the goal of creating a scholarly environment in which theory in social psychology and the behavioral sciences could be applied to address HIV risk behavior and other critical public health problems. CHIP's work would have demonstrable applied implications for fostering health behavior change in those at risk. It would be a place where linking behavioral science theory, rigorous research methodology, and "real world" applications would be the norm, rather than the exception. CHIP would be a research enterprise in which such activity would be nurtured in any way possible. In many academic disciplines, application is paid little more than "lip service," and in fact, is regarded as of secondary importance to theory. CHIP would be different. It would demonstrate repeatedly that applied problem- and solution-focused research questions are exceptional contexts in which to develop powerful theories that actually work to predict and change human behavior.

CHIP would also be multidisciplinary, rather than adopting the typical structure of a university department, which supports only a single discipline. A multidisciplinary approach to health problems (e.g., involving behavioral scientists from different disciplines working together with physicians, nurses, and even patients) could produce sophisticated approaches to health issues, as well as considerable synergies. Many aspects of CHIP would foster multidisciplinary health behavior change research. CHIP would assist its members in forming multidisciplinary research groups, fund pilot work by these teams, and ultimately assist them to identify funders for the resulting large-scale research, intervention implementation, and/or dissemination projects. It would attempt to offer more administrative support to those with grants than did typical university departments so that researchers could focus on what they do best—research and application—rather than grants administration. In contrast to many university departments, CHIP would have a scholarly, an applied, and an entrepreneurial focus. It would also have a somewhat different culture: be faster paced, be more able to react quickly and outside the box administratively, and be more service oriented toward its affiliates. Universities sometimes create "centers" to serve these types of functions, and in some cases, provide them with significant financial support. The University of Connecticut already had several centers, but none of them performed the type of work I envisioned for CHIP. So I petitioned the university to start a new center with the characteristics outlined above.

CHIP'S PREDECESSOR

Bill and I had been involved in HIV prevention research since the start of the HIV epidemic in the early 1980s. We planned our first HIV-related research study sitting around our parents' dining room table in Ohio one Thanksgiving, and we crystallized the ideas that ultimately were reflected in the theoretical model that would guide most of our health behavior change research at a breakfast table at an early HIV prevention conference in Vermont. Our first HIV prevention research, and the initial work of CHIP's predecessor, ARRP, in 1985, focused on the relationship between fear of AIDS and AIDS preventive behavior. It addressed the question, Was a particular level of fear of HIV associated with optimal levels of HIV preventive behavior? The research was funded with a $1,000 grant from the Society for the Scientific Study of Social Issues (SPSSI), followed by a $50,000 grant on this topic from the Social Sciences and Humanities Research Council of Canada and several small grants from the University of Connecticut.

ARRP's—and our—first large grant (for about $2 million) was from the U.S. NIMH, beginning in 1989 and extending to 1995. It focused on a theory-based approach to designing, implementing, and evaluating HIV risk behavior change interventions in college students. As part of that grant, we created an intervention for mixed-sex groups of college students—implemented in dormitories—that was effective in lowering students' HIV risk behavior. The work was based on the Information, Motivation, Behavioral Skills (IMB) model of HIV risk and prevention (J. Fisher & Fisher, 1992; W. Fisher & Fisher, 1993; J. Fisher & Fisher, 2002; W. Fisher, Fisher, & Harman, 2003; J. Fisher, Fisher, & Shuper, in press) initially developed over breakfast in Vermont, which has since been very widely cited and used in health behavior change research at CHIP and internationally. From 1995 to 2000 our work focused on using the IMB model to design, implement, and evaluate cutting-edge interventions to reduce HIV risk behavior in minority urban high school students. It pitted peer-based versus teacher-based HIV prevention interventions against one another in an effort to ascertain the most effective way to perform large-scale HIV prevention interventions in urban high schools. As part of this work, we developed a low-cost HIV prevention intervention for inner-city high school students that changed their AIDS risk behavior and maintained it at lower levels.

The seeds of the much larger entity that CHIP comprises today were sown in 1997 when the university approved the formation of the Center for HIV Intervention and Prevention, the predecessor to the current CHIP. (So in a sense, this chapter is written on CHIP's tenth anniversary.) By 1997 Bill and I were competing with much larger organizations for very substantial grants, and the name AIDS Risk Reduction Project (ARRP) was obsolete. Organizations with similar names were based in the community, not in academia, and were doing a very different type of work, so I asked the university for permission to start a new multidisciplinary center to replace ARRP. I believed this would help us win our next, much larger grant. This project focused on developing, implementing, and evaluating theory-based interventions to change HIV risk behavior in seropositive individuals (people living with HIV/AIDS). It was a huge departure for the HIV prevention field since the bulk of extant HIV prevention interventions were done with seronegatives (people who did *not* have HIV). Typical interventions attempted to help prevent seronegatives from acquiring HIV but ignored seropositives, who—if they did not practice safer sexual and drug use behavior—could spread HIV and damage their own health by acquiring other pathogens. Clearly, a more complete approach to HIV prevention would have to involve interventions for both seropositives and seronegatives.

Based on the strength of our previous work, in 1997 the university agreed to initiate the new multidisciplinary center, without committing any money, and with the stipulation that it must quickly succeed in acquiring substantial outside funding. The document authorizing the center stated that if substantial funding did not follow, the center could be closed. Fortunately, instead, $3.5 million for our seropositives prevention research project was provided by the U.S. NIMH. The project involved teaching physicians theory-based approaches to having effective conversations about prevention with their seropositive patients in order to help lower patients' levels of risky sexual and drug use behavior. The physician-based intervention was successful, and has since been modified for use by other types of health care providers with seropositive individuals. This intervention approach has been disseminated throughout the world.

In addition to the seropositives prevention project, the grant proposals that CHIP submitted for other projects were also successful. Much to CHIP's good fortune, in the next few years, critical new faculty and other PhDs with research interests and/or funding in HIV prevention were recruited to UConn, and they joined CHIP. Adding Blair Johnson, Kerry Marsh, Deborah Cornman, Rivet

Amico, Mike Copenhaver, and Bede Agocha turned CHIP into a much more substantial operation. CHIP also began to receive institutional support from the Department of Psychology, the dean of Liberal Arts and Sciences, and the vice provost for Research and Graduate Education (VPRGE), and began to thrive as an expanded entity.

There were still critical unfilled needs for increased center support, so in 2002, CHIP began to negotiate a successor agreement with the university. Under this new agreement, CHIP would become one of a select few university research centers, and would receive substantial institutional support. The university would provide CHIP with newly constructed, 9,000 square feet of research and office space as well as funds to create a shared research and administrative infrastructure. Since our first grant, all CHIP research administration had been done solely by the Department of Psychology. It was important to have some of our own administrative staff located physically within the center so they could perform essential work "close to home" and still interface with the Department of Psychology. The agreement also included money for seed grants to fund pilot research to provide promising data and to lead to more successful, and larger, externally funded projects. Under the new agreement, CHIP's charge was to become a major multidisciplinary center for health behavior change research throughout the University of Connecticut system.

Consistent with this charge, CHIP undertook an extensive inventory to identify faculty with interests in health behavior change research across the several campuses of the university. Faculty with relevant interests were asked if they wanted to affiliate with the center, and CHIP went from having 5 affiliates in 2002 to over 115 at present. Also in 2002, with the help of the Psychology Department head, the dean of Liberal Arts and Sciences, and the provost, we recruited Seth Kalichman, an important HIV prevention researcher, to come to UConn from Wisconsin Medical College. At that point, CHIP affiliates included psychologists, sociologists, anthropologists, communications scientists, nursing scientists, kinesiologists, nutritional scientists, statisticians, physicians, psychiatrists, computer scientists, and others representing each school and college of the institution (Photo 12.1). In addition, graduate students who received their PhDs with CHIP faculty began to affiliate formally when they received their degrees and continued their affiliation from their new institutions. Faculty from other universities in the United States and abroad with interests in health behavior change joined CHIP as well. To accommodate this influx of new affiliates, CHIP began to hire more of its own administrative personnel and took over a greater share of its administrative work.

Yearly external grant funding for CHIP research grew geometrically. In 2002 total costs expended by CHIP on research comprised about $1.4 million. Dramatically, CHIP research funding has grown almost sixfold, to $8.3 million per year, since CHIP became a university research center in 2002. This was done in several ways. We "primed the pump" and stimulated additional research grant applications in existing CHIP faculty affiliates and research personnel by providing seed grants

Figure 12.1   Some of CHIP's Research Affiliates: from left, Bill Fisher, Michael Copenhaver, Jeff Fisher, Seth Kalichman, Leslie Snyder, Blair Johnson, Kerry Marsh, Bede Agocha, Deborah Cornman. Courtesy of Dollie Harvey, University of Connecticut.

for promising research likely to lead to external funding. Seed grant proposals are reviewed by a panel of CHIP experts using NIMH grant review criteria and rules, and mentoring reviews are provided to applicants. If a proposal is not funded, suggestions are given on how to make it stronger for the next round of seed grants. Moreover, we provide faculty with information on potential external grant-funding opportunities, form groups of researchers to pursue them (when necessary), and support these groups in any way possible. CHIP provides institutional funding for both substantive and statistical/methodological presubmission reviews of CHIP external grant applications by outside experts to give its affiliates an "edge" in the peer review process. CHIP also hosts an active, biweekly lunch time "health behavior change" speaker series with internationally known guest speakers who meet with interested CHIP faculty and students to discuss their interests and stimulate new research.

Universities often do not provide faculty who have grants with adequate administrative support, and therefore having a grant can become a burden. CHIP attempts to provide excellent administrative support to its affiliates after their grants are funded. Because of CHIP's very large increase in outside grant funds, since 2002 there has been substantial growth in the university's funding of CHIP's research infrastructure, which assists CHIP's grant-funded faculty. In the past five years, the UConn administration has provided CHIP with several administrative positions to handle grant- and center-related financial, personnel, and program-related matters, and with additional monies to fund seed grants to support future faculty research. In 2002 the CHIP administrative team had only one employee; in 2007 there were eleven CHIP administrative employees (8.25 FTE). Overall, CHIP's administrative and operations budget from the university has increased from about $350,000 in 2002 to about $800,000 in 2007. There has been a corresponding increase in grant-funded research employees. In 2002 CHIP had a relatively small number of these staff members, but in 2008, there were about 100 grant-funded research staff working on CHIP research projects in Connecticut and around the world.

The more than twofold increase per year in university support and the sixfold increase per year in external grant funding (from $1.4 to $8.3 million) since 2002 have helped CHIP develop new HIV prevention interventions in South Africa, Mozambique, China, Uganda, India, Russia, Thailand, Vietnam, New Zealand, and Ukraine. This work has included HIV prevention interventions that focus on seronegative and seropositive individuals, as well as on heterosexual, homosexual, and injection drug using populations, among others. Other groups that have been the focus of CHIP's HIV prevention interventions have involved adolescents, sexually transmitted disease clinic patients, soldiers in African countries, and prisoners.

Some of CHIP's intervention work is designed to benefit a particular group of individuals in a particular place. But much more often and as a matter of principle, CHIP interventions are built from the very start so that that if they are found to be effective, they can be disseminated nationally and internationally, and reach very large numbers of people cheaply and effectively. Innovative work in this realm has involved interventions that have peers, rather than traditional interveners, intervene to help other peers practice safer sex and drug use. In addition to my own work, this type of intervention has been implemented by Bob Broadhead, Bill Fisher, and Seth Kalichman, among others. Peers have certain advantages as interveners, in that they can "walk the walk, and talk the talk" of the target population, have greater access to them, and perhaps have greater credibility with them than others might have. Peers also have a unique ability to advocate new behaviors and in so doing, to change group norms and expectations for what types of behavior are acceptable, which can help maintain behavior change over time. Although initiating new, healthier behaviors is critical to health behavior change, it is maintaining these new behaviors over long periods of time that is essential for substantial, sustained changes in public health. Effective peer-based interventions developed in CHIP have involved urban, minority, high school students intervening to promote HIV prevention in other students, and even having active injection drug users intervene to promote HIV prevention in other active injection drug users. We have also identified some unique situations in which peer-based interventions may fail (e.g., when peer networks are unstable, or when peer interveners begin to display, over time, antisocial behaviors inconsistent with what they advocated in the intervention).

Peers have been used in other novel ways in CHIP's HIV prevention interventions. We have found that individuals in some groups that practice risky behavior feel invulnerable to HIV—they believe they could never become HIV positive. When asked what it would take to make them feel vulnerable to HIV, these individuals often answer "show me someone who is 'just like me,' who practices the same risk behaviors that I practice, but who has contracted HIV," or "show me that someone who I consider attractive, and could imagine myself having sex with, could be HIV infected." This has led us to create powerful videos of real people living with HIV, some of whom are very attractive, who tell their stories and establish their similarities to high school or college student audiences. Each of these people contracted HIV in high school or college. We have found that exposure to these videos increases HIV testing behavior in the audience, and in concert with the other HIV prevention intervention components, leads to sustained behavior change in young people.

Another area in which CHIP researchers have taken the lead is in interventions to promote safer sex among individuals living with HIV/AIDS. Historically, most HIV prevention interventions have focused on helping HIV seronegative individuals stay uninfected. The most effective way to accomplish this goal involves fielding a "mixture" of interventions, some targeting seronegatives and others targeting seropositives—and promoting safer sex and drug use in *both* populations. Interventions for seropositives can help them practice safer behaviors, so they do not spread the virus to seronegatives *or* infect themselves with other pathogens. CHIP research on understanding the unique HIV risk dynamics of seropositives (which differ in important ways from risk dynamics among seronegatives), and on learning how to harness this knowledge and use it to change risky behaviors in this critical population, has been pathbreaking. The Healthy Relationships and Options interventions for seropositives developed at CHIP by Kalichman and associates, and by Bill, myself, and our associates, respectively, have been disseminated worldwide.

Other interventions for seropositives developed at CHIP have involved helping them to adhere to antiretroviral medications (ARVs), which can save their lives. If people on ARVs don't take the medicines about 95 percent of the time, and many do not, they can develop a resistant virus, which is difficult to impossible to treat, and which can be transmitted to others through unsafe sex or drug use. People infected by these individuals may also contract difficult to impossible-to-treat viruses. High levels of ARV adherence, which are critical to avoid developing a resistant virus and transmitting it through risky behavior, are very difficult to maintain and must be sustained indefinitely. Therefore, creating adherence-enhancement interventions is challenging and at the same time astoundingly important. Theory-based interventions by Kalichman's team and our team, and by others in CHIP, have helped seropositive individuals increase and sustain their adherence to ARVs. One CHIP intervention program, funded by NIMH, involved creating software to assess the dynamics of each patient's nonadherence, and offering highly engaging, interactive, tailored interventions to address and remediate the causes of poor adherence.

With a strong presence in the HIV prevention and ARV adherence fields, CHIP moved to diversify to other health behavior change areas. This was motivated partly by the university's mandate for CHIP to become a broadly based health behavior change center, partly by the fact that CHIP's expertise could easily be applied in other health behavior change areas, and partly because, as in the stock market, a broad grant portfolio protects against a "downturn" in research funding in any one area. CHIP already had excellent research on issues related to research synthesis, by Blair Johnson and associates, in its portfolio. This research involves the use of sophisticated statistical procedures to assess across multiple research studies and determine what types of interventions are most effective for preventing a given health threat. Some of Johnson's research synthesis work was in the HIV prevention realm, and some was in other health behavior change areas. Additional new research outside HIV prevention included work by Leslie Snyder and associates on using social marketing techniques to promote healthy behavior, work on cancer prevention and on assisting individuals to cope with cancer, research on reducing adverse self-medication behaviors in older adults, and work on pregnancy prevention, exercise genomics, and diet and exercise interventions for diabetics, among other studies.

The move to diversify CHIP's research portfolio is still under way, and is critical. In 2005 CHIP introduced the Center for Health Communication and Marketing (CHCM), headed by Leslie Snyder, which is a U.S. Centers for Disease Control (CDC)–funded "center-within-a center" in CHIP. CHCM, like CHIP, addresses health behavior change across several areas. It helps anchor CHIP in a broader domain of health behavior change arenas, expands its depth of expertise to communications sciences (CHIP had previously been especially strong in psychological approaches to health behavior change), and provides a greater diversity of funding streams (most previous CHIP funding had come from the U.S. National Institutes of Health [NIH]).

Breadth of focus is important, and diversity of funders is crucial. As previously stated, CHIP expertise has the potential to benefit public health in many realms, and it would be desirable to be able to do so. Moreover, diversification across health behavior change areas and funders—involving both public funding sources (such as the CDC and NIH) and private sources (such as the Robert Wood Johnson Foundation and the Bill & Melinda Gates Foundation)—is important. To date, CHIP's external grant support has consisted predominantly of public funding. Although CHIP has been very successful obtaining such resources, future efforts to develop more privately funded research are important. Today, some of the most innovative and important prevention work worldwide is being funded by private organizations such as the Gates Foundation.

Although we have attempted to diversify the breadth of CHIP's research portfolio across health behavior change domains, we struggle with the question of how far to move beyond our roots in HIV prevention. In an ideal world, with unlimited funds and personnel, the answer would be clear. But university funds available to CHIP for additional expansion of its faculty and research are limited, and we have to make careful choices. Mostly, CHIP has to rely for new affiliates on faculty recruited to the university for another reason (e.g., the teaching and/or research needs of a university department), who then choose CHIP as the place to base their research. CHIP cannot dictate their areas of expertise, and is fortunate when new faculty interests correspond to CHIP's needs. Such additions, while critical, do not permit CHIP to grow in new areas in a planful way.

With a finite budget, planful growth could mean taking funds from some of our programs (e.g., seed grants, presubmission grant reviews, "brown bag" lectures) and investing them in a new area (e.g., a position to bolster CHIP cancer prevention research and coordinate cancer prevention activities). Should CHIP take resources from current areas of strength—which are providing support for the entire CHIP research enterprise—and put them into new areas, quite possibly at a cost to our current functions? Too much of this sort of activity could be risky. At this point, we have made a commitment to attempt to expand our foci in a few new, health-related areas; with more financial support and the addition of new university faculty with interests in other health domains, broader-based expansion could become possible.

One way for CHIP to diversify successfully and quickly is for it to recruit several new senior researchers with large—and already funded—grant portfolios in select new areas. Rather than being a "university department" hire with a CHIP co-affiliation, such a hire would be a CHIP hire first, with departmental tenure and co-affiliation. This could quickly jump start research in a new domain. We are currently recruiting two senior faculty investigators with research interests in any of these areas: alcohol and drug abuse; prevention, treatment and management of chronic diseases such as cancer, obesity, or metabolic syndrome; health risk reduction in other areas; health communication marketing campaigns; dissemination of effective health behavior change interventions; and intervention cost-effectiveness analysis. Unfortunately, these types of hires are very rare for university centers. If we can use them to add new research foci and simultaneously add synergy to some of our current areas, we will be optimally successful.

THE UNIVERSITY'S MOTIVATION TO SUPPORT CHIP

Aside from small "seed grant" projects, all of CHIP's research expenditures are supported entirely by its success at winning external grants. Simply put, our grants pay the costs of our research. Since 2002 CHIP has successfully competed for over $54 million in new federal grants, and current annual CHIP research expenditures are about $8.3 million. Historically, about 60 percent of the external grant dollars CHIP researchers apply for are ultimately funded, which is an enviable rate of success. This is likely because of the quality of CHIP researchers and CHIP research, as well as the activities CHIP engages in to help its researchers succeed—seed grants, external presubmission reviews of grants by experts, and others.

Outside of research expenditures, all of CHIP's operating expenses have been borne by the University of Connecticut, which has invested about $3.1 million to cover these expenses (e.g., costs of funding personnel and equipment for CHIP administration; expenses for seed grants, furniture, office supplies, and more) since 2002. The university has also invested about $4 million in constructing about 15,000 square feet of new space for CHIP researchers and administration during the past five years. This has made it possible for CHIP to have researchers from different disciplines under one roof, which creates a great deal of synergy in common physical and intellectual space.

Why would a university make such an investment? Universities value research and teaching, as well as providing service to the community, the state, and ultimately the world. In fact, research, teaching, and service comprise a university's stated mission. The work CHIP does is highly consistent with the research mission of a university, the most valued of the three by many academics. CHIP faculty affiliates have performed pathbreaking research with important conceptual and applied significance, and published their work in top-ranking journals. This work has been highly influential in the health behavior change field and has been widely disseminated. Within the research mission of a university, "basic" research has historically been afforded somewhat greater value than applied research— which is CHIP's major focus. In addition to the research mission of a university, the type of work done at CHIP might also favorably impact on faculty members' teaching, contributing new theoretical models and compelling applications and illustrations of them. Finally, research that impacts the public health is quite consistent with a university's service mission. So in terms of consistency with the tripartite mission of a major research university, CHIP's work is appealing, although perhaps not the most appealing type of activity in which faculty members might engage. So what else explains the university's willingness to invest in CHIP over the past several years?

In addition to serving the missions of the university, the type of work CHIP performs, which is funded by external sponsors (e.g., NIMH, the CDC, state governments, and private foundations) confers significant financial advantages to the university. Each grant carries a charge (termed "indirect costs" and ranging from 40 percent to over 60 percent, or even higher, depending on the institution), to pay for the facilities required to perform the work and other necessary activities such as business and accounting services. University research that is *not* externally funded requires the same types of expenditures (e.g., for facilities), but the costs are not paid by outside funders and must be absorbed by the university. Although one might not like to think of universities as businesses, in many ways they are. The money brought into the institution by the grants CHIP receives, and the prestige associated with these grants—in addition to the contributions of grant-funded work to the missions of the university—are major motivators for the institution to support the types of activities in which CHIP engages.

When we initially applied to the university for center status in 1997, without requesting funding, the administration's acceptance of the proposal was likely motivated by the fact that the work the new center would do could enhance the university's mission. Another critical factor was likely that a successful center could attract substantial research funding and prestige. In 2002, after receiving several more very large grants, we petitioned the university for a new agreement requiring the commitment of substantial university resources: startup expenses to support a much larger multidisciplinary center, funds to cover the yearly costs of running the center (i.e., funds to cover the administrative costs of the center, seed grant funds, and other costs), and monies to build a facility to house the center. The 2002 request was for about $350,000 for the first year (to provide startup administrative staff and seed grants), a percentage return on the indirect costs generated by new grants to the center, and a research/office facility that would cost about $2 million. (In subsequent years, the base operating budget was increased, and the percentage return on indirect costs was dropped.)

The university agreed to the request, likely because a strong center could help the institution meet the research and service aspects of its mission, but also because of the financial benefits associated with supporting a center that was clearly highly successful at winning grants and apt to become even more so. The same motivation likely was responsible for the funding of construction of an expanded CHIP facility in 2006 (6,000 square feet, opening in 2007, to augment the initial 9,000 square feet constructed in 2003) at a cost of about $1.5 million. A factor in this decision was also the likelihood that without additional space, it would be impossible for CHIP to continue to grow its grant portfolio. In 2007, to help ensure CHIP's long-term growth and to assist it in expanding its research base, CHIP was provided with two tenure-track faculty positions, described above.

What overall returns to the university can be used to justify these expenditures? CHIP's grant portfolio has grown phenomenally since 2002, when the university began to support the center by funding its administrative operations and constructing space for CHIP. During the period 2002 to the present, yearly CHIP grant funding has grown sixfold. Over $54 million in new funding, some of which extends well into the future, has been obtained, which has supported a great deal of research activity by UConn scholars at CHIP. During the period 2002 to the present, yearly indirect cost returns to the university generated by CHIP's grants, which under Connecticut law can be used by the institution to improve its research infrastructure (e.g., provide research funding to faculty without grants; purchase research equipment for university departments), have ranged from about $0.3 million in 2002 to about $1.9 million in 2007 and 2008, and have totaled in excess of $9 million. The home departments of CHIP faculty affiliates and their deans also benefit from indirect returns from CHIP grants (i.e., each receives a percentage of the indirect costs generated by CHIP grants from members of their faculty). Other nonfinancial benefits to the institution from CHIP grants involve producing exceptional scholarship, contributing to the solution of critical worldwide health problems, helping to recruit and retain excellent faculty and graduate students, and providing graduate assistantships and unique research settings to support training of a very substantial number of graduate students per year.

During the 2002–8 interval, total operating cost expenditures on CHIP by the university have equaled $3.1 million, and construction costs for CHIP facilities have equaled $4 million. At this point in CHIP's history, the university has expended about $7.1 million on CHIP operations and facilities ($3.1 and $4 million, respectively), and has had $9 million in indirect costs returned to it. At present, since CHIP has sufficient space in which to grow, indirect costs recovered from new grants can continue to increase without additional facility costs, and the university may ultimately have made quite a reasonable investment return when considering financial and other benefits (e.g., to its standing among major U.S. research universities, to its research portfolio, to recruiting and retaining excellent faculty and graduate students, and to funding graduate student training). CHIP's operating expenses over time, which are paid for entirely by the institution, have increased at a much slower pace than CHIP's grant portfolio or its indirect cost returns. This suggests economies of scale and provides confidence that, over time, indirect costs generated by CHIP grants will very substantially overtake the funds the university has expended on CHIP operating expenses and facilities construction. (In the years 2002 to present, CHIP's indirect returns to the university from its grants have ranged from twice its operating budget from the institution, to over four times its operating budget).

EVOLUTION OF CHIP'S STRUCTURE OVER TIME

As CHIP has grown over time, its structure has evolved. CHIP was "born" within the UConn Department of Psychology and performed its administrative functions with assistance from that department until September 2007. Until 2004 most major decisions were made by the CHIP director and the Psychology Department chair, with informal consultation from CHIP affiliates. In 2004 CHIP's director began to report to the university vice provost for Research and Graduate Education (VPRGE), and CHIP continued to receive oversight and substantial administrative support from the Psychology Department. Most major decisions continued to be made by its director in consultation with the Psychology Department head and the VPRGE, again with informal consultation from CHIP affiliates. In a sense, CHIP was relatively "closely held" by the university.

The reason CHIP initially received administrative support from the Psychology Department and did not function as an independent entity was because, as a young organization, there were economies of scale in "bundling" administrative services. In addition, CHIP did not have a sufficiently deep or mature business staff to become administratively independent until about 2006. The relationship with the Psychology Department to help administer CHIP's business was critical in the early years; indeed, CHIP could not have thrived without the tremendous assistance it received from the Psychology Department and its chair, Charles Lowe. Later, as CHIP matured and became capable of functioning independently, it became clear that administrative efficiencies could be achieved from separating from the Psychology Department and running its own business operations.

In 2007, in anticipation of becoming administratively independent, CHIP formed a more active executive committee made up of junior and senior CHIP affiliates. This committee meets four or more times a year and broadly advises the director and associate director on matters of interest and concern.

One of the major challenges CHIP faces at present is becoming a center with a number of faculty and staff leaders, not just in research, but in administration. To this end, the position of CHIP associate director Deborah Cornman has been expanded in the past few years. CHIP is also involving additional faculty affiliates in its administrative leadership. Its founding director (the author of this chapter) will likely retire in the next five years, and for CHIP to continue to thrive, its leadership needs to become broader, deeper, and more decentralized. This is being done through having a vital executive committee and generally by becoming a more inclusive organization. Another element that could foster more broad-based leadership would be for CHIP's structure to evolve, over time, to be more similar to traditional NIMH-funded research centers. This would involve the creation of several "cores" that perform critical functions for the center, each with its own leadership (CHIP is not, at this time, an NIMH-funded center, but it may aspire to become one in the future).

In this context, CHIP might evolve to have an active administrative core (led by its director, associate director, and the CHIP business team leader) as well as a formal methods core, responsible for supporting CHIP researchers and ensuring that CHIP grants use state-of-the-science research methods and statistical procedures. CHIP could also develop a formal developmental core, charged with assisting CHIP scientists in the development of new research proposals. This group could also oversee the provision of seed grant funds and presubmission reviews of grant applications, and provide information about external funding possibilities. Since many CHIP affiliates have a serious interest in intervention dissemination—relatively unique among research centers—and since CHIP has had substantial success in this domain, adding a dedicated dissemination core, which would specialize in developing theory and research on the science of successfully disseminating evidence-based interventions, would also be desirable. A center organization in terms of cores, each with its own leadership, could broaden CHIP leadership and encourage more activity on the part of rank-and-file CHIP members, who would belong to the cores. It could create additional synergies within the center, provide new opportunities and benefits for junior faculty, and position CHIP to apply successfully for NIMH or CDC center grant funds.

Some of the challenges CHIP faces involve whether it will be able to continue to grow at its current pace in an environment in which federal grant funding is leveling off and in some cases decreasing (Loscalzo, 2006; Zerhouni, 2006). The fact that CHIP performs multidisciplinary research may help in this respect, since multidisciplinary work is consistent with the "NIH roadmap" and is not targeted for decreased funding (Zerhouni, 2003). As with grant funds, it may ultimately be a challenge for CHIP to continue to obtain increased operating funds from the university to support its programs.

Assuming that CHIP can continue to increase its grant portfolio and operating funds, it is absolutely critical that the center not grow too fast. At times in its short history, CHIP's growth has outstripped its ability to provide services to its affiliates, which has caused temporary difficulties. Geometric growth can create organizational problems and pressures for limited resources and physical space. Too much growth can also change the character of an organization which initially made it appealing. In sum, the challenge for us is to choose the right rate of growth in the face of a myriad of seemingly attractive opportunities.

CONCLUSION

It has been a privilege for me to have had the opportunity to start CHIP, and to have helped create and influence the development of an organization that attempts to aid others in need. In just a few years, CHIP has gone from having a couple of grants, a couple of researchers, and a couple of graduate students, in a couple of rooms on the second floor of the UConn psychology building, to a very substantial enterprise with its own facility. Along the way, I firmly believe that some of our efforts have benefited the public health of vulnerable populations, and, hopefully, saved more than a few lives.

For me, the University of Connecticut has been a place where I was able to have a promising idea (for CHIP) and receive the tremendous and continuing support needed to turn it into reality and to sustain it. Throughout my career, I have continuously been amazed at the "places I've been able to go," to quote Dr. Seuss. Part of this success has been because of wonderful partners, such as my brother, Bill, and others too numerous to name, over a career of thirty-three years. All are terribly important to me, and some are among my best friends. I have had the good fortune to have had truly magnificent collaborators, graduate students, and staff in my own research programs and wonderful staff within the CHIP administration. They wear many hats, work very long hours, and go beyond the call of duty daily. They are committed to the goals of our research and to the vision of the center. Among these folks, Deborah Cornman, associate director, has been an important part of the CHIP administration from the start. My wife and family have always been supportive of my work with CHIP.

My career in psychology has given me the opportunity to contribute to science, build theory, and engage in an ever-changing array of extremely interesting projects with potentially great practical significance. I have been able to have fascinating discussions about what promotes healthy and unhealthy behavior, apply for grants with extraordinarily talented groups of people, and obtain the funding needed for large-scale health behavior change intervention research projects that can benefit public health. I have been a part of the creation of amazing teams of people, who have gone on to do almost unbelievable things. I have met and worked with wonderful people worldwide, and have immensely enjoyed being part of the growth of exceptional postdoctorate, graduate, and undergraduate students and staff at the university and elsewhere. It is a pleasure to watch people grow to do—consistently and well—what they at first never thought they could ever do, just as it has been a pleasure to grow in these ways myself over the past thirty-three years. I have never been bored, even for a moment.

Acknowledgments

Thanks to William Fisher, Wynne Norton, and Beth Krane for the helpful comments on earlier drafts of this manuscript. Thanks to NIMH for over twenty years of continuous research support.

ORGANIZATIONAL SNAPSHOT

Organization: Center for Health, Intervention, and Prevention (CHIP)

Founder/Director: Jeffrey D. Fisher

Mission/Description: The University of Connecticut's Center for Health, Intervention, and Prevention (CHIP) creates new scientific knowledge and theoretical frameworks in the areas of health behavior, health behavior change, health intervention, and prevention. It disseminates theory-based knowledge and new, cutting-edge interventions through research, capacity building, teaching, mentoring, and collaboration at the university, local, state, national, and international levels.

Website: http://www.chip.uconn.edu/int_res_int.htm

Address: Center for Health, Intervention, and Prevention (CHIP)

University of Connecticut

2006 Hillside Road, Unit 1248

Storrs, CT 06269-1248

Phone: 860-486-5917

Fax: 860-486-4876

E-mail: jeffrey.fisher@uconn.edu

lisa.dunnack@uconn.edu (Lisa Dunnack, administrative assistant)

sarah.bothell@uconn.edu (Sarah Bothell, webmaster)

REFERENCES

Fisher, J. D., & Fisher, W. A. (1992). Changing AIDS-Risk Behavior. *Psychological Bulletin, 111*, 455–474.

Fisher, J. D., & Fisher, W. A. (2002). The Information-Motivation-Behavioral Skills Model. In R. DiClemente, R. Crosby, & M. Kegler. (Eds.). *Emerging Theories in Health Promotion Practice and Research* (pp. 40–70). San Francisco, CA: Jossey Bass.

Fisher, J. D., Fisher, W. A., & Shuper, P. A. (In press). The Information-Motivation-Behavioral Skills Model of HIV Preventive Behavior. In R. DiClemente, R. Crosby, & M. Kegler. (Eds.). *Emerging Theories in Health Promotion Practice and Research* (2nd ed.). San Francisco, CA: Jossey Bass.

Fisher, J. D., Cornman, D. H., Norton, W. E., & Fisher, W. A. (2006). Involving Behavioral Scientists, Health Care Providers, and HIV-Infected Patients as Collaborators in Theory-Based HIV Prevention and Antiretroviral Adherence Interventions. *JAIDS, 43*, S10–S17.

Fisher, W. A., & Fisher, J. D. (1993). Understanding and Promoting AIDS Preventive Behavior: A Conceptual Model and Educational Tools. *Canadian Journal of Human Sexuality, 1*, 99–106.

Fisher, W. A., Fisher, J. D., & Harman, J. J. (2003). The Information-Motivation-Behavioral Skills Model: A General Social Psychological Approach to Understanding and Promoting Health Behavior. In J. Suls & K. Wallston. (Eds.). *Social Psychological Foundations of Health and Illness* (pp. 82–105). United Kingdom: Blackwell Publishers.

Loscalzo, J. (2006). The NIH Budget and the Future of Biomedical Research. *New England Journal of Medicine, 354*(16), 1665–1667.

UNAIDS, (2007). *2007 AIDS Epidemic Update: Executive Summary.* Retrieved December 2, 2007, from UNAIDS website: http://www.unaids.org/en/KnowledgeCentre/HIVData/ EpiUpdate/EpiUpdArchive/2007/default.asp.

Zerhouni, E. (2003). The NIH Roadmap. *Science, 302,* 63-64, 72.

Zerhouni, E. A. (2006). NIH in the Post-Doubling Era: Realities and Strategies. *Science, 314*(5802), 1088–1090.

13

REMEDY

William H. Rosenblatt, Teresa
Bartrum, and Myron Panchuk

REMEDY (Recovered Medical Equipment for the Developing World) is an organization dedicated to promoting the recovery of unused medical supplies for the purposes of providing aid, reducing waste, and promoting cost-effectiveness. As a catalyst for change, this group seeks to inspire through education, practice, and example.

REMEDY is committed to cooperating with other charitable organizations engaged in similar activities. By working together, these organizations hope to more efficiently and reliably respond to those in needs.

BACKGROUND

Founded in 1991 by William H. Rosenblatt, MD, professor of anesthesiology at Yale University School of Medicine, REMEDY is a group of health care professionals who promote the nationwide recovery of opened-but-unused surgical supplies. The end goal of their mission is to provide international medical relief and to reduce solid medical waste in hospitals.

During the 1980s, Dr. Rosenblatt was a pediatrician in training at Stanford University in California. He was well aware of the Inter-plast program in Palo Alto: the first program of its kind to perform cleft lip and cleft palate surgery for the indigenous peoples of Latin America. As a trainee in pediatrics, Dr. Rosenblatt did not have the opportunity to participate in mission trips, but when he came to Yale as a trainee in anesthesiology, he found that trip anesthesiology residents were in high demand. He started traveling to Latin America to provide anesthesia for cleft lip and cleft palate surgeries. These medical missions had a profound impact on him. He was exposed to the lack of adequate equipment and the problems that this created. With this new insight, he returned to a modern operating room and noted that the exact same equipment— excess supplies prepared for surgery— was being discarded without ever being used. As a result, Dr. Rosenblatt formed REMEDY in 1988. He began recovering unused supplies from operating rooms at Yale-New Haven Hospital. He discovered that nurses and doctors at other facilities had been attempting to collect unused supplies as well, but without a formalized program. The great disparity in the conditions between operating rooms in countries where medical supplies are lacking and in modern operating rooms where there is an excess of equipment reinforced Dr. Rosenblatt's quest to find a solution that would bridge this gap.

The regulation of medical waste in the United States was also a factor that initially blocked the creation of REMEDY. At about the same time that Dr. Rosenblatt was formulating the concept of a recovery effort, reports of medical waste washing up on the shores of Long Island were appearing in the media. This created a public outcry. A similar mishap was documented at another hospital in Long Island. A barge that was carrying general household waste was found on inspection to be carrying a small amount of medical waste. Eventually, the hospital disposed of the entire barge as medical waste—a costly solution. Medical waste is typically treated chemically and either landfilled or incinerated. When there is chemical treatment, there is the potential for the chemicals to leech into the ground water. When medical waste is incinerated, toxins may also be produced. In the early 1990s, U.S. hospitals decided to no longer risk a small amount of medical waste being found in materials that were labeled "general" waste; instead, all hospital waste was labeled "medical" waste.

Gloves, sutures, drapes, gowns, and many other items are prepared for use during surgeries, but not all are used. These supplies are discarded nevertheless because they are no longer considered to be "sterile." This is true even if there has been no contact with a patient. Because of legal concerns, these supplies cannot be used in the United States, but they are enthusiastically accepted by many charitable organizations for distribution to healthcare personnel throughout the developing world.

For years healthcare workers have voluntarily collected these supplies; however, such efforts are often erratic and can place both the individual and the institution at legal risk. In addition, these isolated efforts could not possibly recover the huge surplus that becomes available in U.S. hospitals.

As a result of these concerns and new procedures, hospitals began producing a tremendous amount of what was designated "medical waste," with a disposal cost six times that of normal hospital waste. If the hospital could send tons of materials to an organization such as REMEDY, a cost savings could result.

REMEDY started as pilot project at Yale-New Haven Hospital (YNHH) in Connecticut. This location also served as a base for research studies conducted by Dr. Rosenblatt in collaboration with Dr. David Silverman. These studies demonstrated the efficacy, cost-effectiveness, and environmental friendliness of supply recovery through the REMEDY program. After the studies were published, inquiries began to pour in from medical professionals from across the United States.

REMEDY became a nonprofit organization committed to teaching about and promoting the recovery of surplus medical supplies. Drs. Rosenblatt and Silverman developed a comprehensive in-service teaching packet with all the information needed to start a standardized recovery program based on the REMEDY model, applicable to any surgical procedure in hospitals throughout the United States. Recovery protocols were designed for easy adaptability in operating rooms and for critical care routines. This educational packet is distributed free of charge to any requesting hospital. Materials can be found at REMEDY's website, www.remed yinc.org/Content/Educational_Materials.asp.

PHILOSOPHY

Rather than reinvent the logistics of charitable medical supply distribution, REMEDY suggested turning to the huge network of U.S.-based nonprofit medical charities to form partnerships. It is the mission of these groups to support and successfully deliver medical assistance and supplies to countries in need. These groups have the staff, knowledge, experience, funding, and overseas contacts to successfully deliver recovered supplies to appropriate medical professionals. REMEDY encourages each hospital's recovery program to target donations to any organization or project they wish.

As of June 2004, the REMEDY programs had donated many millions of dollars worth of supplies from operating rooms alone. This has resulted in a vast increase in medical aid sent from the United States to the developing world.

To date, REMEDY has assisted more than 600 hospitals around the United States in program implementation and the identification of potential recipient charities. REMEDY relies on the expertise of these U.S.–based nonprofit agencies to distribute these materials abroad.

In 2004 REMEDY became an endorser of the Environmental Protection Agency's Waste Wise program. By becoming a partner in this program, the REMEDY recovery programs are able to translate the amount of supplies recovered every year into greenhouse gas reductions. Waste Wise uses the EPA's Waste Reduction Model (WARM) to estimate the amount of gas emissions prevented through an organization's solid waste reduction activities. There is no fee for membership, and it allows groups to set their own goals that are feasible for their individual organizations. (For more information on Waste Wise, see www.remed yinc.org/Content/Wastewise.asp.)

SUPPLY RECOVERY PROGRAMS

In addition to the accomplishments of the REMEDY pilot program at Yale, there has been significant success over the years among the hospitals and groups that have requested the REMEDY in-service teaching packet. REMEDY follows up on all requests for teaching packets and on the progress of those initiatives. REMEDY is not a membership organization, so it can be difficult to get regular feedback from those who have used REMEDY's ideas or resources.

Protocols

REMEDY has developed recovery protocols that are designed to be quickly adaptable to the everyday operating room routine. Although these are the procedures developed for the active pilot program in the operating rooms of Yale-New Haven Hospital (YNHH), they can be modified to adapt to the demands and resources of each healthcare facility. YNHH uses a "case cart" system, where supplies for each surgical procedure are sent to the operating room on a prepared, wheeled cart.

What Supplies Can Be Recovered?

This is a sample list of the items commonly recovered through the REMEDY pilot program at YNHH. This list is offered only as an example, and does not imply that other organizations should recover these same items, nor limit their recovery to items that appear on this list.

- 4 × 4 Sponge
- Absorbable Hemostat
- Absorbent Towel
- Ace Bandage
- Aortic Cannula
- Arthroscope Drape
- Burn Dressing
- C-Arm Drape
- Cast Padding
- Cautery Pad
- Cautery Pencil
- Cherry Sponge
- Chest Tube
- Cone Splash Shield
- Cover Sponge
- Disposable Vascular Clip
- Electrode
- Electrosurgical Dispersive
- Endotracheal Tube
- Extremity Sheet
- Femoral Irrigation And Suction Tip Set
- Foley Catheter
- Heel Protector
- Hemo Clip
- Hemovacimpervious Split Drape
- Intestinal Sucker
- Irrigation Syringe
- Iv Set
- Jackson Pratt Drain
- Lap Set 18x18
- Lap Set 4x18
- Large Drape
- Magnetic Pad
- Mucus Trap
- Open Sponge
- Open Sta-Tite
- Other Syringe
- Paper Towel
- Partial Lap 4 × 18
- Peanut Sponge
- Penrose Drain
- Prep Solution Pack
- Rolled Gauze
- Salem Sump
- Scalpel Blade (No Sharps Exposed/Foil Intact)

- Skin Graft Carrier
- Skin Marker
- Skin Staple
- Soft Suction
- Specimen Container
- Staple Remover
- Steri Strip
- Steridrape
- Sterile Gloves
- Stockinet Impervious
- Straight Catheter
- Suction Hose
- Surgical Gown
- Surgical Patties (In Package Set)

- Suture (No Sharps Exposed/Foil Intact) Sponge-Package
- Tape Roll: Cloth/Paper
- Tissue Stapler And Refill
- Tube & Cord Holder
- T-U-R-Y Set
- Telfa Packaged
- Urine Culture Tube
- Urine Drainage Bag
- Urine Meter
- Vascular Occlusion
- Vasefine Gauze
- Wet Pruf Packaged
- Xeroform
- Yankeur

CHALLENGES FOR STARTING THE PROGRAM

REMEDY has experienced steady and positive growth. REMEDY typically works with one hospital staff member who is motivated to start a REMEDY program. Unfortunately, that individual may find roadblocks at the facility. REMEDY works with invested individuals and helps work through any difficulties they might face.

There are several problems a hospital may experience in creating a REMEDY program, but the most frequent problem is administrative. The administration has to have a clear vision of what needs to be done. One example that demonstrated a need for clear communication was a situation in a hospital in the state of Washington. Although one nurse was diligently working at collecting surplus supplies, the hospital administration thought the REMEDY Recovery Program reflected poorly on the hospital. The concern was that the hospital would be seen as wasting too much material. This was a concern shared by the YNHH administration prior to the start of the Yale pilot program. Fortunately, only positive reporting appeared in the media, the authors of which understood that waste is inevitably produced by hospitals, as in other industries. REMEDY was making good use of that so-called hospital waste.

Other individuals meet resistance from the hospitals' risk management services. The perception exists that the hospital could be held liable for injury to a patient abroad. A legal opinion from the Yale School of Law noted that without the sale of the items and with a clear statement that the materials were donated "as is," the donating facilities were indemnified.

Storage is yet another issue. If a hospital is unable to find a charity to take their unused materials on a regular basis, storage space (a premium in hospitals) is vital.

How REMEDY Handles Challenges

Although REMEDY has been successful, it has grown slowly. The program has been in place for seventeen years. Instead of making giant strides, Dr. Rosenblatt thinks REMEDY has plodded along. REMEDY has not sought to rush development after having seen similar types of programs fail when they tried to jump ahead too quickly.

As Dr. Rosenblatt reflects over REMEDY's past seventeen years, he wishes that he would have tried to secure funding earlier in an attempt to help the program grow faster. He also thinks the hospital projects are too independent, and wishes they would form tighter networks and maintain better communication and ties with each other. This would increase benefits for all involved. The typical hospital's cost of recovering these supplies has amounted to a minor expense of no more than $200 a year. Additionally, by avoiding the discarding of tons of solid medical waste, a hospital should realize a net savings for the length of time the hospital has participated in the REMEDY program. As a byproduct of the program's in-house exposure at YNHH, hundreds of thousands of dollars in new disposables and capital equipment have also been donated to the REMEDY pilot program. The majority of these collected supplies have been donated to the following nonprofit organizations:

- New Haven/Leon (Nicaragua) Sister Cities Project
- Albert Schweitzer Institute
- New Haven/Hue (Vietnam) Sister Cities Project
- New Haven/Freetown, Sierra Leone, Sister Cities Project
- PUMA (Operation Blessing Nepal)
- Knightsbridge International
- Hand Carry Program

In addition to the accomplishments of the original REMEDY project at Yale, there has been significant success in the hospitals that have developed programs based on the REMEDY model.

REMEDY currently has 640 hospitals using the model in the United States. These are either established REMEDY hospitals or hospitals that are just joining the program. During the last six months, they have received REMEDY's written materials and are developing their recovery programs.

REMEDY'S SHOOTING STARS

REMEDY is delighted the following programs have embraced the full REMEDY philosophy, not only by running supply recovery programs but also by disseminating the ideas and methods to others: Duke Recovery, MED World, Supplies Overseas (SOS), Medical Bridges, and MedShare International.

REMEDY TODAY

REMEDY shifted from concept to reality by just doing it. Dr. Rosenblatt's idea of distributing supplies was turned into a working model. Protocols were written and put into a book form to be sent to those interested in the program. There was not a lot of discussion and planning. It was just a question of doing it, and from there, REMEDY simply evolved over time.

HOW REMEDY SUPPORTS ITSELF

REMEDY first acquired funding through personal donations from medical colleagues and friends. At first, efforts were local. The REMEDY annual appeal raises over $10,000 yearly from donators across the United States. Efforts now also include grant writing.

REMEDY supports itself primarily through grants and family foundation gifts. A comprehensive list is available on the website at www.remedyinc.org. A teaching packet and a list of other ways in which individuals can contribute are also available on the website.

REMEDY's work is augmented in various ways, including

- Online donations: https://payments.auctionpay.com/ver3/?id=w022042
- Mail-in donations: www.remedyinc.org/Content/Mail_In_Donations.asp
- In-kind donations: www.remedyinc.org/Content/In_Kind_Donations.asp
- Shop online: www.remedyinc.org/Content/Support_Us.asp
- Wish list: www.remedyinc.org/Content/Wish_List.asp
- Medical supplies and equipment: make donations by visiting the Medical Equipment Donation Agency (Med-Eq) program at www.med-eq.org/

RAISING AWARENESS FOR REMEDY

REMEDY creates educational opportunities for interested hospitals, organizations, and others. By participating in venues that raise awareness, REMEDY shows interested individuals how to start their own programs and network with similar organizations.

REMEDY representatives attend several academic and professional meetings throughout the year. One such gathering is the Association of Operating Room Nurses (AORN). REMEDY attends this meeting annually, and has been doing so since 1993. REMEDY also attends the American Society of Anesthesiologists, the American Medical Students' Association, and Clean Med's annual meetings. Also, in the 1990s, REMEDY published academic articles that appeared in anesthesiology (1996, 1997), orthopedic (1996), and plastic surgery (1996) journals. Dr. Rosenblatt published two articles in the *Journal of the American Medical Association* (JAMA) (1992, 1993), and REMEDY received marked interest as a result.

MEASURES OF SUCCESS

Another indication of REMEDY's success over the past seventeen years is the building of partnerships with students from Yale and other colleges who travel to developing countries for medical and educational projects. REMEDY supplies medical devices for these endeavors. For the Yale students, this is a wonderful opportunity to transport supplies and enhance their experience on these trips.

REMEDY ON DISASTER RELIEF

When a natural disaster affects the world community, REMEDY makes no direct contribution to the relief aid in the affected region. REMEDY has long maintained that the millions of dollars of medical supplies collected by associate hospitals are best suited for the chronic shortages that affect the developing world and are not adequate for acute relief. A coordinated relief effort requires immense organization. Predictability and compatibility are of the utmost importance. When a doctor is working in a disaster area, he or she needs to know exactly what supplies are available and how they must be rationed. The healthcare worker has no use for the heterogeneous and often unpredictable supplies that can be donated through the REMEDY recovery process. There is nowhere to store these supplies until they can be used, and the funds used for shipment are better spent elsewhere. Sending boxes of supplies to a disaster region may make people feel good, but in all likelihood would pose a burden on the recipient. Perhaps REMEDY is missing an opportunity to request "disaster donations" from the public, and to receive media attention, but REMEDY believes that donor generosity would be misguided.

So how does REMEDY respond to crises? After the acute events are over, the affected communities will continue to need help and the equipment and supplies provided through the REMEDY model. When the international community responds to the next tragedy, REMEDY will be there to help charitable agencies that already have an established long-term commitment to the region.

WHAT ARE THE NEXT STEPS FOR REMEDY?

A REMEDY sister project called Med-Eq, which pairs more advanced materials and equipment with charitable agencies, was started in 2005. Begun as e-mail alert system in 1998 (AIRe-mail), Med-Eq is an interactive database website. Items that are not suited to general medical-surgical care are posted on the Med-Eq website. Agencies whose specific mission can deliver an item to an appropriate site are connected with the donor.

REMEDY will be working on revisiting the need for the decontamination of recovered surgical supplies earmarked for donation and will continue its ongoing examination of the legal issues involved in the recovery of surgical supplies from U.S. hospitals.

REMEDY invites readers to visit the website at www.remedyinc.org. Also, REMEDY networks with groups interested in initiating hospital supply recovery programs, such as

- International relief/aid organizations
- Medical waste-reduction and environmental organizations/professionals
- Medical ethics groups
- Government agencies
- Associations of healthcare professionals and facilities
- Supply vendors

REMEDY collaborates with interested readers through the website email at www.remedyinc.org/Content/Contact.asp. Anyone interested in waste reduction in hospitals is encouraged to contact Dr. Rosenblatt.

AWARDS REMEDY HAS RECEIVED

The prestigious Rolex Award for Enterprise was bestowed upon Dr. William H. Rosenblatt in May 1996. The five winners of this award (from an initial field of 2,300) also received extensive international media coverage. As a result, REMEDY received requests for information from many U.S. hospitals as well as from facilities in Japan, West Africa, Mexico, France, Switzerland, India, Pakistan, Cameroon, Kenya, Canada, Germany, Grenada, the Netherlands, Romania, Philippines, and Ivory Coast.

REMEDY received the Cost-effectiveness Award from Anesthesiology News (sponsored by an educational grant from Stuart Pharmaceuticals) in April 1994 for achievement in cost-effectiveness in the operating room.

REMEDY has also been awarded the Green Ribbon Award from the New Haven Chamber of Commerce and the Committee on Environmental Issues. REMEDY won the Current Innovations Award (*Anesthesiology News* magazine) in 1992. In 1999 Alaska state legislature officials honored REMEDY for the introduction of the program to hospitals throughout the state.

BOARD OF DIRECTORS

William H. Rosenblatt, MD, president, is professor of anesthesiology at Yale University School of Medicine, the founder of REMEDY, its volunteer medical director, and primary author of the seminal articles on recovery published in the *Journal of the American Medical Association* and others. Dr. Rosenblatt has been the recipient of multiple awards for his work with REMEDY, including the 1996 Rolex Award for Enterprise in Science and Invention. Dr. Rosenblatt was nominated for the Ford Foundation Leadership for a Changing World Award (2000), the Conrad N. Hilton Award (1999), and the Points of Light Award (1999).

David G. Silverman, MD, vice president, is professor of anesthesiology and director of clinical research, Department of Anesthesiology, Yale University School of Medicine. He is also medical director of the Yale-New Haven Hospital Pre-Admission Center. Dr. Silverman is a highly accomplished investigator with over seventy publications in major medical journals and numerous grant-funded studies; he is the co-author of the seminal articles on recovery published in the *Journal of the American Medical Association* and others.

Chris Ariyan, MPH, director, is the program director for strategic planning with Anthem Blue Cross Blue Shield's East Region. Prior to joining Anthem, he was a healthcare consultant with Deloitte Consulting and Ernst & Young LLP. He was also co-founder and executive vice president of HealthInfo Corp, a Web-based patient and physician education service. Mr. Ariyan received his Master's of Public Health degree with a concentration in healthcare management from Yale University and was the first executive director for REMEDY (1992–97).

Catherine Adcock Admay, JD, director, has been a member of the Duke Law School faculty since September 1996. She teaches comparative and public international law, directs the International Development Clinic, and is affiliate faculty of the Duke Center for International Development (DCID) at the Terry Sanford Institute of Public Policy at Duke University. Prior to her appointment at Duke, she was a lecturer and co-director of the international development clinic at New York University Law School. She has worked for the NAACP Legal Defense Fund, the Office of the Legal Advisor in the United States Department of State, and with private law firms in Washington, D.C.

Darryl Rotman Kuperstock, director, is a past executive director of REMEDY. During her tenure (1995–2003), the organization grew significantly, and her service culminated with the development and launch of the current REMEDY website. She brings with her significant, diverse professional and volunteer experience in the fields of management consulting, program and event planning, nonprofit organizational leadership development, editing, library science, and the visual arts.

Allen Katzoff, director, has spent the past fifteen years managing entrepreneurial initiatives in the nonprofit sector. Before that, he spent many years in executive marketing positions with high-technology companies and founded a start-up data compilation company. Currently, he serves as the director of the Center for Adult Learning at Hebrew College in Boston and is on the board of directors of the Vain and Harry Fish Foundation. He was an important advocate of REMEDY's application to the Fish Foundation, which led not only to an initial gift but also to continued support. He has an MBA from Northeastern University.

Mary Koto, PhD, director, has worked for more than twenty years in marketing, strategic planning, and operations in the medical industry.

Most recently, she served as vice president of marketing for Accumetrics, a privately held cardiovascular diagnostics company. Prior to that, as vice president at LMA North America, she headed marketing and operations, and helped to launch two major anesthesia devices that have influenced standards of care worldwide. During her years there, she was responsible for LMA-NA becoming a significant REMEDY corporate supporter—one of the earliest. Her most important contribution to REMEDY to date was her leading role in the first REMEDY staff retreat in December 2004. At her own expense, she traveled from her home in San Diego to meet with the staff for a one-day session during which the REMEDY mission was focused and strengthened. She has a BA and MBA from Stanford University and a PhD in biology from Yale.

ORGANIZATIONAL SNAPSHOT

Organization: REMEDY

Founder: William Rosenblatt, MD

Mission/Description: REMEDY, Recovered Medical Equipment for the Developing World, is a nonprofit organization committed to teaching about and promoting the recovery of surplus operating room supplies. REMEDY provides proven recovery protocols that can be adapted quickly to everyday operating room or critical care routines. As of June 2006, the REMEDY at Yale University program alone has donated more than 50 tons of medical supplies. It is estimated that at least $200 million worth of supplies could be recovered from U.S. hospitals each year, resulting in an increase of 50 percent in the medical aid sent from the United States to the developing world.

Website: http://www.remedyinc.org/

Address: 3-TMP, 333 Cedar Street

P. O. Box 208051

New Haven, CT 06520-8051

Phone: (203) 737-5356

Fax: (203) 785-2802

E-mail: Will.rosenblatt@Yale.edu

14

Center for Global Initiatives

Chris E. Stout

Of all the forms of inequality, injustice in health care is the most shocking and inhumane.

—Martin Luther King Jr.

The Center for Global Initiatives (CGI) is the first center devoted to training multidisciplinary healthcare professionals and students to bring services that are integrated, sustainable, and resiliency based, with publicly accountable outcomes, to areas of need worldwide via multiple, small, context-specific collaboratives that integrate primary care, behavioral healthcare, systems development, public health, and social justice. The word "global" is not used as a synonym for overseas or international, but rather to indicate local as well as transnational disparities and inequities of health risk and illness outcomes. We seek to eschew the many disconnects between separation of body/mind, physical/mental, and individual/community, and offer instead a synthetic model of integration. CGI's philosophy and approach is always that of a collaborator and colleague. No "West-Knows-Best" hubris. We learn as we teach. We feel as we treat.

We focus on the complex healthcare issues involved in community crises, healthcare inequities, humanitarian emergencies, and relief situations, from the individual care level to a regional scale. All activities are grounded in science/evidence-based practice models and best practices in culturally diverse communities. We will focus on all underserved and economically disadvantaged populations, but hold a special focus on refugees and immigrants both in Chicago and globally. A fundamental approach to all of the center's work is that individuals need to acquire a sense of control over their lives. We see ourselves as being members of a global community of hope, focusing on inherent strengths and augmenting recovery and resilience. The center also works via collaborative relationships with medical schools, graduate schools, undergraduate programs, and schools of public health to provide training that will result in an internationally recognized diploma/certification in global health.

Whew! This is the triumphal rant that one must so often banter in order to gain the coveted 501(c)3 status or the attention of foundations for funding. Put more simply, the CGI works to save lives and teaches others how to do likewise. Period. Full stop.

THE MOST UNIQUE ASPECTS OF THE CENTER

Perhaps the most important aspects of the Center for Global Initiatives are the simplest:

1. We serve as an incubator and hothouse for new projects. We help to nurture, grow, and launch these projects as self sustaining, ongoing interests.
2. After a project has taken hold, we serve as pro bono consultants, fee-free Coopers & Lybrand's, if you will. We help those now managing the work with whatever it is they may need: materials, medicines, case consultation, introductions.
3. About 90 percent of our projects have come about as a result of being invited to do the work. That is, we do not come up with project ideas or toss darts at a globe to determine where to go next. There seems to be a global line outside our door waiting to be the next one to work with us. When we are not a good fit, we work to triage to a more suitable organization.
4. As best we can, depending on the project, we seek to blend primary care, behavioral health, and public health into an ultimately self-sustaining, outcomes accountable, culturally consonant result.

And really, everything else is the details. So here are some of those.

THE PROBLEM

Healthcare services, sciences, systems, education, and research all suffer from disconnections—globally and locally, biologically and behaviorally, in training and in practice—and health inequities are global in scale.

THE SOLUTION

There has not been a truly integrated center that is at once mindful of all the complex aspects of global health inequities; focused on small, outcomes-oriented projects; and also agile, responsive, improvisational, and empowering in the clinical, training, and research domains.

THE MISSION

The Center for Global Initiatives reaches across disciplines and international borders to bring together partners to provide education, training, and research programs that crosscut with primary care, behavioral healthcare, and public healthcare services within a context of social justice that addresses health inequalities. The center works to

- Advance the education and performance of local and international health professionals and students in health-related fields to meet the challenges of health inequalities
- Maintain a philosophy and approach as that of a collaborator and colleague
- Foster a sense of control over the lives of those with whom we work
- Augment inherent strengths and resilience
- Improve preparedness for reacting to human-made and natural disasters and their aftermath
- Strengthen collaboration as well as the sharing of experience and knowledge among various stakeholders addressing global health inequities (primary care, behavioral healthcare, and public health)
- Improve people's lives by decreasing premature death and disability with a special focus on the underserved, refugee, and immigrant populations' needs
- Provide clinical services
- Augment existing medical, psychological, science education, research, and service capacity (including health education)
- Build capacity of local communities to improve health and healthcare access
- Motivate the public and private sectors to drive consensus and action for the improvement of health globally
- Fold in issues of behavioral health, violence, and prevention as public health concerns
- Integrate all the health sciences and services with policy and advocacy at both the governmental and nongovernmental levels in order to create appropriate funding methods and sources, capacity building, and sustainable development

HOW THINGS STARTED

As a little boy, I was not what you would call much of an athlete. I was bit shy and bookish, and I was quite overweight (often the butt of teasing—it is not very cool to be fat and named Stout when you are a child). Adding to this, I had crooked teeth, and then braces (twice). But I somehow developed a spirit for adventure, perhaps in reaction to a rather sheltered (albeit quite loving) household. Fast-forwarding to today, I have taken up mountain climbing (as very much the amateur). In doing so, I have set out to do the Seven Summits—reaching the top of the highest mountain on each of the seven continents. I have been fortunate to have summited three of the easy ones so far: Mt. Kilimanjaro, Africa; Mt. Elbrus, Europe (Russia); and Mt. Kosciusko, Australia.

After my first major climb, Mt. Kilimanjaro, I met a Tanzanian guide who was studying in the seminary. We kept in touch over the ensuing years, and he became involved in running an orphanage for children who had lost both parents to AIDS. I developed a project called Just 'Cause to collect toys and school supplies for them for Christmas. I was successful in amassing quite a shipment, but I was then faced with an unbelievable bureaucracy, high costs, and long delay in shipping everything over to them. So, I thought there had to be a better way.

At about that same time, I went on my first medical mission. It was for about three weeks in Halong Bay, Viet Nam, with the Flying Doctors of America (see Chapter 8 in this volume). I was so moved by doing that work, and I was so miffed at the hassles involved with trying to ship materials to Africa, that the seed for the center was planted. Also during this time, I was fortunate to have been selected to serve as a nongovernmental organization (NGO) special representative to the United Nations via Division 9 of the American Psychological Association. Thus, blending my background in clinical psychology with my UN experiences in sustainable development (I presented a paper that was the result of a year-long project on behavioral health's role in health and sustainable development vis-à-vis a UN document known as the Copenhagen Declaration), mixing in what I had learned in Viet Nam and from the Flying Doctors' organization, along with a passion for public health (as a board of health member for many years and later a public health fellow), in a context of battling the inequities experienced by those less fortunate, marginalized, or disenfranchised, the center was born.

I have been involved in various healthcare start-ups, and I was reminded of what Susan Davis once noted: donors nowadays have recognized the value of entrepreneurial skills in managing a not-for-profit, rather than running a want-ad.[1] I believe that the center is an evolutionary progression from my clinical business ventures and international medical projects. I have been on medical missions with Flying Doctors of America to Vietnam, Peru, and most recently, to the Amazon basin. These impactful experiences taught me that active participation in international work is critical for a real understanding of others and of events.

WORKING TOGETHER TO RESPOND TO GLOBAL HEALTH INEQUITIES

All CGI programs are developed and implemented with public and private, local and international, academic and community-based partners. The objective is to foster interdisciplinary collaboration, pool resources, and integrate methodologies and perspectives from other disciplines, institutions, peoples, and countries. Here are a few of the organizations and universities with which the center is currently collaborating:

    University of Illinois–Chicago, College of Medicine
    Flying Doctors of America (see Chapter 8 in this volume)

International Center for Equal Healthcare Access (see Chapter 7 in this volume)

Jamkhed (aka Comprehensive Rural Health Project—CRHP) (see Chapter 6 in this volume)

Institute for One World Health (see Chapter 5 in this volume)

Sustainable Sciences Institute (see Chapter 4 in this volume)

Rush University's Health Services Management Program

University of Benin

Argosy University/Illinois School of Professional Psychology

Chicago School of Professional Psychology

Adler School of Professional Psychology

College of William and Mary

University of Colorado Health Sciences

Loyola University, Chicago's Center for Experiential Learning

DELIVERABLES

The ultimate deliverable is to save and improve the lives of those suffering from illness. A nice side effect is that we are developing new innovations in the process of doing our work, as in the SMART project: *Sustainable Medical Arts, Research, & Technology* (noted in detail below), wherein emergency first aid and treatment algorithms were developed, including a training methodology and pictograms for generalizability in different countries that would minimize language and literacy limits. This work product can be adapted quickly for use in similar areas of need, globally.

Part of our approach to funding and for being self-sustaining ourselves is to provide training for students and professionals. For students, we provide credits that their universities can consider as transfer or elective. For professionals, we are applying to be accredited and licensed to provide continuing medical education and continuing education credits.

Volunteers may participate in optional international mission experiences. And in the near future, we hope to have completed construction of a global health fellowship that offers certification in international development for U.S.-based students and professionals, and a healthcare and systems development certificate for international students and professionals. Similarly, we are designing a post-doctoral fellowship for graduates in clinical psychology that should blend clinical services with program development and also provide the appropriate supervision to qualify for sitting for the licensure examination in clinical psychology.

And we like to track what we do and write about it, so book chapters such as this one would also be one of our deliverables. We also seek to provide position papers via our website, submit to peer-reviewed journals, and produce books. Use of the media via interviews also helps increase awareness of need and hopefully desire in the audience to volunteer for projects or participate in our educational programs.

FUNDING RESOURCES

It seems that with few exceptions, funding is always a challenge. When I started the center, I paid for everything out of my own pocket, as I think many founders do. Websites, domain name registration, e-mail accounts, a computer, mobile phone and service, Internet service, travel costs, pencils, and paper—you quickly learn there are a lot of expenses. It is just like opening a small business, which in a sense, any organization is. I have been fortunate to make ends meet in the nascent stages through making economical purchases, having lots of volunteer help (see Staffing below), and having a "day job" to pay for the needs of the center as well as my family. But things have been pretty tight at times. As the cliché goes, "no mission without a margin," and the following note some of the ways we are starting to fund our work.

Staffing costs are typically the biggest financial challenge for any organization. Our solution is as robust as it is simple. We do not pay anyone. That is, all our staff members are volunteers, including me. We take no salary or benefit other than enjoying the work we do. Now, honestly, this will not go on forever (we hope), but the work is getting done. We look forward to the day when we can spend less time chasing project dollars and more time doing the projects.

Having come from a background of start-ups and having an entrepreneurial spirit, I am looking to fill a need in the niche of those interested in international affairs and global health inequities—in particular from the discipline of psychology, what I know best. And the early returns are promising. In 2007 (the year this is being written), I had a number of speaking invitations for psychology undergraduate and graduate students and also for students in public health, medicine, and leadership programs. And the buzz seems to be building as evidenced by numerous media interviews (magazines, newspapers, and television), and a wonderful number of contacts from individuals, students, programs, and other organizations wishing to volunteer or collaborate. We plan to channel those interested in workshops and lectures into appropriate trainings that will be income generating. We also plan to seek seminar sponsorships via grants and provide continuing medical education and continuing education credits to licensed professional attendees.

We also have plans to develop a certificate or diploma programs that integrate topics ranging from public health principles and primary care to behavioral healthcare and systems management. Tuition funds would support these programs with margins to additionally support other projects.

Volunteers who wish to travel to work with a international project can deduct their associated travel costs from their taxes in many instances. Volunteers who are in school may be able to use student loan funds to support their travel costs if their universities allow them to gain elective credits for the experience (this often happens if they write a paper or give a presentation on their work and experience upon return).

We worked with another organization I had founded, Summits for Others (see www.SummitsForOthers.org) in the summer of 2007 and embarked on a new approach to fundraising: sponsoring the center in a summit attempt of

Mt. Whitney (the tallest in the continental United States) with graduate psychology students. We plan on doing more traditional types of fundraising as well, such as having various levels of sponsors, seeking good corporate citizens as benefactors, holding events such as in-home dinners and discussions, and seeking support from related organizations such as Rotary to help with travel funds. We also work for specific program funding via the "Adopting an Outcome" model, in which we calculate the cost of making an impact (e.g., twelve cents for an antimalarial to save a life) in order to educate potential contributors and thus hopefully motivate them to contribute in the process.

Our board has also been a source of funding—both in providing funds and acting as conduits to funding sources and pro bono sources ("a penny saved . . ."). The center offers "Academic Memberships" to universities for a annual fee. Membership benefits include the opportunity for students to participate in courses and workshops on International Travel Tools and Methods, Global Health Initiatives, International Humanitarian Interventionism, and others; local opportunities to work with international populations via clinical, research, and specific projects; opportunity for at least one international trip per year; provision of funding opportunities to help defray travel expenses of students; connections with other ongoing projects and learning opportunities; experiences on an individualized basis for students and faculty; opportunities to "seed" the start of ongoing projects; having the center serve as an ongoing resource and informational clearinghouse; student mentoring; access to a vast global network of contacts; collaborative project launching; and collaborative grant and donor procurement. Students from these universities who volunteer for center projects are eligible for center travel scholarships and possible elective credit. Students from nonmember universities do not qualify for such funding opportunities.

STAFFING MODEL

I suppose you could describe our model as an ensemble. We are very fortunate to have many professionals volunteering as staff and on the board of directors (including Dale Galassie, MA, and Edith Grotberg, PhD). Our attorney, Carleen Schrader, JD, worked pro bono to complete all of our incorporation and not-for-profit paperwork, and even paid for all of the associated fees. My mentor, Ralph Musicant, JD, has guided me, encouraged me, and kicked me in the kiester through every step of the center's development. I have been blessed with a volunteer fundraiser, Laura Welch, who has additionally taken on more leadership tasks to move the Center forward.

All our projects are staffed by volunteers. Much of our research and development work is done by a wonderful group of graduate students from the Adler School of Professional Psychology's Community Service Practicum Program. At the time of this writing, we are forging a relationship with Loyola University, Chicago's new Center for Experiential Learning, which is very exciting and a wonderful additional resource.

EXAMPLES OF PAST AND CURRENT PROJECTS

CGI has been fortunate to be involved in many interesting and what we believe are impactful projects. These have been varied, and I expect they will continue to be. I would like to invite any interested reader to contact us if you have interest in learning more about any of the following projects. Also, please frequently check the Projects area of our website (see www.CenterForGlobalInitiatives.org) for the most current information on work going on or planned. Also, feel free to contact us and solicit help for a project you may be working on. We are always open to collaborating or make better connections.

CONTACT (Coordination & ONline Tracking of Activities & Clinical Teams)

The center is currently developing a freely accessible, Web-based database that will serve as a central warehouse of information for groups working in the Equatorial Amazon Basin. This pioneering database will provide the first centralized location for details on medical missions, medication and equipment donations, and guidelines and protocols for services and programs that have proven results within the tribal communities. Our hope is to expand the database to other rural community projects worldwide.

SMART (Sustainable Medical Arts, Research, & Technology)

To combat the lack of primary and emergency care in rural areas of Cambodia, the center aims to teach indigenous women basic public health practices and emergency medical care to aid those in their villages. Women will be trained to stabilize and care for patients until ready for transport to the nearest medical facility.

THRIVE (Tanzanian Health & Resilience Initiative Valuing Education)

Expanding on the kindergarten for orphans created in Moshi, Tanzania, in 2005, CGI now aims to add healthcare education for the children and local medical care providers. In collaboration with doctors, nurses, and staff at Huruma Designated Hospital, the center will develop programs for nursing students, the orphans, and the community that focus on HIV treatment and AIDS prevention as well as on combating malaria, TB, and other illnesses endemic to that area.

Project Niños

In the summer of 2007, the center collaborated with Flying Doctors of America in a pioneering project within several Bolivian prisons. Currently, hundreds of Bolivian children live with their incarcerated parents in both minimum- and even maximum-security prisons throughout this South American country. After treating over 600 imprisoned men, women, and children, the center has begun developing a unique educational and social skills training program in cooperation with teachers in prison-run schools. In addition, programs in parenting skills, noncompetitive play, resilience development, music, and creative/expressive arts will be developed to improve the welfare of the inmates' children in order to maximize the potential for improving their lives. For a look at our 2007 Project Niños beginnings, please visit http//homepage.mac.com/masonimage/ThreeDaysinaBolivianPrison/index.html.

WorldWise

Through a collaborative with partners in rural India who have developed a comprehensive, community-based primary health care approach, CGI is a conduit for recruiting students for summer experiences that will provide a life-changing perspective on healthcare. The project is called WorldWise, and it is being made available only to graduate students in any health discipline and to medical students.

One of the main aims of the project is to reach the poorest and most marginalized, and to improve their health. In reality, perhaps not everyone in the world will be able to have equal health care. However, it is possible to make sure that all people have access to necessary and relevant health care. This concept is known as equity, and it is an important principle of this project. Health is not only the absence of disease but also includes social, economic, spiritual, physical, and mental well-being. With this comprehensive understanding of health, the project focuses on improving the socioeconomic well-being of the people as well as other aspects of health. Health does not exist in isolation, but it is inherently related to education, environment, sanitation, socioeconomic status, and agriculture. Therefore, improvement in these areas by the communities in turn improves the health of the people. Health care includes promotive, preventive, curative, and rehabilitative aspects. The integration of these areas brings about effective health care.

Working at the grassroots level with village health workers and community groups leads to the process of empowerment of women and communities in general. This is an important aspect of community-based health care. Once people have knowledge and can make informed decisions, they have power they can use in constructive ways to transform their communities.

The majority of health problems in rural areas will be basic, but these problems can become worse and may even cause death if not identified and treated at the onset. To a large extent, the problems will be preventable and amenable to health detection. The project began with a view to develop a healthcare delivery program best suited to the needs and resources of this rural area. The essential element of the project is community involvement in the planning and in the activities of the project. The experience is for those interested in the exchange of learning; candidates must be able to handle rugged experiences/adventure, and they must be interested in global health in a pragmatic way.

BASIS (*Bio-pharmacogenomic Access & Sustainable Infra-Structure*)

Good friend and colleague Mariano Levin, PhD, of Argentina, a Howard Hughes Fellow, has received grant funding from the World Health Organization/Pan-American Health Organization (WHO/PAHO) South-South project to search for new drugs to fight African and American trypanosomiasis. This project combines genomics, high throughput, and the design of novel drugs. The center seeks to help expand the resources and the outreach of his work.

ENVOY (*Enabled, Networked Ventures Optimizing Yields*)

This project focuses on neglected diseases and seeks to operationalize projects via collaborations with DzGenes, PAHO, Sustainable Sciences Institute (SSI), Institute for OneWorld Health (iOWH), and Xomix. I am intrigued by the clever Médecines Sans Frontières (see Chapter 1 in this volume) approach of buying cheaper copies of HIV/AIDS drugs in India and using them in Africa, as well as the Brazilian approach to medication patents. And, while it is genuinely wonderful what the Bill & Melinda Gates Foundation is doing, such an approach still smacks of dependency and almost a pharmaco-colonialism of sorts. Although it is immensely important that many such foundations will be providing monies for the global distribution of medications, and these palliative efforts will be indeed necessary, they will be just as surely insufficient and shortsighted. I would offer that it would also be helpful for countries to be able to have the medical technology know-how to work on their own specific needs. We hear a lot about the problem of the "digital divide" between those with technology and those without—this typically refers to computer availability and Internet access. But there is also a divide between the haves and have-nots of medical technology and knowledge.

The center would collaborate with countries to create sustainable medical solutions for their most pressing and neglected public health problems/concerns. In some areas, this may be providing medical services of all disciplines; it may be clinic and hospital establishment or reconstruction; it could be augmentation of medical and science education, research, and service capacity (including health education); or it may include the expansion of medical sciences education to include genomic sciences and drug discovery technologies, such as pharmacogenomics (request a proof-of-concept paper from the center's website, or a reprint of my article on remedying neglected diseases published in the World Economic Forum's journal *World Link*).

Medical InterAction

Contacts and relationships have been developed with colleagues in Benin that crosscut various areas: health and illness, poverty and sustainability, environmental concerns, traditional healing and medical sciences/health treatment, and education. We plan to develop a scientific and economic mechanism of researching the medicinal properties of specific plant materials used by our Benin partners (university scientists and traditional healers) to further develop medicines, use the resultant knowledge to refine the compounds to have fewer side effects and improved dosing characteristics, and develop that intellectual property into concomitant economic value that will provide for economic sustainability, self-sufficiency, and independence for ongoing research. This would be within an overarching context of making resultant products available to those impoverished and in need. We seek to establish not only a groundbreaking mechanism to ensure the perpetuation of traditional medicines but also to further develop medicines for local and global benefit.

A current problem for the big pharma companies is that they have not been internally investing in new medication research—known as "the pipeline." The results of our proposed work will not only serve to fill this critical void via licensing and royalty agreements of the resultant intellectual property that are equitable and mutually beneficial, but this project may also serve as a pilot study that can generalize and scale as a global model for others to mimic.

Additionally, since Benin is a land in transition and under development, there is a new risk of the loss of the current richness of the biodiversity of the region. In order to ensure such losses will be avoided, we also seek to develop a literal "botanical garden" of the species of plants that are promising candidates for pharmacological research. Thus, this work provides an example of the intersection of science, pharmacological development, intellectual property rights offering economic sustainability and capacity building, environmental preservation, public health impacts, medical sciences education, and cultural traditions.

BUILDING BRIDGES

We often use the word "architecting" when we are in the nascent design phases of a project. It seems we do a bit of bridge building—between cultures, peoples, and disciplines—and honestly, this is a wonderful process. I personally enjoy this remarkably frustrating and difficult work so very much. Next to my family, nothing affects me so deeply. I encourage you to honor your gift, and if the center can help you do so, please be in touch.

BIOGRAPHIES
Chris E. Stout

Chris E. Stout, PsyD, is a licensed clinical psychologist who has the necessary entrepreneurial experience in healthcare center start-ups (chief operating officer of YellowbricK and founding chief executive officer of Timberline Knolls). He also is a clinical full professor in the University of Illinois–Chicago College of Medicine's Department of Psychiatry, a fellow in the School of Public Health Leadership Institute, and a core faculty member of the International Center on Responses to Catastrophes at the University of Illinois–Chicago. He also holds an academic appointment in the Northwestern University Feinberg Medical School, Department of Psychiatry and Behavioral Sciences' Mental Health Services and Policy Program, and was a visiting professor in the Department of Health Systems Management at Rush University. He served as an NGO special representative to the United Nations. He was appointed by the U.S. Secretary of Commerce to the board of examiners for the Malcolm Baldridge National Quality Award. He holds the distinction of being one of only 100 worldwide leaders appointed to the World Economic Forum's Global Leaders of Tomorrow 2000. He was invited by the Club de Madrid and Safe-Democracy to serve on the Madrid-11 Countering Terrorism Task Force.

Dr. Stout is a fellow in three divisions of the American Psychological Association, past president of the Illinois Psychological Association, and a distinguished practitioner in the National Academies of Practice. He was appointed as a special (citizen) ambassador and delegation leader to South Africa and Eastern Europe by the Eisenhower Foundation. He is the series editor of *Contemporary Psychology* (Praeger), and *Getting Started* (Wiley & Sons). He produced the critically acclaimed, four-volume set titled *The Psychology of Terrorism*. Dr. Stout has published or presented over 300 papers and 30 books/manuals on various topics in psychology, including the popular *Evidence-Based Practice* (Wiley & Sons, 2005, with R. Hayes). His works have been translated into eight languages. He has lectured across the nation and internationally in nineteen countries, and visited six continents and over seventy countries. He was noted as being "one of the most frequently cited psychologists in the scientific literature" in a study by Hartwick College. He is the 2004 winner of the American Psychological Association's International Humanitarian Award and the 2006 recipient of the Illinois Psychological Association's Humanitarian Award.

He has served as chief of psychology, director of research, and senior vice president of an integrated behavioral healthcare system during a fifteen-year tenure. He served as Illinois' first chief of psychological services for the Department of Human Services/Division of Mental Health, making him the highest-ranking psychologist in the State of Illinois and a committed reformer of psychology within the governmental setting. He also served as chief clinical information officer for the state's Division of Mental Health in 2004—a state cabinet-level position. He is the first psychologist to have an invited appointment to the Lake County Board of Health. The breadth of his work ranges from having served as a judge for Dean Kamen's FIRST Robotics competitions, to serving on the Young Leaders Forum of the Chicago Community Trust. His humanitarian activities include going on international missions with the Flying Doctors of America to Vietnam, Rwanda, Peru, and the Amazon; War Child in Russia; working with the Marjorie Kovler Center for the Treatment of Survivors of Torture (see profile in this volume), Amnesty International, Robert Woods Johnson Foundation, the Elizabeth Morse Charitable Trust, and Psychologists for Social Responsibility. He founded a kindergarten for AIDS-orphaned children in Tanzania and continues as a consultant. He also was a delegate to the State of the World Forum in Belfast. He is a signatory to the UN's 50th Anniversary of the Universal Declaration of Human

Rights. He is the inventor of the *52 Ways to Change the World* card deck. He is listed in *Fast Co.'s* Global Fast 50 nominees and in Richard Saul Wurman's *1000: The Most Creative Individuals in America*. He currently serves on the Illinois Disaster Mental Health Coalition and the Medical Reserve Corp, and he is a member of the APA Disaster Response Network.

His current interests are in the multidisciplinary aspects of global psychology and healthcare, complex systems, and battling mediocrity. He's an ultramarathon runner, diver, and avid (albeit amateur) alpinist, having thus far summited three of the world's seven summits and Mt. Whitney (tallest in the continental 49 states), and founded SummitsForOthers.org.

Ralph Musicant

Ralph Musicant is a Harvard Law School (1971) graduate who has founded and operated start-up companies in a variety of industries: coal mining, comic book and cigar magazine publishing, computerized multiple listing service for commercial office space, and a behavioral health company offering telephone counseling by licensed therapists. He is currently managing director of Ideas and Methods Inc., a Chicago-based business consulting and acquisition firm. His academic career includes an appointment as the Martin C. Remer Visiting Distinguished Professor of Finance (1976) at the Kellogg Graduate School of Management at Northwestern University. Most recently, he was an invited speaker at a Colloquium on E-therapy presented by the Institute of Cybermedicine at Harvard Medical School.

Edith Grotberg

Edith Grotberg, PhD, spent five years in Sudan teaching at the Ahfad University for Women in Omdurman. There, she began her work on resilience, which culminated in an international study of the promotion of resilience, with data gathered from twenty-seven sites in twenty-two countries. Her books on resilience include *A Guide to Promoting Resilience in Children: Strengthening the Human Spirit* and *Tapping Your Inner Strength: How to Find the Resilience to Deal with Anything;* she was also editor of *Resilience for Today: Gaining Strength from Adversity*. She has conducted work with UNICEF, Organization for Economic Co-operation and Development (OECD), UNESCO, and International Chamber of Commerce (ICC). She has worked with colleagues in Argentina, Chile, Peru, and Brazil to enhance resilience skills and behaviors. Her current work involves life-long well-being in the Western Hemisphere.

Carleen L. Schreder

Carleen L. Schreder is an attorney and one of the founders of Levin & Schreder Ltd. in 1988. She graduated from Lake Forest College in 1979 and received her JD from the University of Chicago Law School in 1982. Her practice is focused in the areas of estate tax and income tax planning for individuals and businesses. In addition to her legal work, Ms. Schreder is active in community organizations. She was recognized for her community work by the Chicago Bar Foundation, which awarded her the 1988 Maurice Weigle Award as an Outstanding Young Lawyer. She is currently a board member of Chicago Foundation for Women and is a past board member and officer of Chicago Legal Advocacy for Incarcerated Mothers and Chicago Abused Women Coalition. Ms. Schreder is an author and presenter on topics related to tax planning, including an article on Illinois estate tax apportionment, which appeared in the *Illinois Bar Journal* in June 2007, and a presentation on the same topic at the Chicago Bar Association Probate Practice Committee in November 2007.

Dale W. Galassie

Dale W. Galassie, MA, MS, has served as the executive director of the Lake County Health Department/Community Health Center since 1992, an organization that employs approximately 1,000 staff members with resources of $60 million. It provides a comprehensive array of public health, primary care, behavioral health, and environmental health services in Lake County. Dale previously served as the director of management services for the Health Department from 1981. His pre–public health life was in higher education, serving from 1975 to 1981 as business manager of Lewis University, a Christian Brothers institution in Will County, Illinois.

His years of senior-level administrative experience are complemented by his academic accomplishments, including a Baccalaureate degree in political science and business, an MA in administration, and an MS in social justice from Lewis University; a fellow in the University of Illinois School of Public Health Leadership Institute and a Primary Care Fellow through the United States Bureau of Primary Health Care. He is chair of Midwest American Regional Public Health Leadership Institute, and as a self-committed, life-long learner, ABD in his doctorate degree in administration and leadership through Vanderbilt University.

He routinely speaks to professional organizations, special interest groups, and legislative bodies. He has testified before numerous state and federal legislative committees as an outspoken member of the public health community to promote social justice. He is an active Adjunct Faculty member for Webster University since 1982, teaching graduate courses in Health Administration and Human Resource Management. He is also the proud father of three young adult daughters raised in Lake County, Illinois.

His association affiliations include past chair of the Illinois Association of Public Health Administrators, President 1996–97; Illinois Public Health Association Executive Council, 1993 to 1996; Illinois Primary Health Care Association, past president, and currently serving on the Legislative and Public Policy Committee. He currently serves on the National Association of Community Health Centers Legislative Policy Committee. Other association activities include past co-chair of the Illinois Department of Public Aid, Medicaid Advisory/Managed

Care Sub-Committee. He also serves on the National Association of County & City Officials, Committee to Promote Public Health and Legislative Committees, National Association for Public Health Policy, and other public health advisory committees. He served as the vice-chair of the National Association of County and City Health Officials (NACCHO), Metro-Forum Group, and maintains current membership in that group. He is also an active member of the Northern Illinois Public Health Consortium.

Laura Welch

Laura Welch is a graduate of the University of Wisconsin–Madison with a BA in arts administration. Her earliest work involved fundraising with American Players Theater in Spring Green, Wisconsin; serving as public relations director with the Peninsula Players in Door County, Wisconsin; and acting as the annual fund manager with the St. Louis Symphony Orchestra, where her team raised over $7.5 million. Her desire to be more socially active led Laura to create the Development Department for the Family Resource Center, a child abuse agency in St. Louis, where she initiated a capital campaign for a new building. She moved on to be director of development for the Women's Self-Help Center, a counseling center for abused women in St. Louis. She also was asked to establish the annual giving and special events arm of the Good Samaritan Hospital Foundation in Corvallis, Oregon. She has volunteered extensively, including serving as chair of the Corvallis Arts Center board of directors, consulting on the capital campaign for the Majestic Theatre, also in Corvallis, Oregon, and as chair of the Benefit of Hope for the American Cancer Society of DuPage County, Illinois. She is now home with her two children and husband in Naperville, Illinois, and continues her exciting work on a volunteer basis with the Center for Global Initiatives.

ORGANIZATIONAL SNAPSHOT

Organization: Center for Global Initiatives

Founder and/or Executive Director: Dr. Chris E. Stout, PsyD

Mission/Description:

The Center for Global Initiatives (CGI) is at once mindful of all complex aspects of global health inequities while being focused on small, outcomes-oriented projects so that it is also agile, responsive, improvisational, and empowering in clinical, training, and research domains. It is the philosophy of the center that the optimal way of successfully addressing these injustices and disconnects is by multiple, small-scale projects with a coordinated approaches and outcome accountability.

CGI is the first center devoted to training multidisciplinary healthcare professionals and students to bring services that are integrated, sustainable, and resiliency based, with publicly accountable outcomes, to areas of need worldwide via multiple, small, context-specific collaboratives that integrate primary care, behavioral healthcare, systems development, public health, and social justice. We seek to eschew the many disconnects between separation of body/mind, physical/mental, and individual/community, and offer instead a synthetic model of integration. The Center's philosophy and approach is always that of a collaborator and colleague. No "West-Knows-Best" hubris. We learn as we teach. We feel as we treat.

Perhaps the most important aspects of the Center for Global Initiatives are the simplest:

1. We serve as an incubator and hothouse for new projects. We help to nurture, grow, and launch them as self sustaining, ongoing interests.
2. After a project has taken hold, we serve as pro bono consultants—forever if need be. We help those now managing the work with whatever it is they may need—materials, medicines, case consultation, introductions.
3. About 90 percent of all of our projects have come about as a result of being invited to do the work. That is, we do not come up with project ideas or toss darts at a globe to determine where to go next. There seems to be a global line outside our door waiting to be the next one to work with us. When we are not a good fit, we work to triage to a more suitable organization.

Website: CenterForGlobalInitiatives.org

Address: 120 North LaSalle Street, 38th Floor

Chicago, IL 60602 USA

Phone: +1.847.550.0092, ext. 2

Fax: none

E-mail: Chris@CenterForGlobalInitiatives.org

NOTE

1. Susan M. Davis, "Social Entrepreneurship: Towards an Entrepreneurial Culture for Social and Economic Development" (July 31, 2002). Available at SSRN (http://ssrn.com/abstract=978868).

Afterword

Keith Ferrazzi

If you take the ingredients of social entrepreneurship, venture philanthropy, and social networking, liberally mix with individuals who hold a passion for making a true difference in various aspects of people's lives throughout the world, and then take a sample of some of the best, the result you have is *The New Humanitarians.* Chris Stout has served as a uniting thread to connect these organizations in this three-volume set. While these organizations are all different in their approaches and goals, they share a common aspect of their work: innovation. Indeed, they are the *new* humanitarians. They are born from the power of the individual taking action in a novel way, and then using the power of their relationships to effect impactful change. After all, giving back is a huge part of a life well led.

In the spirit of *Three Cups of Tea*, Chris's adventuresome life has taken him to a variety of exotic and often not-so-safe locales, and the work he has done in these venues has resulted not only in his Center for Global Initiatives, but also *The New Humanitarians.* He has done well with many of the aspects I wrote about in *Never Eat Alone* but applied them in the milieu of humanitarian work. He and I share a kinship, as Chris was a reviewer for the ABE Awards that I founded, a fellow Baldrige Award reviewer, and a fellow "TEDizen" during the Richard Saul Wurman era; was elected as a Global Leader of Tomorrow by the World Economic Forum; and served as faculty with me in Davos. So it is no surprise that Chris has the brainpower as well as the horsepower to have accomplished this wonderful compilation of wunderkinder.

Chris is able to contribute to Davos talks and UN presentations, but he is much more at home working in the field and with his students. He is known for bringing people together in cross-disciplinary projects worldwide—in healthcare, medical education, human rights, poverty, conflict, policy, sustainable development, diplomacy, and terrorism. As the American Psychological Association said about him and his work: "He is a rare individual who takes risks, stimulates new ideas, and enlarges possibilities in areas of great need but few resources. He is able to masterfully navigate between the domains of policy development while also rolling up his sleeves to provide in-the-trenches care. His drive and vigor are disguised by his quick humor and ever-present kindness. He is provocative in his ideas and evocative in spirit. His creative solutions and inclusiveness cross conceptual boundaries as well as physical borders." *The New Humanitarians* serves a testament to this praise.

Simply put, these organizations are amazing. The people behind the organizations are amazing. Their stories are amazing. And as a result, this book is amazing.

Series Afterword

THE NEW HUMANITARIANS

I am honored to include Professor Chris Stout's three-volume set—*The New Humanitarians*—in my book series. These volumes are like rare diamonds shining with visionary perspectives for the fields of human rights, health, and education advocacy; charitable and philanthropic organizations; and legal rights and remedies.

The *New Humanitarians* volumes are of great value to informed citizens, volunteers, and professionals because of their originality, down-to-earth approach, reader-friendly format, and comprehensive scope. Many of the specially written book chapters include the latest factual information on ways in which the new leaders, advocates, and foundations have been instrumental in meeting the critical medical and human service needs of millions of people in underdeveloped and war-torn countries.

Professor Chris Stout has developed a pathfinding set here. A gifted and prolific psychologist who planned and edited these comprehensive volumes, Stout has developed an original concept couched in these three remarkable books. I predict that the *New Humanitarians* will rapidly become a classic, and will be extremely useful reading for all informed citizens and professionals in the important years ahead.

Albert R. Roberts, DSW, PhD

Series Editor, Social and Psychological Issues: Challenges and Solutions

Professor of Social Work and Criminal Justice

School of Arts and Sciences

Rutgers, the State University of New Jersey

About the Editor and Contributors

Chris E. Stout is a licensed clinical psychologist and founding director of the Center for Global Initiatives. He also is a clinical full professor in the College of Medicine, Department of Psychiatry; a fellow in the School of Public Health Leadership Institute; and a core faculty member at the International Center on Responses to Catastrophes at the University of Illinois–Chicago. He also holds an academic appointment in the Northwestern University Feinberg Medical School and was visiting professor in the Department of Health Systems Management at Rush University. He served as a nongovernmental organization special representative to the United Nations for the American Psychological Association, was appointed to the World Economic Forum's Global Leaders of Tomorrow, and was an invited faculty at their annual meeting in Davos, Switzerland. He was invited by the Club de Madrid and Safe-Democracy to serve on the Madrid-11 Countering Terrorism Task Force.

Dr. Stout is a fellow of the American Psychological Association, past-president of the Illinois Psychological Association, and is a distinguished practitioner in the National Academies of Practice. He has published thirty books, and his works have been translated into eight languages. He was noted as being "one of the most frequently cited psychologists in the scientific literature" in a study by Hartwick College. He is the 2004 winner of the American Psychological Association's International Humanitarian Award and the 2006 recipient of the Illinois Psychological Association's Humanitarian Award.

Raj S. and Shobha Arole co-founded The Comprehensive Rural Health Project, Jamkhed, India, in 1970. Both Drs. Raj and Mabelle Arole had a deep commitment and compassion for the poor and marginalized. As medical doctors, with training both at CMC Vellore, India, and at Johns Hopkins in the United States, they returned to Jamkhed, India, to implement a community-based health and development program. As highly motivated public health specialists, their vision was to empower people, particularly the rural poor and women, to take their health into their own hands. Both the Aroles were the recipients of the Magasaysay Award for community leadership in 1979. Dr. Raj Arole also received the Padmabhushan (one of the highest honors in India) for commitment to the rural poor. In 1999, at the age of sixty-four, Dr. Mabelle Arole passed away from heart disease. The program now is still under the leadership of Dr. Raj Arole. Their daughter, Dr. Shobha Arole, is the associate director of the project, and their son, Ravi, is involved in administration. The Aroles were also chosen by the Schwab Foundation as social entrepreneurs in the field of innovative, community-based health and development. The project is committed to empowering people, integrating health, promoting equity, and serving as a replicable and sustainable model for India and the world.

Teresa Bartrum attended Ball State University for her undergraduate studies. She earned a bachelor's degree in psychology and photojournalism. She worked at the *Herald Bulletin* in Anderson, Indiana, and at the *Star Press* as a staff photographer for five years before moving back to the field of psychology. She then worked at the Youth Opportunity Center, a juvenile residential treatment facility, as a frontline supervisor in the Treatment of Adolescents in Secure Care (TASC) Unit of this organization. While employed at this organization, she helped develop and facilitate a therapeutic horseback riding program, served as a therapeutic crisis intervention instructor, and completed multiple in-service trainings. She is currently attends the Adler School of Professional Psychology while pursuing her doctoral degree in clinical psychology. She completed her community service practicum at the Center for Global Initiatives while working on the book project *The New Humanitarians: Innovations, Inspirations, and Blueprints for Visionaries.*

Mary Black, MS, OTR/L, is an occupational therapist with the Marjorie Kovler Center of Heartland Alliance. Her responsibilities include assessment and intervention focused on enhancing the functional skills needed to perform meaningful occupational roles that have been compromised or abandoned as a result of torture, displacement, or injury. She has been extensively involved in working with refugee individuals, families, and children, using individual and group activities to help support the maintenance of cultural identity while coping with the multiple challenges presented in transitioning to an urban lifestyle in the United States. Ms. Black has over eleven years' experience working with refugees and those seeking asylum in the United States, and has collaborated with many schools and numerous community programs including Casa Guatemala, the Community Culture Council of Dance Africa Chicago, Mioghar Eedee Ogoni (an Ogoni, Nigeria, children's group), and Angelic Organics Farm. She has presented at numerous ISTSS conferences and at the National AOTA conference in 2003 and 2007. She has an MS in occupational therapy from the University at Illinois–Chicago and is licensed in the state of Illinois.

Marie Charles founded ICEHA, the global leader in clinical skills rapid transfer to emerging nations in November 2001. Drawing on its pool of over 650 highly qualified infectious disease professionals from fourteen Western countries, ICEHA deployed into ten countries in Africa and Asia within three years of commencing operations, transferring at least 7,500 aggregate human-years of clinical expertise to local colleagues. As one of the world's leading fourth-generation NGOs, ICEHA uses a unique funding model, whereby Western funding catalyzes 300 percent matched funding by recipient developing countries. In recognition of her professional achievements, Dr. Charles received the National Medal of Honor from the president of Vietnam at the opening of the Vietnamese National Assembly in Hanoi in June 2007. She was also named a Henry Crown Fellow at the Aspen Institute in 2006 and served as adjunct professor at Columbia University School of International and Public Affairs in 2004–2005.

Josefina Coloma is a senior research associate in the Division of Infectious Diseases in the School of Public Health at UC–Berkeley. She received a BA in biological sciences from the American College of Quito, Ecuador, in 1983 and a PhD in microbiology and molecular genetics from UCLA in 1997. Coming from a developing country and having had the opportunity to study in the United States, she felt that doing something about the large gap in scientific knowledge between the two was in part her responsibility. Dr. Coloma has been working with Dr. Eva Harris since 1993 to build scientific capacity in developing countries. Dr. Coloma helped envision and fund the Sustainable Sciences Institute (SSI) and has served on its board of directors since 2000. Dr. Coloma believes that her involvement with SSI allows her to give back to her native country of Ecuador some of what she has learned and experienced.

Mary Fabri, PsyD, is a clinical psychologist and director of Torture Treatment Services and International Training for Heartland Alliance in Chicago, Illinois. She is the current president of the National Consortium of Torture Treatment Programs. Dr. Fabri provides consultation and training internationally on the consequences of severe trauma, cross-cultural psychotherapy, and secondary traumatization. Since 2004 she has been collaborating with Women's Equity in Access to Care and Treatment (WE-ACTx) in Rwanda, addressing the needs of traumatized HIV-positive women. She has also conducted trainings in Guatemala and Haiti. She has published on topics pertaining to refugee mental health, cross-cultural treatment modifications, and the psychological consequences of torture. After receiving her doctoral degree in clinical psychology from the Illinois School of Professional Psychology in 1986, Dr. Fabri has devoted her career to working in the public health sector. She worked as a staff psychologist at Cook County Hospital until 1995 when she joined Heartland

Alliance as the clinical coordinator for the Bosnian Mental Health Program; in 1997, she became the training coordinator for the Refugee Mental Health Training Program. In 2000 Dr. Fabri became the director of the Marjorie Kovler Center after fourteen years of providing pro bono services to torture survivors.

Keith Ferrazzi is one of the rare individuals to discover the essential formula for making his way to the top through a powerful, balanced combination of marketing acumen and networking savvy. Both *Forbes* and *Inc.* magazines have designated him one of the world's most "connected" individuals. Now, as founder and CEO of Ferrazzi Greenlight, he provides market leaders with advanced strategic consulting and training services to increase company sales and enhance personal careers. Ferrazzi earned a BA from Yale University and an MBA from Harvard Business School.

Jeffrey D. Fisher is a professor of psychology at the University of Connecticut. He is the founder and director of its Center for Health, Intervention & Prevention (CHIP). Most of his work has involved theoretical and empirical work on social psychological factors that can affect the success of interventions to change human behavior. His early research (with Arie Nadler) focused on how to facilitate the seeking of needed help, and what types of help promote favorable and unfavorable recipient reactions to aid (e.g., self-sufficiency vs. continued help seeking; favorable vs. unfavorable reactions to the donor of help). More recent work has involved similar issues in the realm of health psychology. He has published extensively on factors associated with HIV risk behavior, and has done a great deal of conceptual and empirical work in the area of interventions to increase HIV preventive behavior. His work also focuses on designing theoretically based interventions to increase adherence to antiretroviral therapy, and on health behavior change in general. As principal investigator, he has been awarded seven major NIMH grants since 1989 on HIV risk reduction and medical adherence, totaling over $20 million, and he has lectured and consulted internationally in the area of HIV preventive behavior.

Allan Gathercoal is the president and founder of Flying Doctors of America, which he established in 1990. He travels the globe, but his second home is in Latin America. He has been the team leader on more than 140 medical and dental missions. Allan is an ordained minister and holds a doctorate from Columbia Theological Seminary. He is a private pilot and an aficionado of adventure sports. He was born in England.

Mario González is the clinical supervisor of the Marjorie Kovler Center of Heartland Alliance in Chicago, Illinois. He is a native of Guatemala, where he studied and received his license in psychology from the University Rafael Landivar in 1984. He is bilingual and bicultural. In addition to clinical oversight of the Kovler Center program, Mr. González provides supervision to the case management and clinical staff, consultation to pro bono therapists and immigration attorneys, and evaluation services for forensic psychological documentation for political asylum applicants. He also provides psychotherapy to torture survivors and has special interests in diagnostics and cross-cultural psychotherapy. Prior to working with torture survivors, Mr. González was the director of the Instituto del Progreso Latino's Gang Involvement Prevention Program, where community outreach was an integral part of the services provided. In addition to his training in psychology, Mr. González also earned a bachelor's degree in accounting and administration from La Patria College, Guatemala, in 1970 and a master's in education and psychology from the Universidad Rafael Landivar, Guatemala, in 1978.

Victoria Hale established her expertise in all stages of biopharmaceutical drug development at the U.S. Food and Drug Administration (FDA) Center for Drug Evaluation and Research and at Genentech Inc., the world's first biotechnology company. She presently maintains an adjunct associate professorship in biopharmaceutical sciences at the University of California–San Francisco, is an advisor to the World Health Organization (WHO) for building ethical review capacity in the developing world, and has served as an expert reviewer to the National Institutes of Health (NIH) on the topic of biodiversity. Dr. Hale's recent honors include being elected to membership in the Institute of Medicine of the National Academies and being named a 2006 John D. and Catherine T. MacArthur Foundation Fellow. Other recent achievements include being selected as an Ashoka Fellow for work in leading social innovation (2006) and as Executive of the Year by *Esquire* magazine (2005), and receiving the Economist Innovation Award for Social and Economic Innovation (2005) and the Skoll Award for Social Entrepreneurship from the Skoll Foundation (2005). She was named one of the Most Outstanding Social Entrepreneurs by the Schwab Foundation for Social Entrepreneurship in Switzerland (2004). In 2004 Dr. Hale and OneWorld Health (iOWH) were included in the *Scientific American* 50, the magazine's annual list recognizing outstanding acts of leadership in science and technology.

Eva Harris is an associate professor in the Division of Infectious Diseases in the School of Public Health at UC–Berkeley. She received a BA in biochemical sciences from Harvard University in 1987 and a PhD in molecular and cell biology from UC–Berkeley in 1993. In 1997 Dr. Harris received a MacArthur "Genius" Award for her pioneering work developing programs and working to build scientific capacity in developing countries to address public health and infectious disease issues. To continue and expand this work, Dr. Harris founded the Sustainable Sciences Institute (SSI) in 1998. SSI is a San Francisco-based, international nonprofit organization that supports scientists and public health professionals in developing countries as they work toward meeting the public health needs of their communities. Dr. Harris has published over sixty-five peer-reviewed articles, as well as a book on her international scientific work.

Marianne Joyce is a clinical social worker at the Marjorie Kovler Center of Heartland Alliance. Since joining the staff in 2000, she has conducted clinical evaluations, supervised and trained graduate student interns, engaged survivors in healing therapies, provided consultation to volunteer therapists, and documented and testified to the psychological effects of torture in support of asylum claims. Her first role with the Kovler Center in 1990 was as a volunteer interpreter and co-coordinator of a Guatemalan children's group. She has been involved with survivors bringing lawsuits against perpetrators residing in the United States in collaboration with the Center of Justice and Accountability. She has trained health providers, attorneys, and interpreters in the United States on issues of sensitivity in their work with survivors. She has helped train health professionals from Guatemala, Haiti, and Iraq on treatment issues. She holds a BS in psychology from the University of Illinois–Urbana-Champaign and an MA from the School of Social Services Administration at the University of Chicago. She has taught human rights at the School of Services Administration as adjunct faculty.

Jordan Kassalow is a co-founder of Scojo Vision LLC and the Scojo Foundation. He is also the founder of the Global Health Policy Program at the Council on Foreign Relations, where he served as an adjunct senior fellow from 1999–2004. Prior to his position at the council, he served as director of the Onchocerciasis Division at Helen Keller International. He currently serves on the board of directors for Lighthouse International and on the medical advisory board of Helen Keller International. The recipient of numerous awards, including the Social Innovator of the Year award from Brigham Young University's Marriott School of Management, the Aspen Institute's Henry Crown Fellowship, and a Draper Richards Foundation Fellowship, Dr. Kassalow received his doctorate of optometry from the New England College of Optometry and his master's in public health from Johns Hopkins University. In addition to his position at Scojo Foundation, he is currently a partner at the practice of Drs. Farkas, Kassalow, Resnick, and Associates.

Katherine Katcher is a recent graduate of Columbia College, where she majored in anthropology and studied abroad in Dharamsala, India. She has traveled extensively through Eastern Europe, the Balkans, East Africa, and Latin America and is passionate about sustainable development and finding innovative approaches to ending poverty.

Annie Khan, originally from Trinidad and Tobago, migrated to Toronto, Canada, in 1994. She completed her undergraduate degree at the University of Toronto in neuroscience and psychology. While working in community-based organizations, she felt compelled to do more for disenfranchised populations. She pursued a master's in counseling psychology at the Adler School of Professional Psychology and is currently working on her doctorate in clinical psychology. She worked at the Center for Global Initiatives as a placement student on *The New*

Humanitarians: Innovations, Inspirations, and Blueprints for Visionaries book project.

Graham Macmillan is senior director of Scojo Foundation, a leading social enterprise focused on reducing poverty and generating opportunity through the sale of affordable eyeglasses and complementary products. Prior to joining Scojo Foundation, Mr. Macmillan served as director of business development for the ChildSight program at Helen Keller International. He currently serves on the board of directors of the FISH Hospitality Program and is a member of the Micro-franchise Development Initiative at Brigham Young University's Marriott School of Management. Mr. Macmillan was a 2006 fellow at the Global Social Benefit Incubator at Santa Clara University's Center for Science, Technology, and Society, and has been an invited judge with NYU Stern's Berkley Center for Entrepreneurial Studies business plan competition as well as the Robert F. Wagner School for Public Service's Catherine B. Reynolds Undergraduate Scholarship in Social Enterprise competition. He received his BA in international studies and history from Colby College and his MSc in management of international public service organizations from New York University's Robert F. Wagner School for Public Service. Mr. Macmillan is currently pursuing an MBA through the TRIUM Program (NYU Stern, London School of Economics, and HEC Management School of Paris).

Mehmet Oz received a 1982 undergraduate degree from Harvard and a 1986 joint MD and MBA from the University of Pennsylvania School of Medicine and the Wharton Business School. He is vice-chair of surgery and professor of cardiac surgery, Columbia University; founder and director, Complementary Medicine Program, New York Presbyterian Medical Center; currently, director, Cardiovascular Institute, New York Presbyterian Hospital. Research interests include heart replacement surgery, minimally invasive cardiac surgery, and health care policy. He is a member of the American Board of Thoracic Surgery; American Board of Surgery; American Association of Thoracic Surgeons; Society of Thoracic Surgeons; American College of Surgeons; International Society for Heart and Lung Transplantation; American College of Cardiology; and the American Society for Artificial Internal Organs. He is the author of more than 350 publications.

Myron Panchuk completed his BS degree in psychology and philosophy at Loyola University of Chicago in 1976. In 1982 he was ordained to the priesthood for the Chicago Diocese of Ukrainian Catholics and has actively served this community for over twenty years. His professional work includes designing and facilitating retreats and conferences for clergy and laity, professional development, conflict resolution, and social advocacy. He is a co-founder and member of Starving For Color, a humanitarian organization that provides baby formula for orphans in Ukraine. He is currently a counseling graduate student at the Adler School of Professional Psychology and is engaged in a community service practicum with

Dr. Chris Stout at the Center for Global Initiatives. He intends to continue his studies and pursue a doctorate in depth psychology.

Kevin P. Q. Phelan is a senior communications manager for Doctors Without Borders/Médecins Sans Frontières (MSF) in the United States. Since 2001 he has worked with MSF in Angola, the Palestinian Territories, Iraq, Sudan, Haiti, Uganda, Nigeria, and Niger. Before joining MSF, he worked as a correspondent at Radio France International, as a teacher at the City College of New York, and as a social worker in the Bronx and Queens.

William H. Rosenblatt is professor of anesthesiology, Yale University School of Medicine, the founder of REMEDY, its volunteer medical director, and primary author of seminal articles on recovery published by the *Journal of the American Medical Association* and others. Dr. Rosenblatt has been the recipient of multiple awards for his work with REMEDY, including the Rolex Award for Enterprise in Science and Invention given by the Rolex Foundation in 1996.

Jack Saul is a psychologist who has worked for more than twenty years with individuals, families, and communities that have endured war, torture, and forced migration. Since 1997 he has directed the International Trauma Studies Program (ITSP), now affiliated with the Mailman School of Public Health at Columbia University, where he is assistant professor of clinical population and family health. ITSP provides post-graduate training in trauma theory, treatment, and prevention in New York and Uganda. In 1995 Dr. Saul co-founded the Bellevue/NYU Program for Survivors of Torture and served as its first clinical director. He helped establish the Metro Area Support for Survivors of Torture (MASST) Consortium and created a nonprofit organization, Refuge, which provides psychosocial services to refugee families and communities in New York City. Following the 9/11/2001 World Trade Center attack, Dr. Saul formed the Downtown Community Resource Center with Lower Manhattan residents, and was funded by the Federal Emergency Management Agency (FEMA) as a demonstration project in community resilience following catastrophe. Since 2000 he has worked with the Kosovar Family Professional Education Collaborative to develop community mental health services based on a family- and community-resilience approach. He is a member of the American Family Therapy Academy and received the 2002 Marion Langer Award for Human Rights and Social Change of the American Association for Orthopsychiatry.

Patrick Savaiano is currently enrolled in the doctoral (PsyD) program at the Adler School of Professional Psychology (ASPP) in Chicago, Illinois. He graduated from the University of Notre Dame in 2004 with a BA in history and Spanish, and has since worked in marketing, real estate, and music. In the summer of 2003, he had the rewarding experience of traveling to Costa Rica by himself to work with Habitat for Humanity. Although he still plays guitar in two bands, in 2006 he decided to shift his "day job" away from business and into the profession of psychology. In fall 2007, as part of ASPP's Community Service Practicum, he worked under Dr. Chris E. Stout at the Center for Global Initiatives (CGI). He became an integral member of a team of students and professionals that ultimately put together a book project entitled *The New Humanitarians: Innovations, Inspirations, and Blueprints for Visionaries*. Mr. Savaiano hopes to use the experience he has gained at ASPP and CGI to fuel his desire to help the less fortunate and underserved populations throughout the world.

Jennifer Staple founded Unite For Sight during her sophomore year at Yale University in 2000. Under her stewardship, the organization has grown from a community-based nonprofit organization in New Haven to an international nonprofit organization serving the medically underserved in twenty-five countries. She has created ninety chapters throughout the world, engaging more than 4,000 professionals and students. The goal of the organization is to create eye disease–free communities, and Unite For Sight has provided services to more than 600,000 people worldwide. Currently a medical student at Stanford University School of Medicine, she is a cum laude graduate of Yale University, where she received her bachelor's degree in biology and anthropology in May 2003. For her commitment to public service and leadership, Ms. Staple has been featured in books and received many international awards.

Miriam Stone is responsible for fundraising, communications, and developing franchise partner opportunities. Prior to joining Scojo Foundation, she worked as a consultant to a variety of international social enterprise organizations, including Solidaridad's Latin America program and Tilonia, the U.S. fair trade distributor for the Barefoot College in India. She has also worked as a community eye health organizer in Guatemala and has traveled extensively throughout Latin America. The author of published articles, poetry, and a memoir, Ms. Stone graduated from Columbia University in 2003 with a degree in cultural anthropology and creative writing.

Stevan Weine, a psychiatrist, is a researcher, writer, teacher, and clinician in the Department of Psychiatry and the Health Research and Policy Centers of the University of Illinois–Chicago, where he directs the International Center on Responses to Catastrophes. He is co-founder and co-director of the Project on Genocide, Psychiatry, and Witnessing, which provides family-focused, community-based mental health services to Bosnians; conducts interdisciplinary research on survivors; and engages in mental health reform in postwar countries. His scholarly work focuses on familial, cultural, and historical dimensions of traumatization. Dr. Weine is principal investigator of a National Institute of Mental Health–funded research study "A Prevention and Access Intervention for Survivor Families" that is studying the effectiveness of the Coffee and Family Education and Support intervention with Bosnian and Kosovar families in Chicago, a resilience-oriented, multiple-family group intervention first developed with CCFH. In 2001 he was awarded a Career Scientist Award from the National Institute of Mental Health on "Services Based Research with Refugee Families" for which he is conducting an ethnography of Bosnian adolescents and their families. Weine is author of a book based upon survivors' oral histories, *When History is a Nightmare: Lives and Memories of Ethnic Cleansing in Bosnia-Herzegovina* (Rutgers, 1999). His new book, *Living Histories*, is a narrative inquiry of diverse testimony readings from within four different twentieth-century sociohistorical occurrences of political violence. Weine is also chair of the Task Force on International Trauma Training of the International Society for Traumatic Stress Studies and principal co-author of the "Guidelines for International Trauma Training of Practitioners in Clinical and Community Settings." He is co-founder of the Kosovar Family Professional Education Collaborative and Services, involving CCFH, and scientific director the Services Based Training for Kosovar Community Mental Health and Prevention, which is building family-focused, community-based public mental health services in Kosovo. For more information, see his webpage at the International Center on Responses to Catastrophes.

Martine Zoer, born and raised in the Netherlands, has lived in the United Kingdom and Canada. As a fundraising and publicity associate of the Sustainable Sciences Institute, she has written multiple grant proposals since 2003, including grant proposals for Big City Mountaineers, GirlVentures, National Children's Literacy Group, Venice Arts, and WriteGirl. A prolific writer, she has also published numerous articles in national and international publications as well as two children's books, including *The Kids' Guide to Living Abroad*. She is currently working on a book about Dutch war brides who married Canadian servicemen after World War II.

Index

Note: A page number followed by an *f* indicates that the reference is to a figure.